BAPTIST FAITH & WITNESS
BOOK 5

BAPTIST FAITH & WITNESS BOOK 5

Papers of the Commission on Mission, Evangelism and Theological Reflection of the Baptist World Alliance

2010-2015

Edited by Eron Henry

Copyright ©2015 by the Baptist World Alliance, Falls Church, Virginia, USA. All rights reserved.

Manufactured in the United States of America

Opinions, thoughts and theories are those of the authors and do not necessarily reflect the position of the Baptist World Alliance. The Baptist World Alliance has relied upon the authors and accepts no responsibility for the accuracy or inaccuracy of any statements, quotations or attributions made in the papers published herein. The style and format of the papers reflect essentially the modus of their presentation.

ISBN: 978-1-936945-08-5

All rights reserved. No part of this publication may be reproduced, stored in a retrieval system, or transmitted in any form, or by any means electronic, photocopying, recording or otherwise without prior permission of the author or publisher.

Printed in the United States of America

TABLE OF CONTENTS

Foreword /ix

Focus on The John Leland Center for Theological Studies. /1

Commission on Doctrine and Christian Unity /3

1. "The Church of the Triune God": A Baptist Response to Chapters I and II of *The Nature and Mission of the Church - A Stage on the Way to a Common Statement* (Faith and Order Paper 198) - Curtis W. Freeman /7

2. "The Church: Growing in Communion": Response to Chapter III of *The Church: Towards a Common Vision* (Faith and Order Paper 214) - Elizabeth Newman /25

3. "*Koinonia*: The Church in and For the World" Comment on the Final Part of *The Church: Towards a Common Vision* (Faith and Order Paper 214) - Paul S. Fiddes /37

4. Reflections on *The Word of God in the Life of the Church: A Report of International Conversations Between the Catholic Church and the Baptist World Alliance, 2006-2010* - Stephen R. Holmes /50

Commission on Ministry /65

5. A Tribute to Dr. Duke K. McCall: Denominational Statesman, Baptist Educator, and Global Leader - Robert I. Garrett /69

6. Bible Translation, A Major Component of Emancipation - The Case for a Jamaican New Testament - Courtney Stewart /90

7. Bible Translation, A Major Component of Emancipation - The Significance of Bible Translation into the Mother Tongue - Faith Linton /103

8. Biblical Perspectives on Calls to Ministry - R. Glenn Wooden /111

Commission on Theological Education and Leadership Formation /123

9. Beyond Milk: The Moral Failure and Ongoing Formation of Lay Christian Leaders in the Church and Society - Louise Kretzschmar /127

10. Faithful Thinking: The Role of the Seminary in Promoting a Thoughtful Christianity - Brian Harris /144

11. How We View the Value of Theological Education - "DA" /155

Commission on Christian Ethics /161

12. "But How *Does* the Spirit Work in Moral Action?" A Case for the Utility of Virtue Theory - Samuel K. Roberts /165
13. From Antioch to Santiago by Way of Mars Hill: Acts 11:19-26; Acts 13:13-16, 42-44; Acts 17:16-21 - William M. Tillman, Jr. /178
14. Growth in Grace as a Control Belief for the People of God - Rod Benson /189
15. Unity through Christ: Engaging the Ephesian Household Code - Robert Scott Nash /200

Commission on Baptist Worship and Spirituality /221

16. Evangelical Hymnody in Latin America - Joel Sierra Cavazos /225
17. Leadership Safari: The 21st Century Pastor as Leader in Worship and Spirituality - D. Leslie Hollon /233
18. The Liturgical Participation of Children in Small Churches: The Theology Behind it, and How it Can be Done - Alison Sampson and Nathan Nettleton /247

Commission on Evangelism /257

19. Church Planting and Leadership in Eastern Europe - Daniel Trusiewicz /261
20. Observations of a Church Planting Movement in Northeastern Ghana - John Drummond /269
21. Transformation and Gospel in the New Testament – Contextualizing the Gospel and Transforming the World - Timothy Hyunmo Lee /277
22. Transformations in the West: Some Reflections from 'Down Under' WEST - John Beasy /284

Commission on Baptist Heritage and Identity /289

23. The King James Bible and Baptists Over 400 Years – Brian R. Talbot /293
24. "free indeed!" – Virginia Baptists and Slavery – How a State Baptist Historical Organization Commemorated the 150th Anniversary of Emancipation - Fred Anderson /313

25. Historia de los Bautistas en Chile - Victor Aguilar Reyes /336
26. Identidad Bautista Latinoamericana, Aproximaciones y Desafíos - Jose Parrish Jacome Hernandez /353

Notes /363

Contributing Authors /405

FOREWORD

It is with a sense of joy and privilege that the Baptist World Alliance (BWA), through its Division on Mission, Evangelism and Theological Reflection (METR), offers this Baptist Faith and Witness Book 5 to the Baptist family.

At the Annual Gatherings during this quinquennium, Baptist theologians and leaders presented papers at the meetings of the commissions associated with METR. These papers cover a wide range of topics related to the life and ministry of Baptist churches across the world. Each section of this book is preceded by an introductory article, prepared by the commission chairs, including an overview of the commissions' work.

The purpose of this book is to make available to BWA member bodies and local Baptist churches across the world a sample of the wealth of reflections by METR commission members. These papers do not seek to present the official position of the Baptist World Alliance on the topics being presented. However, they make available insights into their subject matter that arise within the worldwide Baptist community.

I had the pleasure of selecting from among the papers delivered those that are presented in this book and it is my privilege to recognize a number of persons who made this publication possible. A committee including members of the faculty of the John Leland Center for Theological Studies, under the leadership of Jeffrey G. Willetts; and Shannon Cowett, administrative staff in the BWA METR Division, provided competent editorial service. Final editorial review was undertaken by Eron Henry of the BWA Division of Communications.

I am grateful to John Leland Center for Theological Studies President, Mark Olson, and BWA General Secretary Neville G. Callam for their facilitation and support.

May all who read this *Baptist Faith and Witness Book 5* proclaim boldly, in the power of the Holy Spirit, that Jesus Christ is the Door to eternal life!

Soli Deo Gloria!

Fausto A. Vasconcelos
METR Director
January 2016

THE JOHN LELAND CENTER FOR THEOLOGICAL STUDIES: EQUIPPING TRANSFORMATIONAL LEADERS FOR THE GLOBAL MINISTRY OF JESUS CHRIST

The John Leland Center for Theological Studies began as a dream conceived by several church leaders from the northern Virginia region of metropolitan, Washington, DC, in attendance at the annual meeting of the Baptist World Alliance in Vancouver, British Columbia, Canada, in the summer of 1997. At the heart of their dream was the need to provide a school for the cosmopolitan region of Washington, DC, which nurtured and equipped theological leadership for the emerging global community and church. At that initial meeting were figures who played a strategic role in the early development of the school, K. Randel Everett (founding President), Jeffrey G. Willetts (founding Academic Dean), Sheila K. Everett (founding Student Dean), Daniel Carro (the school's first Professor of Divinity), and Michael Catlett (founding Trustee and Affiliated faculty member).

The John Leland Center for Theological Studies was named for the 18th century Virginia Baptist leader, elder and preacher John Leland, who is notable for his defense of the freedom of the Gospel, his opposition to slavery, and his advocacy of religious liberty. From its inception the Leland Center has understood itself as a broadly evangelical, pan-Baptist institution. As such the Leland Center has no single denominational affiliation, but works in cooperation with many Baptist and evangelical institutions that share a common heritage and interest in the development of theological leadership.

The John Leland Center for Theological Studies is located just four miles from downtown Washington, DC, in Clarendon, Virginia. Metropolitan-Washington, DC, is home to more than five million people and Baptists represent the largest denominational grouping among Protestants in the region. African-American, Anglo, and many non-English speaking churches make up the diversity that is the Baptist family of faith in the area.

From the Leland Center's inception, the school has sought to be a community of theologically reflective practitioners within which participants teach and learn from one another in a variety of contexts including the classroom, worship settings, informal gatherings, and even interactions within church staffs. Emerging from the stated mission of Leland Center is a vision for a culturally diverse community of faith and learning, working together within various settings, seeking to integrate scholarship, faith, and Christian service. The members of this community bring a great diversity of knowledge, experience and skill to the learning community in which teaching, learning and research are experienced as a collaborative event.

As its primary mission, the school seeks to "equip transformation leaders for the global ministry of Jesus Christ." In order to accomplish this task, the Leland Center has created for its community a theological curriculum designed to develop theological understanding, which is the proper end of any theological school and for the Leland Center community is the key to transformational leadership. In order to meet this broad expectation, the school brings together scholars, practitioners of ministry, and students throughout our region, as well as from around the world, in order to learn, teach, and research the verities, virtues, and sensibilities that constitute theological understanding. The school offers three theological degrees: The Master of Divinity, the Master of Theological Studies and the Master of Christian Leadership. The Leland Center actively relates to many historically Baptist institutions. Among those institutions are the following: the NorthStar Church Network: an Association of Baptist Churches; the Baptist General Association of Virginia; the District of Columbia Baptist Convention; the Northern Virginia Baptist Association; the Baptist General Convention of Virginia; the Baptist Joint Committee, and others.

The Leland Center has always worked in close partnership with the Baptist World Alliance. Since the Leland Center's inception many members of faculty and staff have served on Baptist World Alliance committees or commissions and understood the school's identity as inspired by the global character of the Baptist World Alliance's ministry and mission.

In 2010, the faculty of the Leland Center served as the editorial committee for Book 4 of the *Baptist Faith & Witness: Papers of the Study and Research Division of the Baptist World Alliance*. Again, in 2015, the faculty of the John Leland Center for Theological Studies is privileged to serve as the editorial committee for Book 5. Contributing to the editorial committee's work were Profs. Daniel Carro, Daniel Dapaah, John Lee, Andre Shirin, Bryan Jones, April Vega and Jeffrey Willetts (Chair).

Jeffrey G. Willetts, PhD, is professor of divinity at The John Leland Center for Theological Studies in Arlington, VA, and pastor of Calvary Hill Baptist Church in Fairfax, VA, both in the United States.

COMMISSION ON DOCTRINE AND CHRISTIAN UNITY

These four essays represent two major concerns of the Commission on Doctrine and Christian Unity over the past five years. The first two essays place in context *The Word of God in the Life of the Church*, the report of theological conversations between the Baptist World Alliance and the Catholic Church from 2006-2010. The other two essays reflect the Commission's interaction with the Faith and Order document number 214, titled *The Church: Towards a Common Vision* (2013). During this quinquennium, the Commission on Doctrine and Christian Unity also took up other issues not represented in this volume, including Bible translation, Baptist ecclesiology, the role of women in the early church and the theology of preaching (in a joint session with the Commission on Baptist Worship and Spirituality).

Paul S. Fiddes served as the Baptist co-chair of the International Baptist-Catholic Conversations. In his introduction to *The Word of God in the Life of the Church*, he notes the continuity between the conversations reflected in this report and an earlier round of Baptist-Catholic discussions that took place between 1984 and 1988. At that time, the concept of *koinonia* was recognized as a point of convergence reflecting the importance of this major theme in many bilateral dialogues following the Second Vatican Council. *Koinonia* is a New Testament term (cf. 1 Cor. 10:16-17) that grounds Christian unity not in church politics but in the participative love and holiness shared among the Father, the Son and the Holy Spirit from all eternity. *The Word of God in the Life of the Church* accepts the ecumenical consensus around the concept of *communion*, but it makes a new move by introducing the theme of *covenant*, a term much used among Baptists. In this context, "covenant community" indicates both the initiative of God in God's redeeming work through Christ and "the willing commitment of people to each other and to God." The report argues for the co-inherence of covenant and communion and calls for its further development among both Baptists and Catholics.

Fiddes also reviews a number of controverted issues that surfaced during the five-year conversation between the two communities. These include Scripture and tradition, the Virgin Mary, baptism and the Lord's Supper as sacraments/ordinances, as well as the shape of ministry and proper oversight in the life of the church. Important differences remain on all these matters, and these are duly noted in the report. But, as Fiddes points out, there was also a significant convergence of belief between Baptists and Catholics on each of these broad themes. The points of convergence are designated by bold type in the report itself.

Reception is a key term in ecumenical work. It involves listening to, receiving, and evaluating the results of theological discourse, precisely the kind represented by *The Word of God in the Life of the Church*. Steven R. Holmes, a distinguished British Baptist theologian, was one of several scholars who responded to this report. He reviews each section of the report and acknowledges the serious – and surprising – points of convergence, but he also notes major areas of difference that remain. Such differences include divergent ways of talking about the church as local and universal; the place of the Bishop of Rome as the focus of ecclesial unity; the extent of the biblical canon; and the later Marian dogmas. Holmes points out that in the report the use of the term "sacraments/ordinances" to speak of baptism and the Lord's Supper reflects different emphases within the Baptist community itself. He also recognizes a basic asymmetry between Catholic and Baptist approaches to ecumenism and the theological weighting of various issues. Baptists have neither a clearly defined "hierarchy of truths" nor a centralized office of magisterial teaching to help adjudicate doctrinal differences.

The Faith and Order document number 214, *The Church: Towards a Common Vision* (2013), reflects ongoing ecclesiological work over the last two decades. The Commission on Doctrine and Christian Unity devoted several sessions to engaging with this important statement. Two members of the commission, Curtis W. Freeman and Elizabeth Newman, presented critical and appreciative evaluations of this statement. Freeman reviews the document under its previous title, *The Nature and Mission of the Church*, and points out three areas where Baptists have special concerns about the emerging ecumenical consensus on the church: (1) the nuancing of trinitarian language to emphasize more clearly the economic and immanent dimensions of trinitarian thought as seen in the scriptural narrative of the unfolding story of the triune God; (2) the development of *mediation* as well as *witness* to represent the presence and grace of God in baptism and the Lord's Supper; (3) the tension in Baptist ecclesiology between individual conscience and local church freedom on the one hand and wider expressions of the one, holy, catholic and apostolic church on the other.

Elizabeth Newman evaluates that section of the Faith and Order document that affirms the holiness of the church – a mark of ecclesial identity with both Christological and eschatological aspects. Newman also points to the potential compatibility between ordinance and sacrament as appropriate terms for baptism and the Lord's Supper. She concludes by pointing to the way "saints" provide both a pathway to unity and a model for holiness. To this end, she brings together two figures not often thought of in consort, Teresa of Avila (about whom Newman has written a book) and Clarence Jordan, a Baptist scholar-preacher who established Koinonia Farms, an integrated Christian community in pre-Civil Rights Georgia.

Timothy George, commission chair, is dean of Beeson Divinity School at Samford University in Birmingham, Alabama, in the United States. He was a member of the BWA Academic and Theological Education Workgroup, 1990-2010; the Commission on Doctrine and Interchurch Cooperation, 1995-2010; the Evangelism and Education Executive Committee, 2000-2005; the METR Advisory Committee, 2010-2015; and chair of the Commission on Doctrine and Christian Unity, 2010-2015.

CHAPTER 1
"THE CHURCH OF THE TRIUNE GOD":
A BAPTIST RESPONSE TO CHAPTERS I AND II OF *THE NATURE AND MISSION OF THE CHURCH – A STAGE ON THE WAY TO A COMMON STATEMENT* (FAITH AND ORDER PAPER 198)

Curtis W. Freeman

What is the church, and where is it found? In December 2005, the Faith and Order Commission of the World Council of Churches issued a study document, *The Nature and Mission of the Church* (NMC), which reflects on these questions.[1] Following the *Pattern of Baptism, Eucharist and Ministry* (BEM),[2] this new document seeks to be a convergence text, enabling churches to recognize much of the current agreement that has emerged as the result of multilateral dialogues and conversations. It also identifies many of the ecclesiological issues that still divide churches today. Yet the subtitle, *A Stage on the Way to a Common Statement*, gestures toward the hope that conversations and responses might take another step toward visible unity of the churches. This paper is a reply to the invitation for a Baptist response to *Section I: The Church of the Triune God* (§§9-28).

The Nature of the Church (§§9-23)

(I) The Church as a Gift of God (§§9-13)

(§9) The NMC begins with a section on the church as a gift of God. The church is God's new creation by Spirit and the Word. God's Word calls the church into being. God's Spirit draws the church into fellowship. This trinitarian vision is a strong reminder that the church is not merely the product of human will or design. The church is both the people gathered by Christ and the people who gather in response to his call. It is the body into which members are joined, as well as the body that members join. But like the bells that ring on Sunday morning, calling the church to the meeting, the initiative lies with God, not humanity. The church is the gift of the triune God. And because the church is God's gift, it belongs to God. Moreover, since the church cannot exist apart from God's life-giving Word and Spirit, it stands in constant need of the life-sustaining grace imparted through Spirit and Word. And given that the church belongs to God, it cannot exist by or for itself, but rather by and for Word and Spirit as a witness to God's reign in the world.

This ecclesial vision follows the lead of the trinitarian resurgence in modern theology that began with Karl Barth (on the Protestant side) and Karl Rahner (on the Catholic side).[3] Baptist theologians have offered careful descriptions of how, through the Spirit and the Word, the ecclesial community is created and sustained by sharing in the inner life of the Trinity.[4] And Baptist missiologists have further shown how the church is drawn to participate in the mission of the triune God.[5] The resonance of these Baptist voices with this trinitarian vision of the nature and mission of the church suggests that a convergence of views is indeed possible. Yet embracing a trinitarian ecclesiology is not without challenge. Indeed, for many Baptists the focus of the faith is almost exclusively on Jesus, leading some observers to ask if it indicates a tendency toward a unitarianism of the Second Person.[6] A more charitable reading suggests that although the Jesus-centered piety of Baptists is sometimes expressed in non-trinitarian terms, it is rarely deliberately anti-trinitarian, signifying that the Trinity is implicitly intended even when not explicitly affirmed.[7] It is also the case that when Baptists invoke trinitarian language, it is more often in economic than in immanent terms. Yet there is good reason for Baptists to heed the call of the NMC for a retrieval of the doctrine of the Trinity, which as Karl Barth explained is what "fundamentally distinguishes the Christian doctrine of God as Christian,"[8] and which (it might be also added) is what fundamentally distinguishes the Christian doctrine of the church as Christian.[9]

($10) The NMC declares that the church is centered and grounded on the Word of God, which is manifested in Jesus Christ as the incarnate Word, the Holy Scriptures as the written Word, and the preaching of the Gospel as the proclaimed Word. This Word reveals the nature of God as Trinity but also draws believers into the life of the triune God. The communion of God thereby creates the communion of the church, and so such ecclesial visions are known among theologians as "communion ecclesiology."[10] The church thus always exists in relation to the faithful who are called into communion with the triune God and one another through the Word of God. Faith therefore is always relational and never merely individual. Yet faith is also personal, though it is never private. Like Mary, the first disciple, who exemplifies both responsive and responsible faith, each person must answer, "let it be with me according to your word" (Lk 1:38). This living Word continues to create and nourish the church as it has through the ages. And so the church bears witness to the Word through Gospel preaching, sacramental observance, and sacrificial service.

Baptists find their ecclesiological touchstone in the statement of Jesus that "where two or three are gathered in my name, I am there among them" (Mt 18:20). For where Christ is, there is the church. Yet as Miroslav Volf observes, the integrity of a Baptist (and baptistic free church) ecclesiology is challenged by individualistic understandings of faith.[11] The trouble is not that Baptists and other evangelical Christians forsake to assemble (Heb. 10:25). Instead they often tend to understand their assemblies as merely voluntary associations. It was Friedrich Schleiermacher who famously distinguished between Protestantism, which makes the individual's relation to the church dependent on a relation to Christ, and Catholicism, which makes the individual's relation to Christ dependent on a relation to the church.[12] The church-as-voluntary-association model is a radical version of Scheiermacher's Protestant type, which results in a deficient social reductionism because it conceives of the church merely as a human community. Baptists, to be sure, contend that to be in the church, everyone must answer as Peter did: "You are the Christ, the Son of the living God" (Mt 16:16). But Baptist understandings of the church, which begin with the conviction that every member must attest to a personal faith in Christ, need not succumb to individualism, because through Jesus Christ, the living Word, each believer is drawn into fellowship with the relational God and other relational beings into a common life.

(§11) This section of the NMC highlights the complementarity of divine action and human response, citing the apostle Paul, that "no one can say 'Jesus is Lord' except by the Holy Spirit" (1 Cor 12:3). It affirms that faith is not merely a human response, but is called forth by the Word and brought about by the Holy Spirit, and thereby attests that the work of the Word and Spirit of God are inseparable. The church is therefore to be understood as a creature of the Holy Spirit every bit as much as it is a creature of the Word of God. Moreover, the incorporation of believers into the church through baptism is equally as complementary and mysterious as the response of faith, because "in the one Spirit we were all baptized into one body" (1 Cor 12:13). For faith is not the only means whereby believers are joined into the church, but through baptism believers are also incorporated into the body of Christ. In baptism, like in faith, the Spirit works in mysterious ways through water in the medium of creaturely existence. And as members of the body of Christ, each and all are fed and nourished from the Lord's Table so that everyone may live into the calling to which they are called.

Baptists have not always been open to receive the work of the Holy Spirit. Indeed, some Baptists are probably not too unlike the disciples that Paul met in Ephesus, who replied when he asked them if they had received the Spirit: "No, we have not even heard that there is a Holy Spirit" (Acts 19:2). Baptists have consequently tended to see themselves at the other end of the spectrum from Pentecostals. Indeed, many Baptists have identified themselves over against Pentecostalism: "We have Jesus. They have the Holy Spirit." Such polarization and suspicion, however, fails to do justice to a trinitarian understanding of God who is Father, Son, and Spirit. Baptists need to be more Spirit-focused, and as a consequence, more trinitarian. Yet in addition to a deeper pneumatology, this section also challenges Baptists to consider a deeper sacramentalism, as they explore the mysterious ways in which God's action and human responses collide through the working of God by the Holy Spirit in baptism and the Lord's Supper.

(§12) Where is the church, and how is it recognized? The NMC commends the four identifying marks (i.e., one, holy, catholic, and apostolic) as a way of seeing the church as a "creature of God's own Word and Spirit." However, these historic marks are not meant to suggest that the church's nature is empirically recognizable for any and all to see. Indeed, their location in the Nicene Creed is a reminder that these essential attributes cannot be seen apart from faith. Moreover, it is important to note that the reason for the church's "invisibility" is that these attributes are ultimately about God and only derivatively about the church. As identifying marks they indicate that the nature of the church flows from and is dependent on God. Yet these are not the terms with which Baptists readily identify or use to describe the church. Baptists have historically emphasized the church as it is visible and gathered, sharing with Anabaptists a sense of the church as *Gemeinde* or community. In 1609, in what is arguably the earliest Baptist statement of ecclesiology, Thomas Helwys defined a church as

> an assembly of believers (*Coetus populi fidelis*) baptized in the name of the Father, Son, and Spirit who have confessed their faith and sins, having the authority of Christ, of preaching the Word, of administering baptism and the Lord's Supper, of selecting and rejecting their own ministers, and of restoring and banishing their members according to the rule of Christ.[13]

W. T. Whitley, the English Baptist historian, went so far as to describe this emphasis on the church as visibly gathered as "the most distinctive feature about Baptists."[14] But given this emphasis on the visible and gathered community, what can Baptists say about the church more widely? How are these local communities related to the church as the whole people of God?

From the standpoint of a gathered church ecclesiology it may appear contrary to fact to confess the church to be one, holy, catholic, or apostolic. The trinitarian ecclesial vision put forth in the NMC, however, provides a way of seeing the church through different eyes. It emphasizes that the communion among members and between communities is grounded in their communion with the triune God. The unity of the church is grounded in the Trinity. The one and the many participate in the fellowship of the Father with the Son (1 John 1:3) and with the Holy Spirit (2 Cor 13:13). From the standpoint of this communion ecclesiology, the divisions among the churches are historical, not ontological. If the church were truly divided there would be, indeed there could be, no church. For the church is one. The holiness of the church is not a quantitative sum of virtuous character or moral excellence exemplified by the individual members, but is rather a qualitative distinctive made possible by participation in the fellowship of the Holy Spirit which indwells the church. The church embodies a quantitative sense of catholicity as a universally inclusive communion of communions spread throughout the world and a qualitative catholicity that names the fullness of Christ and the gifts of Spirit that are determinative of the church's being. The mark of apostolicity suggests that by participation in the triune life of God the church lives in continuity with the faith and practice of the apostolic community.

These four marks of the church are not inconsistent with a gathered church ecclesiology. Indeed, one way of putting it is to say that Baptists affirm that the one, holy, catholic, and apostolic church becomes visible in gathered communities where "the word of God is rightly preached, and the sacraments truly administered according to Christ's institution, and the practice of the primitive church," and where "discipline and government [are] duly executed, by ministers or pastors of God's appointing, and the church's election."[15] In March of 1948, the Baptist Union of Great Britain issued a remarkable statement of Baptist catholicity, which historian Walter Shurden praised as "an extraordinary lucid document" that "deserves serious consideration by Baptists around the world."[16] It declared:

> Although Baptists have for so long held a position separate from that of other communions, they have always claimed to be part of the one holy catholic Church of our Lord Jesus Christ. They believe in the catholic Church as the holy society of believers in our Lord Jesus Christ, which He founded, of which He is the only Head, and in which He dwells by

His Spirit, so that though manifested in many communions, organized in various modes, and scattered throughout the world, it is yet one in Him.[17]

It is a model that contemporary Baptists might follow in thinking about what it might mean to move in the direction pointed by the NMC. Living into such an ecclesial vision, however, is not without challenges. As Australian Baptist ecumenist, E. Roberts-Thomson observed, "catholic" is not a term with which most Baptists readily identify. Yet to deny their part in the catholicity of the church is to revert to a sectarian stance that turns back from the ecumenical vision of John Smyth and the early Baptists.[18] Commenting on these dramatic gestures toward a fuller understanding of the church, Ernest Payne observed that though such views did not receive universal acceptance even among British Baptists, they succeeded in shifting attention toward a vision of catholicity among the early Baptists that had long been neglected.[19]

A consultation of African-American Baptists meeting in Richmond, Virginia, from December 14-15, 1984, offered their reflections on the four marks of the church "toward a common expression of faith." They affirmed "that the unity of the Church not only expresses the unity of the Triune God, but is also a sign of the unity of humankind that holds together in one family the diversity of all races and cultures." But they insisted that unity among Christians "must not be spiritualized, but manifested in concrete behavior, by doing justice and loving service to one another." Citing Acts 2:42 as biblical warrant, the Richmond consultation argued that the catholicity of the church is visible in faith, baptism, apostolic teaching, fellowship, the breaking of bread, and prayers. Therefore, they continued, "No person, group or institution that meets these requirements should be excluded from the visible Church or relegated to an inferior status by human authority, ecclesiastical or secular." And they urged fellow Baptists (white and black) to repudiate as a racist violation of catholicity any discouragement of fellowship with other predominantly black Christian denominational bodies.[20]

A trinitarian framing of Baptist ecclesiology such as proposed by the NMC, has important implications. In his book, *After Our Likeness: The Church as the Image of the Trinity*, Miroslav Volf notes three: (1) Christ is directly present through his Spirit in every gathered community that assembles in his name and professes faith in him; (2) Each congregation is simultaneously independent of and interconnected with other churches through the Spirit which makes Christ present; and (3) The profession of Christ as universal Savior and Lord implies that participation in the church must be open to all people.[21] Such a trinitarian ecclesial vision would surely enable Baptists to see more clearly that their gathered communities of believers are simply local manifestations of the one, holy, catholic, and apostolic church of God. At the same time the fullness of this ecclesial vision awaits the coming eschatological communion of the entire people of God in the new creation, and so it stands over the horizon of that to which the church in its earthly pilgrimage is always moving.

(§13) The NMC states that "the church is not merely the sum of individual believers in communion with God, nor primarily the mutual communion of individual believers among themselves." Rather the church is characterized by the mutual sharing in the life of the triune God, who is the source and center of this life together. At times Baptists tilt toward a democratized understanding of ecclesial existence in which the church is conceived as merely an aggregate of its individual members and congregations are understood simply as voluntary associations isolated from the wider fellowship of God's people. Yet if the church is the image of the Trinity, its ecclesial life is marked by interdependence rather than independence. Nigel Wright offers the following summary of a trinitarian ecclesial vision for Baptists and other free church Christians:

> The church is that community of believers which participates by the Spirit in the fellowship and mission of the Triune God. Through the Son and by the Spirit believers are drawn into the communion of God's own being and become partakers of the divine nature. The word preached evokes response and participation in the Spirit. Inevitably, therefore, the church is a confessing or believers church constituted by the Spirit from those gathered into communion.[22]

Such a vision, as Ernest Payne once argued, stands over against the "exaggerated independence, self-sufficiency, and atomism" that has sometimes characterized Baptist life.[23]

The NMC identifies three subjects about which there are divergent views on the institutional dimensions of the church and the work of the Holy Spirit: (a) whether preaching and the sacraments are means of or simply witnesses to the activity of the Spirit through the Word, (b) what the institutional implications and presuppositions of the church as a creature of Word and Spirit are with regard to ordained ministry and the episcopacy, and (c) how the institutional continuity of the church is understood with regard to the episcopacy as a means and/or guarantee of apostolic faith. (§13a) Baptists have tended to refer to baptism and the Lord's Supper as "ordinances," although they sometimes have also used the language of "sacraments."[24] For example, in the previously noted 1948 statement, the Baptist Union of Great Britain declared:

We recognize two sacraments of Believers" Baptism and the Lord's Supper as being of the Lord's ordaining. We hold that both are "means of grace" to those who receive them in faith, and that Christ is really and truly present, not in the material elements, but in the heart and mind and soul of the believer and in the Christian community which observes the sacrament.[25]

While most Baptists would still likely say that the sacraments confirm rather confer the gifts of God, some wish to say more. They maintain that the sacraments are both a response to God's promise and an expectation of God's action. They view these ecclesial rites as more than acts of obedience that witness to the Spirit (viz. ordinances), but see them as means of grace that participate in the communion of the Spirit (viz. sacraments).[26] For example, the early nineteenth century English Baptist, Robert Hall, criticized as inadequate accounts of the Lord's Table as "a mere commemoration" and contended that the Supper is "a spiritual participation of the blood… and body of the crucified Saviour."[27] Yet the spiritual participation Hall commended begs for a more robust trinitarian pneumatology that makes room for the real presence of Christ through the Spirit in the Eucharistic meal. What might it mean for Baptists to reconsider this question of the communion of the Holy Spirit in the sacraments within the framework of participation in the trinitarian relations?

(§13b) Ordination is practiced among all Baptists, but there is no consensus on its theological and ecclesiological significance. Baptists do not hold ordained ministry as essential for the church to be the church. Yet almost all have supported an ordained ministry for the church's wellbeing.[28] Some Baptists have held a functional view of ministry, while others have maintained that ordained ministry is necessary for the right order of the church, and still others have suggested that in ordination ministers participate in a new way of being.[29] Yet all would seem to agree with eighteenth century Baptist minister Daniel Turner, who contended "that there be some, one or more in every particular church, invested with official power, is necessary, and of divine appointment, for the due administration of the word and sacraments; the maintaining due order in the church, and due execution of the laws of Christ."[30] But why is ordained ministry necessary, and how is the divine appointment to be understood? These are disputed questions. If a trinitarian ecclesiology can move Baptists toward a more theologically coherent account of ministry it would be a great advance.

(§13c) Baptists have maintained a witness to another, and often overlooked, a sense of apostolicity derived from the literal meaning of the word *apostolos* as "one who is sent out." Thus Baptists have held that obedience to the Great

Commission to "make disciples of all nations" (Mt 28:19) is an important strand of apostolic faith and life. Yet they can recognize that there were other strands along which apostolic faith and life has been transmitted down the centuries, and that from the early centuries of Christianity to the present episcopal succession has been recognized by the majority of Christians to be one of those strands.[31] But while Baptists can regard the succession of ministers as an indication of continuity with the apostolic church, they strongly resist the reduction of apostolicity to historical continuity. Still Baptists and other free churches, which rely on the Holy Spirit working providentially to keep the churches in the apostolic tradition, might (borrowing language from BEM) nevertheless welcome episcopal succession as "a sign, though not a guarantee" of continuity with apostolic faith and practice across space and time in the life of the whole church, though they do not regard it as a necessary condition for valid apostolic ministry and gifts.[32]

(II) Biblical Insights (§§14-33)

(§§14-17) These sections of the NMC begin with the affirmation that the One who calls the church into being and unites it unto himself is the triune God: Father, Son, and Spirit. Yet the church is related to each of the divine persons in distinct ways. To explore how these trinitarian relations inform the nature and mission of the church, the report commends the study of Scripture, which provides "a uniquely privileged source" for the church's self understanding. Baptists will find these sections dealing with biblical images of the church to be accessible yet at the same time challenging as they contend that a biblically informed ecclesiology demands a deeply trinitiarian theology. That the biblical witness contains a plurality of insights into the nature and mission of the church illustrates that within the unity of the church there is room for a diversity of gifts. Yet conceiving of church as one body with many members suggests that this underlying unity in diversity is possible only insofar as it is coordinated within the fellowship of the triune God. The report examines four images of the church in the biblical witness: (a) people of God, (b) body of Christ, (c) temple of the Holy Spirit, and (d) *koinonia*/communion.

(a) *The Church as People of God*

(§18) Beginning with Abraham, God has been about the gathering of a people. Through Word (*dabar*) and Spirit (*rû'ah*), God called Israel from the nations as people with whom God made a covenant. In Christ the covenant was renewed by incorporating the church into the people of God. Yet the church does not supersede God's covenant with Israel, but rather in Christ, Gentiles were grafted into it (cf. Rom 11:11-36). This covenantal narration of the biblical story connects Baptists with their ecclesiological origins. For in the year 1606/1607 the Gainsborough congregation led by John Smyth "joyned them selves (by a covenant of the Lord) into a Church estate, in the fellowship of the gospell, to walke in all his wayes, made known, or to be made known unto them, according to their best endeavours, whatsoever it should cost them, the Lord assisting them."[33] Smyth soon maintained that "the true form of the church is a covenant betwixt God and the faithful made in baptism in which Christ is visibly put on."[34] Baptism was understood as a covenanting act, requiring no written covenant to constitute the church or to subscribe to for membership. Similarly, Thomas Helwys argued that those who believe and are baptized are of the faith of Abraham and enter as Abraham did into covenant with God and the people of God.[35] Baptists have largely forgotten the covenant theology that brought their churches into being. Their ecclesiological life only stands to be enriched by engaging the biblical themes of covenant.[36]

(§19) God's promise to Abraham was to bless all nations through him and his descendants. This promise finds its fulfillment in Christ, as the dividing wall between Jew and Gentile has been destroyed (cf. Eph 2:14). In the church, both Jew and Gentile are called to be a "royal priesthood" and a "holy nation" (1 Pet 2:9-10). Missing from NMC is any discussion of overcoming the historic divisions of race, gender, and class that give lie to the one peoplehood of the church. Baptists will no doubt welcome the report's emphasis on the priesthood of all believers, which has its roots in the protest theology of Martin Luther. Yet they will also be drawn to reflect on a more ecclesiological and Christological account of believer priesthood. In The Babylonian Captivity of the Church, Luther linked the priesthood of all believers with baptism, for it is in baptism that Christians hear the words, "You are a chosen race, a royal priesthood, a holy nation, God's own people" (1 Pet 2:9). "Therefore," Luther argued, "we are all priests."[37] And because Jesus Christ alone is the great high priest, no one exercises their priesthood apart from Christ or in isolation from the members of the church.

(c) The Church as the Body of Christ

(§§20-21) This biblical image depicts the church as Christ's body, but Christ is the head of the body, which is animated by the Spirit. Though made up of many members, the body is one (cf. Rom 12:5). By confession of faith and baptism, each person becomes a member of Christ's body through the Spirit (1 Cor 12:3, 13). And in the Lord's Supper each member's participation in the body is renewed, as through the one loaf and common cup they are united with Christ and with one another in Christ (1 Cor 10:16). By drawing on the Pauline imagery, Baptists may begin to see something of what Augustine imagined when he described Christ and the church together as forming the *totus Christus* ("the whole Christ").[38] Such a vision stands as a corrective to individualism that conceives of faith as a one-on-one relationship between God and the individual soul.[39] As the American Baptist church historian, Winthrop Hudson, succinctly put it, the upshot of identifying individualism as the cardinal doctrine of Baptists was "to make every[one]'s hat [their] own church."[40] Hudson warned that such atomization rendered ecclesiology all but impossible except as the voluntary association of free individuals. And, Hudson continued, "No one chooses to be a member of the church; he is made a member of the church. It is not his doing; it is God's doing."[41] The NMC calls for a serious engagement with the biblical image of the church as the body of Christ which if understood curbs the individualist and sectarian tendencies of Baptist ecclesiology.

(d) The Church as Temple of the Holy Spirit

(§§22-23) What makes the church the church? The answer that runs through the New Testament is: the Holy Spirit. Although individual believers are described as being the temple of the Holy Spirit (1 Cor 6:19), the church is depicted as the temple in which God's Spirit uniquely dwells (1 Cor 3:19-17). The same Spirit that became incarnate in the body of Jesus now indwells the church, so that the church is a continuation of the incarnation. The story of Pentecost is paradigmatic of the church being filled with the Holy Spirit to continue the ministry and mission of Jesus (Acts 2). The church is God's instrument as the witness of salvation for the world, and indeed for the transformation of the entire cosmos (Rom 8:22-23).

Yet the successive waves of the Holy Spirit that have swept through the churches, from the Azuza Street Revival to the Toronto Blessing have met with a mixed reception among Baptists.[42] The dangers of pneumatocentric eccentricities notwithstanding, a number of Baptist theologians have suggested that the emphasis on the Spirit in the Pentecostal-Charismatic movement might actually be received as a blessing of renewal for the churches if it is integrated into a more fully trinitarian faith and practice.[43] African-American Baptists are a notable exception to the tendency of resistance to the Holy Spirit. One black Baptist theologian, Willam C. Turner, points to the trinitrian character of the National Baptist Church Covenant that provides an internal critique of the Pentecostal-Charismatic influences on historic Baptist faith and practice.

"Without the Spirit," Turner asserts, "the covenant falls apart, salvation loses all its meaning, and the church disintegrates into a collection of individuals."[44]

In his Systematic Theology, James William McClendon, Jr., adopted a Pentecostal perspective as the hermeneutical motto he called "the baptist vision" (cf. Acts 2:16). This is that: the church is the apostolic community, and the commands of Jesus are addressed to us. Then is now: we are the end time people, a new humanity anticipating the consummation of the blessed hope.[45] But the baptist vision does not belong exclusively to the Baptists. It denotes a way of life in the Spirit that belongs to all churches, and therefore may be rightly described as "universal," "ecumenical," and "catholic." This is the standpoint of baptist catholicity.[46]

(e) The Church as Koinonia/Communion

(§§24-33) The biblical theme of *koinonia*, which is variously translated as "communion," "participation," "fellowship," or "sharing," is crucial for understanding the nature and visible unity of the church. The epistle of 1 John vividly describes the mutual participation in human and divine fellowship (1 Jn. 1:3), and the apostle Paul points to the distinctive role of the Holy Spirit (2 Cor 15:13), not because the Spirit alone brings fellowship in and with God, but because the Spirit opens this *koinonia* to ever-new dimensions of relationship.[47] The image of *koinonia* describes the church as a fellowship that participates in the fellowship of the triune God. Individual members of the church are joined in communion with one another through participation in the communion of Father, Son and Holy Spirit, and the members of the Godhead are also in *koinonia* with one another through their participation in the *koinonia* of the gathered community of believers. Though none of these images of the church can be understood apart from the relations of all three persons of the Trinity, Baptist theologian, Paul Fiddes, notes that each image draws attention to a particular member of the Godhead: the church as people stresses the Father; the church as body focuses on the Son; and the church as temple emphasizes the Spirit, whereas the church as *koinonia* attests to all three persons in relation.[48]

Although it is not a familiar concept to many Baptists, communion ecclesiology gives voice to this conviction of the church as a fellowship in which the church is understood as grounded in the *koinonia* between the Father, Son, and Holy Spirit.[49] Moreover, because in this ecclesial vision, the local church and the universal church participate in the *koinonia* between the Father, Son, and Holy Spirit, they are held together in a perichoretic unity. So whenever a community of believers is gathered in baptismal covenant around Word and Table, Christ is directly present with them and through the Spirit they share communion with the whole people of God. This sense of communion resonates with the earliest English Particular Baptist statement in which seven congregations declared themselves to be distinct bodies yet "one in communion" as they walked together under the Lordship of Christ.[50]

(A) The Mission of the Church (§§34-42)

God has a mission, and the church is called to participate in it. Just as the church is being gathered by Word and Spirit to live under Christ's rule, so God's ultimate design is to gather all creation under the Lordship of Christ (Eph 1:10), bringing humanity and all creation into communion. In this mission the church is not only the image of communion in the triune God, but is the instrument in the fulfillment of this goal. The church is called to bear witness to the good news of God's plan in word and deed. But the mission of the church is not what it does. It is what the church is. Mission belongs to the being of the church, so in a very real sense the mission of the church is simply to be the church. The church thus signifies, participates in, and anticipates the new humanity that God intends for all creation. The description offered in the NMC of the church's participation in God's mission is rich, but it lacks a developed trinitarian account, which ironically might be enriched by reflection on contemporary work on the *missio Dei* and the missional church.

Baptist missiologists, René Padilla, Samuel Escobar, the late Orlando Costas, and others in the Latin American Theological Fraternity have long argued for an understanding of the church that is holistic and missional by nature. They stress the urgency of a missional Christology that is historically situated and responds to the cries of the poor and disenfranchised of the world. Evangelism and social justice are seen as integrally related within this account of the *missio Dei*. Yet for these Latin American Baptist missiologists, questions about the nature and mission of the church can only be answered by addressing the more fundamental question: Who is Jesus Christ? Missional ecclesiology is therefore also integrally related to missional Christology. Determining the nature and mission of the church thus begins with the foundational conviction that Jesus Christ is Lord over everything and everyone. Only then can the mission of the church move from Christology to ecclesiology in which the church is understood as a community that incarnates the witness of Christ's lordship over all of life.[51] Escobar goes so far as to argue that because mission is integral to the nature of the church, "a church that is only inward looking is not truly the church."[52] But the mission of the church is also pneumatological, which first demands pausing to discern the blowing of the Spirit and then running to follow in the same direction as the winds of the Spirit are blowing.[53] Thus the Christological and pneumatological reflections on the church lead to a more fully trinitarian account of the *missio Dei* as is found in the opening statement of the Lausanne Covenant:

> We affirm our belief in the one-eternal God, Creator and Lord of the world, Father, Son and Holy Spirit, who governs all things according to the purpose of his will. He has been calling out from the world a people for himself, and sending his people back into the world to be his servants and his witnesses, for the extension of his kingdom, the building up of Christ's body, and the glory of his name.[54]

In his groundbreaking book, *Transforming Mission*, Baptist missiologist David Bosch offered a historical and theological analysis of the church's mission. Central to the emerging ecumenical missionary consensus is an understanding of the church's mission as participation in the mission of God. In this account the mission of the church begins in the nature of the triune God. From this trinitarian standpoint, the central question is not "What message must the church proclaim?" or "How can the mission effort be supported?" but "Where is God at work?" The *locus classicus* of the *missio Dei* is Jesus' commission to the disciples in John 20:21: "As the Father has sent me, so I send you." These words are immediately followed by the observation that he breathed on them and said, "Receive the Holy Spirit." The classical formulation of the *missio Dei*, then, understands the mission of the church to begin with the mission of the Father sending the Son, and the Father and Son sending the Spirit, which extends to the Father, Son, and Spirit sending the church into the world.[55] The upshot of this shift is a radically transformed understanding in which, "It is not the church of God that has a mission in the world, but the God of mission that has a church in the world."[56]

The theological basis of this trinitarian missional theology can be traced to Lesslie Newbigin who argued that the task of Christian mission is simply understood "as proclaiming the kingdom of the Father, as sharing the life of the Son, and as bearing the witness of the Spirit."[57] This vision of the *missio Dei* also owes much to the theology of Karl Barth who envisioned a radically missionary church sent in the power of the Spirit to attest to the good news of Jesus Christ, the light of life and the hope of all nations. And yet in going to the ends of the earth, Barth explained, the church of Jesus Christ does not bring the light to the world. Rather wherever Christian witnesses go, there they meet the one eternal light of the world and the one true witness of the Gospel, the risen Lord Jesus

Christ, who has been missionally going since before the foundation of the world: The Father sending the Son, and the Father and Son sending the Spirit, and the Father, Son, and Spirit sending the church as witnesses into the world.[58]

(B) The Church as Sign and Instrument of God's Intention and Plan (§§43-47)

Section one concludes with a summary of the one, holy, catholic, and apostolic church as a sign and an instrument of God's saving purpose for the whole world. To speak of the church in terms of these four marks is to recognize that the church is a sign that points beyond itself to the triune God who creates, redeems, and sustains the entire universe. Moreover, through word and deed the church is an instrument of God's mission for the reconciliation and redemption of the world (2 Cor 5:16-21). Yet in its visible manifestations the church always stands in need of wider expressions of ecclesiality so that the world may believe the truth which became incarnate in Jesus Christ (Jn 17:21). Baptists will readily recognize the church as a sign and instrument of mission and affirm the church is beginning of the new creation. Yet like other evangelicals they stress the importance of personal faith and are less inclined to speak of the whole world as being in Christ. Consequently, Baptists place a strong urgency on the need for the Gospel to be communicated to the whole world so that every person might have the opportunity to respond in faith and repentance.[59] Can gathered communities of Baptists find good reason not to join with other ecclesial communities outside their denominational family in seeking visible ways to signify and participate in God's mission for the salvation of the world?

Conclusion

What might it mean for a denominationally divided church to understand and display Jesus' prayer "that they may all be one ... that the world may believe" (Jn 17:21)? Such a question stretches the limits of the imagination, and indeed has led many Baptists to the unfortunate conclusion that the biblical standard of "one Lord, one faith, one baptism" (Eph 4:5) must await the eschaton. While understandable, such resignation is unacceptable given the emerging ecumenical consensus on the nature and mission of the church. The difficult way beyond the as yet unresolved questions is surely through ongoing conversation. To this end, Baptists can welcome this study document and take advantage of the opportunity it provides to reason together with their brothers and sisters in Christ about the nature and mission of the church. Nevertheless, to enter into these conversations

Baptists will face challenges. Three in particular seem worth naming in relation to the section "The Church of the Triune God" (§§9-28).

> (1) The understanding and invocation of the Trinity in Baptist life typically draws upon the economic aspects of biblical revelation that identify God the Father, his Son Jesus, and their Spirit, whereas the underlying communion ecclesiology in the NMC lays stress on participation in the ontological relations within the Godhead. Because the theological and liturgical language of the immanent Trinity is not familiar to many Baptists, it may be difficult to appropriate insights from a more fully trinitarian ecclesiology. To be sure, economic and immanent language names the same three-in-one-God. As Karl Rahner famously observed, "the 'economic' Trinity is the 'immanent' Trinity and the 'immanent' Trinity is the 'economic' Trinity."[60] However, the theological maps of the immanent Trinity and the economic Trinity are not symmetrical and function somewhat differently. Still this challenge is not insurmountable. One possible intermediate step might be for Baptists to learn how to move from the economic language in the triadic narrative of the Bible (God, Jesus, and Spirit) to seeing the narrative of Scripture as the unfolding story of the triune God.[61] Such efforts to render the language of the immanent Trinity more familiar to Baptists would make the ecclesial vision of the NMC more readily accessible, thus providing a common language to talk about the visible unity of the church.
>
> (2) The fact that many Baptists seem to be more comfortable speaking about the ordinances as "outward signs of inward experience" will surely give them pause about the suggestion that these acts may be understood as means of as well as witnesses to the presence and grace of God. Although Baptists and others in the free church tradition recognize that God is mysteriously at work in ways that they do not understand and cannot name, they have resisted accounts which suggest that God works *ex opere operato*. Nevertheless, the interest in finding richer and fuller language for talking about God's action remains very much open. It is a conversation that has been going on for a long time. Trying to explain God's transcendent presence to children, St. Augustine said, "These realities are called sacraments because in them one thing is seen, while another is grasped."[62] If there is more going on here than meets the eye, what language can Baptists borrow to talk about such realities? The contemporary interest in pneumatology offers an opportunity to think anew about what God might be doing in the baptismal waters

and at the communion table. Though the eyes see only water, bread, and wine, what is grasped in and through the Spirit is a sense of the life-giving reality of God. Thinking about the communion of the Holy Spirit (2 Cor 13:14) as participation in the inner life of the Trinity surely opens new lines of communication for considering a more sacramental understanding of God's action through the Spirit.

(3) A third significant challenge Baptists face in addressing the issues of the NMC has to do with thinking about what it means to recognize expressions of the one, holy, catholic, and apostolic church within the associations, denominations, unions, and fellowships of Baptists. The historic stress on the liberty of individual conscience and the emphasis on the freedom of each local church sometimes make it seem near impossible to think about life together for Baptists in ecumenical terms. Yet there are hopeful signs. In March 2007 a group of theologians met in Elstal, Germany, to reflect on the state of ecclesiology in Baptist life. Their statement declared that the foundational understanding of the church is that "Christ is in the midst of His church as its Lord. As the head of the church He empowers and equips it for holistic mission and ministry, and grants it its freedom." But they made the important distinction that "For Baptists, the local church is wholly church but not the whole church." Congregations thus need the wider church "for discernment and action."[63]

The Cooperative Baptist Fellowship, the wider denominational body of which I am part, like many other Baptist groups emphasizes the visible church. But the last night of each general assembly concludes with worship in which the Lord's Supper is observed. From the standpoint of many Baptists, this is an ecclesiologically ambiguous act because the general assembly, not being a local church, is not regarded as an ecclesial body. It remains unclear how these translocal gatherings may be understood as expressions of the church. Yet there the community of the baptized is gathered by word and sacrament. What is that if it is not a visible manifestation of the one, holy, catholic, and apostolic church? It may be a practice without a theology to sustain it, but the deliberate decision to "do this" gestures toward a vision of the church as the *totus Christus*. In a May 15, 2008, article, BWA General Secretary Neville Callam, asked, "What is the precise ecclesiological significance of the BWA?"[64] Callam did not ask whether there is any ecclesial significance, but what the ecclesial significance is. He went on to suggest that the BWA is more than an alliance, an association, a society, or a federation. For the global family of Baptists are drawn together into fellowship with one another through the communion of the Holy Spirit. The new Faith and

Order study document extends the invitation to continue the conversation in search of ways to identify and manifest expressions of the one, holy, catholic, and apostolic church in worship, work, and witness. Can the global Baptist fellowship find a way to participate in the emerging convergence on the nature and mission of the church? For the sake of the Gospel, let us hope so.

CHAPTER 2
"THE CHURCH: GROWING IN COMMUNION":
RESPONSE TO CHAPTER III OF *THE CHURCH: TOWARDS A COMMON VISION*
(Faith and Order Paper 214)

Elizabeth Newman

I am grateful for the opportunity to respond to *The Church: Towards a Common Vision* (hereafter identified as CV), previously titled *The Nature and Mission of the Church*. Our current document, published this year by the World Council of Church's Faith and Order Commission, summarizes convergences in multilateral conversations and explores ways that churches might continue to embrace a shared calling toward visible unity. My assignment is to engage Chapter III: "The Church: Growing in Communion." This section builds upon a key conviction expressed in the first chapter's opening paragraph: "Communion, whose source is the very life of the Holy Trinity, is both the gift by which the Church lives and, at the same time, the gift that God calls the Church to offer to a wounded and divided humanity in hope of reconciliation and healing," (§1).[1] My comments will focus on four topics from this chapter: 1) the holiness of the church, 2) the compatibility of ordinance and sacrament, 3) the mode of baptism and, 4) the gift of authority.

The Holiness of the Church

Chapter Three begins by placing growth in communion within an eschatological framework, thus the opening section is titled "already but not yet." The authors state that, "On the one hand, as the communion of believers held in personal relationship with God, the Church is already the eschatological community God wills" (§34). On the other hand, CV states that "as an historical reality the Church is made up of human beings who are subject to the conditions of the world" (§34). A key challenge that arises from this already/not yet reality, our authors note, is how to interpret the holiness of the church in light of its sin and an unrealized eschatology. While some traditions "affirm that the Church is sinless since, being the body of the sinless Christ, it cannot sin," (§35) others find this language inadequate "since sin may become systemic so as to affect the institution of the Church itself and, although sin is in contradiction to the true identity of the Church, it is nonetheless real" (§35).

Most Baptists would no doubt take issue with a "sinless" Church, a claim that can appear to whitewash the very real sins that distort the church's life. The alternative position can seem, from this viewpoint, to reflect an over-realized eschatology. The document does not resolve these "significant differences," though it concludes this section stating that "holiness expresses the Church's identity according to the will of God, while sin stands in contradiction to this" (§36).

Response

My response addresses two questions: 1) what do those who maintain the church as "sinless" mean exactly? and 2) how might looking at these "significant differences" through primarily a Christological rather than eschatological lens cast on alternative light on them?

To engage these questions, I turn to a proponent of the "church is sinless" language, the Catholic theologian and Cardinal Charles Journet (1891-1975). Journet understands holiness (like the other marks of the church) as "rooted in and growing out of the very essence of the Church, an exteriorization, a normal manifestation, of her mystery."[2] Journet uses "church" to refer not to its empirical aspect (its descriptive and phenomenal standpoint) nor its moral and "deontological" aspect, but rather its theological and ontological reality. Thus Journet's statement – "The Church is sinless, though she contains sinners"[3] – is a theological/ontological one. What does he mean? Journet agrees, in a sense, with Augustine who "could say that [the church] limps, [and] St. Catherine of Siena that she is leprous." But these statements, Journet argues, ought not to be interpreted to mean that "Christ sins in his members."[4]

According to his commentators as well as his own journals, Journet was deeply formed by his early reading of St. Catherine of Siena. One passage was particularly formative: "This is how I want you to act toward those of my ministers who are ... covered with the filth of sin and ragged from their abuse of charity when they bring you the ... sacraments. For it is not my will that they should administer the Sun to you out of their darksomeness."[5] In light of this vivid description of sin – an "abuse of charity" – Journet embraces a "paradoxical [mode] of expression" (church as sinless, containing sinners). He relates this paradox to such Scripture passages as 1 Corinthians 6:15, 19: "Know you not that your bodies are the members of Christ?...Or know you not that your members are the temple of the Holy Ghost..." (NRSV) Journet's statement is primarily Christological rather than eschatological.

To develop this point, we can relate the challenge St. Catherine apparently posed to Journet to the challenge that the Donatists posed to Augustine. As is well-known, the Donatists viewed those priests who denied Christ by surrendering Scripture to their persecutors as traditors. They concluded that because of such apostasy, these priests could no longer serve as priests, and that sacraments administered by them, such as baptism, were invalid.

Augustine classically opposed this position by arguing that the sins of the priests do not negate the validity of the sacraments.[6] This is because, Augustine argued, the "real minister in every sacrament is none other than Christ himself." Augustine cites John 1:33: "This [Christ] is he which baptizeth with the Holy Spirit."[7] Augustine claims more broadly that "...no sin of man, however villainous and monstrous, can interfere with the promises of God, nor can any impiety of any persons within the Church cause the word of God to be made void as to the existence and diffusion of the Church to the ends of the earth, which was promised to the Fathers and now is manifest."[8]

In terms of the relation between holiness and sin, both Journet and Augustine conclude that the church is always holy, not because of her members but because of Christ.

Journet's position is not without critics within his own tradition. Yves Congar (1904-1995) argues that the activity of the church in history is not simply accidental but part of the church's essence.[9] A key concern of Congar's is not to idealize the church, separating it from its lived reality in time.[10] Thus as Dennis Doyle notes, for Congar "the Church has an eschatological nature; it remains unfinished, still imperfect and en route to its fulfillment."[11] In this sense, Congar may be in agreement with CV when it states, "sin may become systemic so as to affect the institution of the Church itself" (§35).

Congar's worry about idealizing the church is, at least in part, addressed by Rowan Williams' engagement with Augustine and the Donatists. Williams argues that "Part of Augustine's gravamen against...the Donatists has to do with their identification of possible states within history as bearers of a goodness that [are] somehow complete or adequate." "The Donatists," says Williams, "[absolutize] the purity of the empirical church ... [They] take the church out of time."[12] In other words, the Donatists refuse to acknowledge the holiness of the church as dependent not on moral purity but on the sufficiency of Christ. They thus idealize a singular state in history as complete. Thus it is the Donatists, in their rejection of the necessity of Christ, that remove the church from history. They remove the church from time, because they fail to see how Christ, the source of all holiness, is present in time.

Baptist theologian Robert C. Walton (1905?-1985) makes a similar point when he states that the life of "our churches… is indeed historically conditioned, but this does not alter the fact that they are God's new creation, since He is the Lord of History…"[13] Walton emphasizes the reality of the church as a "divine creation, led by the Holy Spirit." In discussing the gathered church and the church meeting, Walton emphasizes, "Here, especially, it is necessary to keep firmly in mind the nature of the Church as a divine society and not a human institution."[14] Such an emphasis echoes a hymn familiar to most Baptists: "the church's one foundation is Jesus Christ her Lord, she is his new creation, through water and the word."

Language of Divine creation can call forth the following analogy in relation to the holiness of the church: just as creation is entirely good and sin a privation, so also the church is entirely holy (because Christ is holy) and sin a privation. One might well wonder whether or not, and under what conditions, a church might cease to be holy. If we look at the analogy of creation and of sin as privation, we could follow this Augustinian logic for the church as well. That is, sin is parasitic on the goodness of being and thus cannot negate being as good. So also, the sins of Christians are a privation of their new being in Christ, a privation that distorts the holiness of the church but cannot ultimately negate it.[15]

To say that that holiness is "the *will* of God for the church" (§36, my emphasis) could imply that the church might or might not be holy, dependent upon human response. Holiness is dependent upon human response, but in a secondary sense. To say the church is holy is first of all a Christological statement. It points to holiness as a gift already given to the church in the person of Christ. Such an understanding, in my view, coincides with a Baptist understanding of the church – not as simply a voluntary organization – but as a community that Christ through the Spirit gathers and calls. As such, we are "set apart" (holy), freed from sin to live as faithful witnesses to the Gospel.

The Compatibility of Sacraments and Ordinances

In its conclusion, *CV* emphasizes that the liturgy, "*especially the celebration of the Eucharist*, serves as a dynamic paradigm for … *koinonia* in the present age" (§67, my emphasis). While it is often at the Eucharistic table that ecclesial divisions of the church become at once most obvious and painful, CV maintains it may also be at the Lord's Table that new possibilities for communion open up. Christian traditions, they note, have diverged on terminology used for this practice (as well as for baptism). "The word sacrament ... indicates that God's saving work is communicated in the action of the rite, whilst the term ordinance emphasizes that the action of the rite is performed in obedience to Christ's word and example" (§44). While these have "often been seen as mutually opposed" (§44), CV observes that most traditions affirm both an instrumental and expressive understanding. That is, most "affirm ... that God [instrumentally] uses [these events] to bring about a new reality" and that these rites are also expressive "of an already-existing reality." The authors conclude: might the difference between ordinance and sacrament "be more one of emphasis than of doctrinal disagreement?" (§44) They invite churches to reflect on the Lord's Supper and baptism in light of the "historical roots and potential compatibility of the expressions 'sacrament' and 'ordinance'" (§44).

While some Baptist criticized WCC's earlier document *Baptism, Eucharist and Ministry* (1982) for a tendency toward "sacramentalism,"[16] our present document presents an opportunity, not to abandon the language of "ordinance," but to discern how an understanding of both ordinance and a sacrament might enrich liturgical practice.[17]

Generally speaking, Baptists have tended to place a strong emphasis on the expressive dimension. The strength of this position can be a deep personal involvement in the rites and a strong emphasis on human agency. A potential weakness, however, is a failure to see how such human agency is related to Divine agency, or how the rites are more than human efforts. Conversely, an emphasis only on Divine agency in other traditions can lead to seeing the rites as "magical," or divorced from human participation.

The Lord's Supper

Henri De Lubac observes, for example, that the Eucharist in the Middle Ages came to be seen as an "isolated miracle"—one maintained by people in charge, tending to give them great power.[18] The reformers, De Lubac observes rightly, took issue with such pretensions to power, as if only an isolated hierarchy had access to Divine agency.[19] In a similar vein, Catherine Pickstock notes that in the early modern period, a trend arose in the Catholic Church where "the laity would attend only to see the elevation of the Host."[20]

In contrast to this exclusive emphasis on Divine agency – on the Eucharist as an isolated miracle – stands an emphasis on human agency alone, such as we find in John Leland, a Virginia Baptist minister (1754-1841) and well-known defender of religious liberty in America. While pastoring a Baptist church in Cheshire, Massachusetts, Leland came to the conclusion that he could no longer administer the Lord's Supper. In a letter to his congregation, Leland stated that while he had no complaint against communing, "for myself, for more than thirty years experiment I have had no evidence that the bread and wine ever assisted my faith to discern the Lord's body." He thus asked his congregation to allow him the liberty to "do [only] what I have faith and confidence in."[21] The lens through which Leland interprets the Lord's Supper is that of human agency alone; it is only a "commemorative" rite that may be abandoned if not personally efficacious.

Pickstock argues that these two seemingly opposed positions are in fact related in the following way: "an extrinsically miraculous interpretation of the Eucharist secretly colludes with the merely symbolic interpretation of the Eucharist."[22] The isolated miracle versus symbolic dialectic, she suggests, exists in isolated rather than participatory time. Isolated or synchronic time views an object as a given fact in a "single moment."[23] Such a static understanding of time leads to seeing the Eucharist as either an isolated miracle (a static fact in present time) or as merely symbolic (a symbol of a time long gone). As such it removes the Eucharist from the "narrative action of the ecclesial liturgy as a whole – defined broadly, as a mode of life, as well as a particular celebration."[24]

Pickstock's use of phrases such as "narrative action," "mode of life" and "celebration" resonates with a Baptist emphasis on discipleship as a way of life grounded in the narrative of Scripture. One way, then, for Baptists to think about the compatibility between sacrament and ordinance would be to engage more fully how the Lord's Supper not only represents faith but also produces and sustains a life of discipleship. Baptists might be especially helped here by Orthodox theologian Alexander Schmemann, who begins his well-known book, *For the Life of the World*, by quoting Feuerbach: "man is what he eats." While Schmemann notes that Feuerbach understood this in a purely materialistic way, the Bible, says Schmemann, also begins with man (and woman) as hungry beings, and with the fact that "man is what he eats." Adam and Eve's consumption of food, however, was a rejection of communion with God. From this perspective, the fall, according to Schmemann, is not that humans preferred the world to God, "distorted the balance between the spiritual and material, but that [they] made the world material, whereas [they were] to have transformed it into 'life in God'..."[25] Thus the world became opaque. By contrast, in the Eucharist, food is not only "material" (separated from its Creator), but more fully a gift of communion through Christ. In this sense, the sharing of the bread and cup is neither a magical rupture in present time nor merely a present symbol of time long past, but a diachronic sharing in the blood and body of Christ (1 Corinthians 10:16). Schmemann's understanding, though briefly stated, can provide an alternative to an isolated, timeless approach to the Table. Schmemann places his narration of the Eucharist in the broad sweep of Scripture; Christ recapitulates Adam in the sense that Christ through the Spirit repeats and brings to fulfillment creation as communion with God.[26] As such, the Lord's Supper makes possible a Eucharistic "mode of life," one where, as Walter Rauschenbusch states, "even the common thornbush is aflame with [God's] glory."[27]

But, does this understanding run the danger of placing too much weight on the Lord's Supper, especially for Baptists who typically celebrate this rite only once a month (or sometimes less)? This kind of question indicates that if Baptists and other Christians are to embrace a rich and Scriptural compatibility between ordinance and sacrament, then a similar kind of compatibility needs to be seen between the Word and Table.

Baptism

The challenge of bringing "ordinance" and "sacrament" together for Baptists pertains to baptism as well. As Christopher Ellis notes, "Too often interpretations of…baptism have been reduced to an illustration of the gospel, an expression of subjective faith or an opportunity to encourage commitment."[28]

It is no doubt helpful to point out, as Philip Thompson and others have done, that early Baptists sometimes had a more vibrant theology and practice of baptism than many Baptists today. Thompson cites, as one example, a Baptist hymn, published in 1793, by Eleazar Clay: "Eternal Spirit, heavenly Dove, / On these baptismal waters move; / That we through energy divine, / May have the substance with the sign."[29] The Spirit hovering over baptism calls to mind the Spirit hovering over creation, making new creation possible. "On these baptismal waters move" is a prayer for the Spirit to stir the waters so that all those gathered may be transformed. In praying for "the substance with the sign," these early Baptists were acknowledging a deep compatibility between expressing their faith and receiving Divine grace through baptism.

But what does it mean to receive grace through baptism? Baptists have worried about baptism coming to function mechanistically (apart from faith).[30] Such worries were in part responses to such earlier practices as baptizing dying infants to ensure their entrance into heaven.[31] An emphasis on baptism as "expressive" of one's faith has tended to dominate Baptist life, at least in contemporary time.

An exclusive focus on baptism as only expressive, however, has generated its own problems. Anthony Cross, for example, argues that a Baptist theology of baptism has been subordinated to "evangelistic enthusiasms." He adds that outside of heated debates with paedobaptists, we have "made little of the rite."[32] In practice, this subordination has often resulted in baptism being understood as a spectator phenomenon (i.e., the congregation passively watches what happens to the candidate) or as merely symbolic.[33]

The challenge here, as in the Lord's Supper, is to expand the Baptist imagination by describing 1) how baptism functions already instrumentally in the life of the church and 2) how it might do so more fully, both tasks that have been well underway by a number of Baptist theologians.[34] Ellis, for example, describes baptism as a "sacrament of proclamation," relating baptism to a Baptist emphasis on being a people of the Word. Just as the Holy Spirit is present in the preaching of the Word, so also in the proclamation of baptism, "the Holy Spirit is working – in those who act and those who witness, in those who speak and those who hear."[35]

An analogy between the proclamation of Scripture and baptism could also engage how in Scripture God shapes, sends or pours forth water in order to save His people. In Exodus, for example, when "Moses [stretches] out his hand over the sea" (14:21), God saves a people, Israel, by transforming the water into a way of salvation. It is not the water that saves – God does – but the Creator works within creation so that the Israelites might pass through the waters to new life. An eighteenth century Baptist baptismal prayer reads: "Thou that didst come from Galilee to Jordan come now also from heaven to – and meet us on the banks of this river ... afford us communion with thee in thy baptism; for in the water and in the floods thy presence is promised!"[36] This Baptist prayer places baptism within the context of Scripture's narration of Divine involvement with water, and in so doing includes an understanding of baptism as both expressive and instrumental.

In pointing toward a potential compatibility between ordinance and sacrament, I conclude with Neville Callam's description of Caribbean Baptists who sometimes, he states, put it like this: "'Something happens to us whenever we partake of the Lord's Supper'[Callam then observes] they experience the gracious hand of God upon their lives, forgiving their sins, offering them nourishment for the pilgrimage of the Christian life, and drawing them into ever deeper communion with the Trinity ... ordinance is understood to have sacramental significance."[37]

CHAPTER 2

The Mode of Baptism

The authors note a growing convergence in theological understandings of baptism. Key convergences include 1) through baptism with water in the name of the Triune God, Christians are united with Christ, 2) baptism is a participation in Christ's baptism, life, death and resurrection and 3) baptism is a "basic bond of unity." CV does not directly address a key question about baptism: who may be baptized. In terms of the mode of baptism, CV notes that "the churches" "registered significant approval of BEM (1982)," but they acknowledge as well BEM's recommendation to seek "further convergence on what remained the most significant unresolved issue (related to baptism): who may be baptized (§40). In light of a theological convergence, CV thus invites "churches to consider whether they can now achieve closer convergence about who may receive baptism… "(§44)

From a Baptist perspective, a key statement in BEM can be found in the opening paragraph on baptismal practice: "While the possibility that infant baptism was also practised in the apostolic age cannot be excluded, baptism upon personal profession of faith is the most clearly attested pattern in the New Testament documents."[38] In a similar vein, Catholic theologian Susan K. Wood states, "Since the restoration of the catechumenate after Vatican II and with the promulgation of the Rite of Christian Initiation of Adults, adult baptism is normative for Roman Catholic understanding of the sacrament even though statistically more infants may be baptized than adults. Adult baptism is normative because of the faith engaged and also because the rite involves a conversion of life not experienced by the infant."[39] One might wonder what it means to describe believer's baptism as normative, while still maintaining infant baptism as the typical mode of baptism. One response, common in those churches that practice infant baptism, is to say that faith is indeed present and real, but it is "faith by proxy, the faith of parents, godparents, and the Christian community."[40] Such differences in faith requirements notwithstanding, one sees in these other ecclesial bodies a willingness to acknowledge believer's baptism as the sign that most fully embodies the signified: burial and new life; washing and cleansing from sin; and imitation of Jesus' baptism.

Baptists can welcome these acknowledgements that believer's baptism is, in a sense, normative. On our part we are challenged by the controversial question of whether or not to acknowledge the baptism of infants as a real baptism. If baptism is only a symbol of a prior faith or conversion experience (expressive), then it will likely follow that infant baptism is not a genuine baptism. To see baptism as an ordinance with sacramental significance, however, provides some alternative possibilities. First, it calls into question a rationalism that has sometimes shaped Baptist understandings of baptism. For example, some justify believer's baptism by saying, "He (or she) knew what he was doing."41 If human reason becomes the ground for baptism, however, then not only does this exclude those who seem to lack reason (the mentally handicapped, for example), but it assumes that reason alone provides sufficient ground for the life of faith. Such a view is problematic in that it fails to fully register the mystery of God's providential grace. Secondly, baptism as a grace-filled sign opens up possibilities to see infant baptisms as genuine, albeit not as fully scripturally performed as believer's baptism. Such a view can acknowledge that God's grace and promises are present in infant baptism (along with the pledge of the family and church to bring the child up in the faith), while at the same time maintaining the witness of believers baptism as normative. Finally, baptism as a grace-filled sign provides theological space to see baptism not only as a single event, but as a way of life that we live by the grace of God. In other words, baptism is a lifelong process. As Paul emphasizes, "Therefore we have been buried with him by baptism into death, so that, just as Christ was raised from the dead by the glory of the Father, so we too might walk in newness of life" (Romans 6:4, NRSV).

The Gift of Authority

CV describes authority as a gift, meaning that "all authority in the Church comes from her Lord and head, Jesus Christ" (§48). As a gift, "authority in the Church in its various forms and levels, must be distinguished from mere power" (§50). Baptists who have at times shared a history of seeing an abuse of authority as power will welcome this distinction.

CV identifies "the sources of authority recognized in varying degrees by the churches" as Scripture, Tradition, worship, councils and synods." (§50). They add to these more familiar sources "the lives of saints, in the witness of monasticism and in various ways that groups of believers have lived out and expressed the truth of the gospel" (§50). Through the guidance of the Holy Spirit, CV states that we see authority in "the ecumenical movement [which] has made it possible for authoritative teaching by some Christian leaders to have an effect beyond the boundaries of their own communities. For example, Archbishop Desmond Tutu's leadership in declaring that apartheid was too strong to be overcome by a divided Church, the efforts by Popes John Paul II and Benedict XVI to invite Christians and leaders from other faiths to join in praying for and promoting peace, and of the influence of Brother Roger Schutz as he inspired countless

Christian believers, especially the young, to join together in common worship of the Triune God" (§51).

While continued ecumenical conversation around ordained ministry is vital, I find an inclusion of the authority of saints and of specific Christian communities a compelling way to imagine how different churches might move "beyond the boundaries of their own communities." Geoffrey Wainwright states that, "... a significant step towards ecclesial unity would be taken by the increased formal and mutual recognition of saints."[42] In a similar vein, Pope John Paul II wrote, in *Ut Unum Sint* ("May they be one"), "When we speak of a common heritage, we must acknowledge as part of it not only the institutions, rites, means of salvation and the traditions which all the communities have preserved and by which they have been shaped, but first and foremost this reality of holiness." By "this reality of holiness," he means the saints "who come from all the Churches and Ecclesial communities…This universal presence of the Saints is in fact a proof of the transcendent power of the Spirit."[43]

Thus, the turn to the saints as potential sources of authority and Christian unity is grounded in the acknowledgement that the Holy Spirit is present and working in the lives of persons in order to heal the wounds of division in the church. Stated differently, it is sustained by the conviction that God provides saints across time and space as gifts for the whole church. Such an understanding does not negate the presence of the Holy Spirit in other sources of authority (Scripture, tradition, and so forth), but enhances this authority in a dialogical way. The saints can become windows or "living icons" into Scripture and tradition, even as Scripture and tradition can give us ever more fruitful ways to engage their lives. Thus, the communion of saints – the great "cloud of witnesses" (Heb. 12:1) – is best understood as "dialogical" as various churches continually engage and reread the lives of the saints in light of Christ.[44]

In what ways might saints provide paths toward the healing of ecclesial divisions? Or in what ways might particular Christian communities (such as Taizé) be witnesses of unity for the church universal? Reading histories of division with the saints is not intended to erase painful memories, but rather to remember these in a way that heals. For example, in Baptist life, Clarence Jordan established Koinonia Farms (1942), an integrated Christian community, in the midst of a deeply and tragically racially divided church in southwest Georgia (United States), Jordan's vision of *koinonia*, inspired by such biblical passages as Acts 2, "meant loving your enemies, and that meant staying to be reconciled with them."[45] Jordon's life and Koinonia Farms provide a different way of reading the history/story of the church, not by erasing its painful divisions but by placing these within the context of participation with Christ and the whole body of Christ.[46] Conversely, a saint like Teresa of Avila can speak across ecclesial boundaries in her vivid use of scriptural figures as an alternative to the politics and economics that so easily divide the church today.[47] This shared holiness, CV rightly notes, provides a significant way to build up the unity of the Body of Christ.

CHAPTER 3
"*KOINONIA*: THE CHURCH IN AND FOR THE WORLD":
COMMENT ON THE FINAL PART OF *THE CHURCH: TOWARDS A COMMON VISION* (FAITH AND ORDER PAPER 214)

Paul S. Fiddes

Koinonia and Covenant in Ecclesiology

"A picture shows me at a glance what it takes dozens of pages of a book to expound." So wrote the Russian novelist Ivan Turgenev, and the church of Christ has exemplified this truth by offering a series of images to express the complexities (even the mystery) of its own nature. The Faith and Order paper on *The Church: Towards a Common Vision*, notes early on that an adequate approach to the mystery of the church requires a wide range of images – primarily "people of God," "body of Christ" and "temple of the Holy Spirit," together with other images such as vine, flock, bride, household, soldiers and friends (12).[1] However, it subordinates all these to the idea of *koinonia*. "The biblical notion of *koinonia*," it declares, "has become central in the ecumenical quest for a common understanding of the life and unity of the Church" (13).

The Greek noun *koinonia*, the paper explains, may be understood as communion, participation, fellowship or sharing. *Koinonia*, of course, is also an image, especially when applied to the life of God that can only be approached through metaphors or verbal images. Indeed, the usefulness of the term "communion" is both its capacity for expressing a diversity of human relationships, and its rooting in a vision of God as Trinity. Ecclesially, it can describe the relation of an individual believer to a local congregation, the relating of churches together on various levels of human society, the relation between churches and their leaders (pastors and bishops) and leaders with each other, the communal life created by sharing in the Eucharist, the relation of the local to the universal church, and the participation of all these relations (including the partnership of woman and man in creation) in the loving fellowship of Father, Son and Holy Spirit. In short, it makes clear that the church is a manifestation in time and space of the eternal relational life of God. In harmony with *The Church: Towards a Common Vision*, the report of recent conversations between the Baptist World Alliance and the Roman Catholic Church states near the beginning:

> The church is thus to be understood as a *koinonia* ("communion," "participation" or "fellowship"), which is grounded in the *koinonia* of the triune God. Believers are joined in *koinonia* through participation in the communion of Father, Son and Holy Spirit. At the same time they are in *koinonia* through their participation in the community of believers gathered by Christ in his church: "that you may have fellowship with us. And truly our fellowship is with the Father and with his Son Jesus Christ" (1 Jn. 1:3) . The principle of *koinonia* applies both to the church gathered in a local congregation and to congregations gathered together, whether in a regional association of churches (in the Baptist model) or in a local church (in the Catholic sense), or in still wider expressions of the church universal.[2]

Koinonia has become the "sacred thread"[3] weaving together an ecumenical convergence on the nature of the church, partly because it allows the flexibility of "degrees of communion" or "a certain though imperfect communion,"[4] and so is able to express "the various forms and extent of communion already enjoyed by the Churches"[5] as well as hopes for a fuller visible unity.

The importance of *koinonia* for this paper is underlined in both the Conclusion and the Historical Note on process with which the paper ends. The conclusion declares that the liturgy of the church is the paradigm of *koinonia*, which is manifested in three forms – unity in faith, in sacramental life and in service (67). Sounding the characteristic ecumenical note that brokenness and division contradict Christ's will for his church, the conclusion ends with the vision of *koinonia* as the entire communion of saints, and with the glorious hope that the final destiny of the church will be to be "caught up in the *koinonia*/communion of the Father, Son and Holy Spirit. . .praising and rejoicing in God forever." (68)

In the Note on process, a significant moment in Faith and Order reflection is identified as the 1993 Fifth World Congress at Santiago de Compostela, Spain, with its theme, "Towards *Koinonia* in Faith, Life and Witness." This theme was enhanced by a "new ecumenical momentum created by the growing prominence of *communion ecclesiology* in bilateral dialogues" (my italics, p. 43), and all this launched the new study on what was then called The *Nature and Mission of the*

Church, which was published in 1998. Responses to this text by the churches included the need for integration of the chapters on the "Church as Communion" with the chapter on the "Church of the Triune God." How could the *koinonia* of the church be treated separately from the *koinonia* of the Trinity? A second version of *The Nature and Mission of the Church* in 2006 put this right, with greater emphasis on the biblical insights on the church as communion. Finally, the third edition we have before us, issued in 2010, is claimed to be no longer "a stage on the way" to a Common Statement, but the Common Statement itself, a convergence document that can be sent to the churches as "a common point of reference in order to test out or discern their own ecclesiological convergences." The new title with the words "a Common Vision" echoes the idea of *koinonia*, and the section previously called "The Church of the Triune God" is now headed "The Church of the Triune God as *Koinonia*," so beginning with the concept of *koinonia* rather than working up to it through other images as previously (13).[6] Throughout the document, references to the church as communion or *koinonia* have been liberally increased.

I believe that the image of *koinonia* is indeed foundational to our proper vision of the church. But despite this welcome stress on *koinonia* in the final version of the paper, I want to make two observations that might give us pause for thought. First, there is no attempt to place the ecclesial concept of "covenant" alongside *koinonia*, which I suggest by contrast is a definite achievement of the recent BWA-Roman Catholic conversations. These align the ecumenical convergence on *communio* with the traditional Baptist idea of covenant. The agreed statement affirms:

> The *koinonia* of the church may also be understood as a "covenant community" although this language is less familiar to Catholics than to Baptists. "Covenant" expresses at once both the initiative and prior activity of God in making relationship with his people through Christ, and the willing commitment of people to each other and to God... The fellowship or *koinonia* of the church itself is [thus] both a gift and calling...[7]

From their earliest beginnings in the English Reformation period, Baptists have thought of the church as gathered by a covenant or agreement that has two dimensions. There is first a vertical agreement that relates believers to God, members of the church gratefully receiving the eternal covenant of grace that God makes with all humankind in Christ, and promising for their part to be faithful to God. Second, there is a horizontal dimension in which believers are united to each other in a promise that usually took the form of pledging to "walk together and watch over each other."[8] Often this horizontal promise has taken the form of a written document to which all members of a local church have put their names, while in other places the covenant is understood to be enacted in baptism. The covenant in these two dimensions, eternal and temporal, is certainly sealed in baptism and renewed in the Lord's Supper or Eucharist.

The two dimensions of covenant are, we can readily see, parallel to the two dimensions of *koinonia* – communion *within* the people of God and *between* that people and the triune God. To perceive the parallel with *koinonia* it is important to stress that Baptists have not thought of the local church as a merely voluntary organization; the covenant they make is no mere human choice, but an obedient response to the risen Christ who calls them together; Christ is the covenant-maker, ruling in the midst of the congregation that has the responsibility of perceiving his mind or purpose for them. The capacity of *koinonia* to relate the local church to the church universal is thus echoed by covenant since – as early Baptists put is – all congregations walk together under one rule and one head, that of Christ.[9]

Now, while the word "covenant" occasionally appears in this paper,[10] it is never applied to the nature of the church. Perhaps we can see here the result of there being no Baptist representative in the drafting of the final version of the paper, as the Historical Note shows us (p. 45); the drafting committee consisted of theologians coming from the Anglican, Catholic, Lutheran, Methodist, Orthodox and Reformed traditions – but no Baptist. My argument will be that it would have made a difference if features of covenant had made their way into the discussion of *koinonia* as they have done in the BWA-Roman Catholic conversations.

My second general observation is that, despite multiple references to *koinonia*, there is some evidence that a theology of *koinonia*, and particularly a participation in the *koinonia* of the triune God, has not sunk sufficiently deeply into the discussions of chapters III and IV. A very good start is made in chapter II by drawing upon *koinonia* for illumination of the relation between unity and diversity, and especially of the relation between the local church and the great church universal. But my impression is that there is less theological depth to the references to communion and *koinonia* in Chapter III (headed: "The Church, Growing in Communion") with its discussion of faith, sacraments and ministry, and that the depth grows even more shallow in the chapter with which we are mainly concerned here, chapter IV on "The Church: In and for the World." I am going to make one reference to chapter III in due course, but now we turn to the last chapter and its vision of the relation between church and world.

At several points here this "convergence" document is constrained to notice "serious disagreements" that remain within and between the churches on the issues handled (60, 63, 65). The paper does an excellent job on setting out both convergence and remaining divergences, with both clarity and charity. My argument is that we might be able to move some way toward resolution of these disagreements (without admittedly finally solving them) if first we were to draw more on the theological resources of *koinonia*, and second. if we were to draw on the insights that "covenant ecclesiology" can bring to *koinonia* ecclesiology.

God's Purpose for Creation: The Kingdom

The chapter begins with a splendid vision of the love of God for the world, which means "for every child, woman and man who has ever become part of human history and, indeed, for the whole of creation." The final destiny of the universe is thus affirmed to be the Kingdom of God. Of course, this is gloriously true, but oddly there is no reference in the section (58-60) to *koinonia*, or the Kingdom as *koinonia*, though similar affirmations are made elsewhere in the paper. Does this matter? It does, I suggest, when the language of a divine "plan" appears, both in the heading to the section and in the declaration that God intends the church to "serve the divine plan for the transformation of the world." The language of "plan" has a static quality to it, while the notion of "purpose" is more dynamic.

I mean that God can have "purposes" that are open in the way they are to be fulfilled, leaving plenty of room for the freedom of God and the freedom that God gives to created beings. God can fulfill God's promises in unexpected ways, as Israel of old learned continually, and surprises might come both from the creative imagination of God and from the results of cooperation between God and the world God creates. By God's own desire there is an uncreated Creator, and created creators, working in co-creativity. God's purpose to overcome evil and finally bring about a new creation is certain because of the power of God's love, but the form that the new creation takes will be shaped by the responses that creatures have made to the possibilities held before them. This idea of open-ended purposes rather than fixed plans fits well into the vision of *koinonia*, a fellowship in which each partner is open to the other and humbly affected by the other. It is underlined by the idea of "covenant" in which the covenant-partners each play their part, while nothing can happen in the first place without the initiation of the covenant-maker. So, according to Genesis 9, God makes a covenant for the preservation and flourishing of life not only with human beings, but with "every living creature of all flesh that is upon the earth" (Gen 9:12, 16).

This perspective of a God who has purposes for love, justice and peace rather than fixed plans about the future is an essential context for the discussion that follows on evangelization and religious pluralism. The paper rightly affirms that the church must be obedient in evangelizing, understood as bearing witness to reconciliation in Christ and "the promotion of justice and peace." It must also "always be respectful of those who hold other beliefs." In a fine phrase it affirms that "sharing the joyful news of the truth revealed in the New Testament and inviting others to the fullness of life in Christ is an expression of respectful love," adding in a footnote that "inducing anyone to convert through moral pressure or material incentive" is not. Leaving people free to follow their conscience before God is a historic Baptist principle, and so is what the footnote calls "not hindering anyone from entering into conversion of his or her own free will." The paper lays stress here on respecting human dignity; historic Baptist thinking underlines this, but also adds – from the perspective of covenant – that we must respect the freedom of people to stand before God with their own responsibility. Baptists have grounded freedom of religious belief both in human rights and in the sole lordship of God to whom alone human beings must make account.[11]

My point is that those evangelizing are more likely to be "respectful" of others in this way if they are not made anxious by fixed ideas about plans that have to be carried out, whether human strategies or what is thought to be a divine game-plan for the world. The paper may have undermined its commendation of respectful dialogue by the context of "God's plan for creation" and its failure to explore the theology of *koinonia* and covenant.

This becomes even more apparent when the section treats "serious disagreements within and between churches" on the issue of whether there is any salvation for those who do not explicitly believe in Christ, or "explicitly share Christian faith." Here the paper discerns a tension between New Testament teaching that God wills the salvation of all people, and the affirmation that Jesus is the one and only savior of the world. It does not consider the possibility of meeting Jesus Christ himself through the experience of other faiths, drawing attention as it does only to "the positive truths and values" contained by other faiths, and the need to appreciate "elements of truth and goodness" that are present in other religions" (60). A perspective of the *koinonia* of all people in the life of the triune God allows us to think that Christ is present (often in a hidden way) with and in truths and values, always bringing a challenge to human life and calling for response as the Lord of the universe, even where he is not explicitly recognized within the bounds of this earthly life. It also allows us to think that a response might be made faithfully either within a particular religion, or by changing from one faith-community to another, entering the church of Christ, just as the sovereign Spirit of God leads.

Such a perspective also leaves room for people to be disobedient to the call of God, even within the *koinonia* they inhabit; it is the humility of God to allow those whom God holds in communion to be hostile, ungrateful and self-excluding. As the theologian Hans Urs Von Balthasar puts it, there is only one place where our "no" *can* be spoken, and that is – ironically – within the glad response of the Son to the Father. Our "no" is a kind of "twisted knot" within the current of love of the Son's response, which takes the form of the cross.[12] So Von Balthasar says: "The creature's No, its wanting to be autonomous without acknowledging its origin, must be located within the Son's all-embracing Yes to the Father, in the Spirit."[13]

I am not supposing here that a Christian, or a Baptist Christian, must adopt this view of God's purposes for the world. Many will no doubt disagree with me out of their deeply-held convictions. I am simply urging that it is possible to explore this kind of thinking, keeping faithful to scripture, when we have a view of the purposes of God that is grounded theologically in *koinonia* and covenant, and that this exploration might help a move toward consensus. This brings us to the reference to chapter III that I promised to make earlier. In considering the resistance of some to the idea that there can be any salvation outside the church, the paper records their conviction that Scripture requires "the necessity of faith and baptism for salvation." It asks how the churches might arrive at a greater convergence about these issues, but in the previous section it has failed to set "faith and baptism" in the context of *koinonia* and covenant in a way that might well help.

I mean that baptism, whether infant baptism or believer's baptism, is regarded on its own in this paper as being "the introduction to new life in Christ," and "the water of re-birth" "incorporating" the person baptized into the body of Christ (41). Baptists gladly affirm this of the baptism of a believing disciple, but generally find it difficult to apply to the case of a very young infant whose faith has to be vicariously represented by others, and so generally decline the invitation to make a "mutual recognition of baptism." Once again, perhaps, we see the result of a lack of Baptist representation on the drafting committee. Baptists have in fact been urging in a whole series of bilateral ecumenical conversations that initiation, or beginning a new life in Christ, should be understood not as one point but as a process of salvation, a journey on which baptism is one stage.[14] In the case of the baptism of an infant, Baptists have urged, the journey into Christ needs to be completed in an act of personal faith and commissioning by God's Spirit to share in God's mission in the world. Then a mutual recognition of initiation (rather than baptism) might well be possible; this leans on a theology of *koinonia*, in which people are being drawn more deeply over a process of time into the communion of God's life, and a theology of covenant where covenant-promises need at some point to be made. Whether coming into the *koinonia* of the church as a young infant or as a mature believer for the first time, their salvation is not a single point (baptism or a "decision" of faith) but a process of "being saved," of being transformed into the image of Christ.

Unfortunately there is no trace of this understanding of the journey of initiation in this paper, the lack of which betrays – I suggest – a lack of theological exploration of *koinonia*.[15] The relevance for the question of religious pluralism in chapter 4 is that there is no vision of such a process or journey outside the church either. Those who find difficulty in the idea of a saving encounter with Christ outside the church might consider that faith and baptism have their place within a whole process of being saved. Within the counsels of the God who holds us in *koinonia* we do not know what further steps or stages might be needed in any particular life for a salvation that has begun to be completed; we do know from Scripture that our salvation will come to its fullness only in the new creation, at the Day of Jesus Christ.[16]

The Moral Challenge of the Gospel

The term *koinonia* does appear in the next section of this last chapter about the church in the world. We read: "*koinonia* includes not only the confession of the one faith and celebration of common worship, but also shared moral values, based on the inspiration and insights of the Gospel." The point being made is that churches that share together in *koinonia* need to be accountable to each other for the decisions and attitudes they take on ethical issues. The paper obviously has in mind that fellowship between churches, and ecumenical advances between them, have been broken by taking up positions on certain matters – the question of human sexuality hovers in the air here but is not named. The section speaks of "challenges to divergence represented by contemporary moral issues," but no examples are given.

It seems that these challenges belong to what the section calls "individual moral values." Discipleship, it affirms, demands moral commitment on both the individual and social level, but the paper seems happier to specify social values such as "justice, peace and protection of the environment" than contentious individual values. While one paragraph notes that churches sometimes find themselves "divided into opposing opinions about what principles of personal or collective morality are in harmony with the Gospel of Jesus Christ," it seems that it is the personal values that most divide, since they are not even named here.

The collective values of justice, peace and environmental protection are in fact to re-appear in the next section on the church and society, where the authors note that – despite divisions – Christian churches do work together to promote the values of the Kingdom of God (64).

It seems odd that no individual moral values are named in the paper. Perhaps what the authors are trying to avoid are not values at all but codes or rules of behavior that bind the individual, constructed from values. If we are bound by covenant, we will want to name these values, to which a covenantal life commits us, but not necessarily to construct a tight moral code. If we are to begin identifying the values, there are few places better to begin than with the cardinal virtues named by Thomas Aquinas, largely following Aristotle, which combine to make the good life that serves the common good of all. First among these is prudence, the capacity to make judgements in a particular situation where rules are missing or don't seem to apply. This may also be called practical wisdom, which is both "knowing what to want and what not to want" and deciding to act to satisfy the want.[17] Prudence accompanies and guides all the other virtues, of which the cardinal ones are justice, moral courage and temperance (or moderation).[18] It hardly needs to be underlined that those responsible for the recent meltdown that has befallen the international world of business and finance have sadly lacked the virtues of prudence, justice, courage and moderation.

Thomas then identifies three "theological" virtues of faith, hope and love, three values belonging to a relationship with God.[19] These are also going to be built into covenantal relations, and here I want to suggest that the combination of faith and love issues in trust, which in Baptist terms is absolutely essential for the covenant to work – trust between members and pastor, between individual congregations and associations or conventions. Unfortunately, for Aquinas there is a quantum leap between the "moral virtues" that are given as a basis for all human life through a "natural law," and the theological virtues that are given only to a select group – mainly the Christian church – through being revealed by God. Christian disciples will certainly aim, all the time for the cardinal, moral virtues to be transformed by faith, hope and love. Love of God and neighbor will show us how moral virtues are to be worked out in daily life. But we ought not to expect too great a gap between what is considered moral in the church and what is felt to be moral in society. Paragraph 63 perhaps sounds too great a note of despair about the conflict between moral norms in "the world of today" and the life of the church.

This is where the theological idea of *koinonia* becomes important. When wisdom appears in the Old Testament in the first place it is like the moral virtue of prudence, practical wisdom, the ability to make judgements about what is good in the midst of the maze of life. But is it accompanied by another dimension of wisdom – expressed in the colorful picture of "Lady Wisdom," who invites people to walk with her. Portrayed in the picture of an attractive woman walking through the world, traveling from east to west like the sun, she entices those who are wise to walk in her way.[20] She is seen as a kind of extension of personality of the creator God, who is always present in the world to transform and redeem it, offering possibilities of flourishing to human beings. This is wisdom as communion, as *koinonia*. She is taken up in Christian thinking into an even richer image of movement, an interweaving of relations of love that can only be described as being like a father relating to a son, or a mother relating to a daughter, in the power of a spirit of love and hope. That is the image of the Holy Trinity, based on the unique life of Christ, whom the New Testament claims to be the very wisdom of God.

Now, the belief that all things are held together in *koinonia*, and this fellowship is grounded in God's own *koinonia*, means that disciples of Christ can point all people toward the possibility of a life in which relations are the most important thing, where all persons and even the natural environment are interconnected, and where human beings can actively and intentionally participate more deeply in movements of love and justice in which they are already immersed by living in the world. In their own way, all people can find the moral virtues transformed by faith, hope and love. This transformation will happen in a particular, intense way in the church that is bound by covenant, stands under the word of God and nourishes its life with the sacraments. But these theological values can still appear in surprising ways and unusual forms in the world if we look for them with the discernment of the Spirit.

This section suggests that a primary theological issue in thinking about the moral challenge is the relation between faith, grace and works in the life of a believer, and here it points to the recent consensus achieved between the Roman Catholic Church and churches of the Reformation over the meaning of justification, a church-dividing issue at the time of the Reformation. In the conversations between the Catholic Church and the Lutheran World Federation (1967-present), a notable advance in unity has been the *Joint Declaration on the Doctrine of Justification* (1999), to which the World Methodist Council has also now consented.

Unfortunately, the paper gives no idea as to the content of that consensus. The point is that in the past it has often seemed as if Catholic and Lutheran thought has been polarized between a stress on "justification by faith" of the believer, and "justification by grace" infused into the believer by the Holy

Spirit. Lutherans have stressed that justification is a "declaring" or "imputing" of Christ's own righteousness to believers in faith. Believers are not righteous, but they are *declared* to be righteous by God because God sees them clothed in Christ. Catholic theologians have understood justification as an actual *making* of the believer righteous by the infusing of the Holy Spirit, so that they can perform righteous works. The two communions now confess that "justification is the work of the triune God" since justification means that "Christ himself is our righteousness, in which we share through the Holy Spirit in accord with the will of the Father" who has "sent his Son into the world to save sinners."[21] This means that "by grace alone, in faith in Christ's saving work and not because of any merit on our part, we are accepted by God and receive the Holy Spirit, who renews our hearts while equipping us and calling us to good works." That is, forgiveness by God cannot be separated from inner renewal. Divine forgiveness is not simply an announcement that God regards us as being in the right, but is transformative of human life.[22] Justification is received by faith as God's gift through the Holy Spirit who "leads believers into that renewal of life which God will bring to completion in eternal life."[23]

Baptists have not formally entered into talks about joining Lutherans and Methodists in agreeing the meaning of justification. But we should surely agree that God's declaration of us as being in the right must be accompanied by renewal, and that this is the work of the Spirit. Once again, the paper seems to miss an opportunity by not referring to *koinonia* here. *Koinonia* only appears when the paper is considering the way that differences over moral values (which it does not name) affect unity. But it is surely the theological foundation for moral renewal. If we participate in the fellowship of the Trinity, then we will be changed and transformed by any change of our attitude and relation to God. We will share in the faith, hope and love that characterize the relations between the Father, Son and Spirit. It is not a question, as has often been conceived in the past, of having grace like a celestial fluid "infused" into us, injected into our system. Rather, we dwell in the midst of the interweaving relations of a triune God, and God dwells in us to make us new. All persons in the world know something of that reality, but those who are made daughters and sons through Christ know it with a fullness that anticipates the new creation.

Church and Society

The term "communion" (though not the Greek *koinonia*) appears just once in this section, at the beginning where the compassionate engagement of Christians in the world and their passion for its transformation are said to be grounded in "communion with God in Jesus Christ" (64). Their compassion is to be directed toward the poor, the powerless, the marginalized, victims of natural disasters and war, those suffering from threats to health and from economic inequalities and those discriminated against in every way (64-65). Disciples of Christ have a responsibility, the paper insists, to defend human life and dignity and to care for the environment. In these various ways the church is to promote the "values of the Kingdom of God." What might be added to this by a deeper reflection on *koinonia* or communion than appears here?

Two issues are treated that I suggest would benefit from a theology of *koinonia*. First, this section affirms a number of times that members of the church should work in cooperation with those outside the church: it names "adherents of other religions," "even those of no religious belief" (64), "civil authorities" (65) and "all people of goodwill" (66). This is obviously a recommendation that the authors of the paper feel strongly about, and yet no theological basis is given for it. It is the vision of *koinonia* and covenant that will provide this, and perhaps overcome the tendency of churches to be inward-looking and self-sufficient even in their works of love to others. It becomes compelling for Christians to work with others when we believe that we are all held in the communion that God gives to all humankind (67) and in which the triune God dwells, and that God has made covenant with all living things. There are, as I have mentioned already, different ways of living in the communion and the covenant, and different forms for manifesting the values and virtues of the Kingdom; the church certainly has its own distinctive way that should not be confused with the world beyond the walls of the church. Nevertheless the church must learn to discern the way that those outside the church are joined in communion and covenant with the Creator, and learn to detect what motivations have integrity within that framework, even though they may not be the same motivations as the church that lives by the word and the sacraments. It is only through developing this discernment that the church will know when to resist cooperation with others as well as to offer it gladly. We are to be conformed to the movement of God's triune life, not simply conformed to others, and this may sometimes mean resistance.

The notion of resistance brings us to a second issue requiring a theology of *koinonia* and covenant, the variety of models of relation between church and state to which the paper draws attention. It obviously has in mind various models of establishment, synergy between church and institutions of the state, and "free-church," and it rightly gives weight to "contextual circumstances" that may legitimate one model or another. It also notes the danger of the church thereby abetting "sinful and unjust activities." What the paper does not do is offer any criteria by which models may be assessed. A theology of *koinonia* prompts the question as to whether a particular model promotes the enriching and flourishing of human relations. A theology of covenant prompts us to ask whether a particular model respects the rule of Christ in his church as its covenant-maker. It was this latter aspect that fired the passion of our Baptist ancestors. They objected to the rule of the state in the church – determining its ministry through state-appointed bishops and determining its worship through a state-approved prayer book – and they also objected to the church being given privileges over other citizens. These acts of resistance did not stem from a concept of "autonomous" freedom in which Baptists awarded themselves the right to choose the ministers and worship they wanted, but from a conviction that the rule of Christ was being infringed.[24] The liberty they claimed in areas of belief and practice was based in the conviction that they stood under the rule of Christ in covenant, which meant that nobody else had the right to claim that authority.

Baptists have then tended to stress the element of a "prophetic voice" (and even martyrdom) to which the paper refers (65), and perhaps to under-stress the element of cooperation with others outside the church. We might say that we have allowed covenant to swamp *koinonia*, and we often need to recover a balance between them. Unfortunately this section attempts to discuss issues of cooperation and prophetic witness without exploring either of them.

Conclusion

While the paper does represent a certain convergence between the churches on the role of the church in the world, the reader is bound to find that only five pages on this huge theme is somewhat skimpy. My own comments have far exceeded the length of this chapter IV, but I do believe that the text cries out for a development of its very brief references to *koinonia*/communion. Despite taking the professed perspective of the church as communion, the words *koinonia* and communion appear only once each in this section, both in passing. Further, I suggest that the theology of *koinonia* would be enhanced by placing it in parallel to the traditional Baptist concept of covenant, as urged by the recent BWA-Roman Catholic conversations. However, let us admit that this latter report, despite its announced intentions, failed in fact to progress as far as the theme of the church in service to the world. This paper goes one better in tackling it at all.

CHAPTER 4
REFLECTIONS ON *THE WORD OF GOD IN THE LIFE OF THE CHURCH*:
A REPORT OF INTERNATIONAL CONVERSATIONS BETWEEN THE CATHOLIC CHURCH AND THE BAPTIST WORLD ALLIANCE, 2006-2010

Stephen R. Holmes

Introduction

The *Word of God in the Life of the Church* is a substantial and fascinating record of broad points of agreement between representatives of the Commission on Doctrine and Christian Unity of the Baptist World Alliance and the Pontifical Council for Promoting Christian Unity of the Catholic Church.[1] The fact that formal conversations between these two bodies can take place must be welcomed, and that so many points of agreement can be found is a matter for genuine rejoicing. The report speaks of "an astonishing amount of convergence and common mind" being found (§205), a judgment that seems borne out by the evidence.

The report builds on a number of earlier conversations, detailed in the report itself;[2] one feature obvious to any reader who is familiar with those earlier conversations is the increased levels of trust and understanding that can now be found between Baptists and Catholics. Earlier hesitations from Baptists in South America, based on their experience of poor relations with the local Catholic churches in their context, were in 2006 sufficiently lessened to allow their approval of the new conversations; the goals set for the conversations could presume an already-existing level of mutual understanding, common witness, and shared action on ethical issues.[3] Such progress in understanding, and in shared witness where possible, is of course greatly to be welcomed; it is to be hoped that the reception of the present report leads to further mutual understanding and shared work.

CHAPTER 4

The status of the report needs to be understood; on the one hand, although the conversations that led to it were authorized by the two sponsoring bodies, the report is explicitly the product of the participants, and is to be evaluated by the BWA and the Catholic Church;[4] on the other, whilst assertions of Catholic doctrine that are supported with reference to authoritative documents can be taken as definitive, there is of course no similar authoritative body of doctrine for Baptists. The report often appeals to either seventeenth-century confessional documents, or to claims of a developing consensus amongst recent Baptist theologians. The confessional documents are, of course not often explicitly acknowledged as subordinate authorities by Baptist churches in the present day; more seriously, perhaps, the references are often to a single document, and would perhaps be stronger if a demonstration of a consensus amongst the confessions could be demonstrated. Often, the most that can legitimately be claimed is "Baptist understanding has at least some points in the past encompassed this idea" – and the report sometimes makes that explicit.[5]

The controlling doctrinal ideas for the report are, first, a focus on "the Word of God," and, second, a particular vision of the life of the church as *koinonia* – communion. The report establishes that Baptists and Catholics can agree that "[t]he church in all of its aspects including its ministry stands under the Word of God" (§35), and so this concept becomes an organizing category which enables further points of agreement to be derived. This is particularly evident in the discussion of baptism and Eucharist/Lord's Supper, which are described as "the visible Word of God."[6] Again, as will be discussed under "Ecclesiology" below, the recent development of "communion ecclesiology" is held up as a category on which both sides can agree, and which can interrogate their different understandings for marks of convergence.

Such categories function helpfully in allowing the development of a shared theological vision from which differences may be explored in mutually intelligible ways; that said, the particular categories chosen must also be regarded as provisional, and as subject to challenge or correction. If it turns out that, in one area or another, the categories are inadequate lenses through which to explore convergences and differences, or if it should become apparent that another category brings a richer, broader, understanding of shared basic beliefs, then further discussion must be ready to put aside the present categories in favor of better ones.

The task of ecumenical conversation is twofold: to find convergence where it exists and to clarify disagreement where no convergence can be found. Both tasks involve carefully examining apparent disagreements in doctrine and practice to see the extent to which the disagreement is actual and not, for example, the result of different language being used to express very similar ideas. Where there is real disagreement, there is still useful work to be done in clarifying the exact nature of the differences: if a theological question can be specified with accuracy, it can potentially be worked at, and so the move from a hazy "we disagree about the practice of baptism" to a precise "we differ on the following three points" is a genuine and worthwhile theological and ecumenical advance.

One final comment, familiar to any participant in ecumenical work but often forgotten (it seems) in commentary: the disagreements between two Christian communities are not only on matters of substance but on matters of ordering; the subjects that Baptists will consider to be vital might be seen as rather peripheral to Catholics, and vice-versa. Convergence does not need to happen on such judgments of what is first order, it seems to me: if the use of a proper pulpit when preaching (to take an entirely imaginary example) matters profoundly to a particular Christian tradition, then, for unity, there is no need for others to agree that this matters profoundly, only an ability and willingness on the part of that tradition to accept that the practice of others conforms to their criteria.

With these introductory comments in mind, I turn to the substance of the report. I will treat the five main sections of the report in the order they occur, in each case seeking to indicate the points of agreement found, to note remaining points of disagreement, and to offer some theological commentary on my own that might help to advance discussion between the two traditions. I write as a British Baptist, from an evangelical tradition; this no doubt colors my interpretation in all sorts of ways. Where I am aware of cultural location being important, I have indicated this fact in footnotes, but I suppose that in several other instances my understanding of Baptist practice will be shaped by my context in ways I remain unaware of.

Ecclesiology

The first main section is entitled "The *Koinonia* of the Triune God and the Church," and treats questions of ecclesiology narrowly considered (that is, it deals with the nature of the church, but not with forms of ministry, or with the Catholic theme of the place of Mary in the church, both of which are covered in later sections). The ecumenical re-appropriation of Trinitarian doctrine as an ethical account of how human persons should be in communion is held up as the basis of a *koinonia* ecclesiology that Baptists and Catholics can both affirm; this provides the opportunity to affirm many things in common, before ecclesiological differences are faced. Baptists and Catholics agree that Christ is present when believers are gathered (Mt. 18:20); that the promise of Mt. 28:20 requires belief that Christ remains present with His church; that Christ is Lord of the church; that the fellowship of the triune life is mirrored in the fellowship of the church; that *koinonia* is a reality at both local and universal levels; and that local and universal forms of the church are mutually interdependent. Baptists and Catholics can agree on the unity, sanctity, apostolicity, and catholicity of the church, although differences in understanding these marks have to be acknowledged.

That said, there are real differences, which are here acknowledged. Two in particular stand out: the first concerns the nature of the basic ecclesial unit: for Catholics, the "local church" is the diocese, or even the national church; for Baptists it is the gathered congregation. Second, the question of what makes the church authentically the church is a significant area of disagreement: for Catholics, the ministry of the bishop links the local church to the apostolic mission, and to the catholic church across the world; for Baptists, by contrast, the present and active rule of Christ in the gathered congregation is definitive of the church.

These two points bear some reflection. On the first, I wonder whether there is room for a more creative mapping. The report identifies[7] that the episcopal ministry of oversight is seen by Baptists to be exercised by the ordained minister of the local church; this might recall the immediate post-apostolic Christian situation which, historians seem to agree, centered around one bishop celebrating one Eucharist for one congregation. Patristic practice developed into multi-congregation dioceses, but Baptist practice could be narrated as a return to this primitive situation. That is, if the Baptist (senior) pastor is identified with the bishop of a single-parish diocese (in Catholic terms), there might be more theological convergence between the two practices of church life than is identified in the report. In practice, translocal unity amongst Baptist congregations is often achieved through the fellowship shared by the pastors; this might be argued to map rather nicely onto Catholic claims that the basis of catholicity is the fellowship of the bishops, although the particular place of the bishop of Rome at the center of Catholic unity has no parallel in Baptist life.

Again, the report seems to suggest that the place of the parish is almost anomalous in Catholic ecclesiology:

> We must add that even though Catholics do not identify the parish as the local church, nevertheless as the place of Sunday Eucharistic worship, and as the place of Christian initiation, it is where the people of God experience the church most immediately. The parish is where Catholics

assemble to hear the gospel of Christ proclaimed and to be united with Christ and with one another through the celebration of the Eucharist.[8]

For the Baptist reader, the idea that the place of sacramental celebration, gospel preaching, Christian formation, and *koinonia* is not the local church must seem strange; given the emphasis on communion ecclesiology in the report, the last of these looks strange for Catholics, not just for Baptists, under the doctrinal framework being developed and asserted to be shared.

That said, some recent developments in Baptist – and broader – church life might propose a way forward here. The emphasis on "homegroups" or "cells" that has become common in evangelical church life in English-speaking countries, at least, proposes multiple locations of primary Christian fellowship within each local church; in the development of "cell-church" models, which have been enthusiastically embraced by some Baptist congregations, this extends more widely to the multiple "cells" within the local congregation being the primary loci of ecclesial experience. A Baptist church organized according to a "cell-church" model actually looks rather like a multi-parish Catholic diocese in its practical ecclesiology, suggesting, potentially, the discovery of some unexpected convergences. The same point might be made concerning the rise of multi-campus churches in some strands of Baptist life.

Of course, there are profound disanalogies also. I have already alluded to the place of the Bishop of Rome as the focus of unity, which has no parallel in Baptist life; more seriously, it is very difficult to map the calling, charisms, and recognition of Baptist lay leaders of groups within a congregation onto the high and holy vocation of Catholic priesthood. I would suggest, however, that this idea that the Baptist congregation can be mapped onto the Catholic diocese has purchase in church history, and would help us to find more convergences in our practices than are yet identified.

On the second of the divergences, the report has two long sections, §§14-15, describing the ways in which local churches are authentic expressions of the universal church for Catholics and for Baptists. It is striking to this reader, at least, that the two descriptions simply use different language: Catholic unity and apostolicity is defined in structural terms (parish to bishop; diocese to Pope; local and universal colleges of bishops, etc.); the same realities are defined christologically for Baptists (each congregation shares in the threefold office and is "under the rule of Christ"; the communion of local churches is in Christ: each local church is related to Christ, and so is related to every other local church in him.

It is not news that our denominations differ at a structural level; the Christological language should, however, have more purchase. It is surely simply an ecclesiological necessity that, somehow, our accounts of the nature of the church connect back to the person of Jesus Christ: the church is the body of Christ and the bride of Christ, after all. Perhaps an interesting way forward on this issue, of the extent to which we can recognize the reality and fullness of the church in each other's communions, might be, without denying any of the important doctrinal matters reflected by the structural language used in the present report, to invite Catholic theologians to describe their ecclesiology in Christological terms, and to seek overlap in the two descriptions?[9]

§20 of the report turns to the Eucharist/Lord's Supper. Baptists and Catholics agree, according to the report, that "[c]ommunion with the triune God and the whole church of Christ is continually actualized in the Eucharist/Lord's Supper." Under this head, there is a note of disagreement over the need for the sacrament to be presided over by an ordained minister in full communion with the local bishop; again, I wonder if mapping the Baptist pastor on to the Catholic bishop helps to clarify the precise nature of the distinction here? (It would seem at least a matter of good order for Baptists that, even if the explicit permission of the local pastor is not sought for each particular celebration of the Lord's Supper by groups within a church, there is a sense in which s/he is responsible, as the ordained "minister of word and sacrament," for each celebration.)

That the participants could agree to a statement concerning the Eucharist is impressive; the language found bears reflection: what does it mean to speak of communion with God and the universal church as being "continually actualized" in the sacrament/ordinance? The text following in §20 seems to gloss over this phrase (assuming it is intended as interpretation and not as further points of agreement, which is not entirely clear) through the reflection that, in celebrating the Lord's Supper, those who receive the elements are "sharing communion...with the whole church of Christ in time and space." In describing Baptist understanding, §22 further specifies this christologically: to be joined with Christ in the sacrament is necessarily to be joined with all other true churches of Christ.

This is plausible, and certainly is reflected in a standard piece of British Baptist liturgy, a post-communion prayer that enumerates the blessings given by God in the sacrament, including the line "you have made us one with all your people in heaven and on earth." Given the relative infrequency of celebrations of the Lord's Supper in many Baptist traditions, however, (which is explicitly noted in the report, in the second paragraph of §22), can we really speak of this as continual actualization? The language seems to imply more than I can find warrant for, and it would be interesting to know what lies behind it.

Authority

The second major section deals with "the authority of Christ in Scripture and Tradition." In popular Baptist understanding, this would no doubt be expected to be one of the points at which simple disagreement with the Catholic Church would surface; in fact, the report is able to point to what it describes as "a deepened and striking convergence" (§34) in this area. The section is divided into two subsections, one dealing with "Scripture in the life of the church" and one with the "relation of Scripture and tradition."

It should not surprise anyone who has got beyond the level of old-style confessional polemics that there is considerable agreement on the nature of Scripture between the two traditions. Both confess the Bible to be inspired by the Holy Spirit, revelatory of Jesus Christ, and the basic rule of faith and practice for the church. All this is developed and identified with care by the stated agreements in the report, which at this point turn to a series of very brief affirmations (see §§46, 48, 51, and 53) in order to highlight what can be agreed. On the doctrine of Scripture there are really only two significant points of disagreement identified: the extent of the canon; and the different locations of communal reading.

Whilst the two traditions can agree on the extent of the New Testament canon, and a substantial part of the Old Testament, Catholics of course recognize as canonical the so-called deutero-canonical writings, consisting of several extra books, and of some longer versions of books recognized by Baptists (and other Protestants), notably Daniel. The acknowledgement that Baptists find these books important in understanding the history of God's people, and that some Baptists find them to be powerful as devotional literature, is offered (§45); neither point, however, really addresses what is a simple matter of disagreement. We might, however, ask what material difference the recognition or otherwise of these books makes: what are the points of doctrine or practice affirmed in these books, but not elsewhere, and so acceptable as biblical to Catholics but not to Baptists? The difference cannot be overcome easily, but it could be specified carefully, so that our two communions know what is at stake in our commitments to differing canons of Scripture.

On the second point, the report proposes that both Catholics and Baptists emphasize communal discernment as the right way to read Scripture; the relevant mode of community, however, is on the one hand magisterial and on the other congregational. An unsympathetic reader might feel that the proposed convergence here is rather forced: that the practice of the authoritative interpretation of Scripture by the magisterium, and the attentiveness to the Bible of the local congregation, can, with effort, be described as species of the same reality is not a reason to propose real convergence of doctrine. A defense of the point might come from a wider consideration of Christian practice: is it the case that there is not the same focus on (any form of) communal reading in other traditions? If so, the proposed point of agreement is legitimate.

When we turn to the relationship between Scripture and tradition, the report identifies "a noteworthy trend in Baptist theological scholarship. . .[which] has made it possible for Baptist participants. . .to express an appreciation for the value of tradition" (§55), a trend that enabled significant convergence to be recognized on both sides. Certainly, there has been a move in Baptist theological work to be more self-consciously aware of standing in a traditioned context, and not just to recognize that but to rejoice in it as a good gift of God; whilst this is not an embracing of a full-orbed Catholic theory of doctrinal development, it does mean that Baptist theologians are able to talk meaningfully about tradition. The report notes, however, that "[t]his trend has been largely limited to a small number of Baptist academic theologians" (§55).

This is true in what it affirms, but perhaps something more positive could be said. On the one hand, those Baptist theologians who have been active in recovering an account of tradition would want to claim that a part of what they are doing is making explicit a practiced but tacit commitment to the subordinate authority of the theological tradition that has been a significant feature of Baptist life. Baptists have generally been grateful to receive and affirm the ecumenical creeds (the Apostles' Creed, famously, was recited at the inaugural meeting of the Baptist World Alliance) and, more broadly, ecumenical language and decisions relating to the doctrine of the Trinity and the Person of Christ; more broadly, even the commitment to a canon of sixty-six books that is shared with other Christian traditions having their origins in the European Reformation indicates a tacit acceptance of a traditioned decision. Others would disagree that such a "practiced but tacit" commitment to tradition is a feature of Baptist life, but the debate is there to be had.

On the other hand, whilst (explicit) positive evaluations of the theological tradition are currently limited to a few academic theologians in Baptist life, our communities have been much more ready to receive gratefully the riches of devotional traditions, and the two processes surely should be seen as to some degree parallel. Practices of prayer such as *lectio divina* and spiritual classics such as Thomas à Kempis are widely adopted in Baptist life, and this is surely indicative of a much broader positive evaluation of the riches of the Catholic tradition than is indicated in the report.[10]

The report largely follows the careful account of tradition as the preservation and passing on of the Word of God first delivered in Scripture that is found in *Dei Verbum*, the Dogmatic Constitution on Divine Revelation from the Second Vatican Council.[11] Tradition is not a mode of authority independent of Scripture, but a way of encountering and being open to the authority of Scripture. This is rich and helpful; there is further work to be done, however, in specifying with more exactness the extent to which traditioned interpretations of Scripture remain corrigible: there seems to be a finality about many Catholic dogmatic definitions that would feel foreign to Baptists, but without the sort of careful exploration modeled repeatedly in the present report, that remains impressionistic.

Strikingly, when the report turns to listing remaining open questions about the relationship of Scripture and tradition, it is able to assert that "these are as much issues within each communion as issues which divide us" (§66), and to suggest that the questions that remain are largely missional (§71). One interesting proposal here is the idea that the closest functional equivalent for Baptists to at least some of the uses of tradition in Catholic church life is actually preaching (§68). Tradition, in this context, is the way in which the biblical text becomes applied to very foreign contemporary contexts. (Of course, this raises the corrigibility point made above in an acute form: preaching is an occasional and provisional application, which in its very nature resists becoming permanent.)

Baptism and Eucharist

Baptism and Eucharist are defined in the report under the general category of sacrament/ordinance.[12] The 1984-85 round of talks had identified "the relation between faith and sacraments" as a key problem to be faced; here the rubric that a sacrament/ordinance is "a 'making visible' of the Word of God who rules in the church" (§72) is used to discover agreement and to specify disagreement on this matter.

The report proposes several heads of agreement: sacraments/ordinances are "signs through which God acts" (§73) and points of "intersection between" divine and human activity, with priority of course accorded to the divine (§77). They are transformative "experiences of encounter with Christ" (§85) related to both the faith of the individual and the faith of the community (§91). As such, they are central to the life of the church (§83) and necessarily related to the preaching of the Word (§81).

In the commentary on these agreements there is recognition of a "Zwinglian" strand of the Baptist tradition, which would see the sacraments essentially as enacted parables. The controlling rubric of making visible the word of God sits very comfortably with this, but some of these subsidiary heads of agreement might be seen to stretch it rather. The report pushes against this in a paragraph worth quoting at length:

> In practice. . .Baptist Christians approach the "ordinances" in a way that may seem quite "sacramental" to other Christians. All Baptists approach the ordinances with reverence and expectation, and are ready to pray for the activity of the Holy Spirit as they celebrate them, and will usually hope to experience God's "blessing" there. They think that Christ promises to meet his disciples in the waters of baptism and the bread and wine of the Lord's Supper and that this meeting will change lives. The function of the ordinances as signs does not mean that they are merely *empty* symbols (§75, emphasis original).

This account is probably most valid when considered as a piece of phenomenological description, or "ordinary theology":[13] whatever Baptists might say they believe about the ordinances being merely signs, their enacted practice implies a much fuller, more "sacramental" account of what is happening, and that is spelled out here.

The history of Baptist rejection of sacramental language bears some reflection. I have argued before that, in Britain at least (and at the time British Baptist theology was almost inevitably determinative for Baptist life everywhere except the North American continent), Baptists began to resist and criticize sacramental accounts of the ordinances in part through embracing Enlightenment rationalism, and in part as a reaction against the rise of the Oxford Movement, and Catholicizing tendencies within the Church of England.[14] I further suggested that, whilst historically understandable, there was in fact no good positive theological warrant for this move. The North American situation is more complex but I suspect that good historical work on Baptist understandings of the ordinances would help us to overcome our suspicion of "sacramental" language, and to conform our expressed doctrine to the reality of our practice.

When it turns to baptism, the report draws on some other recent ecumenical conversations in which Baptists, particularly European Baptists, have been involved, to speak of an extended "process of initiation," with different moments (hearing the Gospel and responding; baptism; church membership; reception of the gift of the Spirit); this allows a much greater degree of commonality to be found between Baptist practice and the practice of other Christian traditions – to oversimplify grossly, we do all the same things, but in a slightly different order.

That said, Baptists will find the account of the place of faith in baptism offered in these conversations very interesting. The report claims that "there is a large degree of agreement on the nature of faith embodied in [baptism]" (§98), and suggests that "Catholics and Baptists can agree that the practice of baptism that most fully expresses its meaning is that of a believing disciple, whose faith is supported by the faith of the believing community" (§98). The Catholic practice of infant baptism implies and demands a subsequent practice of catechesis, and a responsibility on the part of the church community to nurture the child baptized in the faith of the church.

The section on the Eucharist/Lord's Supper is a model example of the ecumenical work of clarifying the precise nature of differences. The character of the Catholic Mass as a sacrifice is a famous theological division; here there is care and charity in explaining the differences perceived:

> [Baptists] recognize that understanding the category of amamnesis in a scriptural way clarifies the Catholic insistence that the Eucharist is not a repetition of the sacrifice of Christ. In their act of remembrance (amamnesis), Baptists also think that they are participating in the very events of the death and resurrection of Jesus, and that they are sharing in "all the benefits" of Christ's saving sacrifice. However, they make a distinction between "sharing" in the self-offering of Christ and "presenting" the sacrifice of Christ to the Father, believing that only Christ can present himself (§124).

It may be that, somewhere down this road of understanding precisely what is claimed in the language of "re-presenting Christ's sacrifice," there will be a place where, whilst finding the language unhelpful, Baptists, and others, will discover that they can find nothing theologically problematic in the Catholic doctrine. The report does not get us to that place yet, certainly, but it offers very helpful clarification.

The section on the presence of Christ in the celebration of the Eucharist/Lord's Supper is similarly helpful: Baptists, of course, reject transubstantiation, but nonetheless affirm Christ's presence with his people at all times, and so also at the table. Some Baptists see a "sacramental" reality in the Lord's Supper – "Christ makes *himself* more deeply and intensely present to his disciples through the use of the elements (not *in* them)" (§127, emphasis original); others of us see only a "sermonic" use of the elements: in celebrating the Supper, we are reminded forcibly of what Christ has done for us and given us.

Mary

The section on the Blessed Virgin Mary in the report is entitled "Mary as Model of Discipleship in the Communion of the Church," emphasizing both the communion ecclesiology that informs so much of the report, and the post-Vatican II insistence that mariology is to be considered under the head of ecclesiology.[15] Obviously, there is much Scriptural teaching about Mary that Catholics and Baptists can agree on, and the report makes that clear at length. It further asserts that Catholics and Baptists can agree that "[b]eliefs about Mary should be rooted in Scripture, warranted by Scripture, and not contradicted by Scripture" (§133) – a claim Baptists will welcome.

Some dogmatic claims about Mary are essentially Christological. Classically, the insistence of Cyril of Alexandria and the Council of Ephesus that Mary is properly called *theotokos* was a rejection of a Nestorian Christology that improperly separated the divine and human natures of the Redeemer. Theotokos is literally translated "God-bearer" in §134 and §143; the Latin *mater Dei*, and its English equivalent "Mother of God," are dealt with in §143-5, where it is suggested that "many Baptists have reservations about the term itself, although not about the doctrine for which it stands." The perpetual virginity of Mary (§141-2), her immaculate conception (§147-8), and her bodily assumption (§149) remain points of disagreement; the report stresses the ancient nature of some of these beliefs, whilst acknowledging their relatively recent dogmatic definition.

Baptists might want to ask Catholics about the function of these dogmas: how is life lived differently, or liturgy constructed differently, because of them? Dogmatic definition that has no outworking in the life of the church would seem not to be a significant bar to unity. The report has helpful sections on Marian devotion (§§150-61), but there is no indication of how Catholic practices depend on the dogmatic recognitions. This would be a helpful area to clarify in future conversation: if Catholic practices of devotion to Mary are necessitated by the dogmas, then our divisions here are deeper and more difficult than otherwise.

When it turns to devotion, Baptists and Catholics can find agreement on Mary's role as the first New Testament disciple, and as "a model of discipleship in faithful listening and obedience to God's Word." (§150) Mary is described as a "representative figure of the church," language accepted by French Baptists in a recent report of national conversations with Catholics.[16] Baptists will not accept that Mary is "mother of the church" and (of course) find the practice of praying to Mary, and the other Saints, and asking for her – and their – intercession, unacceptable.

It is important for Baptists to realize that this is what the practice of devotion to Mary and the Saints amounts to: a request for intercession. John Calvin rejected this practice simply because he thought there was no way for the living to speak to the dead;[17] it would seem that Christian opinion could legitimately differ on that question, and so on the appropriateness of seeking intercession from the Saints, without any major doctrinal issues being raised. The Catholic might see the Baptist as needlessly neglecting a source of help, and the Baptist see the Catholic as misguidedly asking someone who cannot receive the request for help, but there need not be any basic theological divide here.

Episcopal Oversight

The final substantial section of the report returns to ecclesiology, with a focus on the ministry of oversight in the life of the church. It begins in Christology, with a point of agreement worth quoting in full:

> Christ is the head of the church, her founder, creator and cornerstone. The church owes her whole existence to Christ and he continues to be her "shepherd and guardian (episkopos)" (1 Pet. 2:25). He nourishes and sustains his church with the proclamation of the Gospel and the celebration of the sacraments/ordinances. Through these means, by the power of the Holy Spirit, the community of the church grows in her communion with God, who is Father, Son and Holy Spirit. (§162)

Here, both the communion ecclesiology that underlies much of the report, and the question of episcopal oversight, are located under the head of Christology. This continues as the section develops. The whole church is called to participate in the threefold office of Christ; the episcope of some is a means to enabling that corporate participation in Christ's ministry to take place.

For Catholics, this episcopal ministry is carried forward by the college of bishops, each one standing in a line of unbroken succession that goes back through the apostles to the direct calling and command of Jesus. Baptists see ministry as arising from within the local congregation, but the pastor of a Baptist church in some ways reflects the episcopal ministry of the Catholic bishop in having a special calling to teach and transmit sound doctrine, and in representing the wider church to the local congregation, and the local congregation to the wider church.

Whilst there is a communal element to episcopal ministry in the Catholic Church, particularly in the post-conciliar stress on the shared ministry of the college of bishops, there is no real equivalent to the Baptist church meeting, which is where the basic episcopal ministry of "watching over" each other takes place. That said, the ancient idea of the *sensus fidelium* is not mentioned in the report, and might make an interesting point of intersection with the role Baptists give to the church meeting.

CHAPTER 4

The section concludes by admitting that agreement cannot be reached over the Petrine ministry of primacy exercised by the Bishop of Rome. There is some helpful untangling of the various issues involved in the claim of Papal primacy, with four questions in particular being identified:

1. What was the particular leadership role of Peter amongst the apostles?
2. Does this role continue after the death of Peter?
3. Does the New Testament teach the need for a particular *episkopos* to exercise a ministry of unity for the whole church?
4. If it does, is it necessary that this ministry be carried out by the Bishop of Rome?

This is very helpful clarification of the various issues tied up in the Catholic belief in the continuing Petrine Ministry, and it should be a great help to future discussions that this untangling has been done. As the report itself comments, "the very clarification of these pertinent questions seems a promising beginning for further work in the future." (§199)

Concluding Reflections

The writers of the report are to be commended greatly for their work. As they claim, the degree of convergence they find can rightly be described as "astonishing" (§205); where there is a lack of convergence, they helpfully and patiently clarify many issues; our understanding of the relationship of our two traditions is greatly advanced by this report. I have indicated one or two areas where I thought the work might have been done differently, and have tried to develop a theme suggesting that Christology might be a useful organizing category for further work – thinking of Christ's active Lordship in church and world, and how that is understood in the structures and doctrines of each of our traditions. That said, none of this should be read as anything more than a few appreciative glosses to a truly excellent piece of work.

It happened that I read the report as I traveled to different places across Europe, and had cause to reflect on the different relationships between Baptists and Catholics in some different contexts. In the United Kingdom, whilst there is a deep shared history of exclusion – and indeed persecution – in the seventeenth century, the more relevant context is rather Baptist complicity in a cultural anti-Catholic sentiment that has been a lasting feature of British life;[18] in other countries in Europe, the story is of Catholic states making life very difficult for tiny Baptist unions, or of Catholics and Baptists alike seeming irrelevant to an essentially secular society. In each of these contexts, the report has something important to say. Where there has been mutual suspicion and incomprehension, the report can offer a resource to help promote understanding; where the overwhelming feature of the context is urgent missional needs, the report might help Baptists and Catholics to recognize that they share enough common gospel themes that they might work together, not apart, in mission.

That said, these advantages can only come if the report is read, or at least if its conclusions are transmitted, at very local levels. The problems of misunderstanding that matter tend to be at the level of the local Baptist congregation that will not join ecumenical instruments alongside Catholics, or the local Catholic priest who regards Baptist evangelists as dangerous, almost cult-like. We have been given a great resource; the process of reception is now vital.

COMMISSION ON MINISTRY

The Commission on Ministry engages in research and discussion on the calling to Christian ministry and the ways in which this vocation can be effectively discharged by Baptists in contemporary society. It investigates the ways in which oversight is exercised in Baptist churches at the local, regional, and universal levels. It makes its insights available to the wider Baptist family.

This is a new Commission of the METR Division in the 2010-2015 quinquennium. The commission met on four occasions during the Annual Gatherings of the Baptist World Alliance.

The first meeting was held in Kuala Lumpur, Malaysia, July 4-9, 2011. The sub-theme of the Gathering was *Consecration through the Spirit*. Presentations were made by Isaac Lim, president of the Malaysia Baptist Convention, providing helpful insights into the *Call to Ministry Process through to Ordination*. The role of theological education was highlighted as well as the integral function of the local church.

Glenn Wooden of Acadia Divinity College, Nova Scotia, Canada, presented a paper, *Biblical Perspectives on Calls to Ministry*. This paper is included in the volume, *Baptist Faith and Witness*. Additionally, Judith Battles from Baylor's Truett Seminary provided a vision for a research project on the relationship between seminaries and churches in the calling, training, and placement of pastors. The commission endorsed this research project as part of its work for this five-year period.

The commission reflected during a public forum on the impact of ministry in Japan as a result of the earthquake in March 2011.

The second meeting was held in Santiago de Chile, July 2-7, 2012. The sub-theme of the Gathering was *Proclamation through the Spirit*.

A significant number of local pastors joined the commission for presentations made by Mauricio Reyes, president of the Union of Evangelical Baptist Churches of Chile; and Robert Carter, seminary president. The commission came to understand the significant leadership role of pastors as part of the path to ministry and ordination within the Baptist convention. The role of the local church in this process was highlighted as well as its role in lay leadership, discipleship, and

Christian education.

Further discussion surrounding the research project led by Judith Battles provided insight through a pilot project. Graham Hill, Morling College in Sydney, Australia, made a presentation via SKYPE regarding his new book, *Salt, Light and a City: Introducing Missional Ecclesiology.*

The third meeting took place in Ocho Rios, Jamaica, July 1-6, 2013. The sub-theme of the Gathering was *Liberation through the Spirit.*

The commission met twice on its own for presentations by Stephen McMullin, Acadia Divinity College, Nova Scotia, Canada; and Marsha Woodard, Palmer Theological Seminary, USA.

McMullin made two presentations: *Overcoming Barriers to Church Renewal: Using Research Data to Guide Church Leaders,* and *Church Renewal in a Changing World: Responding to Needs of a New Generation.* Woodard presented her paper, *The Midwife Leadership Style: Effectively Facilitating Transformational Growth in African American Clergywomen.* The presence of various pastoral leaders from the Caribbean added greatly to the discussion. A planned presentation by church planters from Cuba was not possible.

The commission joined the Commission on Evangelism for a Roundtable discussion on effective evangelistic ministry across the BWA.

The final session was shared with the Commission on Theological Education and Leadership Formation to honor the ministry of the late Duke K. McCall, president of the BWA from 1980-1985. This session was led by former missionary, Robert Garrett, director of the Master of Arts in Global Leadership program at Dallas Baptist University in the USA. There was a brief update on the research project led by Judith Battles as she was not able to attend the meetings in Jamaica.

The fourth meeting of the commission was held July 6-12, 2014, in Izmir, Turkey. The commission met on three occasions during the week. The first session was held at the Izmir Baptist Church, hosted by pastor, Ertan Cevik, along with his wife, Marlene, and several members of the church. Two other pastors, Orhan Picaklar of Samsun and Pastor Sukru of Adanna, shared their remarkable testimonies as well the founding of their churches.

Four Baptist churches have recently formed the Turkish Baptist Convention affiliated with the European Baptist Federation (EBF). The impact of the Turkish pastors and their people was inspirational and resulted in a keen realization of the need for prayer for those who serve Christ under restrictions that most of the Baptist world does not encounter.

CHAPTER 4

Daniel Trusiewicz of Poland, director for mission with the European Baptist Federation, as well as Tony Peck, general secretary of the EBF, made presentations on processes related to helping people with their call to ministry and theological preparation for ministry in the EBF and Great Britain. Recognizing vast differences across the EBF in these practices, the focus on personal support for the pastoral leader through times of ministry preparedness is vital.

While excellent work began with the research project led by Judith Battles, it was not feasible to proceed through the limitations of time and resources of this commission. The commission is grateful for the vision and passion of Judith Battles and a summary of this project is also on file with the BWA METR Reports.

Committed to understand ministry in the regional context of each Annual Gathering has resulted in significant presentations on file in the BWA offices.

It has been a privilege to serve as chair of the commission, and I express my thanks for the honor of working with the vice chair and commission members.

Harry G. Gardner, commission chair, is president of Acadia Divinity College and dean of Theology for Acadia University in Nova Scotia, Canada. He was BWA vice president from 2010-2015.

CHAPTER 5
A TRIBUTE TO DR DUKE K. MCCALL:
DENOMINATIONAL STATESMAN, BAPTIST EDUCATOR AND GLOBAL LEADER

Robert I. Garrett

By every conceivable measure Duke K. McCall was one of the towering figures of Baptist life during the last generation. In his public life he left a legacy that has enriched Baptists from all over the world, and that should be appreciated and valued for the many ways in which his creative genius set down patterns and influenced Baptist institutions in ways that continue to benefit people to this day. This presentation is a tribute to his life and will seek to analyze the significance of his legacy in three distinct dimensions. McCall was a denominational statesman who contributed in multiple ways to his own religious body, the Southern Baptist Convention in the USA. McCall was a Baptist educator whose constant efforts on behalf of theological education shaped the formation of a generation of future pastors and church leaders. McCall was also a global leader with an expansive vision of the role Baptists should play in the world, equally through our missionary efforts to win the lost to Christ and through our fellowship with one another in the Baptist family that we call the Baptist World Alliance.

Duke K. McCall was born in September 1914 in Meridian, Mississippi, a son of Judge John W. and Lizette McCall. He and his four siblings grew up in Memphis, Tennessee. McCall died on April 2, 2013, near his home in Delray Beach, Florida, at the age of 98. McCall left behind his wife, Winona McCandless, a widow whom he married after Marguerite died in 1983, and his four sons, Duke Jr., Douglas, John Richard and Michael.

On a personal note, I consider myself to be simply one of hundreds of students at the Southern Baptist Theological Seminary during the time of his presidency who were influenced profoundly by his ministry. For me it is an honor to be asked to speak on behalf of so many others who have benefitted from McCall's ministry. I learned valuable lessons in private conversation from him, as he shared himself in surprisingly open and frank ways, even while he gave me careful personal attention and affirmed the potential leadership he saw in me. Many students like myself owe Duke McCall a debt of gratitude for the blessing and the example of his life.

It is extraordinary to consider that McCall made contributions to Baptist institutions for a span of nearly 70 years. He started out in denominational leadership as a very young man: at age twenty-eight he became the president of a Bible college that quickly after became New Orleans Baptist Theological Seminary. Willis and Hanbury point out that McCall "exercised denominational leadership over an extraordinary period of time: forty years across five decades of the 20th century" (Willis and Hanbury 2013). In addition to these years of fulltime service, McCall continued to support Baptist causes actively throughout many years of retirement. He was influential in shaping profoundly the institutions and causes that he chose to serve.

One of the merits of giving careful consideration to the life of McCall is that his interests were broad and his influence was far-reaching, so that his career reaches into many of the more pressing matters that Baptists dealt with during his years of service. Thus, in reviewing the key elements of his life and work, we can learn a great deal about Baptists, especially Southern Baptists in the USA, from the post-World War II era in 1946 until the end of the 20th century.

Accolades for McCall

Chris Caldwell, one of McCall's successors as pastor of Broadway Baptist Church in Louisville, Kentucky, says of McCall that "he was a larger than life figure, a charming gentleman." Peter Smith of Louisville's *Courier-Journal* calls Duke McCall "one of the leading Baptist statesmen of the 20th century" (Smith 2013). As a result of his denominational leadership, McCall was highly respected among a wide range of Baptists and among Christians in general. BWA President John Upton said, "McCall was a big influence on my life as a student at the Southern Baptist Theological Seminary while he was president. He was a true Baptist statesman, a world leader and a scholar. His influence will be long-lasting. We are grateful for his leadership and friendship in the BWA" (Baptist World Alliance 2013). Neville Callam stated that McCall will be remembered for "the expansiveness of his vision of the BWA mission, the depth of his appreciation for the extensiveness of the BWA's potential reach, and the deep commitment that marked his engagement to help the BWA secure the physical infrastructure to support its ongoing ministry" (Baptist World Alliance 2013).

CHAPTER 5

Baptist historian Bill Leonard stated upon his death that Duke McCall represented "the height of denominational identity. . .and its subsequent collapse" (Steffan 2013). From Leonard's perspective as Baptist historian, "Duke Kimbrough McCall was an institution, bearing in himself elements of American religious corporate and institutional life across much of the twentieth century." Leonard goes on to state, "In some ways he was the ultimate denominational administrator, presiding over. . .significant organizations – New Orleans Baptist Theological Seminary, the Executive Committee, and the Southern Baptist Theological Seminary," not to mention his key leadership in the Baptist World Alliance. McCall's "style rested in what many have called the 'conservative middle,' a traditionalist approach that reflected a broad spectrum of theological positions and ministry practices, but which keep those at either end of the theological spectrum from dominating the denominational center" (Leonard 2013).

Over his years McCall served Baptist institutions and through them guided the Baptist family through periods of both peace and controversy. Fortunate to begin his days of ministry during the post-World War II period, McCall helped to channel the energies of "the Greatest Generation" into significant growth for Southern Baptists. Duke McCall began his ministry in 1946 precisely as the soldiers were coming home from World War II. This time period certainly marked a time of growth, expansion and optimism among Southern Baptists. In many ways Duke McCall was the embodiment of the healthy optimism of those days.

Frank Page, current president of the Executive Committee of Southern Baptists, a post that McCall himself had held, states, "Southern Baptists are indebted to McCall. He leaves a powerful legacy" (Willis and Hanbury 2013). Forced to serve during a later period shrouded with bitter controversy among Southern Baptists, McCall served remarkably as a strong leader among Baptist moderates. *Christianity Today* notes that as a Baptist leader he was "respected in both conservative and moderate circles." So much so that Al Mohler, current president of Southern Seminary, calls him "a Giant among Southern Baptists" and speaks of "the lengthened shadow that one man can cast over a great denomination" (Steffan 2013). Mohler characterizes McCall as "Southern Baptist to the core" and suggests that "He belongs to that great generation of Southern Baptist leaders who shaped the convention as the 20th century brought new opportunities and new challenges. He, along with Drs. W. A. Criswell and Hershel H. Hobbs, brought the Southern Baptist Convention into the modern age" (Willis and Hanbury 2013).

McCall modeled strong leadership until the very end of his long years of life. Jason Allen notes that "even at his most advanced age, he continued to drive his own car, teach a Bible study through the book of Romans. . .and engage intellectually in political, cultural, denominational, and religious affairs. In fact, his home office looked like a veritable nerve center of Baptist life" (Allen 2013).

A Chronology of the Life of Duke K. McCall

Duke McCall recounts the story of his life in an "oral history" compiled by Ronald Tonks (McCall and Tonks 2001). In that autobiographical treatment, dedicated to the memory of his first wife Marguerite, McCall describes episodes of his life with fascinating candor. The chapters of his life follow chronological periods roughly as follows:

Young Duke McCall (1914-1931)

McCall's earliest memory was of falling off a fence and breaking his arm. While born in Meridian, Mississippi, the family moved to Memphis, Tennessee, for much of his childhood, where his father became a prominent attorney.

College and Seminary Days (1931-1940)

At Furman University in Greenville, South Carolina, McCall was the valedictorian of his class. While there he met Marguerite Mullinnix. They were married after his graduation in 1935. He decided to attend Southern Seminary instead of entering Vanderbilt Law School. Only after a year of study did he come to fully recognize his calling into ministry. Upon completing his M.Div., McCall was convinced to stay at Southern Seminary to complete his doctorate in Old Testament Studies instead of doing a Th.M. at Yale by Kyle Yates, who convinced the school to offer McCall a fellowship. In the second year of his doctoral studies young McCall was asked to preach a sermon as a supply preacher at the prestigious Broadway Baptist Church in Louisville, and they invited him to become their pastor even while he completed his doctorate at the Seminary.

Pastor of Broadway Baptist Church of Louisville KY (1941-1943)

McCall was young and inexperienced, and recalled fondly that most of the members of the church took an almost indulgent or patronizing attitude toward him, even while he was able to steer the church into significant ministries, and to remodel their facilities. McCall learned early on how to listen carefully to more experienced people, but to ask them to let him be his own man in making decisions.

Baptist Bible Institute, New Orleans LA (1943-1946)

When McCall assumed the leadership at New Orleans he was so young that he was about the same age as some of the returning GIs who were coming to study. An incoming freshman asked him in 1943, "Are you new here too?" McCall answered, "Yes, I am. They have just made me president" (Willis and Hanbury 2013). McCall spent two weeks at Moody Bible Institute learning from their helpful staff how to administrate a Bible College. However, when he got to New Orleans he quickly realized that the entire school: faculty, students and alumni, believed that they should be a seminary. He was the architect for ramping up their programs and for proposing the name change to New Orleans Baptist Theological Seminary.

Southern Baptist Convention's Executive Committee (1946-1951)

In later years McCall saw that his appointment to the Executive Committee may have come from writing a hot letter to all the members of the committee for a narrowly conservative stance on enforcing antiquated administrative criteria in an era when a broader approach was required for things to grow. So, they just decided to let him have a chance to implement his ideas and invited him to become the executive secretary. Older leaders like T. L. Holcomb at the Sunday School Board took pleasure in coaching this very young man who knew he was inexperienced and brash, but showed promise.

Southern Seminary President (1951-1979)

M. Theron Rankin, executive secretary of the Foreign Mission Board, writes in The Commission for November, 1951 these words:

> Surely circumstances could not of themselves, without the directing hand of God, have worked out to bring the man and the need to meet at such day as this. And what a day it is—a confused, hungry world so desperately in need of the good news that God has in Christ Jesus for the whole world; an institution with almost a century of rich, strong traditions in the training of ministers of the Gospel of Jesus Christ; a student body of nearly a thousand men seeking to be prepared as preachers of this Gospel; a faculty of strong men of God to lead these students in their training; a superb plant, campus and buildings, in

which to conduct such an undertaking. It is to such a day that Duke McCall has come. He has won the confidence of Southern Baptists to a remarkable degree. We believe in him, in his spiritual and intellectual capacities. We will follow him with our support as he leads the seminary on the road of service in God's undertaking of world redemption (Rankin 1951, 9).

Perhaps history will remember that McCall's greatest achievements at Southern Seminary were: (1) to supervise the growth of the institution from a student body of 800 to 2,600 students during his tenure; (2) to have championed vigorously a need for diligent and free scholarship committed to the Gospel and to teaching how to live out its implications; and (3) to have expanded the school to include African American and then women students in opposition to then prevailing views. It was in fact illegal under Kentucky law in 1952 when the seminary opened its doors to the integration of black students. Women were not only admitted to the Carver WMU School of Missions, but also some years later allowed to study in the School of Theology for all of its degrees, including the M.Div.

McCall discusses with candor the 1958 Controversy at Southern Seminary in his memoirs (McCall and Tonks 2001, 161-211). Without any doubt this crisis with the faculty is one of the most difficult and painful challenges to McCall's leadership during his career. McCall clearly was taken by surprise by the fact that eight faculty colleagues would assume an intransigent position opposing his leadership. For so long, McCall had successfully pushed the envelope to achieve new initiatives at dizzying speed. Somehow he missed that there was a backlog of resentment and concern that the role of the presidency at Southern was shifting. Formerly, the very democratic model John Broadus had brought from the University of Virginia had been practiced at Southern Seminary, so that the faculty believed that in their deliberations they were really the authority of the seminary, and the presidents served as moderators and coordinators to execute their decisions.

The conflict came to a head quickly and eight veteran and well-esteemed faculty left the seminary. In retrospect it seems that when this young leader was confronted by a group of professors, each with decades of experience who were capable of articulating a different perspective than his own most eloquently, he simply could not find a way to manage the situation that would not have placed conditions he considered unacceptable on the exercise of his presidency. Given this failure in his ability to exercise informal leadership, McCall leaned on the power of his office to oppose his faculty and assert the dominance of the presidency at the expense of eight academic careers. After so many successes in forging unlikely partnerships and finding a way toward consensus among multiple constituencies, this incident stands out as an ugly exception to McCall's finesse in asserting leadership.

In 1982 upon McCall's retirement he was the longest serving president in Southern Seminary's history of long-tenured presidents.

President of the Baptist World Alliance (1980-1985)

McCall began his participation in BWA events at age sixteen, when he attended the 1931 Baptist Youth World Congress in Prague, Czechoslovakia. He was elected to the BWA Executive Committee in 1947, and served conscientiously and faithfully in many other roles, such as member of the General Council, member of the Commission on Freedom, Justice and Peace, co-chairman of the Commission on Baptist Doctrine, member of nominating committees, and committees charged with reviewing the BWA constitution.

McCall served as BWA president from 1980-1985, elected at the 15th Baptist World Congress in Los Angeles, and he was a primary mover to achieve several significant developments which occurred during his presidency:

- During his presidency, he endorsed the formation of and inclusion of regional bodies within the global organization, including the All Africa Baptist Fellowship and the Union of Baptists in Latin America
- During his presidency, he advocated providing travel scholarships to facilitate attendance and participation of Baptist leaders from around the world, which resulted in a fund being created in 1985
- During his presidency, the first Baptist International Conference on Theological Education was conducted in the United States in 1982
- During his presidency, the search for more suitable offices for the BWA was conducted resulting in the purchase of a new headquarters building in McLean, Virginia, in 1985

McCall's interest and strong participation in the Baptist World Alliance actually spanned his entire career. Frequently when speaking with students at Southern Seminary he would tell stories from his travels for the BWA. In his mind, the BWA was our network to interact with Baptists globally and to maintain close fellowship among the member bodies.

Wrestling with Revolution in the SBC (1979-1985)

Duke McCall was a clarion voice among the "moderates" of the Southern Baptist Convention who from the start of the fundamentalist movement challenged their methods and their goals. He understood more clearly than his peers among SBC leaders of his time that the movement would ultimately change the Southern Baptist Convention inalterably if left unchecked. McCall defended his professors vigorously from the swirling innuendos and complaints about their supposed liberalism.

McCall did eventually run for president of the SBC in an attempt to stop what he considered to be a fundamentalist juggernaut that had created a political machine to elect the president of the convention and to use his broad powers of appointment to stack the boards of all institutions and agencies with conservatives. He lost by only a narrow margin.

After that defeat, McCall turned to creating an alternative system to allow moderate churches to stay somehow within the SBC funding system and to have the strength of their support be taken into account. McCall describes the ingenious system he devised and implemented in a brief article (D. K. McCall 1993, 241-51).

In words that seem strangely prophetic today McCall stated, "Having lost a billion dollars worth of property and funds, and having no programs administered by compatible people, what will moderate churches support? They will mount their horses and ride off in all directions" (D. K. McCall 1993, 243).

McCall cleverly suggested as early as 1990 that there should be an alternative funding structure, and so created a new corporation incorporated in Georgia called the Baptist Cooperative Missions Program, Inc. Churches could send their CP funds to this organization rather than directly into the SBC channels. The entity received more than $ 4.5 million in its first year of existence. McCall speaks of the unhappy surprise of learning about the hardening of the arteries in the SBC Cooperative Program system. Several key state conventions determined to follow Alabama who advised the new entity, "our bylaws require that all funds received and disbursed by our convention must be for causes approved by the Alabama Baptist Convention or the Southern Baptist Convention." Thus the alternative system that McCall devised was thwarted by a focused administrative resistance from the state conventions. Eventually the structures and funding were rolled into the newly formed Cooperative Baptist Fellowship (D. K. McCall 1993, 248-251).

CHAPTER 5

Duke McCall as Denominational Statesman

Perhaps the tribute of Baptist historian Bill Leonard upon McCall's death gives some sense of his personal significance. Leonard speaks of his "characteristic political and theological insight," and maintains that "throughout his long life and work, Duke McCall bridged multiple generations of Baptist life nationally and globally...He was the personification of the amazing organizational success and regional strength of Southern Baptists in much of the 20th century." In the title of his eulogy Leonard calls McCall "the last denominationalist – a symbol of denominational identity that no longer prevails, even among Southern Baptists themselves." Thus, for Leonard the "death of longtime denominational leader Duke McCall marks the end of an era in Baptist life" (Leonard 2013).

As the executive secretary of the Executive Committee of Southern Baptists, McCall led the denomination in an astonishing chain of achievements in rapid succession. While in this position, McCall converted the *Baptist Program* into a monthly magazine for Southern Baptists. He also launched the Baptist Press as an independent news organ. BP continues to provide news for Baptist events to our present day.[1] Also, McCall revamped the Bulletin Service into a color photo format, and passed this very successful concept to the Sunday School Board. McCall also helped the SBC to purchase the land to create Glorieta Assembly. McCall led the SBC to establish the Southern Baptist Foundation, to invest and administer large donations. However, it was as a fund-raiser that McCall had his greatest success as executive secretary of the SBC Executive Committee. When he arrived in Nashville the first job assigned to him was to raise $3.5 million to get the convention out of the debt that had plagued it since the Depression until after World War II. In three months under McCall's leadership they successfully raised $3.8 million to surpass what seemed like an unreachable goal. By liberating Southern Baptists from the debts that had plagued them for decades, McCall established a new level of confidence in the convention and its work. It is difficult to overstate the significance of this early achievement in his career.

While at Southern Seminary, Duke McCall brokered important agreements with other denominational bodies. When he first arrived the president's home was located on the old Norton estate, which was located adjacent to Cherokee Park. The old mansion, buildings, and grounds were hopelessly too large for a residence, even for an institutional head. He worked very hard to find a way to get out of the residence. Eventually he convinced the Presbyterians to buy the property and to remodel the buildings into a seminary. There were close bonds of cooperation between the Baptist and Presbyterian seminaries in Louisville for all of McCall's tenure as president.

Also, McCall reached out to the American Baptist Convention and was able to convince them that since they did not have a seminary in the region, and since there were many of their churches close by, then Southern Seminary could provide that service for them. Part of this arrangement was a very clear understanding that the faculty at Southern would not try to make Southern Baptists out of students coming from American Baptist Convention churches. This provided a strong boost to student enrollment, since in the heyday of the seminary with some 2,600 in the student body, just over 800 of them came from American Baptist churches. We see an expression of the magnanimity and broad gauge thinking of McCall in his ability to convince leaders from other denominations of his sincere desire to cooperate in ways that were mutually beneficial with other religious bodies.

Furthermore, the decision to really integrate the seminary in Louisville in the early 1950s must also be understood as an important interdenominational link. Of course, from a Christian perspective, as sermons from Martin Luther King were reverberating across the USA, integrating the student body was simply the right thing to do from an ethical standpoint. However, there simply were no black students from SBC churches in those days to invite to the seminary. The first black students in the classrooms of the Louisville seminary were there because of McCall's interactions with the National Baptist Convention. This sister Baptist body of African-American churches sent many of their brightest and best students to Southern to be educated, and it included the school in their budget distributions for many years.

In 2009, in a remarkably magnanimous gesture, McCall returned to the institution that had rejected his own vision for the Baptist denomination. McCall explained his willingness to relate positively even with those whom he vehemently disagreed by saying, "For 150 years, Southern Seminary has navigated the shifting tides of social, economic, and political affairs because of divine favor and dedicated leadership, all guided by the inspired word of God. Those who manned the helm have tacked to port or starboard as their times required, but all have had...their hearts fixed on the kingdom of God." McCall added, "There have been diverse currents running through our community and fellowship. We do not always agree with each other on everything. But what I call upon us to recognize is that the hand of God is on this institution" (Smith 2013). Perhaps in this moment, McCall most clearly demonstrated his statesmanship, by his willingness to work closely with those with whom he sharply disagreed, and who had opposed him in very personal and perhaps painful ways. Many others who have been wounded by denominational politics may have chosen to nurse their wounds and allow bitterness to drive them away from causes they once loved.

CHAPTER 5

McCall believed in the power of forgiveness, and he was too big a man to turn his back on Southern Seminary, an institution he had loved and fought for over so many years.

Duke McCall as Baptist Educator

The faculty members at Southern Seminary never doubted that Duke McCall had earned his doctorate in Old Testament studies and easily could have worked alongside them in the classroom. In fact, he was once offered a position teaching at Southern Seminary as an Old Testament professor and turned it down in order to go to New Orleans. Frankly, it is a rare combination of skills sets that McCall seemed equally at home in preaching in a church, in teaching in a classroom, and in administrating large institutions.

One of the ways in which we see McCall as a Baptist educator is to review the books that he wrote and edited. McCall's first book came out while he was in Nashville at the Executive Committee. It is an attractive book casting a vision for the expanded role of the Southern Baptist Convention. Under the title, *God's Hurry*, (D. K. McCall 1949), McCall develops an eloquently and carefully argued treatment of why Southern Baptists needed to be more deeply committed to kingdom causes in such a time as this.

This book was designated as a study course book, whose purpose was to promote the Advance Program of Southern Baptists by advocating Christian stewardship. The book seeks to educate Baptist Christians on their obligation to share their resources in order to further God's kingdom through their churches. There is no hint whatsoever of simply promoting any specific cause nor program, rather, the book refreshingly reviews the classic arguments for a committed and conscientious financial plan of stewardship for every dedicated Christian. It also casts a compelling vision for the opportunities Baptists have to make a difference in the world.

What is instantly obvious to even a casual reader is the prolific research and breadth of reading and insights that are collected into the arguments that McCall constructs. McCall discusses Toynbee and Norman Cousins' book, *Modern Man is Obsolete*. He uses poetry from Lord Byron to clarify the message of Isaiah. He discusses God's hand of Providence at the Battle of Marathon where the Persians were defeated by the Greeks and by the defeat of Napoleon at Waterloo. McCall models scholarship at the service of the church and Christ's kingdom.

The book begins by pointing to the plight of "one lost world," in which McCall advocates the interdependence of all men. We are connected together so that our own future is connected to that of all others. McCall was influenced by the

Marshall Plan and especially by Wendell Willkie who believed that "we are all bound up in the bundle of life together," and who claimed that "There is not a part of the world which any man can afford to ignore" (D. K. McCall, God's Hurry 1949, xi).

McCall sees a spiritual awakening as the solution to the world's dilemma, suggesting that "the way up is the way out." He asks us to look for "help from above" with a "faith which reaches out to grasp God's helping hand" (D. K. McCall, God's Hurry 1949, xix). In great historical upheavals we see "God's participation in the affairs of history."

There is a "divine haste" that is concerned for the thousands who die every hour who will "stand before the Judgment without Christ as an Advocate and Counselor" (D. K. McCall, God's Hurry 1949, 1). The salvation of the lost is too significant to be the work of any one particular denomination, but is the commission given to all Christians who are to go into the world with the Gospel.

McCall spoke of the influence of missionaries who had converted Solomon Islanders who helped our American servicemen at Guadalcanal, which is astonishing when one considers that their parents had practiced cannibalism. McCall also sees in upheavals of the post-World War II era an unparalleled opportunity for global spiritual harvest. The book directly addresses the conflict between Christianity and communism, and advocates that we choose God over Mammon.

McCall suggests that Baptists are "ecumenical" in the older literary sense, that our purpose is to preach the Gospel to the whole wide world. McCall asks what the sources for the miraculous unity of Baptists really are. Our unity is not to be found in a name, since German Baptists call themselves "The Evangelical Free Church." The unity does not come from the practice of baptism by immersion, since at least ten denominational groups who are not Baptist share our practice. The unity is not geographical, nor based on a creed. Organizationally the Southern Baptist Convention is organized bottom side up – authority resides not at the apex but spread along the base in the churches. In fact, the unity of the Baptist effort develops out of a concern for a lost world (D. K. McCall, God's Hurry 1949, 56).

McCall cites the need for Baptists in every state to work for the conversion of lost people on their home turf. He speaks of the need for more home missionaries to speak to the lost of the USA. However, according to McCall, "The wedge which Southern Baptists would drive into the sin-blackened heart of a lost world comes to a point in the Foreign Mission Board" (D. K. McCall, God's Hurry 1949, 58). McCall proceeds to list careful statistics about our missionaries in the foreign field and explains compellingly how they are not enough to even begin to accomplish the task imposed by the Great Commission. He asks, "What proportion of our resources are we using in this task of world missions?" Advance Together was a plan to move forward as a denomination in addressing the needs of lostness on all these multiple fronts.

The book concludes with a stirring call to action: "Forward march! On the double! Charge! Each Christian must place himself completely at the disposal of Christ, his commander. It is not a question of counting the cost of victory. The cost of failure is all too obvious. The world must be reached with the Gospel – NOW!" (D. K. McCall, God's Hurry 1949, 113).

McCall's second book can be treated better under the topic of global leadership later in this paper.

Soon after becoming president at Southern Seminary, McCall led his faculty to sponsor meetings to consider the Baptist perspective on ecclesiology, or the doctrine of the church. During two successive summers the meetings were convened on the campus of the Southern Baptist Theological Seminary. For the second meeting the symposium was held simultaneously with the Executive Committee of the Baptist World Alliance to encourage global participation. In his preface McCall explains that the reason for the meetings and the book is that "Baptists need to take their bearings on the important doctrine of the church" (D. K. McCall, What is the Church? 1958, vi).

McCall noted that it had been more than fifty years since the nature of the church had been discussed seriously by Baptists, adding that "unfortunately that discussion became so involved in personalities that sight of the real issues was lost. May that never happen again!" McCall further gives voice to the Baptist spirit in stating that "Baptists, however, have no ecclesiastical court or infallible ecclesiastic, and must be able to test the truth of any proposition in the arena of free discussions where the first authority is always the revelation of God" (D. K. McCall, What is the Church? 1958, vi).

Missions professor W. O. Carver penned the first paper collected into the book, introducing the topic by exploring the significance of ecclesiology for Baptists. He claimed that "the nature of the church is at the very center of urgent theological considerations" and that the first item to be considered in understanding the church is "the fact of the unfinished task of the Christian Gospel." Carver laments that "after eighteen centuries of Gospel expansion, humanity is still largely unevangelized and still pagan in its patterns of living." He points out how easily "Christians. . .see how relatively ineffective their influence is on the life of the world" (D. K. McCall, What is the Church? 1958, 1). Curiously, these words can describe our own times just as easily as in 1958, though today we might choose different terminology to describe the tragedy of the human condition.

It is this compelling vision of a lost world in need of the Gospel of Jesus Christ that provides the impulse for what Carver calls "the demand for unity and aim within organized Christianity." Of course, there can be no other "starting point for exploring the possibilities of the church" (D. K. McCall, What is the Church? 1958, 2). In fact, it is apt to say:

> The church is at the core of God's kingdom as being realized in human history. Local churches are the agencies of that kingdom and of its Gospel. They are not only emigration centers for heaven, but are also recruiting agencies and training instruments and supervisory bodies for the recruits as they become active in the Gospel (D. K. McCall, What is the Church? 1958, 13).

A chapter focused on baptism and the Lord's Supper recognized these ordinances as defining the outer boundary of membership in the church and the center of its fellowship.

Theron Price contributes a careful treatment on the Anabaptist view of the church. The rich legacy of Anabaptists reflects this simple truth: "Strong men of simple faith, to whom faithful witness was more important than personal safety, are not to be ignored" (D. K. McCall, What is the Church? 1958, 97). In fact, the substance of twentieth century perspectives on the believer's church could well have been written by sixteenth century Anabaptists. The polemic against Anabaptists by both Lutherans and Zwinglians recognizes that "the Anabaptists represent a. . .distinctive approach to Christianity aspiring more for a restitution of New Testament Gospel than a simple reformation of the church" (D. K. McCall, What is the Church? 1958, 99).

For Anabaptists it was a central tenet that the church was based on "voluntary association," which organizes "life to be free from the state in order that it might be free unto God." Since the present world is submerged in evil, consequently witness to Christ becomes warfare against the prevailing principalities and powers. The martyr-church had a theology of suffering since "no Anabaptist could ignore the probability of martyrdom" (D. K. McCall, What is the Church? 1958, 109-10).

Part of the legacy of Anabaptists is that they were also early adopters of the Great Commission. "No Scriptural passages had more use in Anabaptist circles than Matthew 28:19-20." So, when William Carey argued later in his "Enquiry" that Matthew 28 teaches that Christians are required to use all means available for the propagation of the Gospel, his voice is in reality an echo of Anabaptist forbears. Kenneth Scott Latourette believes that Anabaptists "can be appropriately described as the forerunner of the modern missionary movement" (D. K. McCall, What is the Church? 1958, 111).

Robert Torbet describes how a new movement of Baptists emerges from congregations in Holland and England under John Smyth and Thomas Helwys. Though inspired by both Anabaptists and Mennonites, these Baptist pioneers nevertheless forged a clear new identity. In colonial America, Roger Williams established the first Baptist church, and self-sacrificing men like Isaac Backus and Shubael Stearns preached with untiring zeal to promote Baptist ideals on the growing western frontier.

There are chapters on the Landmark Movement, on Stewardship and a final very complete treatment on discipline in the church. The treatment of church discipline by Theron Price is remarkable, since most local churches in the US were already abandoning this biblical practice. Since the chapter was a conscious corrective on church discipline that has not been taken seriously, it is worth reviewing the basic arguments here.

Discipline in the church begins by seeing that "the Church is called to share in and to show forth the holiness of her Lord." The church's call to be holy "involves the consecration and actual sanctification of its individual members." The church has three principal concerns: "the purity of her doctrine, the holiness of her members, and the unity of her fellowship. This requires, of course, that the church look on nothing with greater apprehension than impurity of teaching (heresy), moral and spiritual lapse (sin), and breach of fellowship (schism)" (D. K. McCall, What is the Church? 1958, 164). Church discipline provides the means to address these significant problems. The goal is to protect against whatever can impair or destroy the church's life and witness. The most important text on discipline in the New Testament was held to be Matthew 18:15-18 where brothers in disagreement must go in person to speak of the matter, then if no agreement can be reached mature brothers are to join in the conversation, and finally the matter can be taken to the church. Price maintains that both 1 Corinthians 5 and 2 Corinthians 2:4-8 are examples of "this sort of teaching in the apostolic church" (D. K. McCall, What is the Church? 1958, 166).

Among Baptists, explicit consideration of church discipline harks back to the London Confession of 1689, which is incorporated entirely into the Charleston Confession and Summary of Discipline in 1774 in the American colonies:

The underlying motifs of this publication are: to witness to the truth in modesty and humility, to be perfectly candid with brethren of other names, to remove rather than to create a possible ground of contention, and to provide for adequate instruction in the faith in Christian homes.

The *Summary of Discipline* claims that because all Christians are one in Christ, it is "for the good and prosperity of all the churches of Christ, in all places, and upon all occasions. . .to hold communion among themselves for their peace, increase of love, and mutual edification" (D. K. McCall, What is the Church? 1958, 176). This statement that underscores the importance of maintaining connections and fellowship among local churches could serve well as a mission statement today for the Baptist World Alliance and for its member bodies around the world.

The 1774 *Summary of Discipline* explains that Christ deals directly with his children to reward and to punish, but that there are some punishments that Christ, by his word, authorized his church to impose upon rebellious and unworthy members, and lists three church censures which are to be applied according to the offense. None of these are coercive measures that can be applied by civic authorities. The censures deal with the spiritual concerns of men and must involve no temporal nor civil penalties. The recommended censures are:

1. "rebuke or admonition" which reproves the offender, points out the offence, exhorts to repentance, and prays for reclamation in love and tenderness with Christian prudence.

2. "suspension" in which a member is set aside from office, and from voting, so that the member is still in union with the church until upon credible profession of repentance the censure is removed.

3. "excommunication" is recognized as the severe and last resort where an offender "remains impenitent and incorrigible." This decision is seen as "awful and tremendous," and to be reserved for members "who are guilty of notorious and atrocious crimes" (D. K. McCall, What is the Church? 1958, 177-79).

There is an explicit list of the kinds of offenses that can and should be addressed by each of these "levels" of church discipline. Prudently, sins that are private can best be dealt with in private, but sins that are public require public responses.

Such discipline was held as necessary, because "by sin the church is the contradiction of her own Gospel." Ironically, the congregation of saints is both righteous and sinful, but knows her Lord's demands, and "must bring that demand to bear upon sin and error." The church must correct itself "in love through mutual instruction, mutual rebuke, and mutual aid" (D. K. McCall, What is the Church? 1958, 182-83).

Theron Price concludes by noting that too often "respectability takes precedence of righteousness in the church of God, when the churches are too self-conscious to maintain discipline." The fervent "prayer and mourning over an erring brother to be reclaimed from the devil" is too often replaced by "a prevalent sense of politeness" that is "gravely shocked at a church meeting where. . .a fellow member's moral lapse is investigated before the congregation" (D. K. McCall, What is the Church? 1958, 182-183).

The careful reader today can easily conclude that if Southern Baptist churches had more carefully applied the suggestions in McCall's book, we could have been saved the spectacle of a sitting US President openly identified as a Baptist who involved himself in spectacularly immoral sexual activity and in which the Baptist church where he was a member found itself paralyzed in knowing how to respond. The matter was exposed in a media frenzy, rather than dealt with redemptively by caring brothers, and we were treated to multiple editorials which explained the moral duplicity of the president as deeply rooted in his Baptist beliefs.

Perhaps among the areas where Baptists need to learn from one another globally, should be treated this difficult matter of how to apply church discipline in love yet with moral firmness. On a personal level, I am so grateful to Argentine Baptists for teaching me in my years among them about how to gracefully manage church discipline along the lines that our Baptist heritage had long practiced, but which the brothers in my own country have long since forgotten.

Duke McCall as Global Leader

Neville Callam has stated that "as BWA general secretary, I have had good reason, again and again, to review McCall's addresses to the BWA Executive Committee and General Council …. Baptists around the world have lost a wonderful brother, a valiant witness and a disciple of Christ who was faithful to the end" (Baptist World Alliance 2013). McCall was a key force in challenging the BWA to find a more suitable office space for its headquarters. Shortly after he was elected president of the BWA he led the organization to purchase a new building in McLean, Virginia. The building was dedicated in 1985, moving from cramped quarters in Washington, DC. The quest for adequate space has continued, since the BWA central office moved to its present location in Falls Church, Virginia, in 2001.

One of McCall's frustrated goals for the BWA was to create an endowed funding mechanism that would help especially to defray the cost of travel to meetings of those who were furthest away and faced financial challenges to attend. This was tied to another goal, which was to broaden participation in the meetings. He was convinced that the only way to do this was to find a way to make it financially possible for more people from conventions other than North America and Europe to attend the meetings.

Duke McCall's global experience got a shot in the arm during a trip around the world that was planned in conjunction with a BWA meeting in Nigeria. In fact, Duke McCall and W. A. Criswell wrote a book together about their experiences (McCall and Criswell, Passport to the World 1951). Soon after World War II had ended, and while they were together in Nigeria for a meeting of the Baptist World Alliance, then executive secretary of the Foreign Mission Board, M. Theron Rankin, convinced the two of them to travel home through the Orient. Missionary doctor Bill Wallace had recently been killed by the Communists in China, and displaced missionaries from China were looking for new fields to enter across Asia and the Pacific Rim. Rankin asked them to go and to visit government officials in several of those countries as a special delegation from Southern Baptists formally requesting that their nations would accept the presence of missionaries. To their credit these two young Baptist leaders changed their plans to seize this once in a lifetime opportunity. So they jumped on a plane and circumnavigated the globe. The book, *Passport to the World*, is a report on what they discovered.

W. A. Criswell and Duke McCall became fast friends on this trip for the rest of their lives, and although later they would disagree sharply on central issues for the Southern Baptist Convention in the future, they never lost a healthy sense of mutual respect for one another.

On one level, the book is a travelogue, but on a deeper level it was an invitation to Baptists to respond to the deep needs of a world that McCall and Criswell had seen firsthand. They were asking Baptists to look out into the fields and to see God's harvest. In fact, the book did play a role in promoting one of the most vigorous times of expanding missionary endeavor in Baptist history.

Chapter by chapter the book relates experiences in their visits on each major continent. In the "Land of the Latins" there was a visit to an impressive new church in Caracas, Venezuela, and stops in Belen and Fortaleza, Brazil. They entered "Unforgettable Africa" by a flight from Recife, Brazil, to Dakar, Senegal, and after resting caught a flight to Lagos, Nigeria. They were impressed by the schools missionaries had built and the size of the churches. So many of the Yoruba had facial scars as tribal markings that Criswell chose to make Galatians

CHAPTER 5

6:17 the text of his sermon: "For I bear branded in my body the marks of Jesus." McCall comments, "The missionaries themselves were illustrations for the sermon. No one serves long in Africa without being able to say, 'Not only in my heart but also in my body I bear the brand marks of the Lord Jesus.'" McCall also remembered vividly that when they arrived in Sepele, they were greeted by a crowd of stamping, singing, hand-clapping Nigerians, and that they were put at the front of a procession and danced their way to the church. They were also granted an audience with the king of Eku,[2] and learned impressive lessons on the protocols used among Africans. The group visited Ogbomosho, where McCall delivered a commencement address at the seminary. They were inspired by the work of missionaries at a leper colony, and learned to avoid driver ants. In Tripoli they pressed a local official to consider receiving Jesus. They were stunned to find him negotiating with them, saying that he would convert to Christianity if both of them would become Muslims.

The chapter on Europe includes visits to Italy and to Germany, Switzerland and Greece. Criswell recoils against the patent distortion of Christianity implicit in the power of the Vatican. They attended the Passion Play in Oberamergau. They visited Dachau. They saw Orson Wells in his version of Faust. The final line stated tellingly, "Damnation is Contagious." In Switzerland they visited sites of the Reformers, and a Baptist seminary newly founded in Zurich.

They visited the newly formed nation of Israel, and the Baptist school in Nazareth, and walked where Jesus walked. They were deeply moved by the spiritual plight of the Israelis, whether Jews or Arabs.

In India, Thailand, and Indonesia they recognized how tragic it is to live without the Ten Commandments as they encountered strange customs and poverty. McCall, with his typical self-deprecating humor, tells a funny anecdote about his address to an evangelistic conference in Bangkok. He had a local interpreter translating his message into Swatow, and on the right a woman translated it into Cantonese. After the service missionary Ed Galloway congratulated McCall by telling him that those were three great speeches, each of them different! McCall had said "As executive secretary of the Executive Committee of the Southern Baptist Convention I bring you greetings from its 27,000 churches." The Swatow interpreter edited his statement into the boundaries of his own experience of possibility and translated "I bring you greeting from the 27 churches of the Southern Baptist Convention." McCall continued, "Last April 8,000 of these churches united in cooperative simultaneous evangelistic efforts, with the result that 71,000 people were baptized." The Swatow interpreter thought about that and translated "Last April 8 of those churches held revivals and seven people were saved." When Baker James Cauthen first heard the story he consoled Duke

McCall by saying "Never in all your life will you be called a liar more politely than that" (McCall and Criswell, Passport to the World 1951, xi-xii).

To a reader today many of the experiences chronicled in the book seem hopelessly naïve about the multiple cultural understandings that one must navigate to become a global citizen, but when one reads the book in its context it shows Americans shaking off their cheerful and glib mono-culturalism. McCall is clearly seeking to understand the larger world, and to apply faith in Christ to the needs of entire nations of lost people and needs that had not really been taken seriously into account until that time.

Finally, McCall and Criswell visited Japan, completing a tour of vanquished enemies in World War II. They found a deep "heart hunger" in Japan and closed their book speaking about the urgency of addressing the world's spiritual needs. In the final lines of the book we hear McCall and Criswell together assessing the significance of their journey:

> While we were going around the world, we were winding the world into our hearts. It is a big world, full of lost people. Their needs are too much for our hearts to hold. We have come home to try to parcel out our concern among our friends. A Christian's concern for the salvation of his fellow man is the Christian's passport to the world (McCall and Criswell, Passport to the World 1951, 139).

In fact, they conclude that we are living on "borrowed time" in trying to complete the Great Commission.

An Enduring Legacy

Duke K. McCall has left a strong footprint on the life of Baptists globally through the Baptist World Alliance. The list of his achievements is truly remarkable, whether serving his denomination, whether teaching as a Baptist educator, or whether calling fellow Baptists to see the larger world and to go out bravely to share the Gospel in it. His example of denominational statesmanship continues as an example for us today. While he was a capable administrator and a visionary thinker, McCall's chief contribution was rooted in his ability to form stable partnerships and trusted relationships with people with whom he disagreed in very important ways. While he never wavered in his own commitment to the truth as best he understood it, he was always willing to listen to another's opinion and to grant them the freedom to hold fast to ideas far different from his own. In that sense Duke McCall was a bearer of the Baptist spirit.

Hopefully, this abbreviated list of the many ways God used his life, will serve as an inspiration to all of us to live with the same intensity in our walk with God, our service to the church, and our witness with the world.

Bibliography

Allen, Jason K. Duke K. McCall: In Memoriam. Press Release, Kansas City: Baptist Press, 2013. http://www.bpnews.net/bpnews.asp?id=40004.

Baptist World Alliance. *Former BWA President Duke McCall has died*. Press Release, Falls Church: Baptist World Alliance, 2013. Accessed on 20 May 2013 at: http://www.bwanet.org/news/news-releases/243-duke-mccall.

Leonard, Bill. *The Last Denominationalist: Can I get a Witness?* Press Release, Jacksonville: Associated Baptist Press, 2013. Accessed on 20 May 2013 at: http://www.abpnews.com/opinion/item/8368-the-last-denominationalist.

McCall, Duke K. God's Hurry. Nashville, TN: Broadman Press, 1949.

McCall, Duke K. "The History of the Baptist Cooperative Missions Program." In The Struggle for the Soul of the SBC: Moderate Responses to the Fundamental Movement, edited by Walter B. Shurden, pages 241-251. Macon, GA: Mercer University Press, 1993.

McCall, Duke K. What is the Church?: A Symposium of Baptist Thought. Nashville, TN: Broadman Press, 1958.

McCall, Duke K., and W. A. Criswell. Passport to the World. Nashville, TN: Broadman Press, 1951.

McCall, Duke, and A. Ronald Tonks. Duke McCall: An Oral History. Brentwood, TN: Baptist History and Heritage Society, 2001.

Rankin, M. Theron. "Two Comrades at Southern." The Commission, November 1951:9.

Smith, Peter. *Duke McCall dies; former Southern Baptist Seminary president*. Press Release, Louisville: Courier-journal.com, 2013. Accessed 20 May 2013 at: http://blogs.courier-journal.com/faith/2013/04/02/duke-mccall-dies-former-southern-baptist-seminary-president/ .

Steffan, Melissa. Died: Duke McCall, 'Giant Among Southern Baptists'. Press Release, Christianity Today, 2013. Accessed 20 May 2013 at: http://www.christianitytoday.com/gleanings/2013/april/died-duke-mccall-giant-among-southern-baptists.html.

Willis, Gregory A., and Aaron Cline Hanbury. Duke K. McCall, Southern Baptist statesman and Southern Seminary president, dies at 98. Press Release, Louisville: Towers, 2013. Accessed 20 May 2013 at: http://news.sbts.edu/2013/04/02/duke-k-mccall-southern-baptist-statesman-and-southern-seminary-president-dies-at-98/.

CHAPTER 6
BIBLE TRANSLATION, A MAJOR COMPONENT OF EMANCIPATION:
THE CASE FOR A JAMAICAN NEW TESTAMENT

Courtney Stewart

The Bible Society of the West Indies (BSWI) is a full member organization of the Global network of 145 national Bible Societies known as the United Bible Societies (UBS). The UBS has been operating since 1946 and is present in more than 200 countries.

BSWI embraces as its mission making the Holy Scriptures and Scripture products available in forms readily understood and to promote engagement with Scripture in the territories it serves, including the Bahama Islands, Belize, Cayman Islands, Jamaica and Turks and Caicos Islands.

Like all Bible societies in the global UBS fellowship, BSWI seeks to carry out its tasks in partnership and cooperation with all Christian churches and with church-related organizations.

BSWI is governed by a board of directors drawn from several confessions. Operationally, BSWI has a small staff, managed by a general secretary who reports to and is held accountable by the board. The organization is a registered not-for-profit charity under the laws of Jamaica.

The translation of the JNT was completed by a team of four persons including two linguists (MPhil degrees), a pastor (MDiv.) and a coordinator (BA in Bible, MPhil (candidate). Exegetical consultants were provided by Jamaica Theological Seminary and United Theological College of the West Indies. The Jamaica Language Unit of the University of the West Indies provided Linguistic consultancy and conducted field tests for the project. A UBS linguist/biblical scholar was assigned to this project and guided the process from beginning to end.

Typesetting of the text was done by the British and Foreign Bible Society and printing was done at the UBS's printing plant in Nanjing, China.

CHAPTER 6

History of JNT

Translating religious texts, including the Bible, into indigenous Caribbean languages goes as far back as the 1700s with the translation of the New Testament and Christian hymns into the Virgin Islands Creole Dutch, also known as Negerhollands. It was not until the 1960s, however, that discussions began in relation to translating the Bible into Jamaican, known to the majority of its speakers as Patois (Patwa) (BSWI, 1996:1).

Three realities moved the BSWI to embark on the translation program. The first contribution came from the efforts of Faith Linton, a BSWI board member. Having become aware of the importance of mother-tongue education in the 1950s and of the benefits of vernacular Bible translation, she advocated for the rights of the vast majority of Jamaicans to experience the Scriptures in their heart-language (BSWI DVD, 2010).

Second, upon learning, in 1980, that Jamaica was one of the world's numerically significant speech communities without a word of Scripture, the United Bible Society (UBS) contacted the then General Secretary of the BSWI, William Edwards, requesting he sought the mind of his Board of Directors "concerning commencing a translation project of the Scriptures into Patois" (BSWI, 1996:1).

Up until this time, the BSWI Board was not moved to undertake the responsibilities for a local translation program as it was believed "the (Jamaican) churches, by and large, would neither be receptive nor supportive of such a project" (BSWI, 1996:2).

"The turning point" for a Bible Translation program into Jamaican, however, came about in 1985, with the linguistic crisis experience of a young, female, Christian social worker. The young woman related to Edwards that, in her experience, "the only way that she could adequately communicate with people [in the inner-city communities in which she worked] on matters of hygiene, family life, relationship, etc., was to speak in Patois" (BSWI, 1996:2).

The translation project begun in earnest in 1993, with BSWI approaching the UBS and soliciting its assistance in launching the local program. A UBS Translation Consultant, Harold Fehderau, was assigned to oversee the program and the Jamaican Bible translation program was launched on the weekend of January 15-16, 1993, at the Immaculate Conception Convent (BSWI, 1996:2).

Productions

Notwithstanding a number of challenges, and prior to 2012, BSWI has been able to release three audio productions:1] *A Who Run Things?* (1996), 2] *Di Krismos Story* (2003) and 3] Jiizas – *Di Buk We Luuk Rait Bout Im* (2010). (The latter was also released in print format.)

On December 9 2012, the Bible Society dedicated and launched the Jamaican New Testament. This is a translation of the Christian Testament into Jamaican. The completion and public launch of this was significant for several reasons, not the least of which being that it took place in the final month of celebration and commemoration of Jamaica's fiftieth anniversary as an independent nation. It is also significant that from a linguistic perspective, the JNT represents the largest corpus of text extant in Jamaican.

Currently, the JNT is available in print and audio formats, as well as on websites such as Bible.is, You Version, and, of course Bible Society. There is even a video representation of the first three chapters of St. John's gospel in which the JNT narrative has been dubbed. See http://www.youtube.com/watch?v=ygEVbmYx2ao.

We are continuing to explore other platforms to reach the widest possible audience including MP4 players, iPhone, Android, SMS, Blackberry, Windows Mobile and Symbian-based phones. All at one's fingertips. Anytime, anywhere in the world!

Partner agencies that cooperated with BSWI in producing the JNT include American Bible Society, The Seed Company, University of the West Indies (Jamaica Language Unit), Wycliffe Caribbean, British & Foreign Bible Society and the UBS.

BSWI's ministry of Bible Translation could be viewed from the perspective of the incarnation of God in Jesus, the Christ, who came to liberate humanity.

Objections

Many objections have been leveled against the Jamaican Creole Translation Programme (JCTP), the BSWI lead initiative that ultimately produced the JNT. Objections included but were not limited to:

1. Jamaican is simply bad English
2. Jamaican should only be used for oral communication as it does not possess a standardized orthography
3. Jamaican is a barrier preventing the learning, speaking and use of standard English

4. To translate the Scriptures into Jamaican demeans the sanctity of Scripture
5. Resources spent on the JNT could be better spent
6. Jamaican is an inadequate vehicle to communicate the nuances of Scripture
7. Persons who are illiterate will not be able to read the Scriptures in Jamaican
8. To promote the Scriptures in Jamaican is to forever relegate its speakers to a life of 2nd class citizenships as they will not be able to function in a rapidly increasing English-speaking world

Perhaps the most poignant of these is the notion that extending the functional domains of Jamaican (i.e. Jamaican Patois) would confine Jamaicans to their local socio-economic context. It is also believed that such an endeavor would limit their educational opportunities and would, hence, impede their ability to participate in the wider global community in which English is the *lingua franca*. In this lecture, I provide a brief overview of JCTP and argue that the BSWI-led initiative is a catalyst for national liberation/emancipation, both religiously and socially. It will be argued, therefore, that those who insist on expanding the functional domains of Jamaican are by no means depriving our people of some of the basic tools needed to participate effectively in the global village.

Incarnational Metaphor

Over the years, Christian theologians have observed a number of parallels between the incarnation of God in Jesus of Nazareth and the church's missional activity. The incarnation, the supreme act of God's self-revelation, is seen as an event that should inform and serve as a paradigm for how Christians do mission in the world. According to Andrew Walls in his book *The Missionary Movement in Christian History: Studies in the Transmission of Faith* (1997:26),

Christianity is built on "a divine act of translation:'the Word became flesh, and dwelt among us' (John 1:14)." "Incarnation is translation," he argues (1997:27), for when God in Christ assumed human nature, "Divinity was translated into humanity, as though humanity were a receptor language."

Walls and others have made it their duty to go further by pointing out that the incarnation is not simply a matter of God assuming human nature, but of God becoming a *"particular"* human individual (Walls, 1996:27). God in Christ became not a generic but a specific human being and was located within a specific locale with its unique set of social features – political, cultural, religious, linguistic, etc. As such, God was able to relate to the realities of his people in first-century Jewish Palestine. He made himself accessible to them in a tangible way (1 Jn 1:1).

In missions, therefore, states Walls (1996:27), it is as if:

> Christ, God's translated speech, is re-translated from the Palestinian Jewish original. The words of the Great Commission require that the various nations are to be made disciples of Christ. In other words, national distinctives, the things that mark out a nation, the shared consciousness and shared traditions, and the shared mental processes and patterns of relationship, are within the scope of discipleship. Christ can become visible within the very things which constitute nationality. The first divine act of translation into humanity thus gives rise to a constant succession of new translations.

In other words, God the Son did not have a generic incarnation. He and his message were rooted in a particular historical context. In similar fashion, the Christian church is not an a-cultural entity that proclaims a generic gospel. The church must, therefore, like its Head, adapt to the living cultural contexts in which she finds herself. She must speak to the social features of the culture, utilising the structural and cultural categories available within that culture.

The ministry of Bible Translation in some ways, therefore, mirrors the translation of God's eternal Word, into a specific sub-group of humanity. As such, the Scriptures that testify to the eternal Word of God are translated into new cultures, taking the Word of God to people in a tangible manner. Christian mission in general and Bible Translation in particular, therefore reflect the character and activity of God.

Durrell Guder (2000:80) summarizes this as follows:

> Confession of faith in all languages is possible because of the distinctive character of God's action, as it leads to faith. God's self-communication takes the form of incarnation in history, events in which God encounters us and enables us to recognize that it is God who is speaking and acting. These events lead toward and find their climax and ultimate purpose in the Word that became flesh, the Son of Man.

> Because this incarnation in history could be witnessed, it could be reported and be put into words. Yet, there are no particular sacred words in a sacred language that must always be learned and used in order to encounter the divine.

CHAPTER 6

In the Great Commission the church, empowered by the Spirit (Matt. 28; Acts 1-2) is given the responsibility to carry on the *missio Dei* the climax of which is God by means of the living Word, Christ, entering into the human experience. In similar fashion, the translation in Jamaican of the written Word about the living Word speaks to an incarnation of God into the reality of ordinary Jamaicans and of him making himself accessible to the Jamaican people.

God in Jamaican Liberates/Emancipates

God in Christ became a human being with a specific ethnicity and was confined within a specific socio-cultural space with its unique features. As a first century Palestinian Jew, God in Jesus was able to relate to and address the realities of the people amongst whom he lived. The translation of Divinity into humanity in first century Palestine had a meaningful effect on the concrete contextual situation of first century Palestine. This was the observation of several Latin Americans Christians, primarily Catholics, such as the Peruvian priest, Gustavo Gutierriez, in his book *The Theology of Liberation* (1969). Liberation Theology has as its core value the concept of Jesus as a "Liberator" who, in his life and ministry, contended for meaningful action to be taken against social injustice, the misuse of power and poverty with a view to bringing freedom to the poor from oppressive structures. Jesus himself understood his calling in Luke 4:18 in light of Isaiah 58:

> The Spirit of the Lord is upon me, because he has anointed me to proclaim good news to the poor. He has sent me to proclaim release to the captives and the regaining of sight to the blind, to set free those who are oppressed.[1]

The Jamaican Creole Translation Project (JCTP) began at a time when significant efforts were being made to standardize Jamaican (c.f. Durrleman 2008:10), in an attempt to extend the language into several functional domains reserved for Standard Jamaican English (SJE) so that speakers could have access to the social and economic benefits of those areas. In Jamaica, it is generally assumed that the Bible is the most formal, prestigious and respected book. Given this reality, the translation of the Christian Scriptures into Jamaican will make it inevitable for the language to take on a standardized form in order to meet the demands of the formal, religious domain to which the Bible is assigned. This involves putting the Jamaican language to new use, sending it in new directions and applying a new standard to our current system of thought (c.f. Walls, 1996:27). It appears, therefore, that the church in Jamaica, through the ministry of Bible Translation could meaningfully address several of our unique challenges as a nation. According to Walls (1996:28):

Bible translation as a process is thus both a reflection of the central act on which the Christian faith depends and a concretization of the commission which Christ gave his disciples. Perhaps no other specific activity more clearly represents the mission of the Church.

This is in keeping with Caribbean Theology which seeks to do theology using the approach that is identical to all theologies of Liberation – the people's reality. With the coming of the Christian Bible into Jamaican, to a large degree, freedom/liberation/emancipation has really come to the Jamaican people. We are now free to have and hear God's word in our own language.

In the experience of the churches ministry of Bible Translation, translation, when done well, has served as a double edged sword:it facilitates Christian spiritual ministry and serves as a catalyst for social liberation and empowerment for the target speech communities.

Spiritual Liberation and Empowerment

Evangelism and Discipleship

The UBS and a host of other organizations involved in Bible Translation have testified that, whenever the Scriptures are in the heart-language of a people, the church grows in terms of evangelism and discipleship (David J. Hargrave, 1978). States Hargrave (1978:36), "Wycliffe Bible Translators has worked from its very beginning with the conviction that the most effective way to complete the commission of Christ is to give the Gospel to every person in his own tongue."

Fifty-six top church leaders from a wide spectrum of Christian constituencies here in Jamaica attended a Breakfast for Clergy hosted by the BSWI in July 2008. Of the fifty-six personnel who attended the function, thirty-five (62.5 percent) completed a questionnaire that was provided. The purpose of the questionnaire was to ascertain the attendees' response to the proposed JCTP. It is not insignificant that 85 percent of respondents were in full support of the project. The other 15 percent indicated hesitation – not opposition. Attendees were also asked to indicate those ministries they deem would benefit most from the project. Needless to say, evangelism and discipleship were amongst the top ministry opportunities indicated. We can conclude, therefore, that a significant number of our church leaders believe the Jamaican Bible will equip them to better serve and minister to their constituents.

Bridge to Indigenous Jamaican Religions

Our indigenous religious expressions such as Revivalism and Rastafarianism are at ease with Jamaican. Those Christian constituencies that are more influenced by North America and Western Europe, particularly British, Christian, religious expressions tend to be the ones who are more averse to the use of Jamaican in the religious domain, for, with the importation of Western Christian varieties came the language used in such groups – English. It remains to be explored to what extent the Jamaican Bible could help us better engage our indigenous, Afro-centric, religious movements.

Please forgive anecdotal evidence. During the translation project, one of our translators was conducting business in Portmore. She had taken along with her a copy of the "Lord's Prayer" in Jamaican. Whilst conducting her business, the copy of the prayer fell from her belongings and was spotted by a Rastafarian. It looked a bit strange to the Dread, so he asked, "A wa dis ya?" The translator told him what it was and used the incident to inform him of the Jamaican Bible. And what was the Dread's response? "So wa yu a se? Rasta man kyahn kom bak a chorch?!" [Translated:"What are you saying? Rastafarians can now return to church?"]

Doing Theology in the Caribbean

An important question we must ask, is, "What is the place of Caribbean vernaculars in the articulation or expression of Caribbean theology in Jamaica?" Seeing we codify our understanding and our experience of the world in our language; seeing we codify in our language our culture, our history, or beliefs and, therefore, our uniqueness, what role does our language play in the articulation of theology from our perspective – in light of our experience as a people? Shall we continue using the language of our colonial masters and ignore those of the vast majority of those for whom we do theology?

In her paper "Teaching Black Biblical Studies in the UK:Special Issues for Consideration and Suggested Hermeneutical Approaches," Lynette Mullings seeks to outline how "Black vernacular" and "Black Hermeneutics" could contribute to the expression of "Black Theology." She writes from the perspective of Blacks in the UK, and uses the BSWI's translation of the Scriptures into Jamaican as a case study. This provided her with an opportunity to:

> address ... the need for the development of a form of biblical scholarship that applies a reading strategy that is distinct to a particular aspect of Black culture ... to make a case for the use of Black vernacular and vernacular hermeneutics for critical dialogue and interpretation of the Scriptures through an assessment of the Bible Society of the West Indies' work, "A Who Run Tings?"... and subsequently the Bible Society's effort to build upon this seminal work in a bid to translate the entire Bible into Jamaican.

Social Liberation, Emancipation and Empowerment

This point will be better appreciated if we look at language and the role of language in society. According to Devonish (2007:1):

> One area in which class conflict expresses itself in language is the relationship between language(s) used as the medium of formal spoken communication among the mass of the population, and the language(s) used for official purposes by the State and those who control it.

The reason for this linguistic divergence, argues Devonish, is the role writing plays in official language use. The result is that the ruling classes identify themselves with the official language and impose it on the masses via avenues such as the education system (Devonish, 2007:1). The unfortunate result, however, is that this effort has been of only limited success. The partial success is reflected in Jamaica in our low levels of literacy.

In 2003, former Prime Minster, P.J. Patterson, lamented over the teaching of English language in our schools:

> "I think we have to face the fact," he said, "that the teaching of English Language at every level now has to be approached as if you are teaching a foreign language. In the daily exchanges on the radio, on television English is the exception rather than the rule" (BSWI, 1996:4-5).

Things have not changed since then as a 2005 study on Language Attitudes in Jamaica shows that Jamaicans are increasingly becoming more accepting of Jamaican. "Given the option of ...schools that teach children to read and write in Jamaican and English as opposed to ...schools that teach children to read and write in English only," 71.1 percent of the population polled would like to have bilingual schools" (JLU, 2005).

We see the elites – the wealthy, the educated and the powerful – within our society formulating and imposing policies and structures that ignore the linguistic reality of 95 percent of Jamaicans (c.f., Sensmeier 2009:10), leaving room open for discrimination on the grounds of language and for exploitation through ignorance. We inherited these structural evils from our colonial masters, the ones, whom to this day, many of our people deem better than us.

By default, God, through the ministry of Bible Translation, empowers us to stand up to the structures that ignore the linguistic reality of our people and its attending social ills. Within our society, the social reality of our people is, to a large extent, linked to their linguistic situation. Thus, translating the Bible into minority languages could have significant social implications for speakers of the Jamaican language. How?

CHAPTER 6

Facilitating Literacy

It goes beyond question that one of our primary educational problems is what Devonish and Carpenter (2007:6) refer to as "the perennial sense of crisis that has affected the post-independence Commonwealth Caribbean in the areas of language education and literacy." Within our Caribbean reality, this usually involves two languages in operation in each territory, a creole language and a lexically related standard European language. Within our Jamaican context, these are Jamaican (Creole) and Standard Jamaican English (SJE). The lexical (not structural) similarities between both languages generate linguistic insecurities within the members. This leads to persons being confused as to the features and boundaries of both languages.

My colleague, Faith Linton, in her presentation, will explore in more detail the literacy opportunities that the JNT provides. Suffice it to say that the failure in terms of language education and literacy has led a number of educators and linguists, over the years, to recommend the formal implementation of Jamaican (Creole) alongside SJE in primary level education as an appropriate response to the national crisis we are experiencing in our educational system. (cf. Devonish and Carpenter, 2007:7).

The translation of the Scriptures into Jamaican is by no means unrelated to the linguistic challenges that plague our education system at all levels, primary to tertiary. In fact, the initiative to address our language education and literacy reality was initiated by our very own, Faith Linton. Devonish and Carpenter (2007:22) summarizes it for us:

> In Jamaica, the first step in the process that resulted in the BEP [Bilingual Education Project] came from an initiative by Mrs. Faith Linton, a retired educator who had been active in the process of Bible Translation into Jamaican. An approach to the MOEYC by Mrs. Linton and a short project sketch presented (Linton 2003) set things in motion...The eventual outcome, in the form of the Bilingual Education Project, was inspired by the commitment and daring shown in the Linton initiative.

Standardization of Jamaican

It is being suggested that the translation of the Scriptures into Jamaican will lead the way in liberating the language by causing it to take on a standardized form in order to take on new roles or be used in formal domains.

Jamaican is what Einar Haugen (in Copeland and Jawsorki, 1997:341-352) would refer to as an "undeveloped" or "underdeveloped" language, that is, a speech variety that has not been developed to meet the wider needs of a the wider society. According to Haugen, an underdeveloped language variety needs to undergo four stages, in order to be deemed a "developed" language and hence, useful to the linguistic demands of society.

The first policy that needs to be made is in reference to the selection of "a model from which the norm can be derived." Accordingly, a particular variety of Jamaican Creole would need to be selected to serve as the standard to be used in formal settings. Secondly, the selected model would need to be codified. This would have to do with the formulation of a functional orthography and lexicon, prescriptive grammars and dictionaries. Implementation and elaboration of function are Haugen's third and fourth criteria respectively. These refer to the spread of the chosen Jamaican variety by means of the continued development of books and other literary material.

Amongst other things, the orthographic standardization, the syntactic elaboration, the lexical enrichment and the functional extension of many languages can be traced back to Bible Translation. Decisions are made during the translation process and are disseminated and reinforced by powerful or influential individuals and institutions (e.g., the church) that impose the newly developed system of communication on a populace. Susanne Mühleise (2005:4-5) reminds us that Bible translation was instrumental in forming "the beginning of many European writing languages and paved the path out of the Latin-dominated diglossia of early medial Europe." Take for example the Great Bible published in 1539 (and revised several times after). This was "the first (and only) English Bible formally authorized for public use in Britain (Kenyon in Hastings:1903). This translation was widely read (ibid) and, over time, it served as a means of familiarizing the vast majority of the English population with a standard form of the language.

Whilst the role of religious texts in the standardization of many of the world's major languages cannot be denied, it must not be assumed that translation of such texts was the only contributor to the standardization of such languages. Also, it must not be assumed that the translation process was without its linguistic difficulties. In relation to the latter, Albert Cook (1907-21) tells us that, not long after the Authorised Version was issued, critiques of the translation said, "The Bible is translated into English words rather than into English phrases. The Hebraisms are kept, and the phrase of that language is kept" (Ward, Waller, et al, 2000).

Changed Attitudes toward Language and Language Users

In a bilingual society such as Jamaica, the vast majority of the population generally deem the Creole inferior to and/or an aberration of the lexifier language. As such, both languages are allotted functional complementary roles, that is to say, they are used in contexts that are mutually exclusive (Alleyne, 1985:157). In such contexts, linguistics refers to the Creole as the L(ow) variety and the lexifier language as the H(igh) variety. The H-variety is used in government services such as education, administration and legal affairs and is used in formal contexts (c.f. Devonish, 2007:2). The L-variety, on the other hand, is the mother tongue of the vast majority of the population and is used in all other domains:the family, popular culture and other informal settings (ibid).

The abovementioned linguistic reality creates socio-political, ideological, attitudinal, technical and practical challenges for translation initiatives such as the JCTP. There are at least two reasons for this. First, the Christian Scriptures belong to a functional domain traditionally reserved for the H-variety. It therefore follows that the translation program is empowering the language to breach its socially pre-assigned functions. Second, for the purpose of translation, those facilitating the program will need to make important linguistic choices that will have significant implications for the language, if the translation is accepted and sufficiently imposed on the target audience. The latter of these relate to linguistic codification, which we have already looked at; the former relates primarily to language attitudes, to which we now turn our attention.

Enhancing and Sustaining a Sense of Identity and Worth

This has to do with the issue of language ideologies or beliefs. Some of the language ideologies we have today in Jamaica date back to the colonial era. We keep passing them on to our children in subtle forms such as when we say things such as "Yu chat bad, iihn?" If you speak a particular language, how it is treated, viewed and valued it will affect someone's perception of whom you are. Thus, one of the things about language ideology is that the perceptions of the language are transferred to the people who speak it. In our context, Jamaican is associated with the lower echelon of society, the uneducated, the low, consequently, our primary perception of those we hear speaking Jamaican is that they have limited socio-economic power, are uneducated, etc.

The Jamaican New Testament will use the elevated status inherent in the Scriptures and elevate the Jamaican language and, consequently, its speakers. Thus, validating the people – we can directly hear and understand God on their own linguistic terms.

In her article, "Caribbean Theology, Self-Esteem and Black Identity," Desecree Whittle (2002) discusses the need for Caribbean Theology to address the issue of low self-esteem.

Unfortunately, the author says nothing concerning the need to affirm Caribbean nationals in terms of their own languages. The linguist and translator, Tasheney Francis, is noted to have said in a verbal communication that translating the Scriptures into a minority language such as Jamaican is like looking at a black person and saying, "You are beautiful. Your language is worthy. It is what you speak. You have something that is worthy."

We could go further than this for language is not just a personal, but also a sociological issue. Therefore, by raising the standard of Jamaican to formal, important domains by means of the Scriptures, we seek to validate our people not only in relation to God but also in relation to others within society. It is the experience of translators, that prior to Bible Translation, many persons believed God would be more likely to hear someone who belonged to that segment of society that uses the "high" language variety – the one used in education, in the courts, and in public and formal speaks to him, using the official language – not someone who speaks the language of the socio-economically disadvantaged.

Conclusion

The church in Jamaica has, within her mandate to continue the *missio Dei* in the world, the ability to lead the way in liberating our people though the ministry of Bible Translation, in spite of the varying levels of structural and cultural differences that exist between Jamaica and the Greco-Roman world in which the Christian Testament is located. This is an extension of Caribbean theology that seeks to honor God in Christ who liberates.

CHAPTER 7
BIBLE TRANSLATION, A MAJOR COMPONENT OF EMANCIPATION:
THE SIGNIFICANCE OF BIBLE TRANSLATION INTO THE MOTHER TONGUE

Faith Linton

The translation of the Scriptures into a new language for the first time has proven over and over again to be the agent, indeed the driving force, behind a moral and spiritual transformation of the speakers of the language. Moreover, as a direct consequence of the moral and spiritual breakthrough, there has usually been remarkable evidence of positive change and development culturally, intellectually, socially and economically among the people of that language community.

Christians understand this phenomenon as the impact of the Spirit of God working through the Word – both spoken and written – bringing life and healing to every facet of human society. This is just what Jamaica needs right now, hence the timeliness of the publishing of the JNT.

At this point, someone might well ask: Isn't Jamaica an English speaking country? Hasn't the Bible been available to Jamaicans in English for more than 150 years? Churches abound on this island. Surely that in itself is evidence of the effective ministry of the word throughout the length and breadth of this country.

On what grounds therefore do we justify the effort and expense involved in the translation of the JNT? This is the question I hope to address in this presentation.

There is actually a very simple answer to this question: We justify this translation on the grounds that the Jamaican Creole is the mother tongue of the majority of our people.

The Importance of the Mother Tongue

The critical importance of the mother tongue, has, in recent decades, been increasingly affirmed by studies and research carried out both in Linguistics and

Neuroscience. Linguistics is the scientific study of language and its structure. Neuroscience deals with the structure and development of the human brain and its functions.

The neuroscientist Lise Eliot, in her book, *How the Brain and Mind Develop in the First Five Years of Life*, provides detailed information of interest to parents and educators in a fascinating chapter titled, "Language and the Developing Brain." Eliot declares, "Learning to talk is probably the greatest intellectual leap of an individual's life," and she asserts that language is "the critical foundation for much of what we consider to be intelligent behavior." These statements apply specifically to the role played by the mother tongue.

The mother tongue is the language the child acquires automatically, naturally and informally during the first five years of life, simply by being part of a community that speaks a particular language. That language is the foundation laid down in the child's brain from which develop the skills that contribute to intelligent behavior-skills such as literacy, critical thinking and the ability to engage in meaningful discussion.

It is therefore not surprising that no less an organization than UNESCO has put on record its unequivocal support for mother tongue instruction. In its Position Paper 2002 concerning language and education in the 21st century, UNESCO states, "UNESCO supports mother tongue instruction as a means of improving educational quality by building upon the knowledge and experience of the learners and teachers".

The position paper elaborates on this statement by adding, "Mother-tongue instruction is essential for initial instruction and literacy and should be extended to as late a stage in education as possible."

"Every pupil should begin his (or her) formal education in his (or her) mother tongue".

"Adult illiterates should make their first step to literacy through their mother tongue, passing on to a second language if they desire and are able."

As Christians, we have not needed to wait for the results of studies done in the last two centuries, in order to recognize the importance of the mother tongue. More than two thousand years ago on the Day of Pentecost, the birthday of the church, God himself dramatically demonstrated the essential role of the mother tongue. On that day the Gospel message preached by the Apostles was translated supernaturally, simultaneously into the mother tongues of about fifteen people groups present in Jerusalem on that day.

The mandate to the church could not be more clear and specific. "Make sure you give each person the message of God's love in his/her heart language, that is, in the mother tongue." As linguists and Bible translators will agree, it is in the sounds and structures of the mother tongue that meaning at the deepest level, first becomes established in the mind and emotions of the child.

Illiteracy – Jamaica's Major Education Problem

Jamaica is a particularly disturbing example of the negative impact of ignoring the mother tongue, especially in the education system. Our major educational problem is illiteracy.

Commenting on the seriousness of the problem, former Prime Minister of Jamaica, now Chancellor of the University of Technology, Edward Seaga, stated in March 2011, that after almost fifty years of independence, Jamaica had failed to become a functional nation. He pointed to the root cause as our failure to create a literate society.

Seaga noted, "Sixty percent of those who enter secondary school cannot cope with secondary education because of illiteracy." He further said that between 60 and 70 percent of secondary school graduates are unable to cope with the demands of the economy and society, because of illiteracy.

What is the root cause of the chronic failure of the Jamaican education system to produce a literate society? It is this: we have largely ignored the children's mother tongue in the education process and have instead prioritized the use of Standard English as the language of instruction.

A large proportion of Jamaican four year olds who enter school for the first time are fluent in Jamaican Creole only. They have not yet had enough exposure to Standard English to enable them to understand even simple sentences such as "What is your name?"

When we teach such children to read English, they may eventually learn to pronounce the sounds of the words on the written page, but the meaning of the phrases and sentences often eludes them. They have no accurate or precise comprehension of what they are reading; some are simply calling words.

The problem manifests itself throughout their primary, secondary and even tertiary years. College and university tutors and lecturers complain that too many of their students lack the ability for logical and critical thinking. These students may be very knowledgeable but they are unable to use their knowledge creatively and intelligently. These skills are the product of language development. Language development begins in the home with the mother tongue. It must continue in school with the mother tongue. It is virtually impossible for the child to learn to read with meaning or even to think, in a language to which he/she has never been adequately exposed.

There is no substitute for mother-tongue education. Our problem is that for reasons arising mainly out of our early history, the idea of using the Jamaican Creole (the patois) in education is totally unacceptable to many Jamaicans. Moreover, we have the mistaken idea that if we choose to use the patois, we will lose English. It has to be either one or the other. In our anxiety to make our children competent in Standard English we therefore ignore the patois. The desire to learn English is not confined to Jamaica. We find it in countries as widely dispersed as Denmark, China, and Argentina. Do those countries ignore the mother tongue and make English the main language of instruction? Most certainly not. They educate in the mother tongue and teach English as a second language. That is the way to go.

Indeed, competence in a second language is largely determined by the fact that cognitive skills have been and are being developed in the mother tongue. Literacy, logical thinking and intellectual creativity are some of the skills that a person transfers from his/her mother tongue to any other language to which s/he is adequately exposed. It takes at least twelve years of active stimulation for these skills to be developed in the mother tongue. There is no substitute for mother tongue education. Our children will only become fully literate in English when they become fully literate in the mother tongue.

The disastrous effects of illiteracy are not confined to the educational field only. Illiteracy is a major factor in our unsatisfactory economic situation.

Illiteracy also accounts for a fair proportion of our psychological and social ills. The importance of school and literacy is highlighted in a recent report titled, "Children in Conflict with the Law," prepared by the Office of the Children's Advocate (OCA) in Jamaica. Identifying why children are in conflict with the: Law, practitioners working with at-risk youth pointed to poor parenting (60 percent), lack of adequate supervision (60 percent) and frustrations with school or being illiterate or semi-illiterate (64 percent) as critical factors.

Some practitioners also pointed out that poor literacy leads to poor reasoning. This results in violence where even simple conflicts might deteriorate into a fight.

Illiteracy, weak comprehension skills, poor reading ability and failure to read widely or even enjoy reading, also take their toll on the quality of the teaching ministry of the church. A quick illustration from my own personal experience; Some years ago I heard a sermon preached on the text 1 Corinthians. 4:9, "We have become a spectacle to the world to angels and to men." The main points made by the preacher were based on the interpretation of spectacle as eye glasses.

CHAPTER 7

The Relevance of the JNT

The question is, can the JNT make a difference? I believe it could become the catalyst for change in this desperate situation.

Already we have seen evidence of the potential for change inherent in these Scriptures now that they speak the language of the people. Much of this evidence has surfaced as a result of an initiative by Wycliffe Caribbean, which forms part of Wycliffe Bible Translators International.

Under the direction of its CEO, John Roomes, Wycliffe Caribbean carried out in Jamaica a Biliteracy and Bible Reading Project between 2011 and 2012, as their contribution to the promotion and ministry-effectiveness of the JNT.

The Bible Society had carried out the mammoth task of translating the NT into Jamaican and making it available. But the JNT needed to be read, and Jamaicans were complaining that they found it hard to read Jamaican Creole, their own mother tongue.

Everyone needs to be taught to read their mother tongue. However, learning to read the Creole has never been part of the Jamaican school curriculum. Therefore, the purpose of Wycliffe's Biliteracy and Bible Reading Project was mainly to teach our people to read, understand and appreciate the Scriptures in the mother tongue. The word biliteracy indicates that in the end, each participant will be able to read both languages found on each page of this diglot publication of the New Testament.

Twenty-three Bible Reading groups were set up across the island, with nineteen continuing to the end of the project. Immediately before the start of the reading groups, a series of meetings was held with pastors and church leaders in parishes all over the island, to inform them of the project and invite their support. These meetings revealed how ready most of these leaders were for the mother tongue translation. They recognized the importance of validating the mother tongue. Some commented on the negative consequences of our society's failure to do so, and pointed out the benefits we would derive from the use of the language in the church, the education system and the society in general.

Concerning the Scripture translation itself, one pastor said he couldn't wait to receive the diglot publication of the Scriptures giving the Jamaican translation side by side with the KJV. He explained that currently when he is teaching and preaching, he reads the Scripture in more than one version, for this brings greater clarity and increased understanding. He clearly implied that the proposed diglot publication would suit the purpose better than anything else.

The feedback at the end of the project was particularly encouraging. Participants expressed not only a sense of achievement from learning to read their mother tongue, but also intense delight and satisfaction with what they were reading in the Scriptures. In many cases they were already familiar with these Scriptures in English, but hearing them in the mother tongue brought greater understanding and enjoyment of the word. One participant wrote of a deeper relationship with God and added, "I understand God's measuring stick."

Yet another new reader described the experience of greater clarity of understanding in these words, "It is like reading the Bible with a stadium bulb" (she was referring to the extremely bright lights of our National Stadium).

On another occasion outside of this project, one listener gave a revealing explanation for the light bulb experience which she herself had just had. She said something to this effect. "You see, I don't think in English, so when you give me the Bible in English, I have to take time to process it, and therefore I lose much of what you are saying." Is it any wonder that the Scriptures in the mother tongue make such a dramatic impact?

Perhaps the most moving testimonies come from those who have experienced deep change within themselves and in their relationships. One participant shared that her relationship with her husband had improved, because her attitude to him had been changed through reading the Scriptures in the mother tongue (patois). In the past she had looked down on him and treated him with scorn because he could only speak patois. But now, her perception both of the language and of her husband had been transformed.

Another participant said that before she started attending the group meetings she did not go to church. She did not understand the preaching or reading of the Scripture. Realizing that Jesus spoke her language, and could identify with her and her language, she started attending church again and now attends regularly.

The book of Luke was the first part of the JNT to be published and distributed. One lady, recognizing its potential, committed herself to taking the "Luuk Buk" on the bus with her on her way to work each day; and she would introduce it to whoever sat beside her. She had some remarkable stories to tell.

On one occasion the passenger began laughing aloud as she read to him from Luke chapter 11. He explained that his laughter had nothing to do with mockery or derision. It was a spontaneous expression of release from tension and strain. That morning he had felt unusually stressed, and the reading had brought him healing. "Yu hiil mi tide," he said. He then gave his contact information so that he could get a copy for himself. This is only one example of several others who have requested their own copy. They call the distributor "The lady with the book."

There are several stories such as these. They have brought forcibly to our attention the fact that Jamaicans who are fluent only in the Creole, have for generations been seriously marginalized and even damaged emotionally at home, at school, in church and in the wider society.

The Gospel deprivation suffered by Creole speakers is the subject of the following feedback comment: Many persons in many parts of Jamaica need to get the Gospel and the ministry and life of Jesus in their own language in their own setting so they can appreciate what God has done through Jesus. It's one aspect of bringing the Gospel to everyone.

Here is an even more succinct comment on the matter, "Many Creole speakers have never really heard the Gospel"; meaning that though they may have heard many Gospel messages in English, none brought the understanding or made the impact that the mother tongue makes.

However, the JNT is already making a difference and showing the way forward. The following is an excerpt from a first-hand eye witness report of what happens when people hear the Bible read in their own language for the very first time. The report, dated August, 10, 2012, was written by Tyler Vanderveen of the USA who at the time was doing an internship with Wycliffe Caribbean in Jamaica.

He writes, "While returning with my boss John Roomes from a Wycliffe retreat we passed through the town of Kendall, about 70 kilometers east of Kingston. We stopped to participate in a March for Righteousness gathering in the town square at which John had been asked to speak. John, however, did not speak in English as two previous speakers had done, but spoke in Jamaican patois. He also focused his preaching, not at the group of Christians near the stage but at the group of men playing dominoes across the street, at the taxi drivers in the parking lot, and at the people in the market.

Soon a small crowd gathered at the edge of the market, listening intently. In the first minute that John began to read from the Gospel of Luke, recently translated into Jamaican, a homeless man ran all the way from the back right to the stage, his face alight with understanding. At the same time, some Rastafarian men who were listening to the event from behind a tree came around to the front to listen.

It seems that every time the church in Jamaica moves toward being more Jamaican and less British, Rastafarians are interested. They are watching and waiting for a church they can be a part of. John says that when the whole Bible is finally translated into Jamaican and churches begin to preach from it, many Rastafarian people will come to the Lord.

John Roomes is not the only church leader who has broken with church tradition by preaching in patois. Lloyd Millen, who is part of the JNT Translation team, takes every opportunity to do so, both in the church he pastors, and elsewhere. He has said that his Standard English sermons have never received the kind of response that his patois sermons now receive.

Friends, the JNT has sparked a movement, which by the working of the Holy Spirit, could bring to the Jamaican people a measure of healing and spiritual renewal beyond what we could ask or think. So be it Lord.

CHAPTER 8
BIBLICAL PERSPECTIVES ON CALLS TO MINISTRY

R. Glenn Wooden

Introduction

Among many Baptists (and others) there is the strong belief that those aspiring to pastoral and other ministries must experience a call of God before pursuing that ministry. Many seminaries and theological colleges will ask applicants to write about their call. The ministries can be varied, including pastoral ministry, mission, chaplaincy, etc. As well, to many people in ministry, discerning a call from God is important before ending or beginning ministries, such as moving to a new congregation or out of congregational ministry to a denomination or teaching ministry. As I have listened to those in my own tradition (the Convention of Atlantic Baptist Churches in Atlantic Canada) and to others in Baptist circles and in other denominations, the call of God to ministry is often understood as a strong or overwhelming compulsion, sometimes it is experienced as a literal call, a voice instructing one to become a minister, such as those experienced by Abraham, Moses, Amos, Isaiah, Paul.

It is talked about in various ways: the "tap on the shoulder" or the voice of the LORD, or a sign, or prophetic word. However, among others within Baptist circles and in other denominations, God's call is discerned through the recognition of giftedness – a recognition driven by the need or desire to find leadership from within the congregation. In some Christian contexts, people without a special call of God are not taken seriously.

In this paper I will highlight some biblical passages used as the basis for the concept of the special call to ministry, and I will offer two other call paradigms that are also biblical. In addition, I will highlight some Scriptural passages that mandate both a personal and corporate (congregational or denominational) scrutiny of those who claim to be called by God to a ministry.

Biblical Models of Calls to Ministry

I became a Christian and was nurtured in a church culture that highlighted the special call as the valid way to enter ministry (and I actually did experience such a call). However, my study of Scripture has led me to see that there are three biblical paradigms: the internal call (the prophetic model), the natural call, and the external call.

Internal Calls: Moses (Judges, Prophets)

The type of call often focused on by writers and speakers (in my experience) is the personal, dramatic call. The call of Moses to lead the people of Israel out of Egypt to a new home is possibly the most famous:

> When Yahweh saw that he had turned aside to see, God called to him out of the bush, "Moses, Moses!" And he said, "Here I am." Then he said, "Come no closer! Remove the sandals from your feet, for the place on which you are standing is holy ground." Then Yahweh said, "I have observed the misery of my people who are in Egypt; I have heard their cry on account of their taskmasters …. So come, I will send you to Pharaoh to bring my people, the Israelites, out of Egypt" (Exodus 3:4-10).[1]

This is the model of call that seems to have been experienced by prophets, as for example Amos:

> Then Amos answered Amaziah, "I am no prophet, nor a prophet's son; but I am a herdsman, and a dresser of sycamore trees, and Yahweh took me from following the flock, and Yahweh said to me, 'Go, prophesy to my people Israel'" (Amos 7:14-15).

The nature of these calls seems to be aural, something heard with the ears. Moses was having a conversation with God. I used to imagine a booming voice that echoed through the hills and valleys. But further reflection on other biblical accounts has made me aware that these are more likely internal calls, for which there were no divinely-created sound waves conveying a voice to human ears, but rather these calls were of the same nature as visionary experiences, something produced by God only for the individuals. Several examples from scripture will help to illustrate the nature of this kind of call.

In a well-known narrative, Samuel the prophet went to the home of Jesse to anoint Saul's successor as king, as instructed by God. He told Jesse to marshal his sons and the following event takes place:

CHAPTER 8

> When they came, [Samuel] looked on Eliab and thought, "Surely Yahweh's anointed is now before Yahweh." But Yahweh said to Samuel, "Do not look on his appearance or on the height of his stature, because I have rejected him; for Yahweh does not see as mortals see; they look on the outward appearance, but Yahweh looks on the heart." Jesse made seven of his sons pass before Samuel, and Samuel said to Jesse, "Yahweh has not chosen any of these." Samuel said to Jesse, "Are all your sons here?" And he said, "There remains yet the youngest, but he is keeping the sheep." He sent and brought him in. Yahweh said, "Rise and anoint him; for this is the one." Then Samuel took the horn of oil, and anointed him in the presence of his brothers; and the spirit of Yahweh came mightily upon David from that day forward (1 Sam. 16:6-13).

In this account, Yahweh and the prophet Samuel have a conversation in the company of Jesse and his sons. After the first son is rejected, Yahweh and Samuel have a conversation about the criteria that will be used, and then they work through all the sons who are present, and each time Yahweh renders judgment, and Samuel or Yahweh states, "Neither has Yahweh chosen this one." From the way the narrative is written, it is clear that Jesse and others are not privy to the conversation, because Samuel must finally inform Jesse that none of those presented were God's choice. Finally, after David is summoned, Yahweh tells the prophet to anoint him. There is no indication in the text that Jesse and the others around the prophet hear this conversation between the prophet and God.

In Ezekiel 8-11 we read about a visionary encounter in which Yahweh speaks, but only the prophet hears it:

> In the sixth year, in the sixth month, on the fifth day of the month, as I sat in my house, with the elders of Judah sitting before me, the hand of Yahweh God fell upon me there. I looked, and there was a figure that looked like a human being; It stretched out the form of a hand, and took me by a lock of my head; and the spirit lifted me up between earth and heaven, and brought me in visions of God to Jerusalem. Then God said to me, "O mortal, lift up your eyes now in the direction of the north" (Ez. 8:1-5).

The vision continues as Ezekiel sees what was happening inside the temple and learns about the judgment of God on those remaining in the land of Israel, and of the departure of the Spirit of God from the Holiest place to outside the city. The section concludes in chapter 11:24-25:

> The spirit lifted me up and brought me in a vision by the spirit of God into Chaldea, to the exiles. Then the vision that I had seen left me. And I told the exiles all the things that Yahweh had shown me.

All the time that Ezekiel is being taken to heaven, shown inside the Temple in Jerusalem, and conversing with heavenly beings, he seems to have been physically sitting before the elders in Babylon (Chaldea). He experienced a vision (8:3), but those around him hear or see nothing.

A slightly different experience is related from an incident during Passion Week:

> (Jesus said:) "Now my soul is troubled. And what should I say—'Father, save me from this hour'? No, it is for this reason that I have come to this hour. Father, glorify your name." Then a voice came from heaven, "I have glorified it, and I will glorify it again." The crowd standing there heard it and said that it was thunder. Others said, "An angel has spoken to him" (Jn. 12:27-29).

In this instance, by-standers hear the voice of God as an indistinct, thunder-like sound.

And as a final example, in Acts 22 Paul testifies to his encounter with the risen, ascended Jesus on the road to Damascus, and he clearly notes the private nature of the voice of God:

> "While I was on my way and approaching Damascus, about noon a great light from heaven suddenly shone about me. I fell to the ground and heard a voice saying to me, 'Saul, Saul, why are you persecuting me?' I answered, 'Who are you, Lord?' Then he said to me, 'I am Jesus of Nazareth whom you are persecuting.' Now those who were with me saw the light but did not hear the voice of the one who was speaking to me (Acts 22:6-9).

So, to go back to the call of Moses in the desert: if there were others watching, they most likely did not hear a distinct voice. So, calls to people like Moses, Samuel, and the prophets were vision-like experiences; they were divine auditions. This, then, makes such spectacular calls internal calls, given by God only to the person being called.

There is an important note that I believe I must add to my comments on this call. In the Bible, the people who received this kind of call did so in extraordinary circumstances. I refer to them as "God's crisis managers." In the Old Testament, they were mostly people called only after God abandoned trying to use other means to summon his people back to Torah living. When the priests did not carry out the duties entrusted to them; when the Levites did not teach the people, as they were tasked to do; when the kings did what was right in their own eyes; when the elders and other leaders of the people acted corruptly; only then did Yahweh send his specially-called crisis-managers to speak. Even, Paul was creating a crisis as he actively pursued and persecuted followers of Jesus and then was changed in his dramatic Damascus road encounter with the risen, ascended Jesus Christ. That conversion led to him becoming an apostle to the Gentiles which was part of what required the first Christians to work out what it meant for the people of God to include believers from all nations, not just from among Jews. God called these individuals into special service in special times, through this auditory experience, but they were not the regular spiritual leaders of the people. It was after I had started teaching Old Testament studies that I was challenged to rethink this model as the preferred one for pastors, missionaries, chaplains, etc. Are pastors, for example, to be thought of as God's crisis managers among his people? Were there other kinds of calls in Scripture? My questions and investigations led me finally to see two other models.

"Natural" calls: Levites (Apostles)

The second, but most frequent "call" to ministry among God's first-covenant people was the natural call. Let's begin with a New Testament account:

> In the days of King Herod of Judea, there was a priest named Zechariah, who belonged to the priestly order of Abijah. His wife was a descendant of Aaron, and her name was Elizabeth. Both of them were righteous before God, living blamelessly according to all the commandments and regulations of the Lord. But they had no children, because Elizabeth was barren, and both were getting on in years… Now the time came for Elizabeth to give birth, and she bore a son (Luke 1:5-7, 57).

John the Baptist was, among other things, a priest. But his call to this high and holy position in Israel was not spectacular. He was merely the son of a priest, and so would be a priest. We can imagine the women who were present when John was born, and others as the news spread, exclaiming: "Another priest to work in the temple of God!" As a calling to ministry among the people of God, it was quite commonplace. Every male child born to a priest or Levite was called to holy service. For this reason it is easy to say that the overwhelming majority of people called to ministry by God under the first covenant were set apart to Torah ministry in this very ordinary way.

This is what I have titled a "natural call." One could call it hereditary, which it was under the first covenant. But that misses where we might find a parallel to priests and Levites in the role they had as the spiritual leaders and teachers of God's people. They were not only the mediators between Yahweh and the people as they offered people's sacrifices. They also served as the pastors of the flock of God and were charged with leading the people in worship, teaching them about Torah living, and acting as experts in Torah legal matters when there were questions or matters of dispute. In that way, they were the pastor/shepherd, the teaching elders of God's people.

It is important to note again that this mundane, natural call is overwhelmingly the most common means of call to ministry under the first covenant. It is true that there are more examples of the "internal" call highlighted in Scripture, because so much of the Old Testament literature is focused on the crises of the people. But failure to place those special calls into the larger context of the whole range of first-covenant ministers leaves us with the impression that the "internal," prophetic call was the dominant one, but it was only sporadic and mostly for time of crisis.

The church does not have a tribe of Levi, so where might we find parallels to this mundane call? Firstly, every Christian is gifted for some ministry (see 1 Cor. 12:7), and it is a gifting that comes with the new birth. That is one parallel. However, there are also more mundane calls to full-time ministry. Many readers of this article probably have heard of someone who has known from their earliest recollections, that they were destined to be a missionary, or pastor, for example. Could this not be an equivalent calling to that of the priests and Levites? Similar at least in the sense that it was from very early in life, and it did not involve any spectacular point of "calling" by God.

External Calls: Paul and Barnabas

The third type of call is one that does not come directly to the person being called, but is conveyed through others at God's prompting. Acts 13 is the example:

> Now in the church at Antioch there were prophets and teachers: Barnabas, Simeon who was called Niger, Lucius of Cyrene, Manaen a member of the court of Herod the ruler, and Saul. While they were worshiping the Lord and fasting, the Holy Spirit said, "Set apart for me Barnabas and Saul for the work to which I have called them." Then after fasting and praying they laid their hands on them and sent them off. (Acts 13:1-3)

Here a group of leaders in the Antioch congregation received an audition from the Spirit – or possibly a common compulsion – to name Barnabas and Saul [Paul] to a new missionary endeavor. Note that it does not come directly to Barnabas and Saul, but the Spirit speaks about them to the other members of the group. The first high priest, Aaron, was called in this way through Moses, at the direction of God. Other examples would be God's selection of Saul and David as kings, through Samuel.

In more and more instances, our seminary is training people who have already been recognized as gifted for ministry by others in their congregations and convinced and commissioned to lead ministries; and then they go on to pursue training that will prepare them for denominational ordination. Such calls to ministry need not be uncommon; and women and men following such external calls should not be thought of as somehow inferior to those who have a spectacular and very personal call (whether internal or natural). It would be difficult to diminish the call of God on the lives of Barnabas and Paul [Saul] because it was not a prophetic-like call; both were used by God to take the Gospel outside the bounds of Judaism to the Gentiles and that was hardly insignificant to us Gentiles!

So, I have highlighted three different patterns of calls to ministry in the Bible:

1. The internal call: the supernatural voice in the night, or vision.
2. The natural call: the knowledge from earliest recollections that one is supposed to be a missionary, or pastor, or some other ministry leader; people who are naturally gifted for ministry roles.
3. The external call: when a woman or man is convinced by other believers that they have the necessary gifts for some ministry and after prayer and seeking God's will become convinced of it.

Rather than give prominence to just one of these calls, we need to see them as complementary, and be open to each of them. The person who says that she has heard a voice telling her to do something should not be given a higher regard than someone who had not heard a voice. The man who is naturally gifted and who seems to have known what he wanted to do from early childhood should not be assessed as having a less important call, or as not having a call at all. And we should be encouraging groups of believers to take note of members of our church families who demonstrate gifts for ministry and encourage them to consider a possible call of God to ministry.

Personal and Corporate Scrutiny of Giftedness

This then brings us to the second part of my paper: the scrutiny of those who claim to be called. I will use the role of the pastor-teacher, only because the New Testament has that particular ministry in its focus in the places where such matters are discussed. Ministry today, as in the times of the Early Church, covered a variety of fields: "The gifts he gave were that some would be apostles, some prophets, some evangelists, some pastors-teachers" (Ephesians 4:11 NRSV modified). But that of pastor-teacher will be the focus, as an example.

Personal Assessment of Gifts

1 Timothy 3:1 refers to people aspiring to the office of overseer, which I understand to be that of a pastor: "If someone desires to be overseer, he desires a noble work" (Author's translation). Clearly, this refers to individuals who have an internal desire or a strong compulsion to become overseers. Such people must have believed that they possessed the necessary gifts or had experienced a call. Paul talks about such self-assessment in Romans 12:3-8:

> For by the grace given to me [the "grace" is Paul's apostleship] I say to everyone among you not to think of yourself more highly than you ought to think, but to think with sober judgment, each according to the measure of faith that God has assigned ....We have gifts that differ according to the grace given to us: prophecy, in proportion to faith.

So, we each have graces, or gifts for ministry, and we are to think "soberly" about our gifts. We are not to over-assess our giftedness, nor should we downplay what God has given us, but we are to make balanced judgments about our levels of giftedness. Aspiration and self assessment are good things!

But, what if a person feels called for the wrong reasons? What if someone misjudges? The fact is there are many people who do not have the necessary level of self-awareness to evaluate themselves. I remember a woman who was adamantly convinced that God had gifted and called her to be a soloist. She paid for voice lessons; she practiced, and prepared. Finally, she was offered a chance to sing a solo during a Sunday morning service. It was painfully embarrassing for everyone, except her. She could not sing in tune, and could not follow the organist. Reality TV programs, like American Idol, make use of such people in the audition phase of the programs, and it is painful to watch non-gifted people who seem to be truly convinced that they have what it takes to win the competition. Self-delusion is not something that an individual can easily overcome because of its very nature, and so assessment by others is necessary.

Corporate Assessment of Gifts

"But, how can a group of men and women scrutinize my call? It's God's call that I have heard. Who do they think they are to question God?" I have heard this sentiment expressed throughout my Christian life. As spiritual as those sentiments sound, they are not in accordance with the New Testament, which does not leave the discernment of a call to the individual. In the advice given to the regional leaders, Timothy and Titus, there is another level of scrutiny that is mandated. 1 Timothy 3:1 begins with self-assessment, but it quickly moves to more objective, external assessment: "If someone desires to be overseer, he desires a noble work. Therefore, an overseer must be ..." (author's translation), and the subsequent characteristics are qualities and skills that Timothy and Titus were to use as criteria when they discerned who should actually become overseers of congregations. It was clearly understood in the Early Church that not every person aspiring to be an overseer was actually qualified, and if they failed to live up to the personal, communal, and ministry qualifications, then their aspiration should not be affirmed, regardless how strongly they might aspire to it.

So, note how 1 Timothy 3 continues:

> above reproach, monogamist, temperate, sensible, respectable, hospitable, an apt teacher, not a drunkard, not violent but gentle, not quarrelsome, and not a lover of money. He must manage his own household well, keeping his children submissive and respectful in every way-- for if someone does not know how to manage his own household, how can he take care of God's church? He must not be a recent convert, or he may be puffed up with conceit and fall into the condemnation of the devil. Moreover, he must be well thought of by outsiders, so that he may not fall into disgrace and the snare of the devil. (1 Tim. 3:1-7, author's translation)

Among these criteria there seem to be two foci: first, candidates for ministry leadership must have a good Christian character. Most of the qualifications are characteristics that pertain to every Christian. To choose a few items from that list, what Christian is free to be a polygamist, not respectable inside the congregation or in the community, inhospitable, a drunkard, violent, quarrelsome, one for whom the acquisition of money is more important than doing what is right? Leaders were not expected to be super Christians, but they could not be living questionable Christian lives. They were to be examples of how to live as a follower of Jesus.

The second focus is evidence of the gifts necessary for the ministry in question. Those aspiring to lead a congregation had to be able to "manage" their own household and family. If someone could manage the complexities of marriage, children, finances and planning for their own household, then this was evidence that they might be able to deal with the complexity of a church. And, because of the significant teaching role of pastor-teachers, candidates were to be assessed for their ability to teach. Neither of these criteria would be required of all Christians.

In Scripture there is no sense that people who claimed to be called were not also scrutinized. Even prophets had to be subjected to criteria to sort out who were the true prophets and who the lying prophets: there are criteria in Deuteronomy (Deut 13:1-5; 18:15-22), and restrictions throughout the biblical material. In fact, history was also a scrutinizer: a prophet like Jeremiah "competed" as a prophet in the market place of public opinion. There were other prophets speaking the word of Yahweh, as in Jeremiah 28. Both Jeremiah and Hananiah claimed to speak the word of Yahweh ("This is what Yahweh says…."), but it was Jeremiah whose prophecies came true and proved him to be a true prophet. It was not the self-claim of Jeremiah that proved he was a prophet, it was the accuracy of what he said. He felt called; he exercised his ministry; but others observed his ministry, and they agreed with what he claimed, and so we have the words of Jeremiah preserved today in a book given his name, but we do not have the prophecies of Hananiah, who was judged to have spoken when Yahweh had not told him to do so.

Even Paul instructed the believers in Corinth to pass judgment on prophets:

> Let two or three prophets speak, and let the others weigh what is said. If a revelation is made to someone else sitting nearby, let the first person be silent. For you can all prophesy one by one, so that all may learn and all be encouraged. And the spirits of prophets are subject to the prophets, for God is a God not of disorder but of peace. (1 Cor. 14:29-33)

Prophets were not to be believed if the other prophets did not agree with them.

So, calls to minister are never merely personal, there must be scrutiny by others to confirm that the sense of call is grounded in the reality of giftedness. Those who claim to be called by God must demonstrate the godly character expected of all Christians, and must have the gifts and skills necessary for the ministry. If someone felt called to pastoral ministry, then others had to verify that they were able to teach and lead the people of God.

At Acadia Divinity College (Wolfville, Nova Scotia, Canada) I talk to potential students about "calls to ministry." I share the previous ideas, and then as practical advice for discerning a call, I pass on the following suggestions, and as a closing I commend them to readers.

CHAPTER 8

In addition to prayer and Scripture study:

1. Be involved in ministry in your local church. How else can you discover and confirm your gifts?
2. Assess your own abilities. Maybe you should just be a good layperson.
3. Assess your motivations. Maybe you are attracted to power; maybe you have some deep-seated psychological need that a ministry position would fill.
4. Ask others to assess your abilities and motivations. Tell people that you are seeking to know if you have gifts for ministry; invite them to observe you. Be truly open to people's comments on your ministry. If people are openly positive, it is a good sign. If people are reluctantly positive, they may be trying to protect your feelings. Give them permission to not recognize gifts in you; and respect their opinions.
5. Find out what it is like in full-time ministry. Talk to pastors/chaplains/pastoral counselors about what they do; can you honestly picture yourself doing everything that is involved?
6. Be willing to go through the process of recognition in your denomination.
7. Train at an accredited seminary or in some other accredited training program.

COMMISSION ON THEOLOGICAL EDUCATION AND LEADERSHIP FORMATION

Over this quinquennium our intention was to provide both research and practical help for participants who were present and to provide those who could not attend copies of all papers through email. Also, we determined to provide teaching materials for training new pastors who were starting new congregations across East Asia and other parts of the world. These training materials were prepared by and gathered from East Asian missionaries and were sent to Baptist convention and union leaders and individuals over the Internet.

The chair of the commission led in developing the program of presenters each year. Vice chair of the commission, Tomás Mackey of Argentina, also shared input and presided over one or more sessions. Also, he usually conducted a panel/symposium each year with participants of the commission who were present. The chair was ably assisted by various members of the commission and by Fausto Vasconcelos. In addition, the chair appointed one of his grandsons, Aaron Bush, as page for each session for 2011, 2012, and 2013 and Alec Bush for 2014. The chair's wife Pat assisted with each session and also made all travel arrangement for all four years.

Finally, each session was planned with a view of the theme for the quinquennium, *In Step with the Spirit*. Highlights for each year are outlined below.

In 2011 the BWA gathering was held in Kuala Lumpur, Malaysia. Papers and reports for this session are listed below:

1. Rachel Tan, Taiwan: "Leadership Formation for Pastors and Lay Leaders: East Asia," from Asia Baptist Graduate Theological Seminary.

2. Pablo Marino, Columbia: "Creative Ways Baptist Churches and Theological Schools Are Using for Christian Formation of Leaders in Latin America," Baptist University.

3. Joyce Chan, Canada: "Leadership Formation for Pastors and Lay Leaders in East Asia."
4. Robert I. Garrett, USA: "Rethinking Theological Education in the 21st Century."
5. Brian Harris, Australia: "Faithful Thinking: The Role of the Seminary in Promoting a Thoughtful Christianity."
6. Sananu Patro, India: "The Local Church and Theological Education with a Focus on Developing Teaching Material, Teaching Methods, and Managing Resources."
7. Thomas Sanders, USA: "Generational Issues Related to Younger Ministry Students in the USA: How They Differ from Previous Generations."
8. Darren Cronshaw, Australia: "Australian Re-envisioning of Theological Education."

In 2012 the BWA gathering was held in in Santiago, Chile. Papers and reports for this session are listed below:

1. Pablo Moreno, Columbia: "Contrasts in Theological Education in Our Region."
2. Chris Liebrum, USA: "Curriculum for Online Minister Training."
3. Darren Cronshaw, Australia: "Re-envisioning Theological Education and Missional Spirituality."
4. Scott Bryant, USA: "Theological Education in the 21st Century: Passing Along the Spirit of Wisdom."
5. Michael Arrington: Report: International Association of Baptist Colleges and Universities.
6. Tommy Sanders, USA: "A Lifetime of Spiritual Formation and Faith Formation."
7. A. K. Lama, India: "Doon Bible College Theological Curriculum Customized for Church Planters."
8. David Wyman, Canada: Report: "Home Church Online Curriculum."
9. A. K. Lama, India: "Interpreting Scripture in the Northeast India and in Arunachal Pradesh in Particular."
10. Tony W. Cartledge, USA: "David and Leadership in Today's Church."

In 2013 the BWA gathering was held in Ocho Rios, Jamaica. Highlights for this session included papers by:

1. Alistair Brown, USA: "What We Don't Teach, Hardly Teach or Can't Teach But They Need."
2. Eng Parush R Parushev, Czech Republic: "The Current State and New Developments in Theological Education in Germany and Bulgaria."
3. Chris Liebrum, USA: Report: "Curriculum for Online Minister Training."
4. Symposium/Panel: Topic: "Lay Leadership and Theological Issues around the World."
5. Nicolas Aime Simplice Singa-Gbazia, Central African Republic: "Lay Leadership Development in Africa."
6. A. K. Lama, India: "Lay Leadership Development in India?"
7. Report by Bernie Spooner: for Mike Arrington, USA: International Association of Baptist Colleges and Universities.
8. Report by Bernie Spooner for David Wyman, Canada: Home Church Curriculum Update.
9. Robert I. Garrett, USA: Presenting Joint Session Celebrating the Contribution of Duke McCall, Sr.: "Duke K. McCall as Denominational Statesman, Baptist Educator, and Global Leader."

In 2014 the BWA gathering was held in Izmir, Turkey. Highlights for this session included papers by:

1. David Page, Turkey and the Middle East: "How theological education and leadership formation is done in Turkey, in particular, and an overview of Persian work."
2. A. K. Lama, India Report: "Theological resources around the world with a particular focus on the development of theological education in North East India."
3. Robert I. Garrett, USA: "Possibilities and Viability of Theological Education through Online or Internet Teaching."
4. Panel: Tomas Mackey, Facilitator: Tony Cartledge (USA), Ben Uche Eyioha (Nigeria), Robert I. Garrett (USA), Elijah Brown (USA), Sunday Odunayo Oke (Nigeria), and David Wyman (Canada).

---"How are we encouraging churches to conduct weekly Bible study and to use Sunday School to mobilize and develop lay leadership?"

---"How is leadership formation taking place in your part of the world?"

The idea was to share reports and developments related to ministry and lay development/training in the areas from which persons come.

1. JOINT SESSION with the Commission on Christian Ethics – Richard F. Wilson, chair: Louise Kretzschmar – "Beyond milk: The moral failure and ongoing formation of existing Christian leaders in the Church and Society;" Bernie Spooner presiding with Richard Wilson presenting Kretzschmar.

Bernie Spooner, commission chair; former professor, dean, and associate dean, Graduate School of Ministry, Dallas Baptist University, Dallas, Texas, US

CHAPTER 9
BEYOND MILK:
THE MORAL FAILURE AND ONGOING FORMATION OF LAY CHRISTIAN LEADERS IN THE CHURCH AND SOCIETY

Louise Kretzschmar

A Story: Reuel Khoza

I wish to commence this paper with a story. Reuel Khoza is currently the non-executive chairman of Nedbank Limited and Nedbank Group Ltd, director of many companies and the author of several books. In 2012, Reuel Khosa[1] said this of the leaders of the ruling party in South Africa, the African National Congress (ANC) in the bank's annual report:

> South Africa is widely recognized for its liberal and enlightened Constitution, yet we observe the emergence of a strange breed of leaders who are determined to undermine the rule of law and override the Constitution...Our political leaderships moral quotient is degenerating and we are fast losing the checks and balances that are necessary to prevent a recurrence of the past. We have a duty to build and develop this nation and to call to book the putative leaders who, due to sheer incapacity to deal with the complexity of 21st century governance and leadership, cannot lead.

The satirical cartoon drawn by Zaphiro that appeared shortly afterwards,[2] shows Khoza being severely castigated by Gwede Mantashe (Secretary General of the ANC), Jimmy Manyi (then the Cabinet Spokesperson) and Nathi Mthethwa (then the Minister of Police Services). Nevertheless Khoza was supported by the Nedbank Board and was a speaker on May, 26, 2014, at a conference organized by the Ethics Institute of South Africa. He has said this of himself and his views:[3]

> My personal belief is that life, work and moral values are indivisible – particularly for those in positions of leadership. African humanism, or

Ubuntu, is my compass, along with Christian values. In the current state of the world I believe that we must recommit humanity to a vision of shared destiny and collective effort for a better future.

With reference to his new book, *Attuned leadership* (2011), he said:[4]

Leaders are not just born to the role. They are born, then made – and sometimes unmade by their own actions. A leader who is not attuned to his or her followers soon becomes a leader in limbo and invariably then fails. Connectedness, compassion, empathy, integrity, humility, reasonableness and a determination to be effective are the keys to attuned leadership. An attuned leader can step boldly into an uncertain future with the certainty that followers will lend their support.

Reuel Khoza, and others like Archbishop Emeritus Desmond Tutu and Thuli Madonsela, are examples of Christian leaders in South Africa who exemplify personal integrity, endeavor to work fairly and generously with colleagues, seek to use their position to promote ethical leadership and the well being of the country and are not afraid to speak out when they believe it to be necessary. Within an African context, their approach to leadership is the exception that proves the rule.

The Aims and Approach of this Paper

This paper has three objectives. The first is to note the challenges facing Christian leaders who are not ordained ministers but who hold positions of responsibility in the world of business, law, medicine, education, government, labor organizations, NGOs (Non-Governmental Organizations) or CBOs (Church Based Organizations).[5] Even though the particular contexts and interests of each of these sectors will not be discussed in any detail, they form the work context that frames this discussion.[6] Second, this paper seeks to identify the perils that can result in moral failure and, third, it discusses some of the means of moral formation that need to be embarked upon intentionally by Christian leaders. In this paper I do not seek to address ministerial formation or the Christian leadership of theological educators and pastors per se, but much of what I say is relevant to their ministries as it addresses their contribution to the training of lay leaders.

In this discussion Christian leaders are understood to be leaders who seek to follow Christ in thought, word, character and action, and who influence the views and actions of others within both Christian organizations and society at large. They may hold specific leadership positions or else be persons of moral

CHAPTER 9

authority to whom others turn for advice, encouragement and mentoring. The terms "formation" or "development" are used as leadership is understood to be an ongoing process of growth in spiritual maturity, character, skill, experience and competence, bearing in mind that leaders are influenced by other people, their contexts, experiences, and their formal and informal studies. Christian leaders are further expected to be spiritually and morally formed. Spiritual formation is initiated by God's grace, requires a human response to the regular prompting of the Holy Spirit and results in mature persons and communities of faith. For Christian leaders, spiritual formation is the foundation, motivation and principal means of moral formation, which is the development of moral virtue, character, behavior and lifestyle.

This topic been chosen because of the influence such leaders exercise. Some Christian leaders manage large companies or departments, hold sway over significant numbers of staff members and have access to enormous sums of money. Their decisions impact regions, nations and sometimes even the global community. Along with other leaders, they are further expected to exercise ethical, responsible and transforming[7] leadership in complex work contexts (Spangenberg &Theron 2005:1-18; Van Aswegen & Engelbrecht 2009: 221-229). But, how is ethical character and leadership to be formed in them (Vadaracco 2003:307–329)? The vast majority of them will not have attended a seminary where they could have gained, inter alia, a grounding in theology; completed studies in ethical decision making and moral formation; learned how to work with many kinds of people; developed the skills of communication, finance, leadership and administration; been helped to attend to their spiritual growth; and nurtured in ways of integrating faith and life. Such lay leaders may attend churches where they receive very little in the way of discipleship, support, intellectual input and spiritual formation. As a result, some may have developed a "split" spirituality that separates their faith from their workplace activities. Some may have developed their business and other skills to a high degree of competence, but find that their understanding of the Christian faith, and their own moral character and spiritual maturity is not commensurate with their leadership responsibilities. Others, of course, may have made it their business to explore what it means to be a Christian leader in such contexts and have become exemplary leaders in largely secular contexts.

A further reason why this topic was chosen for discussion is that most of the literature on the formation of Christian leaders focuses on ministerial formation. Thus many articles and books (e.g. Lamoureux 1999:141–156; Trull & Carter 2004; and Kretzschmar 2015) discuss what seminaries ought to do to form students who are seeking ordination and who desire to enter the Christian ministry. But, even among church leaders and theological educators there is a need for ongoing or "continuing education." Thus, it may be asked, who is "pastoring" the pastors and facilitating the formation of lay leaders?

Below, I employ an inter-disciplinary approach, combining insights drawn mainly from articles, books and Internet sources from the disciplines of Christian Ethics, Business Ethics and Leadership Studies. As this paper addresses an international audience, and interest in leadership is a global phenomenon, it is important to draw on the wisdom and experience of people from a variety of contexts and sources. But, it is also important for such discussions to be rooted in particular social contexts, so that the discourse is not only theoretical but also concrete. Hence, this paper further seeks to address my own African, and Two-Thirds World context. Given that the church is growing rapidly in terms of numbers in Africa, Christian leaders are required to do all they can to ensure that moral integrity and spiritual maturity are increasingly features of this growth. As Mwauru (2006:181) asks, "... why is there a deterioration of moral propriety at a time when Christianity is said to be growing? Why is there disregard for human life through perpetuation of ethnic violence, gender based violence, sexual abuse of children and drug abuse?"

The phrase "beyond milk" in the title of this article alludes to a passage in Hebrews 5:11-14:

> We have much to say about this, but it is hard to explain because you are slow to learn. In fact, though by this time you ought to be teachers, you need someone to teach you the elementary truths of God's word all over again. You need milk, not solid food! Anyone who lives on milk, being still an infant, is not acquainted with the teaching about righteousness. But solid food is for the mature, who by constant use have trained themselves to distinguish good from evil (NIV).

Probably written before AD 70 by an unknown author, the book of Hebrews is a rich and complex text. Addressing mainly Jewish Christians, it contains many references to the Old Testament, including the priesthood and sacrifice, and it makes much of the person and saving work of Christ. The author addresses the problem of believers falling away from the Gospel in various ways and calls upon them to progress in their faith. It challenges the easy assumption of a theology of "once saved, always saved," and offers both warnings and encouragement (e.g. 2:1-4; 3:7-4:11; 6:4-8; 10:26-31; 12:14-17). The immediate literary context of this quotation is chapters 5:11-6:20, which is a call to Christians to learn and grow; the author exhorts them to be diligent to the very end. Christians are expected to develop beyond a need for the milk that is fed to infants; they are to be mature Christians who can teach others, live morally righteous lives and have the spiritual insight to "distinguish between good and evil." If this is true for Christians generally how much more can be expected of Christian leaders?

The Perils Facing Christian Leaders and the Contribution they Can Make Within the Complex World of Work

In what follows I seek to discuss these perils and contributions across the personal (micro-), communal or organizational (meso-), and the socio-global (macro-) levels of a leader's existence. However, these perils and challenges are neither static nor uncomplicated. Nell (2009:160-170) has written of leaders who find themselves "lost in transition." He (2009:160, 162) defines liminality as "a fluid transition phase" or, "the condition of being on a threshold." He also refers to Armour & Browning's (1995) discussion of the "four big C's" of our day, namely, change, complexity, confusion and conflict. In my view, in order to deal well with change and complexity, Christian leaders need to be rooted in the stability of a relationship with God and the simplicity of a life that is straightforward and open. This rootedness in a God-centered life of righteousness can enable them to face the confusion and conflicts that arise as a result of morally wrong motives, relationships and actions, and to be peacemakers (Mat 5:9; Jam 3:18).

The Micro Level: Becoming a Better Person, Friend and Family member

Examples of the perils of moral failure abound in the lives of leaders at all levels.[8] Most obviously these include the abuse of power, sexual misconduct and an avaricious love of money. Often, arrogance, self gratification and indifference toward the needs of other people and the planet are at the root of moral failure. Also important is self-protective withdrawal, a sense of despair, fear, the unwillingness to take a stand on a matter of moral principle and the jettisoning of ethical principles for the sake of profit or promotion. But these perils and vices can be avoided or overcome by Christian leaders. In the process, they never stop discovering who they are and who they can still become.

In order to reach an advanced level of competence in one's work, much time is required to engage in formal and informal studies, gain experience and build competence. Hours need to be spent poring over documents, writing policy statements, devising strategies, attending to financial management, motivating and supervising staff members, being away from home and many more.[9] However, Christian leaders need to be aware of the attendant perils of over-scheduling, burnout, a loss of faith and direction and family breakdown.

Deliberate reflection on what one admires and desires can safeguard the personal moral character and decisions of Christian leaders. Based on the responses of 160 senior executives, De Vries (2009:1-12)[10] identified "Eight major categories of success .... family, wealth, work/career, recognition/fame, power, winning/overcoming challenges, friendships, and meaning." From a Christian perspective, the notion of what constitutes "success" definitely needs to be evaluated and contrasted with biblical notions of faithfulness and stewardship. Overall, Christian leaders ought to aim to respond to God's love, grow in their knowledge and service of God, love their neighbors and relate well to the planet. While the wellbeing of family and the value of friendships as mentioned by De Vries can readily be appreciated, they cannot be reaped without effort and love. The longing for meaning in life cannot be distanced from God's purposes for humankind. Thus, what these leaders value most deeply needs to be questioned because it will determine what they choose. The desire for wealth, recognition/fame and power can be significant moral perils. With reference to the temptations Jesus faced (Mat 4 and Luke 4), Drushall & Flora (2008:36-38) warn against a desire for self-gratification (what's in it for me), the presumption that values style and dazzle over substance, and power grabbing. Kaminiów & Haenze (2013:119-126) tell the story of how following the suffering experienced by Daniel and Teresa Wotkiewicz, after the loss of business and home, God opened up a Christian ministry for them to the homeless and lost. This ministry has since grown into the second largest social assistance organization in Poland. Pain, loss, uncertainly, suffering and persecution are often followed by purification and renewal by the God who brings good out of evil (Rom 8:31-39). Further, while many challenges need to be overcome and work is important,[11] the importance of winning and the relentless pursuit of a career could also lead to a leader's downfall. By way of contrast, the desire to be a leader of moral integrity or righteousness will lead Christians along a very different path. Similarly, leaders who engage in prayer and self-questioning will develop honest self-awareness and learn to detect the perils already mentioned, rather than falling prey to them. The struggle that comes from self-awareness will also enable them to discern good and evil motives in others.

Leaders are called upon constantly to make decisions, including moral decisions. Tiredness, stress, lack of proper reflection and unresolved psychological problems can result in poor decision making that can have serious consequences. But Christian leaders who are self-aware, competent in their work, live healthy and emotionally balanced lives and are able to reflect on the moral elements of decision making, can add significant value to their family life, communities and the world of work.

CHAPTER 9

The Meso Level: Communal and Organizational Life

To begin with, Christian leaders are part of the community of the church. Churches can benefit from the expertize of leaders in, for example, the areas of planning, administration, contracts and finance. However, such leaders cannot assume that the church operates in the same way as a business or legal firm. Nor can churches simply use the expertize of such leaders and fail to meet their own needs for moral direction and nurturing support. Pastors and theologians need to provide teaching that both critiques elements of the secular mindset in which these lay leaders work and provides relevant and constructive insights to guide and support the decision making and actions of these leaders. Vigilance is required lest leaders uncritically imbibe mindsets, goals and methods that conflict with Christian norms and values. Lay leaders can contribute to the church's understanding of the world to which it seeks to minister and enable it to be more in touch with the needs of the organizations that operate in its community. In turn, Christian leaders benefit from being part of the church that is a complex organization that operates at local, national and international levels. They can further form a network of friends and colleagues that can be drawn upon for advice and mentoring.

At an organizational level, Christian leaders face a multitude of perils and problems. No matter in which sector Christian leaders are active, many temptations and perils can cause them to lose their way and deny their faith. For example, the overriding desire to gain or remain in power and the failure to understand the influence of malign group interests can result in poor decision making. Leaders in government may be pressurized to follow the party line against their own consciences. Or, judges pressured to make decisions that will benefit companies owned by their relatives or prominent government officials.

Dealing with relationships among staff members is a major area where a contribution can be made. Because of their own struggles with sin, Christians have a deeper and more nuanced understanding of the positive and sinful aspects of human nature that is extremely important when one is seeking to "discern good from evil." They will have learned in the church how to nurture what is best in others while being able to detect both psychological problems and/or moral evil. Christian leaders operate at various levels of management, hence leaders at a junior level have less authority over others than directors. Nevertheless, all leaders can learn to detect the negative influence of colleagues who are malingers, impossible to please, unduly suspicious, unfair, accusatory, poor communicators, power seekers, abusive toward others and manipulative gossips. Such behavior is unjust, damaging and frustrating; it diminishes the well being, commitment and creativity of other members of staff.

Conflicts within organizations result not only because of negative staff interactions but also because of competing visions and values. For example, senior managers may want to make a company "lean and mean" to increase profits, whereas others may stress the value of institutional memory and loyalty to long-standing, reliable staff. What is to be valued more highly – sustaining a business during hard economic times and ensuring that workers do not lose their livelihoods, or laying off large numbers of staff to maintain significant financial returns?[12] Christian leaders can assist organizations to become ethical environments through persuasion and their own example. They can argue that organizations are good employers when they offer just treatment, fair wages and good working conditions to their employees. Such organizations can also make available educational opportunities and better facilities to the members of the communities in which they operate and enhance, rather than destroy, the physical environments in which these communities live.

But nothing can be achieved if the leader relates to others in a heavy-handed or hypocritical manner. It is useful to remember the advice of St Francis of Assisi, "preach always and sometimes use words." Christians who are in leadership positions can help organizations adapt to new challenges without fear, drawing on the core values of their faith and relevant new knowledge that emerges within their sector of work. They can further identify how major problems such as poverty, inequality and unemployment can be addressed by Christians who engage in business to provide jobs, education, products and services to the community (Heslam 2002).

Christians can make a contribution also to relationships between organizations. For instance, while competition is useful to unleash creativity and encourage efficiency, it is not the only valid criteria. As in nature, interdependency is another criteria given that the work of lawyers, for instance, is inseparably linked to that of the police or justice system and that of an NGO with the political stability of a nation and its physical and electronic infrastructure.

It is vital to realize that not all leaders actually desire a focus on ethical questions within their departments, businesses or organizations. This means that a Christian leader will have to manage a conflict of values. Their leadership position may be such that they can insist upon the importance of ethical conduct and appoint colleagues that implement this vision. However, Christian leaders at the middle and lower levels of management structures may find themselves marginalized and even denigrated by more senior leaders who wish to hide their own theft, corruption or fraud. Hence, establishing an ethical organization is not dependent on the decisions and actions of an individual alone; it will not succeed without the cooperation of the senior management and others within the organization.

CHAPTER 9

The Macro level: Overcoming Problems and Contributing to National and Global Well Being

21st century leaders are faced with challenges, such as conflicts within and between nations, global warming, massive economic disparities, health issues, and many more. How can this complexity be not simply managed but addressed in a manner that enhances human and environmental wellbeing? Christian leaders are compelled to address not only ethical issues of social justice but also the equitable and sustainable use of the earth's resources at a local and global level. Thus, leaders require intellectual, psychological and social capital in order to address these challenges (Miller 2013:4).

For example, at the macro-level, Christian leaders need to evaluate the ethical content of governing ideas or ideologies. The word "ideology" is used here in its more descriptive (not pejorative) sense to mean a framework of thinking. Capitalism is as much an ideology as are socialism or communism. Values such as short-term "profit-maximization" are in conflict with a Christian norm of the stewardship of the earth and what is good for society as a whole. Of course, one may argue that there is more than one form of capitalism but the dominant, current mode is one that looks merely at the economic bottom line. How can a business leader challenge this narrow view whilst still ensuring the continued existence of the business and satisfying both shareholders and other stakeholders? Indeed, what ought the vision and aims of business to be and should social capital, environmental concerns and corporate responsibility be more than terms bandied about for the sake of appearances?

Kohl (2009:75) contrasts the Christian notion of stewardship with the materialism of our time:

> During his three years of ministry, Jesus Christ spoke more about stewardship, sharing, giving, possessions, money, etc. than about any other subject. Our capitalist, consumer culture needs to hear a loud, clear voice saying that all we are and all that we have belongs to God, not to us human beings. Global injustice begins with the failure of individuals to understand the distinction between what we need and what we want.

In short, Christian leaders can endeavor to run their companies or departments in such a way that they serve the genuine interests of their own society, other nations across the globe and the natural environment upon which we all depend.

Similarly, within national, regional and local government, how can terms like the "the needs of our people" or "the common good" be understood, policies devised and their workable implementation ensured? Are there Christians in political leadership that are credible in the eyes of the broader electorate because they work to improve the lives of citizens and neither hide their faith, nor use it to pander to the interests of particular groups in order to gain votes? While the history of the church has revealed the dangers that arise in the political sphere as a result of the misuse of faith, Mwaura (2006:169) asks the important question: "... how does the church in Africa bear witness to the Spirit of God and conduct her mission with integrity in its contextual realities of HIV/AIDS, refugee crises, poverty, corruption and abuse of human rights?" This broad question about the mission of the church raises questions also for Christian leaders who are active in the sectors of health (Popovici 2012), politics and economics.

Another area in which Christian leaders can make a contribution is to include the marginalized and neglected. Many groups are in this position including the poor, women, children, those who are illiterate and groups with low social status. For instance, Kohl (2009:77) says this about the challenges faced by children:

> About 35 percent of the world's population is under 20 years of age. In some countries of Asia, the number is above 50 percent. Our churches focus on adults. . .Church leaders should not only minister to children and youth, they should also be a voice for them, especially in a culture of violence and exploitation. Leaders of our churches should speak out against sex with children, child pornography, child labor, child soldiers, [and] all instances of child exploitation.

If this is true for church leaders, it is also true for lay leaders who often have the networks and resources to contribute significantly to amelioration of the lives of children across the world.

Finally, a significant contribution can be made in the area of the natural environment. Leaders in government, business, NGOs, etc., need to pay attention to issues related to pollution, the exploitation of natural resources, such as water and air, the denuding of natural species that are dependent on the land, rivers and seas and address the sustainability of the planet. "Green" business is a major way in which a contribution can be made, but care needs to be taken to ensure that issues are properly addressed and not entered into for the sake of appearances. In short, the integration of social, economic, political and environmental concerns is an essential part of Christian lay leadership. Motivated by the values and goals of the Kingdom of God, Christian leaders need to critique views and actions that are wrong and work to make a difference in the lives of people and on behalf of the much exploited environment upon which we all depend.

CHAPTER 9

Some Means of Facilitating Moral Formation

Ken Blanchard (2004:115) highlights five disciplines that can assist the formation of Christian leaders:

1. Solitude: spending time alone with God
2. Prayer: speaking with God
3. Study of Scripture: preparing for the challenges that are yet to come
4. Faith in God's unconditional love: proceeding with confidence grounded in trust
5. Involvement in accountability relationships: having truth-tellers to keep you on track and with whom you can share your vulnerability

In my view, all of these are vital means, but their focus needs to be expanded beyond the micro level to include the organizational and global levels and they can be supplemented by other means, as noted below.

Forming the Micro Level of Personal Moral Identity

In order to avoid the perils discussed in the previous section and, more positively, to make a contribution to our world, a deep commitment to self-enquiry, reflection, prayer and meditation on God's word are vital. Self knowledge is essential and it must include a profound understanding of the impact of one's family and early life experiences on one's personality and values. A central goal for lay leaders ought to be the deepening of their spiritual and moral identity. Admittedly, for busy leaders, time is always a factor. But time spent in this way will save the leader from expending much more time and energy putting right what has gone wrong because of a lack of vigilance and attention to God's teaching and correction.

Whether a leader is single or married, relaxation, emotional support and friendship are vital needs. It is not by accident that much attention has been given to emotional intelligence in recent years. But, Christians nurtured in the Scriptures should not have been deluded by modernism into believing that reason, calculation and so-called neutral analysis are sufficient to sustain life. In addition, burnout – whether acute or chronic – can only be avoided by ensuring that one gets exercise, works reasonable hours, takes shorter breaks or longer holidays and enjoys weekly Sabbath worship, restoration and rest. In particular, regular times of connection and celebration (and listening to their feedback) with one's family and friends ought to be regarded as a priority.

It is incumbent on lay leaders to take personal responsibility for their own nurture and holistic formation and pro-actively search for guidance and help. For instance, leaders could communicate their needs to their pastor and request him/her to preach on key subjects such as conflict, jealousy, ambition, work ethics and the stewardship of the earth. In both Germany and the UK, for example, it is possible to book into a monastery for one to three days to rest, pray and reflect. Some church leaders offer "spiritual consulting," for example, priests in the state church in Germany spend 50 percent of their time with business leaders, not all of whom are Christians. Similarly, Father Dermott Tredgett[13] works from Douai Cathedral in the UK, giving courses and offering retreats for leaders. These are important means to combat confusion and search for clarity and wisdom. Spiritual direction and retreats (Culligan 1983), once only common among priests and those in religious life in the Catholic, Anglican and Orthodox traditions, are now being sought after by many others who are starved of deep communion with God and wise nurture from theological educators and church leaders.

It is significant that Manfred F. R. Kets de Vries, who has written and consulted widely and combines an interest in economics, management and psychoanalysis,[14] recommends that each manager should have a "fool" who will tell him the truth – at any cost.[15] As Christians, we ought to know that without truth and honesty, we cannot please God or make genuine progress in our lives.

Means of Formation at the Organizational Level

Belonging and relating are part of our humanness; human beings need to belong and be in relationship with others. This is why marital and family breakdown is so painful and work conflicts so debilitating. But, paradoxically, we find ourselves and others only when we lose ourselves for God's sake (Jn 12:23-26).

A key form of belonging is being part of a church community; occasional attendance is not enough. Lay leaders need to enter fully into the teaching, fellowship and mission of the local church. For Baptists, the importance of the evocation of all five senses and the inner depths of our spirit in ritual is much neglected and misunderstood. Light, color, texture, shape, music, silence, the smell of candles and incense, the touch of the water of baptism, soaring architecture, the taste of the sacraments of communion – all of these are means that enable us to enter into the mysteries of God's grace and presence to feed our souls. In addition, the active membership of a small Bible study or cell group alongside other Christians who seek to grow is essential. Such "soul friends" both support and call each other to account. Foster (1992:270-271) suggests that these questions be asked:

1. What experiences of prayer and meditation have you had this week?
2. What temptations did you face this week?
3. What movements of the Holy Spirit did you receive this week?
4. What opportunities to serve others did you have this week?
5. In what ways have you encountered Christ in your study of the Bible this week?

Other means of nurturing the relational life of lay leaders include modelling,[16] mentoring and coaching. Within an organization mentoring usually refers to the advice, support and provision of information given to an emerging leader by a senior leader in a company, but not the staff member's line manager. Mentorship can also be provided by another group, external to the company. One example is that of LOI (Leaders of Influence) in Europe that seeks to link younger, less experienced leaders to more mature and experienced leaders in a similar field of work, but from a different company. LOI is based in Germany, but applications are done online. Their motto is "inspiration, motivation and vision."[17] Interestingly, in their brochure, they quote from the servant leader passage in Mark 10:42-43.[18] Again, mentorship is well known in the Bible, with that of Eli (1 Sam 3:1-21) and Paul (Phil 2:19-30) being but two examples.

Coaching is often done in small groups of twenty or less, and may be followed up by one-on-one communication between the coach and class members a month or more after the initial training sessions. Depending on the requirements of company and its staff, the focus of such coaching may differ, but is often aimed at clarifying values, work expectations, organizational structure and facilitating better understanding and cooperation. Of particular interest to this paper is the clarification of values – which values are identified, are the (often religious) roots of these values discussed, what is done in the case of a conflict of values, and what attention is paid to the moral formation of the leader?

In this regard, it is important to distinguish between personality and character. The former draws on psychological insights of personality types which indicate preferences of how energy and information are obtained, how data is processed and how decisions are made by different people. Character, on the other hand, deals with the growth of moral virtue in the dispositions, motives, relationships and actions of the leader. For instance, does the stated value of justice find expression in the relevant virtue – just or fair behavior within the home, church and workplace?

Another possibility is that of a co-mentoring a group of Christian leaders who meet twice a year for a weekend of open sharing. Issues of spiritual formation, character, work conflicts, family relationships and many others can be addressed. Such times can be real eye-openers as information and insights are shared and matters can be confronted in a friendly, supportive and honest way.

The Macro Level: Engagement and Sacrifice

According to Kohl (2009:77-78):

> Theological schools must focus more on training laity and must offer courses in training for marketplace ministry. The voice of a pastor should be heard not only from the pulpit but also in the board rooms of banks and businesses and in the halls of government and secular institutions.

This can happen as a result of a much closer relationship and cooperation between ordained and lay leaders. Leaders grow by constantly learning. Such learning can be formal (e.g. university degrees or short courses) and informal (learning from the example of others and significant experiences).

In recent years, the astute use of the Internet can provide a rich source of comment, video clips and lectures on many subjects as well as a host of biblical commentaries and spiritual writings. Christian leaders need to engage with other thinkers from a variety of fields and disciplines. It is not enough to read, for example, business management texts, but it is also important to read in the fields of ethics, history, psychology and sociology. Good novels, too, reveal much about people, organizations and international affairs.

Leaders grow not just by reading about people's problems, but by engaging with the world, struggling to resolve their own problems and seeing at close hand the suffering of others. Hence, Christian leaders, as already argued, need to engage with people as individuals and communities about social and environmental issues at local, national and international levels. Through active participation within the workplace, in projects and with other people, lay Christian leaders are morally, emotionally and intellectually formed so that their faith is deepened and the action that flows from this faith is extended.

Finally, as Christians, such leaders can draw on the wisdom and experience of global bodies such as the Baptist World Alliance, the World Council of Churches, the Lausanne Committee for World Evangelization, Doctors without Borders, the various Commissions of the United Nations, the Organization of African Unity, Oxfam, Christian Aid and many more.

CHAPTER 9

Conclusion

The intention of this paper is to identify the moral needs and challenges of lay Christian leaders. It began with an account of some of the actions and views of the South African businessman, Reuel Khoza. Thereafter both the moral perils faced by Christian leaders and the contribution they can make at a personal, organizational, national or global level were identified. Finally, some of the means that can be employed to enhance the spiritual and moral formation of Christian leaders at the micro-, meso- and marco-levels were identified. It is my prayer that these thoughts will be of some use to Christian leaders, both lay and ordained, as we seek to provide the type of ethical leadership that is so needed in our world.

Bibliography

Armour, M. C. & Browning, D. 1995. *Systems-Sensitive Leadership: Empowering Diversity Without Polarizing The Church*. Missouri: College Press Publishing Company.

Blanchard, K. 2004. "Reflections on encourage the heart," in J.M. Kouzes and B.Z. Posner, *Christian reflections on the leadership challenge*. San Francisco: Jossey-Bass, John Wiley and Sons, 101-118.

Ciulla, J.B. 2000. *The working life: The promise and betrayal of modern work*. New York: Three Rivers Press.

Culligan, K.G. 1983. *Spiritual direction: Contemporary readings*. New York: Living Flame Press.

De Vries, Manfred F.R. Kets, 1989. "The organizational fool: Balancing a leader's hubris," from: https://flora.insead.edu/fichiersti_wp/Inseadwp1989/89-37.pdf, accessed 1 July 2014.

De Vries, Manfred F.R. Kets. 2009. "The Many Colors of Success: What do Executives Want out of Life?," *Organizational Dynamics*, 39:1, 1-12.

Drushall, Mary Ellen & Flora, Jerry R. 2008. "Exemplary Christian Leadership: Beyond Mastery to Joy," *Epiphany International*, 35-45.

Foster, R. 1992. *Prayer*. London: Hodder and Stoughton.

Gomez, Pamela Wesley. 2010. Life's Lessons of a Lay Leader, *Anglican Theological Review* 92:1, 141-145.

Hall, T. 1997. "The personal functioning of pastors: a review of empirical research with implications for the care of pastors," *Journal of Psychology and Theology* 25, 240-253.

Heslam, Peter S. 2002. *Globalization: Unravelling the New Capitalism*, Grove Books, London.

Kaminiów, Karolina & Haenze, Paul D. 2013. "The Christian charity organization, Poland," *Christian Education Journal*, 3:10, Supplement, 118-126.

Kohl, Manfred W. 2009. "Regaining a prophetic voice for the Church today: Training leaders to impact postmodern culture," *International Congregational Journal* 8.2, 73-78.

Kretzschmar, L. 2006. "The indispensability of spiritual formation for Christian leaders," *Missionalia* 34:2/3, 338-361.

Kretzschmar, L. 2007. "The formation of moral leaders in South Africa: A Christian-ethical analysis of some essential elements," *Journal of Theology for Southern Africa* 128, 18-36.

Kretzschmar, L. 2008. "Christian spirituality in dialogue with secular and African spiritualities with reference to moral formation and agency," *Theologia Viatorum* 32:1, 63-96.

Kretzschmar, L. 2010. "Cultural pathways and pitfalls in South Africa: A reflection on moral agency and leadership from a Christian perspective," *Koers - Bulletin for Christian Scholarship*, 75:3, 567-588.

Kretzschmar, L. 2012. "Towards a Christian ethic of work in South Africa," *Acta Theologia* 2012, 32:2, 125-146.

Kretzschmar, L. 2015. "The education of prospective ministers as an invitation to life: Moving from moral failure to moral excellence through a process of moral formation," *In die Skriflig/In Luce Verbi*, 49:1, Art. #1868, 10 pages. http://dx.doi.org/10.4102/ ids.v49i1.1868.

Lamoureux, P. 1999. "An integrated approach to theological education," *Theological Education* 36:1, 141–156.

Meier, Elke Annette. 2014. Shedding light on a muddled field: A Christian ethical appraisal of transforming and transformational leadership, Unpublished MTh Dissertation in Theological Ethics: With Specialisation in Christian Leadership in Context. Pretoria: University Of South Africa.

Miller, Sharmane C. 2013. "Global Leadership and the Call to Authentic Christian Leadership," *Leadership Advance Online*, Issue XXIII, 1-13.

Mwaura, Philomena Njeri. 2006. "Integrity of mission in the light of the Gospel: bearing witness of the Spirit among Africa's gospel bearers," *Exchange* 35:2, 169-190.

Nell, I. A. 2009. "Leaders lost in transition: A case study in leadership, ritual and social capital," *Dutch Reformed Theological Journal/Nederduitse Gereformeerde Teologiese Tydskrif* 50:1&2, 160-170.

Popovici, Alice. 2012. "Shift to laity sparks formation needs." *National Catholic Reporter* February 17 March 1, 2012, 15-16.

Rigby, Rhymer, "Worn-out executives need a place to think," 2008, http://www.ft.com/cms/s/0/8b6bed84-d63c-11dc-b9f4-0000779fd2ac.html#axzz36CwtZwv4, accessed 1 July 2014.

Spangenberg, H.1 & Theron, C. C. 2005. "Promoting ethical follower behaviour through leadership of ethics: The development of the ethical leadership inventory (ELI)," *South African Journal of Business Management*, 36:2, 1-18.

Thoman, Rick. 2009. "Leadership Development, Part 1: Churches Don't Have To Go It Alone," *Christian Education Journal*, Series 3, 6:2, 282-299.

Trull, J.E. & Carter, J.E. 2004. *Ministerial ethics: Moral formation for Church leaders*, 2nd edn., Grand Rapids: Baker Academic.

Vadaracco, J.L. 2003. "The discipline of building character," in Business leadership: *A Jossey-Bass reader*. San Francisco: Jossey-Bass/John Wiley and Sons, 307–329.

Van Aswegen, A. S. & Engelbrecht, A. S. 2009. "The relationship between transformational leadership, integrity and an ethical climate in organizations," *South African Journal of Human Resource Management*, 7:1, 221-229.

CHAPTER 10
FAITHFUL THINKING:
THE ROLE OF THE SEMINARY IN PROMOTING A THOUGHTFUL CHRISTIANITY[1]

Brian Harris

It is alleged that George Bernard Shaw once quipped "5 percent of the people think, 15 percent of the people think they think, 80 percent of the people would rather die than think!"

If Shaw was even remotely accurate, we might well question the need for our topic "Faithful Thinking: The Role of the Seminary in Promoting a Thoughtful Christianity." Many of us who are engaged in theological education are conscious that our intellectual efforts are often viewed with suspicion – even antagonism. I well remember a sermon I once endured when the preacher of the day flung a copy of Moltmann's *Theology of Hope* from the pulpit, ordering one of his elders to burn it immediately because of its supposed heresy.[2] I've no doubt that many copies of Rob Bell's *Love Wins* are facing a similar fate.[3] Generally speaking, when theologians raise new questions or point to problems with old answers, they are greeted with little enthusiasm. Not that a thinking Christianity would uncritically accept new ideas, but it would be refreshing to operate in an environment that was not instinctively opposed to and threatened by the new.

And so the question for today. Do we need a thoughtful Christianity and if so, what role do theological educators and the seminaries they are part of, have to play in promoting faithful thinking?

While we could argue as to what constitute the current major missiological blocks to the Christian faith, my suggestion would be that two significant obstacles are that Christianity is increasingly portrayed as being morally bankrupt and intellectually vacuous. While Anselm argued that faith should seek understanding, we seem to have birthed a generation where faith simply seeks new experiences.[4] The morality and relevance of those experiences is often uncritically embraced, and over time this frequently leads to toxic expressions of faith. There is a link between thinking and doing – and faulty theology leads to blemished lifestyles and flawed faith communities. While we might lament the manner in which the new atheists are ridiculing Christianity, we need to be willing to explore our role in having provoked the onslaught.[5] On its own, exploration is never enough. We need to find the courage and will to change where change is necessary.

Let's then look at the accusations of moral and intellectual poverty and explore the possible role of the seminary in turning this tide, as it promotes a thoughtful Christian faith.

Beyond Moral Poverty

While in the past atheists were usually content to justify their lack of belief in God's existence on the basis of intellectual objections, it is now increasingly common for that justification to be based on moral objections. To quote from the title of Christopher Hitchen's bestselling book, it is alleged that God is not great and that religion poisons everything. Some would have us believe that religious faith is an evil akin to greed, poverty and disease and that it is a significant social problem to be obliterated if we are to attain a more utopian existence. While the famous G.K. Chesterton paradox claims "The Christian ideal has not been tried and found wanting. It has been found difficult; and left untried," a growing tide impatiently dismisses the sentiment as escapist and is unwilling to endure what they claim is the poisonous harvest of religious faith.

That harvest is described in different ways, but ten common components (in no particular order) include:

1. Religious warfare
2. Colonial exploitation
3. Racial bigotry
4. The oppression of women
5. Homophobia
6. The exploitation of the environment
7. Retarding the progress of science, especially medical science
8. Academic censorship with a resultant intellectual dishonesty
9. Intolerance of anything new
10. Hypocrisy

Clearly there is nothing attractive about this list, and if it is seen to be the normative result of religious faith, evangelists should expect audiences who are increasingly hostile to their message – presupposing they can find any audience at all.

David Kinnaman's study of the attitude of 16-29 year old Americans toward Christians saw six recurring images.[6] They considered Christians to be:

1. Hypocritical
2. Interested in "saving" people rather than in relating to them
3. Anti-homosexual
4. Sheltered
5. Too political
6. Judgemental

Again, the list is far from winsome, and represents significant barriers to the likely receptivity to messages about the love and mercy of God.

We could argue that these negative images are the fruit of the Christendom era, when membership of the Christian faith was assumed for almost all who lived in the Western World. Christendom was often more about sanctioning the status quo than following Jesus, and we could be hopeful that its demise might free the church to find more authentic expressions of faith in this "after Christendom" era.[7] If the harvest of Christendom was our poisonous list of ten (and I acknowledge that it is excessively one sided to suggest that the list is fair),[8] is it possible that in the post-Christian era a Christianity that more closely represents and reflects the teaching of Jesus might emerge?

For this to occur, it is important that we recognize and renounce those elements of religious belief that leave us vulnerable to developing a toxic faith. Given that the seminary has a key role in affirming what constitutes valid Christian faith, is it too much to expect the seminary to have a comparable role in stemming the tide of dysfunctional counterfeits to the message of Jesus?

To be fair, not all the fruit of Christendom was negative. Christians can claim credit for many of the positive social advances made in the last 2000 years. While multiple social factors are invariably at work in societal evolution, it is not fair to explore the abolition of slavery, the protection of the rights of women and children, the development of the welfare state or the shift in focus from retributive to restorative justice, without repeatedly referring to the Christian faith that motivated and inspired most of those who championed these causes. And they represent a small selection of an impressive array of humanitarian achievements.[9]

CHAPTER 10

Sadly, there is also a shadow side. There have been many times in the history of the church when it has been supportive of an oppressive agenda, which on occasion has revealed itself in racism, sexism, homophobia, militarism, ecological and economic exploitation, cultural insensitivity and more beside.[10]

Even if not actively supporting exploitation, faith can easily wear unattractive masks.[11] Let's explore three masks that will have to disappear if a more authentic Christian faith is to be birthed, and let's ponder the role of the seminary in ensuring their demise.

First, there is faith as escapism. While it is perhaps understandable that African American slaves longed for the day when the sweet chariot would swing low to carry them home, it is more difficult to understand why those whose lives are saturated with material abundance are sometimes so heavenly minded that they are of little use to those on the fringes of life, indeed those who are specially dear to the heart of God. A thoughtful Christian faith will ensure that eschatology is used not as a crutch justifying escapism, but as a motivator of daring obedience. As people who have been privileged to see the end of the story, we know that ultimate victory belongs to the people of God. This should give us the courage to live in the light of God's coming Kingdom in the present. Baptist theologian Stanley Grenz suggests that all theological construction should be eschatologically oriented, and his insight is important.[12] Allowing the future to guide the present will see a radically new form of Christianity birthed. Imagine, for example, if we truly lived backwards from the Pauline insight that the ultimate reality is that in Christ "there is neither Jew nor Greek, slave nor free, male nor female, for you are all one in Christ Jesus" – to quote Galatians 3:28. This would indeed birth an infectiously different Christianity, one worth following. That this vision flows from good theology must not be overlooked. While it is true that many in the pews are enthralled by the *Left Behind* series, those of us in the seminary have a responsibility to extend their eschatological horizon. Our silence when profound doctrines are reduced to silliness is not acceptable. In the end, error is best combated with truth. We need to paint a compelling portrait of a thoroughly engaged and incarnated Christian faith, one able to strive in the present because it has had a glimpse of the future.

A second caricature left over from the Christendom era is that faith is often confused with the status quo. This mask bears no resemblance to what's required to be an authentic Christ follower, but nonetheless for many people things are good provided they've been around for more than 20 years. Nostalgia, rather than a commitment to a daring faith agenda, is the driver. Onlookers fail to find it inspiring. Perhaps we should stop thinking of ourselves as Christians, but as

Christ followers. This is not a pedantic quibble. To stop viewing ourselves as static nouns and to introduce images of action might help to remind us that the Christian vision is of a daring journey of discipleship. It is a journey that does not bypass the cross and it is one that would never be undertaken without the assurance that resurrection follows crucifixion. If any of this sounds like the status quo, then the status quo is not what it used to be!

Again, the role of the seminary in this paradigm shift is critical. For years we have focused on producing pastorally sensitive graduates. Without sacrificing these gains, perhaps we can evaluate how effective we have been in producing prophetically sensitive graduates. If we are not satisfied with the harvest, perhaps we can look at what we have been planting. After all, we reap what we sow, and if our own vision of the radical agenda implicit in being a Christ follower is inadequate, the harvest will reflect the shortfall.

Third, there is faith as smugness and self-righteousness. While most have renounced the wagging finger, the image of Christians as people who see themselves as morally superior to lesser mortals and who tut tut at the folly of those who don't share their faith, persists. That is not to suggest that we are people without a moral vision. However, a thoughtful Christianity is not proclaimed in "Thou Shalt" terms. It is portrayed invitationally. It recognizes that it is one vision amongst other competing visions and that it needs to woo others by the winsomeness of those who have been captured by its contours.

Yet again, the seminary has an important role to play in brokering this change. By our own hospitality and willingness to think through the likely outcome of alternate moral visions, we model an engaged involvement in the issues that matter to those around us. Rather than simply saying no, we thoughtfully explore the moral issues of our day with the community in which we are incarnated. Because it is a genuine exploration, we do not proclaim our answers in advance. We will indeed be guided by the biblical text and the traditions of the church, but at times we will be surprised at the way in which contemporary issues highlight areas of biblical truth we have previously not observed. Clark Pinnock has alerted us to the possibility of discovering not only past, but also future meanings in the biblical text and his insight is one with which we should creatively engage.[13]

These three false masks – faith as escapism, faith as the status quo and faith as self-righteousness – alert us to an important truth. Faith can spark life's loftiest journeys but paradoxically, can also accompany and bolster its most misguided and tragic detours.

Because of the potentially abusive nature of faith it is important that the seminary highlights some of the warning signs that it is at risk of proving toxic.

CHAPTER 10

Many of our students start with the quaint assumption that so long as something is cloaked in Christian language, it must be good. The harvest of this naivety is often devastating. While an exhaustive list is beyond the scope of this talk, danger signals that point to toxic faith include an insistence on unquestioning faith, or faith as compulsion instead of faith as invitation, or where there is legalism without love, or any form of faith that aims for power and control and attempts to justify the unjustifiable in the name of God. By simply alerting Christ followers to the possibility of toxic faith the seminary makes an important contribution to its destruction. Robust Christ following is the call of the day. Nothing less will persuade a cynical world to revise its largely negative verdict on the previous 2000 years of church history.

Beyond Intellectual Poverty

If the seminary has a role in pointing toward a Christian faith that will move us beyond our moral poverty, its role in articulating a thoughtful Christian faith to move us beyond our intellectual poverty is even more important. Not that it is a role we automatically embrace.

I saw it in an ethics class I taught at an institution I'll leave unnamed. Prior to lecturing on some of the ethical issues raised by genetic engineering, I asked the class of around 50 students how many of them were in favor of this growing discipline. While I had expected the majority to express reservations, I was a little surprised that without exception they all declared their opposition. Wondering how I would provoke interesting discussion in a class with such a homogenous view, I asked if someone could tell me a little bit about genetic engineering and what it involved. An awkward silence settled over the group. It soon became painfully obvious that the only thing the class knew about the subject was that they were opposed to it. While I would like to think that such examples are rare, I fear they are not.

Don't misunderstand me. As I got to know the students in that class I discovered them to be delightful, spiritually committed, good hearted and intelligent human beings. They had simply never realized the need to seriously engage with the issues of the 21st century – indeed, they didn't really know what those issues were. Being taught from a syllabus that had seen little development in the last 30 years, and being educated in an environment suspicious of all things new, their response was hardly surprising. My sad conclusion was that the institution they were part of was actually acting as a brake on their intellectual development. Rather than producing faithful thinkers ready to engage the questions of our time, they were forming pious graduates best suited to an intellectual ghetto where they could hibernate in splendid irrelevance. It was such a waste of excellent potential. Stephen Carter has suggested that the great problem with religion in the United States is not its neglect, but its trivialization.[14] There is no need to limit his observation to the USA, as this example makes clear.

This is all the more disturbing when we remember that we live in an era of the democratization of knowledge. In my country, Australia, the second recommendation of the Bradley review into Higher Education is that by 2020 40 percent of Australians between the ages of 25 and 34 should have at least a first degree, and it outlines the steps the country must take to make this possible.[15] Several countries already exceed this target, including the United Kingdom, Ireland, Sweden and Finland.[16] Globally we are seeing an explosion of higher education. While old timers might lament that the quality of graduates is not what it once was, the reality is that more and more people are highly educated and capable of evaluating ideas. This trend is not limited to some of the planets more privileged countries. In China the number of undergraduate and graduate enrolments quintupled between 1998 and 2005, and there is no sign of this slowing down.[17] By its emphasis on higher education, China is pointing the way to the many countries who aspire for a better future for their population.

With increasingly well-educated congregations, preachers can no longer stand in pulpits "six feet above contradiction" and must expect their views to be challenged. This is especially true when they move to areas outside of their expertise. Are pastors the font of all wisdom on raising children when there are six psychologists and four social workers in the congregation? Views expressed from the pulpit will no longer be accepted uncritically.

In the light of this it is particularly disturbing that some denominations are downplaying the importance of a rigorous theological training for their pastors. While we undoubtedly need to review what is taught at seminary, it is clear that we need clergy who have a depth of biblical understanding and who are theologically insightful. This depth cannot be gained via attending the occasional inspirational seminar or conference. At a time when the training demands for all professions are increasing, it sends an awkward message to the community if we appear to think that our clergy need less training. Are we implying that we are propagating a faith with little substance and content, and that the only skills required in furthering it are those of being able to motivate the credulous?

Not that the seminary should only train potential clergy. With the democratization of knowledge, an increasing number of lay people long for a depth of understanding of the Christian faith that it is unrealistic to expect the local church to provide. We should welcome this development, and ensure that we have sufficiently flexible training pathways to allow for the participation of thoughtful laypeople in our programs.

If we accept the need for thinking faith, we should ask to whom the seminary should speak.

First, the seminary should do theology for and on behalf of the church.[18] We might need to overcome some suspicions here and will sometimes come across a "Jesus yes, theology no" mentality. Rather than lament this, those of us in the seminary need to be willing to work at finding the right tone for our communication, or put slightly differently, how to find our voice. At present the theologian's voice is sometimes portrayed as a pedantic whine. The unspoken fear in many congregations is that what starts as a quibble will escalate into an unseemly brawl, with a church split not far off. Rather than discuss issues, we therefore often bury them. Only the lowest common denominator of completely non-controversial beliefs remains, and as a result we become used to never exploring anything in depth. It is only a small step from here to assuming that we never explore in depth because depth does not exist. The seminary can help reverse this trend by speaking respectfully of alternate views, by welcoming the richness of nuance, and by validating the importance of exploring new ideas. We need to do this in tones of humility. Let's remember that 2000 years of church history support the hypothesis that we might be wrong!

Second, the seminary should do theology for the marketplace. We live at a time of a hardening secularism. Most secularists will tolerate faith communities so long as they remain in their ghettoes. It doesn't take much thought to realize that secular atheism is as much an ideology as is religious faith. It makes no sense to allow the one into the public arena while we banish the other to the religious cloister. If faith communities abandon their role in the public arena, this trend will continue to harden. It is only stating the obvious to note that if the seminary, which employs those who are the best educated in the insights of the Christian faith, says nothing about the major issues of our day, people will conclude that it is because the Christian faith has nothing to say.

For the seminary, the entry to the marketplace will often be via the academy. Rather than only speak at theological conferences, we should prepare ourselves to present papers at conferences on education, philosophy, business ethics, public policy. The list goes on and on. George Marsden speaks supportively and enthusiastically of "the outrageous idea of Christian scholarship" and we should be willing to support this quest.[19] It should not be limited to conference participation. Why should theologians only teach theology students? Should we not raise our hands to teach courses in ethics and philosophy or to participate in class debates about the care of the environment, the eradication of poverty and the appropriate use of wealth? Belief in the Christian God makes a significant difference to the way in which each of these subjects is handled, and if we do not make ourselves available to explore this difference, who will? As we contribute relevantly in this arena, it is only a matter of time until we will be invited to contribute in yet wider arenas. Why should the new atheists be the only ones who get a public hearing?

Embarking upon this journey will take courage. It involves transforming the seminary from a place of quiet reflection (and sometimes escape) to an active participant in the hurly burly of life. I love Philip Dick's words in *The Dark Haired Girl*. "I finally reduced all human virtues to one: BRAVERY....if you aren't brave, it doesn't matter what other virtues you have, because you aren't going to act them out. What good does it do to be able to see the truth if you're too [scared] to act on the basis of what you see."[20]

Let me summarize. If we are to promote faithful thinking, the seminary must

1. Believe in the importance of an educated, thoughtful clergy. If we don't believe in what we do, or worse still, if we don't produce skilled, faithful thinkers, we will vote ourselves out of existence.

2. Create pathways for thinking laypeople to engage with the training provided by the seminary.

3. Work on the interface between the seminary and the church. The seminary should help the church deal with complex issues of faith and practice, and in doing so should model appropriate ways of dealing with difference and nuance.

4. Work on the interface between the seminary and the marketplace. The initial entry point will often be via the academy, but there is no reason why it should be limited to this arena. The goal should be active involvement in all of life.

Increasingly, people dismiss the Christian faith as morally suspect and intellectually shallow. It is not enough for us to lament such lopsided caricatures. Those of us in the seminary are well placed to serve the church by promoting faithful thinking. Faithful thinking is usually a precondition of faithful living, so in birthing a thoughtful Christian faith the seminary can help combat two of the great missiological stumbling blocks of our day. If we don't meet this challenge, who will?

CHAPTER 10

References

Andrews, Dave. People of Compassion. Blackburn, VIC: TEAR Australia, 2008.

Bell, Rob. Love Wins: A Book About Heaven, Hell, and the Fate of Every Person Who Ever Lived. New York: HarperOne, 2011.

Bradley, Denise, Peter Noonan, Helen Nuggent, and Bill Scales. Review of Australian Higher Education. Canberra: DEEWR, 2008.

Carter, Stephen L. The Culture of Disbelief: How American Law and Politics Trivialize Religious Devotion. New York: Basic Books, 1993.

Dawkins, Richard. The God Delusion. Boston: Houghton Mifflin, 2006.

Dick, Philip K. The Dark Haired Girl. Shingletown: Mark V. Ziesing, 1988.

Grenz, Stanley J. Revisioning Evangelical Theology: A Fresh Agenda for the Twenty First Century. Downers Grove: Inter Varsity Press, 1993.

_____. Theology for the Community of God. Nashville: Broadman and Holman, 1994.

Grenz, Stanley J., and John R. Franke. Beyond Foundationalism: Shaping Theology in a Postmodern Context. Louisville: Westminster John Knox Press, 2001.

Harris, Brian. "When Faith Is the Problem." The Advocate, April 2007, 4.

_____. "Beyond Bebbington: The Quest for an Evangelical Identity in a Postmodern Era." Churchman 122, no. 3 (2008): 201-219.

Harris, Sam. Letters to a Christian Nation. New York: Random, 2006.

Hitchens, Christopher. God Is Not Great: How Religion Poisons Everything. New York: Twelve, 2007.

Kinnaman, David, and Gabe Lyons. Unchristian: What a New Generation Really Thinks About Christianity...And Why It Matters. Grand Rapids: Baker, 2007.

Li, Yao, John Whalley, Shunming Zhang, and Xilang Zhao. "China's Higher Education Transformation and Its Global Implications." Vox (2008).

Marsden, George The Outrageous Idea of Christian Scholarship. New York: Oxford University Press, 1997.

Moltmann, Jürgen. Theology of Hope: On the Ground and the Implications of a Christian Eschatology. Translated by James W. Leitch. London: SCM, 1967.

Murray, Stuart. Church after Christendom. Carlisle: Paternoster, 2004.

_____. Post-Christendom. Carlisle: Paternoster, 2004.

Pinnock, Clark H. "Biblical Texts - Past and Future Meanings." Journal of the Evangelical Theological Society 43, no. 1 (2000): 71-81.

Schmidt, Alvin J. Under the Influence: How Christianity Transformed Culture. Grand Rapids: Zondervan, 2001.

Wallis, Jim. The Call to Conversion. Herts: Lion, 1981.

CHAPTER 11
HOW WE VIEW THE VALUE OF THEOLOGICAL EDUCATION

"DA"

I have included a rather informal visual that explains our goal in theological education. Here a case study of sorts that shows how this model works.

Peter the Plumber is a believer who loses a child to Sudden Infant Death Syndrome. His wife is understandably distraught and begins having doubts as to whether God even exists and expresses those doubts to her husband. One of the members of the church says that the death of his child is likely a judgment of God against some undisclosed sin in the life of Peter and/or his wife. How should Peter respond? Peter isn't really sure what to believe so he calls a church leader to help work through this. We will call him Clyde the Communicator. Clyde's church has been studying the book of Job and has been reading some helpful material from thinkers who have struggled with similar questions. He formulates a response that addresses Peter's theological concerns, but does so in a pastoral manner – casting the academic conclusions in language that speaks to Peter's heart – not just his mind. As a result of these conversations, Clyde the Communicator decides to teach a series on a biblical theology of suffering.

What really is happening here is discipleship. Peter the Plumber is facing complex questions concerning his faith in light of life's circumstances. He wants to follow Jesus well during these difficult days, but he is struggling to find answers. Clyde the Communicator's job is to help Peter stay faithful in this part of life's journey, so he finds materials produced by Elbert the Egghead. Elbert is a trained theologian who has been formally trained in the academic arena. Elbert has written articles and books on these kinds of topics and it helps Clyde formulate a thoughtful response. Elbert is discipling Clyde to secure in his own mind the biblical truths of suffering. As Clyde begins to understand the informational side of this topic, he begins to transfer his understanding in a way that encourages Peter to remain a faithful follower of Jesus.

East vs. West

In the West, we have a long and stellar line of Elberts. From the early church fathers to the reformers to more modern scholars like Bruce Metzger and A.T. Robertson. When we have complex issues to unpack, we become disciples of scholars who guide us. We also have gifted communicators who digest complex theological thought and disperse it to church members in meaningful ways. The Iranian church worldwide has only a few Elbert Eggheads and some Clyde Communicators – but inside the borders of Iran, there are almost none of the former and only a select few of the latter. For the church inside Iran to maintain health, this needs to change. We need Elbert Eggheads on the inside who can navigate the complexities of the Christian faith within the Iranian cultural context. We need Eggheads and Communicators who are living out their faith inside the country to work together to maintain healthy churches. That means identifying insiders who have the gifts to be either Elberts or Clydes and then training them to sharpen those gifts for the good of the church (for the sake of Peter the Plumbers). While we appreciate the impact Western eggheads can have on the church of Iran inside the country, we believe developing eggheads inside is far superior. This means learning how to do theological training that keeps theologians inside the country. This means letting our insiders determine the course of theological dialogue, for what is theologically relevant in Fort Worth or Louisville inth United States may not be theologically relevant in Esfahan or Tehran in Iran. This means that we should not only strive to see important theological works translated, we should strive to see theologians inside Iran produce their own theological works to help the church steer clear of heresy and, at the same time, engage the culture in a way that expands the kingdom throughout the country.

Scholastic Discipleship

I consider theological education something different than just discipleship. It is by no means VOID of discipleship, for all theological struggles should lead us to think, act and speak more like Jesus, but the expectations and the processes of theological education are much more demanding. Theological education should include the classic educational disciplines such as biblical languages, biblical studies, church history (including the Eastern church), philosophy and ethics.

Who Should Take Part in Theological Education?

I see theological education as a funnel. Our team spends a good bit of time training nationals to be followers of Jesus by understanding God's word. We see

CHAPTER 11

these folks entering into the top of the funnel. We will eventually identify people (particularly among church leaders) who have some giftedness when it comes to enduring the demands of scholastic discipleship. Some of those become communicators (remember Clyde!). Eventually we will discover a few who seem to have the skillset to receive a high level of scholastic training (Elberts!) The problem is – we do not have an organized system in place yet to develop these kinds of leaders. Ideally, I would like to keep folks passing through the funnel and those who come out on the other side will in turn help us develop others. Eventually, I would like to have a stable of ten or twelve communicators and about five egg-heads who can help develop and deepen the theological process among Persian speakers worldwide. (When I say Persian speakers – I am including Dari/Afghan speakers as well).

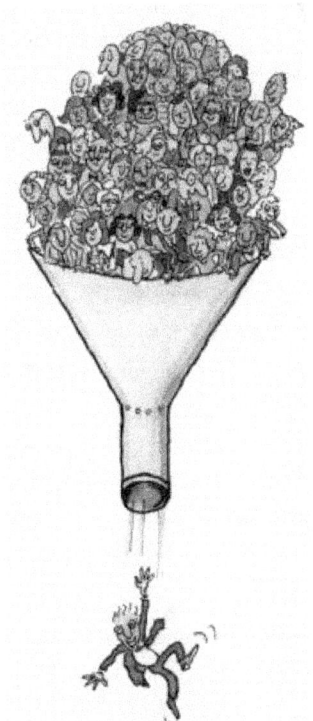

What steps are we taking to see this happen?

Online Seminary

Our team currently has two couples enrolled in an online, English-speaking theological education for their Master of Arts degree. The online seminary is meant to provide the students with access to limited theological resources and theological lectures and participate in the learning process through assignments and tests. All materials will eventually be offered in Farsi (that is our highest priority). Ideally, we would like our students briefly to leave Iran or Afghanistan and go to another Central Asian country for some of their course work. That would mean sending professors to this region to fulfill that requirement. Think of the class work for nationals as an I-term on a campus extension. They receive pre-assignments, receive classroom instruction for two weeks and then receive post-class assignments. This keeps the students in their own country and in their culture (as opposed to being a residential student). Due to the high level of persecution, this is not always possible. Inside the borders of Iran, the government keeps a hostile eye on people who show interest in any drift away from Islam. All our efforts would be surreptitious in nature. That means offering a secure mechanism for delivering the materials and the completed assignments. We have a secure place in a Central Asian city for hosting training events – a three-bedroom villa that can house about ten to twelve people comfortably. Of course the cultural/language barrier is a daunting challenge. Our students have excellent conversational English skills but do not have the literary English to efficiently manage their assignments (both written and reading). Indeed, it is not just the English that is a problem, but theological/academic English, which can feel like a whole other language! There are two ways we can meet this challenge.

1. We would like to secure an Iranian who has the English/Farsi acumen to bridge this language/cultural gap. We envision this person as serving in the seminary as a professor who meets all accreditation demands.

2. We would like to speed up the theological resources by producing audio translations rather than just depending on literary translation. We believe these two initiatives can propel us forward in providing quality theological education to Persian-speakers no matter where they live.

We need to develop those Persian speakers who are already in Western environments so they can serve as partners in this effort. There are more than one million Iranians in Los Angeles. Dallas, Atlanta and Baltimore/DC are other areas of concentration. Many of these Iranians are highly educated, possessing fluency in both English and Persian and could serve as mentors/tutors to help our theological students work through their academic degrees.

One other notable effort in this arena is PARS Theological Seminary, a Farsi only online seminary: http://www.parstheology.com. This London-based ministry is run by some great people in the Persian-speaking community.

CHAPTER 11

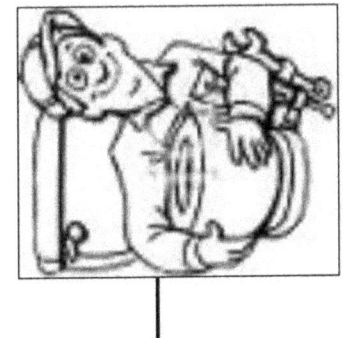

Peter the Plumber. Peter represents every person in the church. He wants to know how to be a good father and a good husband. He wants to live out his faith in the market place. Peter doesn't understand much in the egghead's world so he depends on Clyde to deliver the truths of our faith in language the he can both understand and pass on to others.

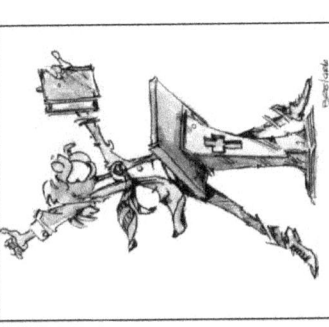

Elbert the Egg-head—This is the guy who lives and breathes theological research, theological scientist that devotes his life to mining the depths of the complexities of our faith in a fallen world. Elbert's ultimate goal is to serve Peter the Plumber by managing the details of the truth of the Christian faith.

Clyde the Communicator—This guy has his feet in both Elbert and Peter's world. He can converse with Elbert about important theological truths, but is required to reshape those conversations in a fashion that helps Peter the Plumber understand better how to be more like Jesus.

COMMISSION ON CHRISTIAN ETHICS

The work of the Commission on Christian Ethics from 2010-2014 promised an adventure as we sought to find our rhythms "In Step with the Spirit." Our steps carried us to Kuala Lumpur, Malaysia, in 2011; to Santiago, Chile, in 2012; to Ocho Rios, Jamaica, in 2013; and, finally, to Izmir, Turkey, in 2014.

We tried something new over these years. The we should be spread across all of the commissions. From year-to-year we had different time allotments. Sometimes we met on four days, and sometimes we only met for three. A second innovation, more specific to the Commission on Christian Ethics, was to invite participants to invest more time with fewer presentations, with the hope of generating meaningful conversation around a subject or topic consistent with the sub-theme of the binding theme of the quinquennium.

Furthermore, the Commission on Christian Ethics intentionally arranged for joint sessions with other gathered BWA groups. In Santiago, Chile, it was appropriate for us to meet with the Commission on Human Rights Advocacy and hear from the 2012 Denton and Janice Lotz Human Rights Award recipient, Edgar Palacios, whose life has been a proclamation in step with the Spirit through the tribulations of the oppressed in El Salvador.

Two years later the Commission on Christian Ethics joined with the Commission on Theological Education and Leadership Formation during the gathering in Izmir, Turkey. Louise Kretzschmar (South Africa) challenged both commissions with a paper and presentation under the title, "Beyond Milk: The Moral Failure and Ongoing Formation of Lay Christian Leaders in the Church and Society."

A final innovation of note that emerged – without our planning for it – was collaboration on some papers. Bill Tillman (Texas, USA) and Allen Reasons (West Virginia, USA) proposed a joint paper, "Bob Marley, Freedom, and the Bible," for the 2013 gathering in Ocho Rios, Jamaica. I'll not soon forget the presentation! While health issues prevented Reasons from being present, Tillman delivered the paper. At one point he began to read the lyrics of a Bob Marley song and our Jamaican friends broke into spontaneous song. For the rest of the session we relied upon the local audience to deepen and broaden the experience of all of the non-island people in attendance.

The four papers included in this section, one from each convening of the Commission on Christian Ethics: Kuala Lumpur, Santiago, Ocho Rios, and Izmir, provided a faint image of what happened in those locales.

I would have preferred to have been able to present in print all of the papers. Better yet, I would have preferred to make available a video of each session. Perhaps someday technology will allow us to stream our sessions in an interactive way.

Meanwhile, you have before you a sample of what transpired during the 2011-2014 meetings of the Commission on Christian Ethics.

In Kuala Lumpur, Samuel K. Roberts offered a helpful, critical, and pastoral paper on the development of an agenda for moral action. His paper, "But How Does the Spirit Work in Moral Action? A Case for the Utility of Virtue Theory," is worthy of broad reading.

In Santiago de Chile, William M. Tillman, Jr. showed his characteristic critical skills –paired with an astute biblical, theological, and cultural sensibility – that encouraged readers and hearers to see the creative risks of Antioch (see Acts 11 and 13) as a model for ever-renewing approaches to proclaiming the Gospel in concrete ways. His paper/essay, "From Antioch to Santiago by Way of Mars Hill," is delightful and provocative.

In Ocho Rios, Rod Benson bored into the admonition of 2 Peter to "grow in grace" as an ethical imperative. His paper/essay, "Growth in Grace as Control Belief for the People of God," could open a new vista for practical Christian Ethics.

Robert Scott Nash joined us in Izmir. By training and practice Nash is a New Testament scholar, a teacher of Greek, and an archaeologist. His paper/essay, "Unity through Christ: Engaging the Ephesian Household Code," nudged us toward a more holistic understanding of the relevance of the biblical texts and contexts in the twenty-first century.

One other event from the quinquennium, not reflected in the agenda and schedules of the proceedings of the Commission on Christian Ethics, deserves modest attention. In 2012 the chair of the Commission on Christian Ethics received an invitation from Chilean Baptist pastors to participate in an open forum on how to address the growing issue of responses to homosexuality in the churches. The chair agreed, but made it clear that his presence and comments were not under the umbrella of the BWA. The meeting was well attended, fifty or so pastors. The conversation generated quite a bit of positive response, leading our METR director, Fausto Vasconcelos, to offer a brief report.

Richard F. Wilson, commission chair, is the Columbus Roberts Professor of Theology and chair of The Roberts Department of Christianity at Mercer University in Georgia, USA, as well as president of the Liberia Baptist Theological Seminary in Paynesville City, Liberia. He has been active within the BWA since 1995 when he joined the Academic and Theological Education Workgroup, which he served until 1999, and again from 2005 until 2010. He began serving as a member of the METR Commission on Christian Ethics in 2005 and transitioned to commission Chair in 2010, when he joined the METR Advisory Committee.

Yvonne Martinez Thorne, commission vice chair, is a renowned faith-based psychologist in Pennsylvania in the United States. She is founder and CEO of Cultivating Wholeness Counseling Associates, PC. Dr. Martinez Thorne is also a Philadelphia Baptist Association Consultant for Area Ministry and Communication. She began serving the BWA on the Commission on Christian Ethics as vice chair in 2010. She is also an active member of the METR Advisory Committee and the Resolutions Committee.

CHAPTER 12
"BUT HOW *DOES* THE SPIRIT WORK IN MORAL ACTION?":
A CASE FOR THE UTILITY OF VIRTUE THEORY

Samuel K. Roberts

In Memoriam

Baptists are hardly unique in their affirmation of the person and power of the Holy Spirit as a co-equal participant in the Trinity. One has only to peruse the many faith statements attributed to Baptists and our theological kin to appreciate just how much Baptist beliefs about the Holy Spirit have been within the mainstream of Christian orthodoxy. For example, the Orthodox Creed of 1678 betrays a doctrinal lineage that goes all the way back to the Nicene Creed:

> We believe that there is one holy spirit, the third person subsisting in the sacred trinity, one with the father and son, who is very and true God, and of one substance or nature with the father and son, coequal, coeternal, and coessential with the father and son, to whom with the father and son, three persons, and but one eternal and almighty God, be by all the hosts of saints and angels, ascribed eternal glory, and Hallelujahs, Amen.[1]

To be sure, Baptist theological sensibility has always affirmed a belief that the Holy Spirit was effectual in the life of the church. Well before the Reformation, the writing of Petr Chelcicky, the Bohemian Reformer who had been influenced by Jan Hus, affirmed the role of the Holy Spirit in forming and sustaining the communion of believers gathered in the church. "The Holy Spirit," wrote Chelcicky, "makes this communion of fellowship among the saints, the union of the members with each other and to Christ's spiritual body."[2]

In addition to enriching the common life of believers, Baptists have also believed that the Spirit animates the moral life of believers as well. The New Hampshire Confession affirms that "sanctification is the process by which…

we are made partakers of [God's] holiness; that it is a progressive work; that it is begun in regeneration; and that it is carried on in the hearts of believers by the presence and power of the Holy Spirit."[3] In all likelihood, most Baptists would agree with Bill Leonard's assessment that 1) the Spirit inspires persons to speak and act in the world; and that 2) the Spirit bestows spiritual gifts for living, among these being the various charismata (gifts) of the Spirit noted in Galatians, that include "love, joy, peace, patience, kindness, goodness, fidelity, gentleness, and self-control" (Gal. 5:22-23).[4]

If, as scripture suggests, the virtues are the result of the Holy Spirit's work, we would be justified in looking to virtue theory to help us understand more fully how this mysterious aspect of the Spirit's work comes into being. Moreover, we would hope that virtue theory would shed light also on the moral agents, the putative virtuous persons who ultimately engage in practices consistent with the virtues. This paper presumes that fruitful results may be in the offing if Christian theological ethics is able to appropriate the aims and methods of virtue theory as a means of explicating the work of the Holy Spirit. As an exercise in theological ethics, the paper proceeds on the presumption that humans must respond to divine action inherent in the gift of sanctification, the theological context in which the virtues ultimately come forth. As Basil of Caesarea says, "all who are in need of sanctification turn to the Spirit; all those seek him who live by virtue, for his breath refreshes them and comes to their aid in pursuit of their natural and proper end."[5] More contemporaneously, William Alston is not far from the mark when he suggests that "[a] crucial function of the Holy Spirit [is] the transformation of the believer into a 'saint,' into the sort of person God designed him/her to be."[6] Such a person would perforce bear the marks of the work of the Holy Spirit, the inculcation of the virtues.

The perspectives of William Alston and Basil of Caesarea suggest that virtue theory, or Christian virtue theory might be marshaled to explain how the Holy Spirit works in the moral life of believers. This paper is an inquiry into these questions and the extent to which Baptists have contributed to an understanding of the Holy Spirit's work. I will explore the extent to which selected writings of three Baptist personages on this subject implicitly employ a Christian virtue theory in ways consistent with the direction suggested by William Alston and Basil of Caesarea.

Christian Virtue Ethics

Christian virtue ethics builds on the Aristotelian preoccupation with refining raw, morally untutored human nature and transforming it to a state such that humans become fit to live a life of *eudaemonia*, or the good and flourishing life. Unlike the Aristotelian project, however, Christian virtue ethics understands that the Christian's chief good is seeking to become a person whose dispositions and subsequent actions are consistent with the will of God. Christian virtue ethics can be traced within Catholic moral theory to Augustine and Thomas Aquinas.[7] However, with the publication of Stanley Hauerwas' *Character and the Christian Life: A Study in Theological Ethics*, in 1975, and Alasdair McIntyre's *After Virtue*, in 1981, Protestant theological ethicists began to engage in a lively conversation about the promise of virtue ethics for giving us a full and robust account of the Christian moral life.[8] Unlike its chief rivals[9] in moral theory, virtue ethics goes inward into the human and essentially asks what must be transformed within our being so that good moral action will ensue. With virtue ethics, being precedes doing. Thus, as Stanley Hauerwas declares, "morality is not primarily concerned with quandaries or hard decisions; nor is the moral self simply the collection of such decisions."[10] This does not mean, however, that Christian virtue ethics is unconcerned with the decisions and the moral actions of believers. As Hauerwas explains:

> To be a person of virtue, therefore, involves acquiring the linguistic, emotional, and rational skills that give us the strength to make our decisions and our life our own. The individual virtues are specific skills required to live faithful to a tradition's understanding of the moral project in which its adherents participate. Like any skills, the virtues must be learned and coordinated in an individual's life, as a master craftsman has learned to blend the many skills necessary for the exercise of any complex craft. Moreover, such skills require constant practice as they are never simply a matter of routine or technique. For skill, unlike technique, give the craftsman the ability to respond creatively to the always unanticipated difficulties involved in any craft in a manner that technique can never provide. That is why the person of virtue is also often thought of as a person of power, in that they moral skills provide them with resources to do easily what some who are less virtuous would find difficult.[11]

Since Christian virtue ethics has staked its legitimacy on this inward journey into the moral self, this method of doing ethics is not fearful of positing a vigorous concept of human self-agency as a springboard for moral action. Hauerwas affirms that any such "self-agency" as we may possess is always shaped through "beliefs, intentions, and actions, by which a man (*sic*) acquires a moral history befitting his nature as a self-determining being."[12] Among such beliefs for

Christians would surely be the power and presence of God and the Holy Spirit in the moral life. Thus there will emerge at some critical point a confluence of our own sense of agency and the power of God and the Holy Spirit in our lives. Christian virtue ethics acknowledges that it is only in response to divine action that human agency will ever achieve a level of moral legitimacy. After all, as I have suggested earlier, the chief good for the believer in Christian virtue theory is becoming a person whose disposition and actions are consistent with the will of God. Toward this end, a Christian virtue ethic will always affirm a vigorous sense of human agency supplemented by divine agency. In the moral life there will always be a balance between human effort and our beliefs about the power of divine will. A noted Baptist preacher, Martin Luther King, Jr., captured this confluence of divine and human will in this way: "Man is not able to save himself or the world. Unless he is guided by God's Spirit, new-found scientific power will become a devastating Frankenstein monster that will bring to ashes his earthly life."[13] William Alston advises that an account of how the Holy Spirit facilitates the inculcation of the virtues must ultimately steer between two extremes: on one hand there is what he calls human moral action as a result of "divine fiat" or, on the other hand, human moral action naively regarded as the result of human effort alone. Alston notes that while Galatians 2:20 does speak of "Christ now in me and the old me having been crucified," Paul does not give up a sense of self, a level of human agency in the ongoing process of sanctification. Christian virtue ethics therefore willingly accepts the challenge of recognizing this balance and the interplay of these critical factors – a vigorous sense of the human self in moral action done in response to divine action.

A second critical aspect of Christian virtue theory holds that human beings attain levels of moral excellence relative to the expectations of specific communities. Our nature as social creatures is a basic presumption of the Christian virtue theory. Whether understood as the church universal or the local congregation, virtues are recognized as such within the normative milieu of a community. Moreover, the task of securing the good and flourishing life that is consistent with the will of God can never be accomplished apart from human community. As Joseph Kotva puts it, "relationships and corporate activity are also central to the human good."[14] Noteworthy within any community in which the virtues are celebrated are persons who are particularly prominent in embodying them. These moral exemplars, known sometimes in our colloquial vernacular as "paragons of virtue," provide a valuable role in providing identifiable "markers" as to the kind of moral behavior that is worthy of emulation.

Generally speaking, treatment of the work of the Holy Spirit by Baptist theologians in the recent past have been approached from the standpoint of doctrine, specifically pneumatology.¹⁵ But by no means have Baptist theologians and ethicists been hostile or indifferent to the notion of a Christian virtue ethic. It may be that many theologians simply feel that the connection between the Christian life and the Christian virtuous life is simply too obvious to warrant extended treatment. James McClendon, Jr., in his *Biography as Theology*, ¹⁶ clearly shows a preference for what he calls "character-in-community" ethics as opposed to a focus on decisions. Unfortunately, he does not provide an extended discussion to justify a theological basis for his preference.

But might not the use of virtue theory within the writings of Baptist writers be a bit more subtle? In the course of consulting the writings of Baptist voices on the work of the Holy Spirit, it became increasingly clear that three thinkers have expressed views in which the outlines of Christian virtue theory were apparent. My aim was to investigate the extent to which such writers employed the ideas, images, and concepts of Christian virtue ethics as they sought to explain how the Holy Spirit works in moral action. I was keen to discern to what extent Baptist writers have understood the confluence of human agency and the powerful work of the Holy Spirit in the believer's moral life as well as the extent to which community plays a critical role in formation of the virtues. My argument is that insofar as the writers – one from the 19th century and two from the 20th century – show these tendencies, their views seem to support the direction suggested by William Alston and Basil of Caesarea. While the choice of Wayland, Graham and Maston may seem a bit arbitrary, it can be defended on the grounds that all three represent varying levels of access to doctrinal discussions to which Baptist believers have been exposed in at least two historical periods. And, to the extent that their views have influenced a significant segment of Baptist believers, the critical assessment of their views should serve a valuable function.

The Work of the Holy Spirit in the Moral Theory of Francis Wayland (1796-1865)

Francis Wayland was an influential American moralist during the middle years of the 19th century as well an important Baptist educator and minister. After serving as president of Brown University from 1827 to 1855, he served as pastor of the First Baptist Church of Providence, Rhode Island, for five years. An early advocate of the temperance movement and eventually a strong anti-slavery proponent, he left a remarkable legacy of moral reform. Wayland Seminary, founded as a school for former slaves in 1867, was named in his honor.

Prior to assuming the office of the president at Brown, Wayland was assigned the task of offering courses in moral philosophy at the institution. Upon assuming those duties, he discovered that the text then in use was one by William Paley, perhaps the 18th century's most notable proponent of utilitarianism, with which he was in strong disagreement. Wayland's objections to utilitarianism soon found their way into lectures, which in turn were eventually published in 1835 under the title, *Elements of Moral Science*.

In his objections to utilitarianism as a basis for the moral life, Wayland affirmed that the pursuit of virtue was more in harmony with the very nature of human beings, particularly insofar as he understood humans to be creatures of God. "Man is created," he wrote, "with moral and intellectual powers, capable of progressive improvement. Hence if he uses his faculties as he ought, he will progressively improve; that is, become more and more capable of virtue."[17] Deeply imbedded within our nature is our tendency toward habituation; for Wayland, we are literally creatures of habit. It is within this rather natural tendency within human nature that Wayland sees a way in which to conceive of divine-human relationships. Listen to this opening to the chapter on the Cultivation of a Devotional Spirit: "From what has already been said, it will be seen that the relation which we sustain to God imposes upon us the obligation of maintaining such an habitual temper towards him as shall continually incite us to do whatever will please him."[18] And indeed, as virtue theory asserts, the more one becomes habituated in an act, the greater facility one experiences in executing it. Wayland affirms this dynamic in no uncertain terms: "The repetition of a virtuous act," he asserts, "produces a tendency to continued repetition; the force of opposing motives is lessened; the power of the will over passion is more decided; and the act is accomplished with less moral effort."[19]

There is within Francis Wayland a clear sense that humans have been fashioned by God to exercise agency in moral development. But while Wayland clearly affirms a vigorous sense of human agency in moral improvement, he nevertheless is adamant that human agency must respond at some point to divine agency. For Wayland, human ability to respond to divine agency is facilitated through divinely implanted conscience within us and also with the love shown to Christ in response to Christ's love to us. It is by virtue of conscience and the love toward Christ that he accounts for our determination to keep divine law. "A twofold motive now impels us to keep it [divine law] with all our heart. In the first place, an enlightened and quickened conscience prompts us in all things to do the will of God: in the second place, the love of Christ constraineth us, because we thus judge, that we should not live unto ourselves, but unto him who dies for us and rose again."[20]

It is a vigorous Christology and acknowledgment of the work of the Holy Spirit that accounts in good measure for the moral action of believers. We see these views at length in Wayland's writings that were devoted to the pastoral context and the moral lives of congregants in churches. A volume of sermons, entitled *Sermons to the Churches* (1858) reveals very clearly these concerns. One notable idea comes through in the sermons and that is that ministry must be cultivated by "relying upon prayer and the Holy Ghost"[21] Yet, Wayland gives an account of the moral challenges that everyday believers confront as well as ordained clergy. The believer "has become a member of that body of which Christ is the head, and the vitality which animates the head animates the remotest extremity. Christ dwells in his heart by faith, a soul within his soul, inciting him to copy the example which he set before us when he was manifest in the flesh. Such is the mold into which the believer is cast."[22] The Christological impetus for moral action is further articulated when he confesses: "I open the New Testament, and there learn that the Son of God left the glory which he had with the Father to establish a spiritual kingdom in the hearts of men, to accomplish a perfect revolution in the moral character of our race, to transform the enemies of God into living and obedient children, to make every human soul a temple of the Holy Ghost."[23]

Christian virtue theory affirms the importance of certain practices in the life of believers, developed and nurtured within the context of community. There is with Wayland a rather conspicuous role for the practice of prayer as a means of positioning oneself to secure guidance in the pursuit of the virtuous life. The last sermon in this volume is a veritable paean to the practice of persistent prayer. With the assurance that God will answer prayer, the believer is admonished to constantly engage in this Christian practice.

> Just in proportion as we abide in the love of Christ, and his words abide in us, his Spirit dwells within us, teaching us how to pray, and what to pray for. The desire which the Spirit of God kindles in the soul, must be according to the will of God. The Spirit helpeth our infirmities, for we know not what we should pray for as we ought, but the Spirit maketh intercession for us. The desires of a soul pervaded by the indwelling of the Holy Spirit must be holy, and they can not but be gratified by a holy God. Our prayers are then nothing nothing else than the perfections of God reflected from the soul of the believer, and he must act in harmony with them, unless he deny himself. The desires of a holy soul in heaven must be gratified, for they are emanations of the divine will. The desires of a soul in hell must be ever unsatisfied, for they are, of necessity, perfectly at enmity with God. And so, between these two extremes, wherever prayer proceeds from a loving and obedient spirit it will be answered; and the abundance of the answer, will, according to

the condition in the text, be measured by our attainments in holiness. It is the effectual fervent prayer of a righteous man that availeth much.[24]

Francis Wayland's objections to utilitarianism and his focus on our nature as creatures of God led him inexorably to virtue theory as a means of exploring the ethical life of believers. A Christian virtue ethic emerges in his conviction that since we have been created with faculties and capabilities for progressive improvement, our responsibility to God impels us to act upon them.

The Work of the Holy Spirit and the Revivalist Piety of Billy Graham

Beginning with a revival in Los Angeles in 1949, Billy Graham (b. 1918) would, in the middle years of the 20th century, come to personify America's fascination with public revivalism. This period was fraught with much international tension and post World War II anxiety. As a burgeoning Cold Warrior, Graham framed his call for spiritual and moral regeneration as a means for America to prove itself more worthy than its arch enemy, the Soviet Union. Ever mindful of the need for a theological framework in which to couch his moral crusade, he affirmed a role for the Holy Spirit in the lives of believers. His book, *The Holy Spirit*, composed some thirty years after he came on the national scene, was a popular success in good measure because of his continuing popularity with mainstream evangelical circles.[25] Within the book, we may see a glimpse of the outlines of a Christian virtue theory as has been suggested above.

Interestingly enough, Graham's starting point in his analysis is very similar to the starting points of virtue theory in general. Virtue theory always juxtaposes a vision of human nature as it is and human nature as it could become. "We have two natures within us," he affirms, "both struggling for mastery."[26] As to the question, "Which one will dominate us?" Graham answers: "It depends on which one we feed.[27] If we feed our spiritual lives and allow the Holy Spirit to empower us, He will have rule over us. If we starve our spiritual natures and instead feed the old, sinful nature, the flesh will dominate."

Graham's use of language and imagery reveals a conception of human agency that is decidedly more limited than that of Francis Wayland. Within Graham's thought, while the self is charged with certain actions, those actions are in essence rather passive. We are advised to feed the spiritual nature in order to allow the Holy Spirit to empower us. Graham insists that we should become "filled with the Holy Spirit," and make ourselves "available"[28] to the Holy Spirit.

To be sure, with Graham the prominence is given to the Spirit in this overall work of regeneration. Not only has the Holy Spirit "come into my heart," but "He has given me new life – God's quality of eternal life. And He Himself is in me to break the old habits, to purify my motives, set my eyes on new goals, especially the goal of becoming like the Lord Jesus Christ (Rom. 8:29)."[29] While Graham does acknowledge that "as we progress in the Christian life there is a 'progressive sanctification,'"[30] he is no advocate of "works righteousness" and takes a rather dismal view with respect to the capabilities of the moral self. This self, steeped in selfishness, is incapable of any morally laudatory works. "We try to educate self, to train and discipline. We pass laws to compel it to behave. But Paul said that the flesh has a mind of its own and that 'the natural mind' is not subject to the law of God. The moment we realize this and yield to the dictates of the Holy Spirit in our lives, greater victory, greater spiritual maturity, greater love, joy, peace and other fruits will manifest themselves."[31] Later on, Graham will explicitly say that "If we as Christians try to make ourselves better or good or even acceptable to God by some human effort, we will fail. Everything we have and are and do comes through the Holy Spirit. The Holy Spirit has come to dwell in us, and God does his works in us by the Holy Spirit. What we have to do is yield ourselves to the Spirit of God so that He may empower us to put off the old and put on the new."[32]

And yet, as if implicitly acknowledging the importance of human agency as one moves toward a greater level of spiritual and moral maturity, Graham does make an allusion to human agency and a quickened will in the awakening process. Ultimately we must evidence "a renewed commitment on our part to seek and do the will of God."[33] Graham writes: "We can be convicted of sin – we can pray and confess our sin – we can repent – but the real test is our willingness to obey. It is no accident that true revival is always accompanied by a new hunger for righteousness. A life touched by the Holy Spirit will tolerate sin no longer."[34]

Moreover, despite the extensive use of passive language in his analysis of the self, one does see a faint glimmer of human agency at some point in the encounter with the Holy Spirit. For Graham, the process of feeding the better part of our nature begins with the awareness that one is confronting sin, and for him this is a salutary development; it is proof "that the Holy Spirit has come into your life, illuminating the darkness of sin, sensitizing your conscience to sin, awakening in you a new desire to be clean and free from sin before God."[35] Prior to the Holy Spirit's coming into a person's life, such a person would not have even been aware of the problematic nature of moral quandaries. In Graham's language, "those old temptations were there strongly before, but they didn't appear evil to you then."[36] Thus the Holy Spirit begins its work by enlarging the moral vision of the person, providing awareness or consciousness that some acts are moral and others are not.

Finally, there are moral exemplars within the community of believers whose behavior can be referenced as manifestations of the faithful life. In doing so, they clearly demonstrate that a recognizable level of agency is ultimately required – and expected – among the faithful. One such exemplar is evoked by Graham in the following way:

> Over 100 years ago, two young men were talking in Ireland. One said, "The world has yet to see what God will do with a man fully consecrated to him. The other man meditated on that thought for weeks. It so gripped him that one day he exclaimed, "By the Holy Spirit in me I'll be that man." Historians now say that he touched two continents for Christ. His name was Dwight L. Moody.[37]

Perhaps we should not be too surprised that Graham would extol another revivalist preacher as an exemplar of what happens when quickened consciousness responds to the Holy Spirit. My concern is not with the identification of the exemplar but rather with the fact that even within Graham's analysis in which the Holy Spirit has decided prominence, an expected role for human agency is nevertheless expected.

The Work of the Holy Spirit in the Thought of T. B. Maston

Over the course of at least four decades, Thomas Buford Maston forged an admirable career as professor of theology at New Orleans Baptist Seminary and as a popular lecturer to countless Baptist congregations. In his written work, he sought to forge a creative link between his work as a practicing theologian and that of a pastoral advisor to his readers. Many readers, students as well as laypeople, were deeply influenced by his classic little volume, *Why Live the Christian Life*, originally published in 1974.[38] As a practicing Christian ethicist, he was keenly aware of the challenges that believers faced as they sought higher levels of spiritual and moral maturity. The *Conscience of a Christian* (1971) dealt with issues as varied as family planning and race relations. The special problems young people faced in their moral development were addressed in *Right or Wrong* (1955).

In many respects, Maston resembles Francis Wayland in his general approach to the role of the Holy Spirit in the moral lives of believers. Like Wayland, Maston presumes that the capacity for conscience is a gift of divine origin. "Man has a sense of oughtness in life. He innately feels that there is such a thing as right and wrong."[39] However, for Maston the "content of the rightness and wrongness is not innate. It is quite possible for one to follow one's conscience and yet be morally wrong, as was Paul when he persecuted Christians. Thus conscience "is not inerrant or infallible."[40] Therefore, conscience needs to be gradually informed by influences and factors external to the person. "The content of what we term conscience is determined for each man by his total moral experience: by the decisions he has made in the past, by his family background, his community relations, and other influences that have touched his life."[41] Within community is the resource of "the aid we can receive from others, particularly those who are older, more experienced, or morally and spiritually more mature."[42]

Maston is sensitive not only to the environmental context in which moral formation takes place but also the developmental aspects in the process of moral formation. For him, the process begins at the most elemental level, that of instinct, followed by the level of custom. The third level, which he calls the "conscience level," evidently connotes a burgeoning level of autonomy in the individual. Such persons are "those who have thought through to clear-cut personal convictions concerning what is right and wrong in their lives."[43] Yet, even this level begs for a greater level of fulfillment, that level being what he simply calls the "Christian level." And it is at this point that Maston seems to incorporate the vision of virtue ethics that notes the distinction between our nature as it is and our nature as it might become. "Only when man lives," he asserts, "on the Christian level does he become most completely man, realizing in himself the divinely ordained potential for his life."[44]

Unlike Billy Graham, T. B. Maston is not as fearful of the internal resources for progressive improvement that are within us. Among what he calls the "three sources of light," that is, resources for guidance in ethical matters, is:

> the light from within ourselves. God has created us with certain innate or inborn powers. "This means that even in the maturing process, God expects us to use every inner resource we have to determine for ourselves what is right and wrong. He is not going to reveal, in some miraculous way, his will to us without our cooperation.[45]

Echoing as well a contention of Christian virtue ethics that our chief good is doing the will of God, Maston affirms that our determinants for what is right and good must be inherent in the will of God. "Our conclusion is that the right is not necessarily what man's reason dictates but what God commands. It is not what man intuits but what the divine voice says. It is not what society sanctions but what the sovereign God approves."[46] Thus "the Christian should make his decision primarily on the basis of what he considers to be the will of God."[47] God's will is "not arbitrary. It is in accord with our natures and in harmony with the nature of the society God wills for the world."[48] Maston's elaboration on how he understands the "will of God" seems to suggest that he is concerned that ethical method should comport with our nature as human beings. Since virtue theory is concerned with our being and the developmental steps needed to reach our better nature, Maston's understanding of how God's will comports with this hope seems rather significant. For him, aside from the fact that it is "all-inclusive," meaning that it covers all of the aspects of human life, it is "a continuing experience." Such a hope is clearly within the parameters of moral development as projected by Christian virtue theory. He goes on to say:

> Frequently, one decision is preparatory to another. If we are responsive to the leadership of the Lord, we shall have a deepening understanding of his will. This, when properly understood, will tend to give us a constant sense of tentativeness, of expectancy, of open-mindedness.[49]

Now, having affirmed that the believer must seek the will of God as a means of determining the normative basis for action, Maston assures us that the Bible and the assistance of the Holy Spirit are available. "The Bible is," he affirms, "the main tangible, objective source for a knowledge of the will of God."[50] How does the Holy Spirit factor in encountering and understanding the Bible? Apparently, for Matson, the Holy Spirit aids in one's ability to interpret Scripture. "The Holy Spirit is the main subjective source for such a knowledge. Both the Scriptures and the guidance of the Holy Spirit are needed in man's (*sic*) search for an authoritative word from the Lord." Thus, "to be guided by the Spirit is to be led into a knowledge of the will of God as revealed in the Scriptures and climaxed in Christ."[51]

For T. B. Maston, the availability of the resources of the Bible and that of the Holy Spirit presumes that there will be a human response. He affirms that "…if we are willing to do his will and start to move in the direction that we have interpreted to be the will of God, that the Lord will not permit us to go far astray. Even in the process of interpreting his will, we should keep our minds and hearts open for additional light, our faces set toward the open road of God's fuller revelation."[52] It is this movement in "the direction that we have interpreted to be the will of God" that is so consistent with the regimen that is the pursuit of virtue. Echoing the evocation of prayer in a fashion similar to Francis Wayland, Maston affirms this Christian practice as a necessary corollary in our attempts to respond faithfully to God's will. As we attempt to discern God's will through the aid of the Bible and Holy Spirit "we should do so in the spirit of prayer."[53]

Conclusion

Faithful response to God's gift of sanctification constitutes in a very real sense the essence of the Christian ethical life. As believers, we have always affirmed that the Holy Spirit works within us as we attempt to respond to the will of God. In this respect, the focus on becoming the kinds of persons whose lives are consistent with a response to God's gracious acts constitutes the essence of the virtuous life.

This paper has tested a thesis that inquiry into how the Holy Spirit works in the moral life of the believer might be fruitfully pursued through the framework of Christian virtue theory. While Baptist scholars have not been widely recognized as receptive to virtue theory, it has been suggested that the writings of at least three Baptist thinkers seem to show the board outlines and implicit use of concepts and problems that are resident within the theory. The fact that Wayland, Graham and Maston represent three rather distinct styles and sensibilities within Baptist history would seem to corroborate a notion that virtue theory approaches just might be particularly useful as we seek to understand with great clarity our rich theological and ethical heritage. For example, Baptist fidelity to the theologically and ethically grounded norm of "soul liberty," attributed to Francis Wayland, would seem to constitute a rather natural context in which to explore the feasibility of Christian virtue ethics within a Baptist sensibility. Inherent within that concept is an expectation of a rigorous sense of self-agency and self-scrutiny that is so consistent with the focus on the morally maturing person – one of the great concerns of Christian virtue ethics. My hope is that those of us who do our theological reflection within the community known as Baptist believers will continue to "think on these things."

CHAPTER 13
FROM ANTIOCH TO SANTIAGO BY WAY OF MARS HILL:
ACTS 11:19-26; ACTS 13:13-16, 42-44; ACTS 17:16-21

William M. Tillman, Jr.

Introduction

My father had several sayings. One of these was, "Those people act like they get up in a new world everyday!" His intent was to take note of people who apparently were sporadic, did not seem to know where they were, wandered literally and in their thinking, mostly useless in his given work context. When they came in it was like two good workers left.

Maybe you have had some of the same experiences. We have to be careful for we can become cynics with this kind of thing. After all, we do get up in a new world every day. We should begin each day with a prayer of gratitude to God for letting us be able to see and feel this day, unlike in many ways, any of the other days that have come through time. Each new sunrise, each new sunset, is different from the others – and on and on.

I know too many Baptists who utilize the former approach, though more Rip Van Winkle like than being appreciative of the creation unfolding before our eyes. Too many Baptists I know are simply puzzled and befuddled by our current context of trying to do and be the church. Some of the puzzlement, in my estimation, stems from the lack of being able to read the culture in which we find ourselves. They have not kept up with things going on around them, even recognizing what they have inherited, that which we call Baptist theology, ethics, and ecclesiology.

Even still, there is a nagging sense we should be doing something, but just what? Lots of spoken and unspoken comments are, "Well this is a new world; not much in our repertoire seems to be working." Thrown into this mix are those who keep telling us, "Be a New Testament church." I have to ask, "Which one?" We pick through a church's personality, match its admirable traits with our selective reading about churches in the New Testament, and conclude we are that. Thus, we sacramentalize everything that we say and do, the style of worship, those whom we hire to lead us, those whom we admit to the fellowship, formally and informally. Enough centuries of such, even among Baptists, and some of us act as if we are the epitome of "the New Testament Church." But, again, which one?

We have to make distinctions here. There was the Syrian Antioch church (Acts 11) and the Antioch of Pisidia (Acts 13). Each and both reflected a strong Christological centering, though. In Antioch of Syria followers of Christ were first called Christians; in Antioch of Pisidia, Luke related Paul preached in this manner: "You Israelites, and others who fear God, listen" (Acts 13:16). Paul built upon Hebrew history for his exposition and moved quickly from Abraham, Moses and David to Jesus Christ. We need to recognize that Paul began with those people in the cultural and theological context they already had.

I propose that in the millennia since Paul too much attention has been given to these Antioch contexts and styles, with not nearly enough attention given to Paul's approach in Athens. We need to include for our sense of doing church the matter of Paul's visit to Athens and particularly the time highlighted by Luke, Paul's conversation around and on the Aeropagus, Mar's Hill (Acts 17).[1]

Contemporary preachers I know love to declare about this occasion that Paul really told off the Athenian philosophers, and yes theologians, that day. Those preacher declarations are delivered, of course, using the current replication of the Antioch churches – lots of language that apparently only the real believers can understand or everyone assumes is being understood. What gets missed, and what I want to emphasize is that, indeed, Paul's communication – style of preaching, teaching, and evangelism – at Mars Hill was not the same approach he used in the churches in the two Antiochs.

What follows is my attempt at unpacking the ramifications of Paul's conversation, dialogue, sermon and lessons taught at Mars Hill. I do have the presentation generally outlined around the questions of What was Paul's message? Why was Paul's message, delivered that way, important? and How do we emulate Paul's style of proclamation? I will add quickly, however, that exploring something like this topic has to be perceived as an organic, vitality holding concept and that certainly as Paul was involved in this event on Mars Hill, he understood the conversation was anything but a static, formulaic, automaton produced experience. Thus, the what, why, and how questions will find a necessary blending along the way.[2]

What Was Paul's Message?

Whether he was at one of the Antiochs or at the Areopagus, Paul's central message was about Jesus the Christ. For the purposes of this paper and to fit with the Proclamation theme of our BWA meeting this time, I have chosen to use the word *kerygma* instead of *evangelion*. The reason is *evangelion* has been too closely linked to being content only, whereas *kerygma* becomes a style of delivery as well, most usually associated with the act of preaching; thus, a more dynamic connection than that of an objectified content.

A classical definition of kerygma is too rigid for my purposes here. My preference is to define kerygma by recognizing the effects, the impact, the application, emitting from the particular proclamation. In this approach, I have found Howard Thurman's statement particularly helpful as Thurman referenced not Christianity but the religion of Jesus: "Wherever his spirit appears, the oppressed gather fresh courage; for he announced the good news that fear, hypocrisy, and hatred, the three hounds of hell that track the trail of the disinherited, need have no dominion over them."[3]

Paul used, from my vantage point, by his time Aristotle's centuries old methodology of rhetoric to provide the what, the content, the message, he had for the Athenians. One would have to say this content was no different in quality, maybe in quantity, than his conversation in the Antiochs. His kerygma, proclamation style, was different, though. This content/style combination is important for any generation, though. The *logos*, or message for Aristotle, the words used, is important. Edward Farley opined some years ago that one of the main ways for the church and its people to get off track is to lose a sense of how to state, much more what is the "meaning and power" of its Master Narrative – the Gospel.[4]

We can re-learn the lessons from Paul's delivery at Mars Hill. Evidence abounds that Paul's cultural context, what can be called a pre-modern one, in basic principles is very much like our own twenty-first century global culture – a mix of all kinds of cultural dynamics. The Epicureans and Stoics mentioned in the passage are still with us. The Cynics who were surely there at Mars Hill are certainly with us. Notice Paul connected with those people from a different starting place than with those in the cities Antioch.

Harry Emerson Fosdick maintained many years ago that Paul addressed matters that these philosophers, philosophers of any age, including our own, were attempting to understand. Fosdick considered that Paul pressed them to find resolution from realms of their personalities which they had not yet

CHAPTER 13

researched. "(Paul) was not thinking of any far-off deity .... He was thinking of the inner deeps of personal religion, where faith gives life meaning and purpose, where character is unified and organized, integrated and directed, so that we find things worth living for an adequate resource to live by."[5]

Is it possible these philosophers worked on a one dimensional level, as do people with whom we live in the same stream of time? We must recognize Paul's delivery, his style, his content, his kerygma, was multidimensional.

There was a beginning place however, to get to this multidimensionality. John Claypool noted that the Gospel story must begin "with an image of primal joy and the assertion that Creation was at bottom an act of generosity, not an act of selfishness. The fear that we humans ultimately have to do with an exploitive Reality simply is not true."[6]

Thus, there is where Paul began, with Creation, a connection, an association those Greeks who were the successors to Aristotle, a Renaissance person before the Renaissance, could understand. Paul brought those somewhat univocal, linear thinkers to their own time by expanding upon a cultural paradigm. For us, we should recognize the points of adaptation of the kerygma both to provide opportunity to expand but also to be able to recognize the points of resistance to the expansion.[7]

In this Mars Hill narrative, we can recognize also that which Claypool noted in his Beecher Lectures that preaching is an event. Moreover, authentic preaching catches up all the faculties of the human beings involved in the process – their minds and bodies and emotions as well as their tongues and ears. Thus it can rightly be called an event, something that happens so holistically that it leaves the kind of impact on one that accompanies participation in any sort of decisive happening.[8]

Too much of our preaching, teaching, and evangelism these days miss such holistic application. Rules-laden religion perpetuates because of insecurity and fear. An Age of Enlightenment, a direct successor to the Hellinistic approach to life, dwells on either-or, this or that, reductionist thinking.[9]

The Mars Hill approach is a less secure starting place for many of us, but we need to figure out how we can move in this global culture we have now, taking our message into the free market place of ideas and offer the Gospel on its own merits proclaiming it as clearly and cleanly as we can.

Unfortunately, what is showing up is that our traditional, church jargon is not making it across the cultural divide. At least that is the case in the United States, and can be reflective of many places where American missiological styles have and are being used. Adapting to starting where other people are in their understanding of what spirituality is, their search for significance and meaning, their need for community and relationship, there was Paul's methodology. Note that whether in one of the Antiochs or in Athens at Mars Hill, wherever he started, Paul always got to Jesus, and not just his death, burial and resurrection, which those in my Baptist church history emphasized, but a living Jesus who could pick up wherever Paul's audiences might be able eventually to get to Jesus, the source of Good News, the Gospel.

Why Was Paul's Message, Delivered That Way, Important?

Paul understood that which drives delivery of the Gospel, kerygma, essentially is God's redemptive purposes toward human beings and the expectations of God that redeemed human beings communicate these purposes to other human beings. As well, the kerygma that redeemed humans communicate will have a degree of abstract facets but also personal, specific facets. There are values all through those two sentences, and they are values that need to be focused upon and developed. At the least, I think we can maintain that whatever values we live by, truly live by, do shape our attitudinal selves, which in turn shape our actions. For Paul, the Good News was really good news for all of what we are and what we are becoming.

I have known too many Baptists who have a knack for turning the Good News into Bad News. Usually such persons have not investigated the context in which they find themselves and figured out or asked, "What is good news for the people to whom we relate the Gospel?" The answers we are able to find can begin the form of our kerygma for those particular ones. A starting place can be, "What would be considered 'good news' for each of us here and now, today?"[10]

For the Athenians at Mars Hill, we cannot forget they perceived life to have been reduced to that of reflecting on "the good old days." That day's dialogue took place a long stone's throw from the Acropolis, with remnants of the glory days still apparent. Also, this once majestic edifice, the center of the Greeks' politics and theology, reflected the mutilations of the Persian invasions. By this point, they had been taken over by the parasitic Roman Empire.

Barely beneath the surface for the Areopagus Athenians was almost certainly a deep sense of despair over what might have been. I do not have a difficult time imagining them using their philosophical arguments on each other as a defense mechanism so as not to have to think about why they were in the context in which they found themselves. In some ways they were struggling with some of the same ultimate questions of life we find in Job. Is not this struggle endemic to humanity? Perhaps the "how we should live life" is being asked, but the "why should we live life any particular way" question is embedded in the discussion that the Athenians initiated with Paul. Those people were looking for values by which to think and act. Again, Paul's beginning with Creation and the Creator is an example for us. Paul put the "Ground of all Being" in front of the Athenians, certainly; but, at least in retrospect, we should recognize he presented to the philosophers the "Ground of all Doing" as well. In short, the values by which to live life are found incarnated in the God Paul described to them. Those values can be reviewed by us as we read Acts 17. Certainly, we can begin to make associations into the Pauline literature to see those values delineated more specifically. At the least, those values form what we would call the kerygma not only for individual evaluation and assimilation but also for a communal, congregational, perspective.

In an abbreviated way, Paul introduced the Athenians to Christ-centered moral discernment. Only a few of those Areopagus types determined that Jesus Christ was the reference point of life for which they had been searching. They allowed their worldview to change.

We have no record that anything like a congregation ever generated in Athens. However, those few did recognize another of Aristotle's points of rhetoric in Paul, that of pathos – the ability of the speaker, communicator, proclaimer to establish rapport with an audience. That rapport happens as those few recognized Paul was not simply spinning tales, talking about the next, new faddish thing, as their colleagues did day by day. Rather, Paul exhibited, incarnated, the values to which he pointed. Questions for all of us who are proclaimers are, "What are the effects of our own preaching upon ourselves? Is there transformation happening in me?" We must stay attuned to whether or not the kerygma is embedding deeply in our own lives. Any number of combinations may occur, but we should be able to observe that what we preach is to be what we practice and the more we practice the Gospel, the more the Gospel revitalizes what and how we preach. In short, we should more and more become the reflection of the Gospel.

This becoming more the reflection of the Gospel prods us toward informing our proclamation so as to deal with the necessary value conflicts people face. The objective of moving a congregation toward being a community of moral discernment provides some of the rationale as to why Paul delivered his message as he did. At least one caution must be raised in these regards, however, for the proclaimer. David J. Schlafer and Timothy F. Sedgwick in *Preaching What We Practice: Proclamation and Moral Discernment* advise:

> ... preaching moral discernment requires a community of moral discernment. Sermons are too short and too infrequent to bear the full

weight of moral discernment, just as they cannot bear all the weight of providing comfort in digress, or of teaching Scripture and the story of faith. Preaching moral discernment should raise questions and engage individuals in what are the distinctive and compelling claims about our lives as faithful Christians, but it cannot stop there. Preaching discernment must continue in the formation of a community of discernment.[11]

One danger is the preacher may attempt to carry too much of the weight toward congregational moral discernment. This temptation to become the center of the efforts can overtake the preacher. Too many congregations have been deflected on their progress toward communal moral discernment because their preacher operates from a self-centered perspective.

So, we must soberly evaluate how we deliver the Gospel. The Gospel cannot be a means to build our own egos. John Claypool makes the case that the kerygma is for the people; and, the preacher's ego is to be laid aside.[12] A most interesting, and in this writer's estimation, seminal study at Baylor University sets some of the contours of life about which especially preaching ministers must be aware. The emphasis is self evident in its title, as described in a Baylor University release, "Narcissism Impairs Ethical Judgment Even Among the Highly Religious, Baylor Study Finds."[13]

This potential toward narcissism should cause us to pay more attention to spiritual formation being a part of our kerygma, what we say and what we assimilate, for we proclaim out of who we are. This formation likely does not occur in one dramatic, quick event, rather it begins to unfold proportionately to each individual.[14]

How Do We Emulate Paul's Style of Proclamation?

We, as disciples of Jesus Christ, are charged with proclaiming, giving kergyma wherever and whenever we can. Diligent, deliberate attention is needed toward how we may proclaim with the best and most impact.

"Give Attention to the Art and Craft of Preaching," Stanley Hauerwas in his *A Cross Shattered Church: Reclaiming the Theological Heart of Preaching*, a book of his sermons, which he describes as some of his best theological work, contends, "... I am convinced that the recovery of the sermon as the context for theological reflection is crucial if Christians are to negotiate the world in which we find ourselves."[15] We need renewed energy and discipline given to the art and craft of preaching. We are at a point where recovering the place of preaching in the life of the church may be more true to reality than revitalizing our preaching. Good and great preaching can be seen as the beginning point, especially in our global context, for what is the gathering point for the rest of the ideals to be lived out.

That is, the Gospel is both personal and social in application. Beginning with kerygma, we should naturally see develop *koinonia, didache* and *diakonia*.[16] However, the insightful proclaimer should recognize each of these facets of the Gospel applied present a beginning point to get to the other dynamics. Diakonia, ministry, extended in the name of Christ may be, for example, exactly the touch point for those looking for fellowship and a group for mutual support and care.

We cannot forget Paul was an extraordinarily well educated person of his time. No doubt he had learned from Gamaliel, as he had many other things of Jewish tradition and theology, the rabbinic style of teaching. He had acquired the skills of persuasive rhetoric along the way, likely reaping some of the benefits of being a Roman citizen and educational opportunities open to such. Between the Antiochs and Mars Hill and beyond he apparently was in a constant mode of refining and honing his preaching skills.

Can we do anything less? My first suggestion is that one becomes as educated as possible in the disciplines I call theological education. A constant self-reminder is that each of us cannot simply emulate an admired preacher. Each of us must find and build upon the natural gifts and skills we bring to the events of proclaiming, and combine those with the best of what we can learn from others.

What Is Going On in the World?

If we do wake up in what amounts to a new world everyday, how do we adapt to such a phenomenon? The style attributed to Karl Barth is not a bad one to adopt, that is, face life with the Bible in one hand and the newspaper in the other. I am concerned with the North American penchant toward not being informed by local, state, regional, national, and global news.

In their own way the Athenians were keeping up with one segment of news and cultural events. Some of the genius that Paul brought to the setting was his experience, for that time, of widespread travels. He had learned to adapt quickly to the place where he found himself. I have watched too many former students move from the school setting to a church setting and find difficulty with the congregation early on, mainly because the graduate has not learned ahead the sub-cultural setting into which he or she has moved. In a manner that can only be called provincial, the former-student-turned-church-staff-person attempts to bring the congregation to his or her presuppositions of how the meeting schedule should be, details of the worship order, what style of worship should be followed, or place of the newly hired person in the setting. Little effort or energy is expended toward building authenticity and rapport with the congregation.[17]

We have joined into an exclusivistic, even xenophobic, or fear of the different, enterprise. One result is being out of touch with the cultural context in which we typically move, all the way from local to global. One result is that as any system, organization, institution – the church, for instance – becomes an end in itself. Such entities will begin to erode, fragment, and ultimately hardly resemble its originators' visions.

Good preaching builds upon the context in which one finds oneself. According to James Childs: "... all good preaching, like all good theology, is contextual. It frames the Word of God in terms of the human situation it addresses and it frames the human situation in terms of how it is addressed by the Word of God."[18]

Be Willing to Call into Question Prevailing Cultural Paradigms

Good proclamation also is going to put in place a tension between where the constituencies are and where the message content is pointing. From Walter Brueggemann:

> Preaching is foolish, dangerous, and exposing, because what must be said in proclamation constitutes a daring alternative to the ideological passions that may be present in the congregation, to the powers that conduct surveillance, either inside or outside the congregation, and to the preacher's own sense of self. The occasion of preaching is risky on all counts, inherently risky because something other happens in preaching besides the echo of our preferred ideologies, our studied interest, or our personal inadequacies.

Further from Brueggemann:

> Our circumstance permits and requires the preacher to do something we have not been permitted or required to do before. Ours is an awesome opportunity: to see whether (the) text, with all of our interpretive inclinations, can voice and offer reality in a redescribed way that is credible and evocative of a new humanness, rooted in holiness and practiced in neighborliness.[19]

Even with ironically a somewhat, lowest, common denominator beginning place, Creation, Paul poked at the Athenians' way of thinking about life. With his attention to Creation he still asked the Athenians to re-imagine life, this world, and humanity's part in renewing Creation. Thus, Paul pushed beyond their usual ways of reflection, gave them some common symbols but with new content toward any of them picking up on the Gospel. The message, as Daniel C. Maguire said was "... God is trying to 'reign,' to get us to re-imagine everything, to make everything 'new.' God's purpose is to try to rescue the potential and beauty of this miracle of an earth from the mess we are bent on making of it."[20]

I do not think it too far a stretch that Paul attempted to address the Athenians style of thinking not only from the perspective of being the people who refined geometry, but also those who produced timeless sculpture and theater, not only deductive, but inductive perspectives; not only the immanent, but the transcendent matters of life. Paul used all these venues of thinking to draw upon and help reform the Greeks' imaginations.

Last But Not Least: Proclaim Scripture through the Spirit

Our kerygma must be more than a well stated sociological treatise, more than conjectural, psychological counseling, and reflect more than a superficial biblical hermeneutic. Even as we proclaim to draw others to Christ, we should be drawing closer to Christ ourselves, becoming yet more mature disciples. This dynamic has been described as "... the Spirit-empowered effort on the part of the disciples of Jesus Christ to discern and to practice a way of life that conforms to the will of God and advances the kingdom of God."[21]

A practice offered by John S. McClure comes this way:

> Implicitly or explicitly, each Sunday morning, preachers transport themselves and their hearers (back?) to this (original) scene. Even though we know that the words on the page barely scratch the surface of it, in an act of memory we gather at this scene for some event, encounter, or manifestation signaled in the biblical words. We hesitate there, knowing that others past and present have been and are at that same imaginary scene, in a similar situation of desire and deferred fulfillment. Movement to this (original) scene is somehow crucial to our memory—and our negotiation of tradition.[22]

Such practice calls for understanding the power of narrative, metaphor, and language that clarifies rather than stupefies. Sider and King enunciate:

> Much contemporary preaching is weak because it is opaque, when what it most desperately needs is to be transparent—to the transcendent, the sacred, the divine. Other ways of putting it might be that much

preaching remains mired in the immanent, this worldly, purely historical or profane dimension of existence.[23]

Transparent preaching should draw attention to beliefs or facts that people hold, convictions or principles by which they live, but also call for a transformation of one's worldview. Paul Heibert, a missiologist, contended in his last book:

It is becoming increasingly clear ... that transforming explicit beliefs is not enough to plant churches that are faithful to the gospel. People often say the same words but mean different things. Underlying explicit beliefs is a deeper level of culture that shapes the categories and logic with which people think and the way they view reality .... Conversion to Christ must encompass all three levels: behavior, beliefs, and the worldview that underlies these. Christians should live differently because they are Christians .... It is important, therefore, to disciple them (people) into Christian maturity. This includes a transformation not only in the way people think and behave but also in their worldviews.[24]

Indeed, we are charged with giving a message that can transform each of us toward recognizing a new World, in fact, a new way to look at and relate to all things, all people, and especially to God. Ah, the promise of hope, a way to see through what otherwise can be a dreariness and drag upon our existence, persona, our very souls.

Conclusion

Let us pray that when we lay our heads down this evening we are recognizing in some ways the end of the world as we know it; and we do wake up in a new world the next day; let us pray that we wake up with a sense of hope and adventure spawned by the Spirit of God to try to engage this new world leaning into the future, with the wisdom of the past, to meet God wherever we find ourselves. Amen.

CHAPTER 14
GROWTH IN GRACE AS A CONTROL BELIEF FOR THE PEOPLE OF GOD

Rod Benson

This paper examines the need for ethical control beliefs for theological method, outlines options suggested by Stanley Grenz and Brian Harris, and commends "growth in grace" (2 Peter 3:18) as a potential control belief or "norming norm" for an ethically fortified theological method.

Since the theme for the Baptist World Alliance in 2013 is "In step with the Spirit: Liberation," and I am about to commence work on a large project on theological method and Christian ethics, it seemed helpful to critically consider the suggestion of my Australian colleague, Rev Dr Brian Harris, that the liberating function of the good news of Jesus Christ might function as a control belief for theological method. On January 1 this year, I made the mistake of posting some thoughts about theological method on my blog, and the chair of the BWA Commission on Christian Ethics happened to read the piece and invited me to say some more. And here we are.

Why We Need Theological Method

With few exceptions, attending to theological method does not appear to be a key concern of professional theologians committed to upholding the four essential qualities of evangelical Christian communities articulated by David Bebbington, namely a particular view of Scripture, crucicentrism, conversionism and activism.[1] Yet throughout church history, "the kinds of theology most faithful to Scripture have been those that variously combined and balanced the demands of the academy with those of the church."[2] This remains true today. We need both rigorous intellectual discipline and vibrant spiritual expression if the church is to remain true to its mission in the world and be effective in accomplishing it.

Yet as a 1987 study by Lewis Mudge and James Polding observed:

> if a typical congregation of Christian people is simply told to go and 'do theology,' what will come out will be a mishmash of favorite scripture

verses quoted out of context, superstitions, fragments of civil religion, vague memories of poorly taught Sunday-school lessons of long ago, and the like.[3]

Some scholars dismiss theological method as dangerous or at best irrelevant. Karl Barth, for example, reacting against the late nineteenth and early twentieth century liberal enthusiasm for theological method, argued that "the persuasiveness of theology is seen in the display of its content rather than its methodological prowess before the content is ever reached."[4] Similarly, and more recently, Dan R. Stiver likens theological method to "one of those cases where a foreign plant is imported to provide ground cover and ends up being a persistent weed that cannot be eradicated."[5] For Stiver, theological method is central to the assumptions of modernity. He argues instead for "doing theology rather than talking about how to do it."[6] He then outlines a framework for doing theology based on a synthesis of postliberal (Yale School) theology and an appeal to the hermeneutical theories of Gadamer and Ricoeur. In other words, he seems to embrace a particular theological method while arguing that such a method is unimportant for the task of theologizing. However, Stiver acknowledges that he retains an interest in theological method as a "clarifying tool rather than a foundation or proof."[7]

If theology is often considered to be an academic discipline, it is also arguably a wider activity encompassing various forms of discourse and the visual and performing arts.[8] Theology (or "theologizing") is also a process of practical moral discernment for which theological method provides structure and clarity. In their book, *The Art of Theological Reflection*, Patricia O'Connell Killen and John de Beer suggest that

> we miss much that the [Christian] tradition offers to enrich our lives and much of the revelatory power of our lived experience when we keep our theological reflection solely at the spontaneous level. We are invited as Christians to a disciplined approach to bringing our religious heritage into our reflection on life experience.[9]

Now theological reflection is not synonymous with theological method. I regard theological reflection as one aspect of the broader agenda of theological method. Such reflection has three primary tasks:

1. induction and nurturing of members: informing the processes that enable the formation of Christian character;
2. building and sustaining corporate identity: assisting the growth and maintenance of the community of faith (including determining

where the normative boundary of faithful practice might lie, and thus the distinctiveness of the collective identity of Christians);

3. communicating the faith to a wider culture: enabling the faith community to relate its communal identity to the surrounding culture, and communicating that faith to the wider world.[10]

This indicates the significant pastoral function and public dimension of theology couched as "a body of knowledge designed to articulate the nature of God in order that people might lead godly lives."[11] Moreover, as Ellen Charry observes:

> Christian doctrines function pastorally when a theologian unearths the divine pedagogy in order to engage the reader or listener in considering that life with the triune God facilitates dignity and excellence.[12]

But that is not all. In addition to defining or explaining doctrinal orthodoxy within a particular tradition, and serving that faith community in pastorally sensitive ways, theology also informs public life with a view to public issues and the common good. As Brian D. Robinette notes, "Christian life ... entails two movements at once: ongoing spiritual formation with others in community, and a commitment to fostering reconciliation and justice in a world that desperately needs it."[13] For such an enterprise to bear godly fruit in personal, faith-community and public contexts, I argue that awareness of issues relating to theological method is essential.

Which Method? Whose Vision?

Several important books exploring questions of theological method have been published since the turn of the century.[14] For the purposes of this paper, however, I will interact with a 2009 review article by Brian Harris, titled "Why method matters: Insights from the theological method of Stanley J. Grenz."[15]

Harris claims that evangelical Christians often view theological method as "the death of spiritual passion, and at best, a dangerous enterprise."[16] Similarly, Stanley J. Grenz and John R. Franke assert that while

> Theologians in mainline theological circles have been in need of a reminder that theology involves more than simply reflecting on method ... Evangelical theologians have ... given little attention to methodological concerns.[17]

Harris outlines how reflection on his personal situation as a young adult in South Africa led him to explore methodological issues and eventually led him to discover Grenz's distinctive evangelical theological methodology. He draws specifically on four of Grenz's books,[18] and suggests that Grenz's theological method has "the potential to genuinely revision evangelical theology." Most of Harris's article summarizes key elements of Grenz's methodology, and suggests some minor "revisioning" to address perceived weaknesses.

Grenz and Franke knew they were making a bold claim that would be contested when in 2001 they published the book titled *Beyond Foundationalism: Shaping Theology in a Postmodern Context*, seeking as it did a secure place for theologizing beyond the demise of foundationalism. They expressed optimism that their project would

> nurture an open and flexible theology that is in keeping with the local and contextual character of the discipline, that remains thoroughly and distinctly Christian, and that fosters a renewed listening to the voice of the Spirit speaking to the churches through the scriptures … [a] further realization of what Hans Frei referred to as a 'generous orthodoxy.[19]

Scripture as a Source for Theology

As an alternative to the Wesleyan Quadrilateral model, Grenz proposes a model whereby Scripture, tradition and culture function as "sources" for theology, with the Trinity, community and eschatology serving as "focal motifs." These sources are used in the same way in which Scripture, tradition, reason and experience are used in the so-called Wesleyan model to develop a cogent and coherent theology. The focal motifs facilitate the application of this theology to the "postmodern situation."[20]

As a Baptist and an evangelical, Grenz's first methodological commitment was to Scripture.[21] He views Scripture as theology's "norming norm,"[22] but modifies the conventional evangelical commitment to the Reformation catch-cry *sola scriptura* by transferring ultimate authority from the text of Scripture to the culture of the believing community. Thus, for Grenz, theology should be conceived as "reflection on the faith commitment of the believing community," since the community of faith is "the source for the symbols, stories, teachings and doctrines that form the cognitive framework for the worldview of the believing community."[23]

Grenz defends this apparent diminution of supreme biblical authority by suggesting that the Bible's status as the foundational text of the faith community guarantees its place of importance in the theological enterprise.[24] Harris notes that this seems a short step from relegating Scripture to the place of a non-authoritative source; and suggests that it is not self-evident that Scripture possesses enduring significance as a source for theology merely because it is viewed as "the repository of the original kerygma of the faith community."[25]

An important aspect of Grenz's revisioning of evangelical theology is his emphasis on the Holy Spirit as mediator of the meaning and impact of Scripture for the community of faith. Grenz endorses the Pietist conviction that "talk about the truth claims of the Bible was less important than the fact that 'truth claims' – that the Scriptures lay hold of the life of the reader and call that life into divine service."[26] Thus "Grenz shifts the subject-object locus, calling evangelicals to pay as much attention to the doctrine of illumination as they do to inspiration."[27] Critics argue that such an approach undermines the authority of Scripture by placing the locus of authority within the community of faith; D.A. Carson goes further, questioning whether Grenz's approach to Scripture can even be called evangelical.[28]

Tradition as a Source for Theology

Tradition (or what I call the historic resources of the church) is at times either valued or eschewed by evangelicals, largely on pragmatic grounds. Grenz outlines what I view as four persuasive reasons for regarding tradition as a useful source for theology:

1. past doctrinal statements and theological methods are instructive for the present theological quest and help avoid the pitfalls of the past;
2. traditions serve as a reference point for contemporary theological reflection and dialogue;
3. some doctrinal formulations have withstood the test of time; and
4. as a second order task, theology is undertaken by theologians who are themselves usually members of a faith community which spans the centuries.[29]

Grenz appears to leave unresolved the important problem of identifying valid criteria for testing the authoritative status of a theological tradition.

Culture as a Source for Theology

Harris suggests that Grenz uses the term "culture" in three ways – in calls for a "culture-sensitive theology"; as a "re-source" for theology; and as one of three conversation partners sourcing theology.[30] For Grenz, "the Spirit and community mediated interaction between culture and scripture enriches the understanding of scripture and unearths aspects of biblical truth that would otherwise be overlooked."[31] He uses the three focal motifs mentioned above (the Trinity, community, and eschatology) to structure, integrate and orient his theology (derived from the three sources of Scripture, tradition, and culture) in relation to postmodern culture. This is evident in his systematic theology, *Theology for the Community of God* (1994), and in some of his later works.

The use of these three motifs presents a methodological problem: how does one prevent one of the three "conversation partners" from speaking too loudly? Harris cites fellow theologian Thomas Oden who described the relative weight appropriate to sources in terms of a pyramid with Scripture at the base (occupying the largest – and, one might say, foundational – significance), followed by the patristics and others in chronological order, with modern theologians forming the apex (and therefore the smallest relative significance).[32] Harris also suggests that a more nuanced approach to that of Grenz "would acknowledge that while three sources are conversing, they have significantly different amounts of influence."[33] Grenz does not appear to have discussed this problem.

Theological Method and Control Beliefs

Harris observes that Grenz's tradition and culture, as sources for theology, serve as what John Macquarrie called "formative factors." He also notes Nicholas Wolterstorff's concept of "control beliefs" and views Grenz's notion of Scripture as theology's "norming norm" as such a belief.[34] Thus, for Grenz, Scripture functions as both a source for theology and a control belief adjudicating between the truth claims of the various sources. Harris argues that a more helpful way forward would be to adopt a control belief that acts "as a lens through which the contribution of all sources of theological construction is filtered."[35] His solution, for evangelical theologians, is to adopt as a control belief the *evangel* (the "good news" that comes through Jesus Christ and to which the Christian Scriptures witness). Grenz interprets this as "participation in what frees," and Harris synthesizes Grenz's notion with the phrase, "the gospel liberates."[36]

Harris further notes that this solution may be viewed as merely another way of privileging foundationalism, but he argues that employing "the gospel liberates" as a control belief in this context should be seen as "a statement encapsulating an ethos and projecting a vision."[37] Further, as Harris crucially points out in his conclusion:

> Evangelicalism's track record in the social arena is reflective of an under developed theological method. Whilst evangelicals usually cite biblical

references to justify doctrinal and ethical stances, the lens that drives the selection of the supporting biblical material is rarely acknowledged or examined. Acknowledging and privileging the control belief "the gospel liberates" as the lens through which all assertions are filtered would result in a transparent and consistent method. A critiquing lens calls for accountability for the morality that inevitably flows from all theological construction. While the control belief ultimately critiques what is proposed, the lens adopted shapes construction at all stages.[38]

Harris adds that "[p]rivileging a hermeneutic of liberation allows shifting volumes for each conversation partner, depending on the issue at stake … for example, in ethical reflection on homosexuality, … [a]lerted to the subtle innuendos unpacked by culture, the conversation is able to deepen as broader biblical themes interact with the insights of the social sciences."[39] I would argue that Grenz's model and the Wesleyan Quadrilateral model already allow for this to occur.

For my part, as someone who highly values Grenz's progressive approach to evangelical theology and methodological creativity, I view the methodological problem identified by Harris as significant, but I also regard his solution as ultimately unconvincing. I would ask: Liberation from what? To what end? For whom? Who decides, and who is excluded from deliberation and decision? And there may be other important questions worth asking where his preferred control belief is applied to particular cases.

Harris's articulation of "the gospel liberates" as a control belief appears to me too open to capture by special interest groups for partisan political or theological ends. That may always be the case for control beliefs. But there may be a more nuanced and fruitful way of stating the solution. Perhaps James W. McClendon's emphasis on ethics in his systematic theology (an emphasis arising from methodological reflection, and in part reflected in the structure of Grenz's systematic theology) indicates a productive way forward.[40] I am not arguing against the notion of liberation as a control belief (in the context in which Harris employs the term), but for a more persuasive expression of an ethically fortified control belief encompassing freedom and perhaps other essential qualities that resonate with the biblical witness and strengthen the mission of the church in the world.

Growth in Grace as a Control Belief for Theological Method

We need a bigger ethical imagination. The liberation perspective needs to be complemented by a more personal and character-based motif or principle if it is to be most effective. One way of moving forward is to ask why we believe the Gospel possesses the power to liberate people from bondage to limiting factors and for qualities and actions informed by the embrace of freedom. I believe the key is the grace (unmerited benevolence) of God, a gift freely available to every person and community. Just as God reached out in grace to us, so we have the opportunity to reach out to others bearing the same grace. In one sense, as we reflect the reconciling perspective and will of God, we are co-creators and co-liberators with God, participating in the new creation through concrete actions and realizing the kingdom of God in the world. To champion and model the unmerited benevolence of God is about as counter-cultural as one can get, especially in a radically individualist society and an advanced liberal democracy such as the country I call home.

But liberation must encompass more than self-determination if it is to be genuinely Christian in character. It must embody love of the kind that comes from God and blesses those in need without partiality and with a view to God's eschatological vision. As Miroslav Volf has said, "Every act of reconciliation, incomplete as it mostly is in this world, stretches itself toward completion in the perfect world of love."[41] Further, such divine love and grace extends through and beyond persons in community to embrace and reconcile the whole cosmos to Christ.

As is well known, grace is a prominent biblical theme. In the New Testament, grace is intimately linked to the character, words and actions of God, including the goodness that God expresses toward the whole creation (Pss 33:5; 119:64; 145), God's compassion for those who are deprived and hurting (Pss 25:6; 103:8; Lk 1:72; 2 Cor 1:3), God's forbearance in the face of human sin and rebellion (Ex 34:6; Ps 145:8; Rom 2:4; 9:22), and God's redemptive mercy and reconciliation demonstrated and offered through the saving work of Christ (Jn 3:16-17; Rom 5:1; 1 Cor 15:10; 2 Cor 6:1; 8:1; 2 Tim 2:1; Tit 2:11).[42]

The Ethical Vision of 2 Peter

One of the most profound yet overlooked references to grace in the New Testament is in 2 Peter 3:18, "But grow in the grace and knowledge of our Lord and Saviour Jesus Christ. To him be glory both now and forever. Amen." Here is a call for followers of Jesus to be imitators of him. Both 1 and 2 Peter call Christians to imitate Christ, both in their moral disposition and in the mission of God in the world. Each of these general letters indicates the vital importance to the leaders of the early Christian community of the practice of imitating Christ through maintaining moral purity and godliness in personal character and the inner life, and from that basis cultivating the fruit of the kingdom of God in individual lives, communities and social structures (1 Pet 1:13-16, 22; 2:21-25; 4:1, 13; 2 Pet 1:1-4; 3:11-12, 14, 18).

One of the chief purposes of both 1 and 2 Peter is to stimulate the readers to wholesome and virtuous thinking that results in faithful Christian living. This is also arguably one of the chief purposes of theology, as I indicated above. The key to this way of thinking and acting is the experience of the grace and peace of God, and continual growth in the grace and knowledge of Jesus Christ, empowered by the indwelling Spirit of Christ in the life of the one who follows Jesus, evidenced in the greeting and benediction in 2 Peter (2 Pet 1:2; 3:18).

When I looked for scholarly wisdom to better understand the final exhortation and doxology in 2 Peter, I was not at first convinced of its relevance to theological method. The biblical commentaries were not much help; 2 Peter is never one of the first published titles in a commentary series, nor does this general epistle feature prominently in the preaching and teaching in our churches. That is understandable due to its scope and the fact that the Gospels and the Pauline epistles especially occupy such prominence in the Christian canon and in the theology and ecclesiology of the church. The Smyth and Helwys commentary has this to say on 2 Peter 3:18: "The benediction is encouraging and hopeful. It needs no commentary."[43] The four other commentaries I consulted on this passage offer little more help than to point out obvious connections with other passages in 1 and 2 Peter and the rest of the New Testament.

However, in the latter section of his book, *The Unformed Conscience of Evangelicalism: Recovering the Church's Moral Vision*, J. Daryl Charles devotes three chapters to exposition of what he calls biblical resources for ethics, under the headings "the Pauline model" (Acts 17), "the disciples' model" (the Sermon on the Mount), and "the Petrine model" (2 Peter). Charles observes that

> One of the great, though little appreciated, contributions that the General Epistles have made to New Testament study and preaching is their representation of the heart of the New Testament ethical tradition. The documents emphasize the ethics of Christian faith – that is, right living. While it is true that Paul's letters typically end with ethical admonitions, the bulk of his writing is devoted to a definition of Christian belief, hence its theological trajectory ... The church's lack of attention to these writings, correlatively, robs us of irreplaceable resources that we need for life and service.[44]

The text of 2 Peter addresses the problem of a lapse of ethical behavior by encouraging a growing awareness and deployment of the spiritual resources available through Christ, characterized by grace, which yield self-mastery of ungodly appetites and a corrective to unethical social values and relationships. As Charles notes, "grace operative in our lives will curb the human passions arising from within as well as enable us to withstand the forces of surrounding culture from without."[45] Charles also observes that the ethical language of 2 Peter preserves the tension between divine sovereignty and human moral agency (for example, 2 Pet 1:5-7; 3:17). Thus while grace has its origin in the mind and heart of God, and is a gift from God, those who follow Christ must actively apply its resources in order to obtain its benefits and share it with others.

This is the burden of the final exhortation in 2 Peter 3:18. The letter closes as it began, with a prayer that the readers would grow in their knowledge of God through the personal and practical experience of grace. The message of the letter is summarized in 2 Pet 3:17-18. In 3:11-16, destructive libertine behavior was seen to result from a denial of Christian eschatological convictions, while godly behavior was the result of an apprehension of divinely revealed eschatological expectation. The writer of the letter is concerned with a clash between false teaching and truth, vice and virtue, moral darkness and light.

The Christian's responsibility is to learn more of Jesus (cf 2 Pet 1:5-10). Those who profess to follow Jesus are called to progress in the Christian life, to "increase in spiritual understanding by growing deeper in our knowledge of the person of Jesus Christ and conforming to his mind and life" – in outlook, aim, attitude and lifestyle.[46] The writer assumes that, if diligently followed, this exhortation will result in a continually increasing understanding of the meaning of Jesus Christ in our lives until the Parousia delivers a full and final revelation of him (cf 1 Cor 13:8-9, 12).[47] This is not a response to incipient Gnosticism but a call to faithful discipleship leading to Christian maturity and fruitfulness in thought and action.

Conclusion

The desire for liberation as a control belief for theological method is admirable, but needs to be emphatically grounded in, and shaped by, Christian ethics if it is to function effectively as a lens through which to define and clarify methodological issues as they relate to Christian theology. And Christian ethics must take seriously the two imperatives of being good and doing right (character formation and the pursuit of duty or obligation), as well as the communitarian dimension of ethical claims, if it is to be true to the fullness of the Christian vision of the good life and the common good as attested by Scripture and expounded by public theology.

CHAPTER 14

Can the notion of "growth in grace" be applied as a control belief for theological method, encapsulating an ethos and projecting a vision of the purpose of the sources of theology, adjudicating between their various truth claims? Or is Grenz's reliance on Scripture as interpreted by the community of faith sufficient as a control belief for theological method? Or is Harris's suggestion of "the gospel liberates" to be preferred? It may be claimed that the term "grace" is not sufficiently defined to be deployed consistently as a control belief for theological method. However, this is a practical advantage as long as the link to the biblical witness to the teaching and example of Jesus remains clear, and as long as there remains freedom to interpret the biblical witness and apply the fruits of such interpretation to particular social and cultural contexts.

Why, in practice, do Baptists hold the ethical views and project the ethical stances they do? Why do Baptists typically vacate the ethical playing field on certain problems and issues? Why is it that we support or oppose this or that moral sentiment or ethical behavior or doctrinal belief or public policy or political theory? Perhaps a re-examination and reassignment of control beliefs for theological method would go some way toward answering these questions. Perhaps the biblical notion of "growth in grace" could prove helpful.

None of us has arrived at our destination. We all need more of God's grace in our lives. We all need a fuller understanding and experience of Jesus Christ, mediated by the Holy Spirit who indwells and guides and empowers the people of God. It is my contention that theological method is also in need of this grace.

Find Rod Benson on Twitter @ozbap.

CHAPTER 15
UNITY THROUGH CHRIST:
ENGAGING THE EPHESIAN HOUSEHOLD CODE

Robert Scott Nash

---

*The RSV is the base version for my biblical quotations, but I have often altered it based on my own translation.

In 1978, Baptist scholars Evelyn and Frank Stagg published their joint investigation of the role of women in the ancient world as depicted in the literature of Jewish, Greek, and Roman writers.[1] In their study, titled *Woman in the World of Jesus*, they also gave an extensive analysis of the various perspectives on women that appear in the New Testament. They concluded that, despite occasional exceptions, the literature of antiquity generally cast women as inferior, subordinate persons. The Staggs argued that much of the New Testament, especially the Gospels and the undisputed letters of Paul, championed the freedom, dignity, and equality of all persons, including women. The main departure from the New Testament norm, according to the Staggs, can be found in those letters containing domestic codes regulating the relationships of members of the household. The Staggs argued that these household codes reflect the church's concern for order, which had become an issue in part because of excesses stemming from the church's proclamation of liberation. In response to the challenges of freedom in Christ, the church retreated to some degree behind the protective social traditions of the male-oriented and male-dominated world in which it had to exist. Reflecting on this reaction, the Staggs noted: "The church has tended to trust controls more than freedom, and it seems that woman has suffered disproportionately in the result."[2]

In 1980, Frank Stagg led a graduate seminar at The Southern Baptist Theological Seminary on Paul's method of regulating behavior in his letters. Following my submission of a paper on Paul's use of *parenesis* in Colossians, Dr. Stagg encouraged me to pursue the question of the function of the domestic code found in Col 3:18-4:1. I later expanded the investigation to include the parallel material in Ephesians. The study culminated in a dissertation on the role of the domestic codes in Colossians and Ephesians.

Discussions of the Household in Antiquity

In that study I analyzed the form and function of similar material found in the relevant Greek, Roman, and Jewish writings of antiquity. Two important conclusions came from this analysis. First, no exact literary parallels to the Colossian and Ephesian household codes exist in the ancient texts. In terms of their form, the two New Testament codes are unique. Secondly, where the ancient texts do include discussions regarding the regulation of relationships between members of the household, these discussions typically occurred in relation to some broader area of inquiry. Management of household behavior provided a model for ancient writers' discussions of other topics.

A good example of this may be found in two of Aristotle's major works, the *Nichomachean Ethics* and the *Politics*. These two works were intended to be companion volumes, with the goal of prescribing the best possible form of government that would be most conducive to attaining what Aristotle considered "the good life." Whereas the *Ethics* examined the character of a person who achieved the good life within the sociopolitical context of the state (*polis*), the *Politics* focused on the structure and management of the state itself. Because Aristotle saw persons as essentially social creatures, any discussion of the nature of the person had to include consideration of the social context in which the person existed. Thus, considerable overlap exists between the two works.

In the *Ethics*,[3] Aristotle discussed household relationships in two ways. First, he used the example of the subordinate members of the household to delineate his view regarding the rights of citizens within a just state. Second, he used the different types of relationships within the household (husband-wife, master-slave, father-children) to identify the different types of constitutional patterns that might exist in a given state. He continued this method of argumentation in the *Politics*,[4] referring to household relationships as examples of similar or different types of rule that should exist within the state.

Aristotle's aim in the two works was to show how the social order might be construed so as to promote the attainment of virtue and the good life. His focus was on the state's constitution. He offered no prescription for how a household should be managed. He assumed that certain parties were subordinate and inferior and that other parties (the free, adult, males) were dominate and superior. He used what was considered a given (the well-run household) as a model for evaluating different types of states and for arguing how the best state should be constructed.[5]

What emerges from a survey of the relevant parallel literature are two conclusions regarding the function of so-called household codes, beside the previously stated point that no actual literary parallel can be found. First, only rarely do we find any ancient writer intending to give instructions to members of the household. In general, they all assumed that in any relationship one party was dominate and the other subordinate. Within the household proper, the free, adult, male was assumed to be in charge, though occasionally the everyday management of the household might fall to the wife, the slaves, or even the adult children. This arrangement was practically a given for ancient society. As such, particular rules or guidance for managing household relationships were unnecessary. Second, because the arrangement of the household was almost universally assumed to be according to an established set of relationships, the topos of the household held considerable flexibility and adaptability for use as an illustrative tool for discussing other topics.

Discussions of the Household in the New Testament

Having observed the general function of domestic-code-like material in other ancient texts, I then investigated how the most complete household codes in the New Testament, those of Colossians and Ephesians, functioned within the context of the writings themselves. John Elliott had recently argued that the domestic-code material in 1 Peter had been deconstructed from its original form and function as it existed in the oral or written traditions used by the author and had been reconfigured by the author to give illustrative support to the main argument of that letter.[6] My inquiry into the function of discussions of the household in nonbiblical writings suggested to me that 1 Peter was basically following the same pattern as those writings.

I wondered, "Is it possible that the same could be said for the household codes in Colossians and Ephesians?" If so, the implications for contemporary hermeneutics would be significant. The household codes as they stand pose challenges for the church today. Basically, two options for interpretation and application hold. One option reads the codes as an expression of God's eternal will for the household and to apply the instructions for the various members of the household in a rigid fashion. While interpreters in some cultural contexts find little problematic about this approach, many others do. In fact, many people find this reading and use of the codes offensive and oppressive. Indeed, what appears to be a simple set of instructions for the smoothly-run home has become an instrument of division and disorder within the household of God.

In those cultures where the patterns of relationship differ drastically with those found in the codes, especially in regard to husbands and wives, hearing a relevant word in the biblical text proves difficult. For this reason, many pursue the other option of trying to distill some theological essence or some ethical principle from the codes that might prove applicable for personal relationships in the contemporary world. Doing this, however, usually results in a distortion of the text itself, especially, for example, when the master-slave relationship of the codes is translated into an employer-employee context. I suggest, instead, that we read the household codes in Colossians and Ephesians in light of the larger texts in which they are found and uncover their functions in their own contexts. Then, I think, we can find in the codes a message for the church today that is far from rigid, oppressive, or divisive. In short, I suggest that the household code in Ephesians, especially, supports a vision of the church that promises and promotes greater unity through Christ.

Colossians

While this paper is primarily concerned with the household code in Ephesians, some attention to Colossians is helpful. Scholars have long noted the numerous literary similarities between these two letters and have tended to see one letter dependent on the other. While the direction of dependency is debated, most scholars favor seeing Ephesians dependent in some sense on Colossians. I agree. In fact, when it comes to the household codes, I think it is strongly evident that Ephesians contains a reworking of the code found in Colossians. Furthermore, I think this reworking confirms the function of the codes in both letters.

I will briefly summarize some conclusions I have made regarding Colossians.[7] Examining the literary features of the letter in terms of epistolary structure and rhetorical analysis has led me to conclude that the household code of Col 3:18-4:1 functions as an exemplum, a type of proof used to support the main proposition of the letter, which I think is stated in Col 2:6-7:

> As you therefore received Christ Jesus the Lord, so live in him, grounded and built up in him and firmly founded in the faith, just as you were taught, abounding in thanksgiving. See to it that no one makes a prey of you by philosophy and empty deceit, according to human tradition, according to the elemental spirits of the cosmos, and not according to Christ.

The author then presents a series of proofs to support this proposition. Among them is the pointed repetition of a theme presented earlier in the "Cosmic Christ Hymn" of 1:15-19, namely that Christ has already conquered any "powers" that they might fear. This hymn is generally considered to be traditional early Christian liturgical material that has been revised by the author and inserted into this letter. Whatever the exact nature of the elusive "Colossian Heresy" was that this letter attacks, its proponents apparently argued that the Colossian believers need to submit to certain regulations and rituals to be protected from dangerous cosmic forces (Col 2:16-23).

Against this heresy the author asserts the sufficient lordship of Christ, to whom alone is submission needed. As the hymn affirms, Christ is the head of his body, the church, and the head of all powers. Submission to his lordship is sufficient. The series of proofs that follows the proposition repeats the call for submission to Christ, often using parenetic ethical instructions that depict what a submitted life entails.

The final proof in the argument for submission to the lordship of Christ comes in the household code of 3:18-4:1. Three pairs of relationships are given, and six groups of household members are addressed. In each pair, the "submissive" member is addressed first, in a sense giving priority of place and emphasis to the act of submission. Each instruction to the "submissive" member is support by a Christological reason. These instructions are all brief, except for the instructions to slaves, which are extensively elaborated. Among the instructions to slaves, the most pointed word is this: *tō kyriō Christō doulete* = "you are slaves to the Lord Christ" 3:24b). Interpreters have often assumed that the slaves in the church received extra instruction because their behavior posed the greatest potential for problems. Nothing else in the letter suggests that this was true. Instead, we have repeated references not to earthly masters but to the one master/lord (*kyrios*), the kyrios in heaven who is Lord even of earthly masters (4:1). We also find allusions to the church not only as Christ's body but as a body "built up" (*epoikodomoumenos*) by the Lord. In short, the church is Christ's household (*oikos*). Christ is the master/lord of the household. If so, then what are the members of the church? They are his slaves and servants. Hence, the words to slaves in the household code are directed to the church as a whole. In fact, most of the particular words addressed to slaves in the code are addressed to the whole church elsewhere in the letter in some form. Also in the letter, the author "Paul" presents himself and others as models of submitted servants, referring to himself and other individuals known to the church as "slaves, servants, and bond-slaves" (1:25; 4:7, 9, 12, 17).

In short, as in most uses of household instructional material in ancient writings, the household code in Colossians functions as a model illustrating the themes of a larger concern. The larger concern here is the lordship of Christ and appropriate submission to that lordship. As the hymn earlier marks the use of traditional liturgical material to exalt the cosmic lordship of Christ, the household code marks the use of traditional parenetic material to illustrate, somewhat metaphorically, the nature of the church as the household of God and the role of church members within this household as the slaves submitting to the lordship of Christ.

Ephesians

When we turn to Ephesians, I think we find a similar function for the household code of 5:21-6:9.[8] Before discussing the function, though, let us compare the forms of the two codes.

Col 3:18-4:1	Eph 5:21-6:9
Wives, be subject to your husbands, as is fitting in the Lord.	Being subject to one another in fear of Christ, wives to your own husbands, as to the Lord. Because a husband is head of the wife as also Christ is head of the church, himself savior of the body. But as the church submits to Christ, thus also the wives to the husbands in everything.
Husbands, love your wives and do not be harsh with them.	Husbands, love the wives, as also Christ loved the church and gave himself over for her, so that he might sanctify her, having cleansed (her) by the washing of water by word, so that he might present to himself the church glorious, not having spot or wrinkle or any such thing,

Col 3:18-4:1 cont.	Eph 5:21-6:9 cont.
	but that (she) might be holy and unblemished.
	So, the husbands ought to love their wives as their own bodies.
	The one who loves his wife loves himself.
	For no one ever hates his own flesh,
	but nourishes and cherishes it,
	as also Christ (does) the church
	because we are members of his body.
	"For this a man leaves father and mother and is joined to his wife, and the two will be unto one flesh."
	This mystery is great, and I refer (it)
	to Christ and to the church;
	however, also you, according to one (flesh) let each of you love his own wife as himself,
	and the wife that she may fear the husband.
Children, obey your parents in everything, for this pleases the Lord.	Children, obey your parents in the Lord, for this is right.
	"Honor your father and mother,"
	which is the first commandment with a promise
	"so that it may be well with you and you may live long upon the earth."

CHAPTER 15

Col 3:18-4:1 cont.	Eph 5:21-6:9 cont.
Fathers, do not provoke your children, lest they become discouraged.	And fathers, do not provoke your children, but raise them in discipline and instruction of the Lord.
Slaves, obey in everything your human masters, not with eye-service, as people-pleasers, but in singleness of heart, fearing the Lord. Whatever your task, work heartily, as serving the Lord and not people, knowing that from the Lord you will receive the compensation of your inheritance; you are slaves to the Lord Christ; for the wrongdoer will be paid back for the wrong he has done, and there is no partiality.	Slaves, obey the human masters those who are with fear and trembling in singleness of the heart, as to Christ not according to eye-service as people-pleasers, but as slaves of Christ doing the will of God from (the) soul. With good will serving as to the Lord and not to people, knowing that each one, if he does good, will receive this (same) from the Lord, whether slave or free.
Masters, treat your slaves justly and fairly, knowing that you also have a Master in heaven.	And masters, do the same to them, ceasing the threat, knowing that both their Lord and yours is in heaven, and there is no partiality with him.

Even a cursory comparison reveals both similarities and differences. Both codes have the same six groups arranged in the same three pairs, with the subordinate group addressed first. The initial instruction for each group is essentially the same for both codes, with the imperatives to masters differing slightly. Each set of instructions in the Ephesians version is slightly longer, with the exception of the words to the slaves. The main reason for this is that part of the Colossian message to the slaves has been moved to the instructions to the masters (note the theme of impartiality). Some of the wording in the Colossian message to the slaves has been rearranged in Ephesians, but the bulk of it is still present.

The major difference is evident in the first pair of instructions to wives and husbands. The verbal form for the word "submit" does not actually appear in Eph 5:22; it has been moved to a preliminary statement introducing the entire code and calling for all members to submit to one another. This, I think, reflects two things. First, the author of Ephesians identified the emphasis on submission that is most pronounced in the Colossian household code and recognized that the code in Colossians was structured so as to stress the need for members of the household of Christ to submit to the lordship of Christ. In other words, I think that the author of Ephesians read the Colossian code in the way I have suggested above. Second, the theme of submission that dominates the function of the code in Colossians was not the theme that the author of Ephesians wished to stress. While the call to submission to Christ was still applicable to the Ephesians audience, the author of this letter wished to make another use of the code. The verbal form for "submit" became a preface to the code proper in Ephesians. The expanded instructions to slaves, which had been the focal point in Colossians, was retained but summarized more succinctly. Where the Ephesians code is most expansive when compared to Colossians reveals where our Ephesians author's interest lay, namely in the instructions to wives and husbands. Both sets of instructions are much longer in Ephesians than in Colossians, and the major expansion of the Colossian precursor comes in the words to the husbands. I do not think this is accidental, nor do I think that the author of Ephesians had a special interest in regulating the relationship of wives and husbands. Instead, I think the expanded words to this first pair in the code reveal the function of the code in the context of the epistle to the Ephesians.

The Context of the Letter to the Ephesians

Examination of the "context" of a letter usually involves trying to identify the historical circumstances in which a letter was written. We ask such questions as these. What problems had arisen in the church community to whom the letter was addressed? What was going on in the life of the author at the time of writing? What was the history of the author's relationship with the church in question? What individuals were involved in the issues addressed, and to what degree did the author support or try to correct them?

When we try to identify the historical context of the Letter to the Ephesians, we encounter several problems. We do not know for certain that this letter was originally addressed to the church in Ephesus. The earliest manuscripts include no reference to Ephesus, nor do the earliest citations of this letter identify the audience. The words "in Ephesus" were apparently added some time after the fourth century. The letter itself does not seem to address any particular historical circumstance. Paul's letter typically addressed some particular problem or problems in the church to which he was writing. We find no direct reference to any such problem in Ephesians. We see no attack on any particular theological view or behavior. Except for the greetings at the end, the letter includes no personal references other than to "Paul" himself. In many ways, the letter seems to be directed toward the church in general without regard to specific time and place. We cannot know the answers to the types of questions we usually ask about the historical context of a letter.

What we can identify with greater certainty are the sociological and theological contexts of the letter. In fact, the lack of historically contingent information assists us in recognizing the distinctive social orientation of Ephesians. Ephesians addresses the church universal as a community beyond specific location. Matters of community identity are paramount. This unusual feature of the letter may alert us to the particular concerns and objective of the author.

The Sociological Context of Ephesians

Ephesians contains distinct descriptions of the church as a community that fall into two broad categories. Some references to the church focus on the radical break with the past that it had experienced. Sociologically speaking, these references deal with "social discontinuity." Other parts of Ephesians stress the unity that should characterize the community. We may label this dimension "social integration." The church experienced social discontinuity because of disruptions with the past, pre-Christian existence and social integration through the formation of new relationships within the body of Christ. These outward and inward movements were serious matters creating internal and external problems, matters urgent enough to merit the attention of the letter to the Ephesians.

Social Discontinuity

The markers of social discontinuity served to identify the church's position apart from its past and other groups. The opening blessing (1:3-14) enumerates the new identity. They were blessed, chosen, and predestined for "sonship." They had received redemption, forgiveness, and enlightenment to the purposes of God. They were selected for a special role in God's plan and had received the Holy Spirit as a sign of their eventual reward.

Two motifs express the difference of their new identity from their previous standing. First, they had moved from death to life (2:1-10). They had been dead in their sins and had walked according to the age of this world. They had submitted to the dictates of their flesh and mind as children of disobedience. But they no longer belonged to this world of death. They had been raised up with the resurrected Christ; they now lived with him. Second, those who had been far are now near (2:11-22). As gentiles in the flesh they had existed apart from Christ and alienated from Israel. Estranged from God and God's people, they had been strangers to God's promise, living in a hopeless, godless state. Now, they were no longer excluded from the rights and privileges that belonged to the people of God. No longer strangers (*xenoi*) and aliens (*paroikoi*), they were fellow citizens (*sympolitai*) with the saints (*hoi hagioi*). They had access to the Father and possessed the promises of God.

The change in social identity resulted in a certain tension regarding their previous identity. They had become strangers to their former life. Previously separated from God, they were now separated from those who remained estranged to God. This separation also brought new responsibilities as well as privileges. Social discontinuity meant adopting a different manner of living, one that reflected their new identity.

The call to this different lifestyle appears halfway through the letter in 4:1ff., and it serves as the rhetorical proposition for the letter as a whole: "Lead a life worthy of the calling to which you have been called." The new, discontinuous worthy life is vividly articulated in terms of dualistic moral instructions, many of which are in the form of antithetical statements that contrast their behavior with that of outsiders. They were no longer to be "babies" subject to craftiness; rather, they were to grow toward maturity in Christ. They should no longer live as gentiles with futile minds, darkened in their understanding and separated from God. They should put off the old nature and put on the new natured patterned after the likeness of God. Specific injunctions in Ephesians 5:1-15 identify behavior no longer permissible, warning of the exclusion befalling those who engage in such practices and urging separation from those who still walk in darkness. Sharply dualistic imagery intensifies the boundary between the church and those outside: "children of light" versus "sons of disobedience"; "you are light" versus "you were darkness"; "the fruit of light" versus "the unfruitful works of darkness"; "the saints" versus "the immoral person"; and "wise" versus "unwise." Social discontinuity required a new lifestyle that revealed the new identity.

Social Integration

Claiming this new identity also required an inward movement of social integration, or unity. The theme of unity is prominent in both the doxological half of the letter (chs. 1-3) and the mare parenetic half (chs. 4-6). The opening doxology (1:3-14) proclaims the disclosure of the divine "mystery" of God's intention to unite all things in Christ (1:10). God's plan (*oikonomia*) for the fullness of time included the unification of heaven and earth. God had already incorporated the readers into Christ as a part of this grand scheme of unification (1:11-13). God had also subjected all things under the feet of Christ, who had "headship" over everything pertaining to the church, which represented in itself the fullness (*plērōma*) of the one who fills all in all (1:22-23). The church had become part of a communion that embodied the divine plan for unifying all things. Its social cohesiveness was vital since in itself it was to reflect the unity intended by God for the whole cosmos (1:10).

Ephesians 2:11-22 demonstrates the relatedness of the church's cohesion to God's *oikonomia* of universal unity. God brought two estranged groups, Jews and gentiles, together in the church by the death of Christ. By removing the separation between them, God transformed them into "one new person" (2:14-15). God had miraculously brought to them the peace that made union possible (2:16) through the blood of Christ in his flesh through the cross (2:13, 15, 16). Unlike Paul's reference to the "grafting" of gentiles into Israel in Romans 11, in Ephesians God has actively created a new social community and has radically reoriented the order of social existence. Old lines of division (ethnicity, class, sex) no longer hold.

The integration and unification of different groups into one new body gives the premise for the exhortations that come in the parenetic half of the letter. The central appeal in 4:1-3, to walk worthily of their calling characterizes that walk as one that promotes social integration. It requires humility, meekness, patience, and loving forbearance. It requires striving to keep the unity of the Spirit in the bond of peace (3:3). The series of "ones" in 3:4-6 supports this appeal to oneness. Actualizing the unity so eloquently affirmed requires utilizing the gifts given to each one for the up-building of the body of Christ (4:7-12). Then, together, all would attain the unity of the faith and knowledge of God and grow up into Christ (4:13-16). The specific injunctions name actions that would affect the good of the community. The stated motives for not lying, stealing, or engaging in evil talk focus on the effects such behaviors have on others (4:25-29). The actions encouraged, on the other hand, all contribute to the attainment of a unified community (4:31-32).

The unification of the community was accomplished through the death of Christ. This event also permitted another miraculous union – thee reconciliation of the unified body to God (2:16). As Christ and the church were joined, in Christ the church experienced a new mode of connectedness with God as the dwelling place for God's Spirit (2:22). This union also carried responsibility for the church called to be a holy temple in the Lord (2:21). Thus, Ephesians expresses concern about moral purity as well as community cohesion and preservation. Numerous ethical injunctions speak to this concern. Believers are admonished not to live any longer as "gentiles," notorious for their immorality, living separated from the life of God, and filled with lusts (4:17-19). The instructions in 5:1-7, in particular, focus on behavior that is incompatible with intimate union with God. In the household code that follows a few verses later, the purification of the church is identified as the intention of Christ who wished to present a holy and blameless bride. The metaphor of the armor of God that follows in 6:10-18 reveals the intensity of the struggle for purity and the necessity for total absorption in the power of God.

This analysis of the sociological context of Ephesians suggests that the intended recipients of the letter were experiencing a high level of social discontinuity and considerable social integration. Former bonds had dissolved, and new ones had developed. The separation from their past with all its significant ties of family, position, and identity – which may have been extremely painful – became endurable by gaining a clearer understanding of the darkness of that past. They could find strength in recognizing also the importance of that community to which they now belonged. Forging the new bonds of this community, however, did not occur without interior struggle. A variety of persons from different backgrounds had been called into this community. Its very existence was part of the mystery of God as God achieved the incredible by uniting Jews and gentiles as one new person. Through Christ, the church had been brought into union with God; indeed, God's Spirit dwelt within the church. The church also experienced union with Christ, an intense, intimate union. Joined to Christ, the church was part of God's grand design to unify all things. This new existence called for behavior appropriate for a holy temple and a pure bride.

CHAPTER 15

The Theological Context of Ephesians

Again, while we cannot know the particular historical situation that prompted this letter, we can follow the verbal clues contained in it and conceive of the kind of sociological context that such a letter might address. We can engage in a similar method for arriving at a view of the theological context of Ephesians. In fact, when we observe the theological issues most prominent in Ephesians, we may hear the author speaking imaginatively and persuasively. New identities and lifestyles called for new theological images, or at least a recasting of major themes of the church's message. This refocusing of their theological lens is most pronounced in the letter's depictions of Christ, the church, and the relationship between the two.

Christ in Ephesians

The Christ of Ephesians is the exalted Lord of the cosmos. God has raised him from the dead and lifted him up to the heavenly places where he now sits at the right hand of God lording it over every other rule, authority, power, dominion, and everything named now and forever (1:20-21).[9] Through Christ, God will eventually unite all things in heaven and earth (1:10). In the meantime, Christ exercises power and authority over the entire cosmos, as well as over the church.

This exalted state of Christ, however, has a distinctly soteriological force in Ephesians. God has put everything under the feet of Jesus for the church (1:22). In him, the church receives the spiritual blessings of the heavenly places (1:3). Through him, the church has become God's children (1:5). In him, God has lavished grace upon the church (1:7-8). Through him the church has received the word of truth (1:13). The exaltation of Christ has a salvific purpose.

The soteriological triumph of God through Christ has occurred through the union of Christ and the church. The church that has been seated in the heavenlies with Christ is also the body of Christ on earth (1:23). Christ's dominion over all other powers leads the church to engagement with the cosmic powers not yet subdued (6:12). The church lives where those powers still operate, yet because the church is united to Christ, the church has the capacity not to submit to those powers.[10] The church's continued existence upon this earth means that even the exalted Christ still abides within his church on earth. God's cosmic plan involves the unification of all things in Christ; this plan has already found partial realization in the union between Christ and the church (1:23, 3:17, 5:23). God's ultimate objective of cosmic unification finds implementation through the creation of a new people united with Christ in anticipation of the eventual unity of all things. The creation of this new people is itself a great feat of unification. Through the death of Christ, God brought those formerly separated together with those who were already recipients of God's covenant of promise (2:13-15). This sacrificial death of Christ removed the obstacles separating these peoples and the barriers to mutual access of both to God (1:13-16; 2:16, 18; 3:12; 5:2, 25). The exalted Christ's central role in the divine plan for unification, then, was primarily soteriological.

This strong emphasis in Ephesians on union, especially the union of two separated peoples into a new person, may have been directed toward gentile believers who had lost sight of or willfully rejected ties to historical Israel. Paul seems to address a similar problem in Romans 9-11. Thus, the orientation of the union depicted in Ephesians is rooted in historical reality and not in myth. Unlike other religions whose understanding of union might involve the mystical reunification of male and female into the primordial Androgyne, the enlightened into the body of the Cosmic Redeemer, or the obedient faithful into the body of the Cosmic Adam, the union accomplished in Ephesians occurred in a moment in history and involved historical persons, namely, Christ, Israel, and gentiles. The stress on the historical grounding of the union that occurred in and through Christ, though, may have had as its target not gentiles departing from their ties to Israel but rather believers who were losing their ties to historical reality altogether.[11] Some similarity may exist here to the super-spiritualism Paul faced in Corinth. Whatever the author's concern may have been, the soteriological significance of Christ is based on his earthly achievement. It is here, on earth within history, and here alone that the church now has access to God through Christ and experiences its life in Christ.

The cultic imagery of sacrifice conveys the soteriological importance of Christ's death for the church. This and other imagery also expresses the continuing salvific work of Christ in the church. In Christ, God created the church for good works (2:10). As the cornerstone of God's house, Christ provides the stimulus for the church to grow (2:20-21). Christ has imparted gifts for the edification of the church (4:9-13). As the head of the body, Christ has enabled the church to up-build itself (4:16). Christ's sacrifice on behalf of the church provides a primary example for imitation to the lifestyle advocated by many of the ethical injunctions (e.g., 5:2). In the household code (5:26-27), Christ's sacrifice has its clear purpose as the moral purification of the church. The exalted Christ of Ephesians, then, is a Cosmic Lord whose primary orientation is ecclesiastical.

Church in Ephesians

Ephesians expresses one of the highest christologies to be found in the New Testament. Its view of the church is even more lofty. The church originated in

God's election and is predestined to be God's children (1:4, 5; 4:1). God redeemed the church, forgave it, and lavished riches on it (1:7-8). The mystery of God's will, in process of disclosure to the cosmos, has already been revealed to the church (1:9; 3:9-10). God sealed the church with the Holy Spirit in anticipation of its full inheritance (1:13-14). God had transferred the church from death to life (2:1) and had made them alive with Christ (2:5-6). Through Christ, the church has full access to the Father (2:18). God dwells spiritually within the church (2:22), and Christ dwells within the hearts of its members (3:17). God works through the church to accomplish the divine will (3:20).

As noted above, God's election of the church led to its exaltation. This heavenly exaltation, however, carries heavily consequences for the everyday, earthly life of the church. Much as the Christology of Ephesians is soteriologically-oriented, the ecclesiology moves toward mission and ethics. God elected the church so that it might appear holy and blameless (1:4). The church's members have been appointed to live for "the praise of glory" (1:12). God delivered them out of previous bondage to sin so that they might walk in the good works for which they had been created (2:1-10). In Christ, the church is to be a suitable dwelling place for God's Spirit (2:21-22). Through the church, God will manifest divine wisdom to the heavenly powers (3:10). All of this obligates the church to a holy lifestyle (4:1). Above all, it must preserve the union accomplished by God in Christ (4:3; cf. 2:16). This union was the foundation for the church's calling, nature, and purpose in the world (4:4-6). Because God elected and exalted the church, the earthly church must manifest its exaltation within its daily, earthly existence. The church's "head" may be in the heavens, but its feet must still walk straight on the cold, hard ground (4:1).

In order to walk worthily of its calling, the church must live in accordance with Christ's example (4:20-21; 5:2). From him it receives its impetus for growth (2:21; 4:15-16), and toward him the church is to direct its moral maturation (4:13). The old nature of life outside of Christ must give way to the new nature of life in him (4:24). In the struggle against the old nature, the church must recognize that the real battle is waged against the powers that formerly ruled their lives (2:2; 6:12). The struggle requires being strong in the Lord and donning the attributes of God as armor (6:11-17).

The moral implications of the church's union with Christ appear most profoundly in the description of the church as the "household of God" (2:19-22). The social concept "household" becomes a theological metaphor depicting the completeness of God's reconciliation of the church to God through Christ. In 2:19-22, the idea of a household under the sovereignty of God morphs into the image of the church as a building in which God dwells. The household, a social entity, becomes a temple, a religious structure (2:21). As a temple in the Lord, the church stands obligated to provide a suitable habitation for God's Spirit. This vision of the church as God's temple certainly has eschatological overtones, for it is a work in progress, not one achieved in fullness.[12] Nevertheless, the eschatological vision impinges on the present. The church is called to walk worthily now (4:1) so that it might become what it is already called. Hence, the parenesis of the letter delineates the kinds of behavior that would detract or contribute to the realization of this identity as the household/temple of God. Expectantly, parenesis regarding the "household" would appropriately appear in Ephesians as a guide for accentuating the moral obligations of the church in "household" matters. The household code in 5:21-6:9, however, does more. Because the household/temple imagery of 2:19-22 lucidly signifies the intrinsic union of God and God's people in Christ, the code as a distinct unit functions to illuminate the nature of the union between Christ and the church.

The Function of the Household Code in Ephesians

The close unity that exists between Christ and the church is depicted in two metaphors in Ephesians: the church as Christ's body and the church as the household/temple of God in Christ. These two images converge in the household code where the relationship of wives and husbands provided the author with a set of fertile images for developing the implications of the union between Christ and the church. My proposal that the primary function of the household code in Ephesians is to illustrate the closeness of the union of Christ and the church is supported furthermore by observing the differences between this code and the one in Colossians.

As noted previously, the Colossian version of the code includes expanded instructions to slaves. I argued that this reflects the author's intent to emphasis the lordship of Christ and the role of the church as submissive members of the household of God. As in Colossians, the household code in Ephesians reinforces the lordship of Christ over the cosmos and over the church, but this is not the author's main point in using the code. The emphases on the lordship of Christ and submission to Christ were already present in the form of the code used by the author of Ephesians. The form of the code in Ephesians reflects exactly the kind of revision we might expect in a letter stressing intimate union between Christ and the church. Using the topos of the household as an *exemplum*, or illustrative device, was characteristic of other ancient writers, as we have seen above in the case of Aristotle, so it should not appear so unusual that the author of Ephesians could follow the example of the author of Colossians and make a similar use of the code in Ephesians.

The perspective of the code in Ephesians regarding the nature of the household also follows suit with the prevailing views of antiquity. Neither Colossians nor Ephesians directly challenges the ancient world's assumptions that the husband was the "head" of the wife and the "ruler" of the household. As noted before, this was a "given" for ancient society. Both versions of the household code in these two letters, however, do include elements that at least begin to question the absolute nature of the prevailing view. The Colossian code calls for ultimate submission to Christ by those who are "slaves" in the household of God, which includes everyone in the church. The Ephesian code takes this a step further and calls for mutual submission of all church members to each other "in fear of Christ." The old-world social standard of specialized submission is indirectly challenged by making submission a responsibility for all members of Christ's body. Ephesians, by prefacing its version of the code with a call to mutual submission, actually moves the whole matter of submission into the background. What receives emphasis here is not the set of instructions to slaves but rather those instructions that best speak to another matter more urgent for the author, namely the intimate union of Christ and the church as exemplified by the wife-husband relationship.

The disproportionate exhortation to the husbands (5:25-33) explicitly reflects the Ephesian emphasis on union and unity between Christ and his church. The author developed two particular aspects of this union. First is the emphasis on the moral obligations this union entails. Christ loved the church and gave himself for it (5:25). His purpose in doing so was to effect the church's sanctification so that it might be presented to Christ in perfection (5:26-27; cf. 4:1). As stressed elsewhere in Ephesians, Christ gave himself for the church. The desire of Christ that his bride/wife appears before him may have some allusion to the Old Testament theme of the marriage of God and Israel. If so, then the affirmation in 2:11-22 that the church has assumed the position of intimate union held by the bride Israel is reaffirmed here.

After repeating the initial admonition that husbands are to love their wives (5:28), the author developed another aspect of the union between Christ and the church. By referring to the love of a husband for his wife as his own "body," the Ephesian code focuses on the intensity of the union of Christ and the church. The love of a husband for his wife involves the cherishing and nourishing of his own flesh (5:29). Because the church is his own body, Christ cherishes and nourishes the church. The quotation of Genesis 2:24 substantiates the emphasis on the intimate nature of the union of marriage. The two become one flesh (5:31), mirroring in a fashion the merging of two separated peoples into one new person in Christ (2:14). At this point the author states unequivocally that the real meaning of the Genesis passage cited here is to describe the mystic union between Christ and the church: the two are one. The author's revelation about what is actually going on in these verses is similar to Paul's use of covert illusion in 1 Corinthians 4:6 where he divulges to his readers that his whole previous discussion about Apollos and himself was actually about the Corinthians. What our author has been writing in regard to husbands' loving their wives is really about Christ and the church.

A common interpretation of the reference to Genesis 2:24, and the whole section addressed to husbands, is to see it as an example of how husbands should love their wives. As Christ sacrificially loved the church, so husbands should love their wives. As Christ loves his own body the church, so husbands should love their wives. As Christ became one with the church, so husbands should be of one flesh with their wives. This interpretation gets it backwards. As the author reveals, this is about Christ and the church. As the husband loves his wife, so Christ loves the church. As the husband loves his own body/flesh, so Christ loves the church. As the man and woman become one flesh, so have Christ and the church become one.

The household imagery in Ephesians 2:19-22 culminated in the depiction of the church as the dwelling place for God's Spirit. In the household code, the idea of God's dwelling within God's people finds a perfect analogy in the intimate union between husband and wife. The union is between Christ and the church because that is how God relates to and operates in the life of God's people. The church exists in and through Christ. The church and Christ are one, but they are not identical; Christ remains the head of his body. Nevertheless, a close, mysterious union exists between the two – a union best exemplified by that intimate, mysterious union that is experienced between wife and husband.

Epilogue

During the summer of 1990, while the Intifada was still evident in Jerusalem, I walked through the Old City with a Palestinian friend who had been a faculty colleague at the Georgia school where I then taught. Though he had been born in Jerusalem, inside the Old City, he had never before been to some of the places we visited that day. We went to the western wall of the temple mount and to the plateau of the mount itself to see the Al-Aksa mosque and the Dome of the Rock. Having visited these places a few times previously, I acted as something of a guide for my friend, who took in their splendor as an amazed child. We left the temple area and eventually made our way down the Via Dolorosa to the Church of the Holy Sepulchre. On the way, Samir said, Scott, I have always admired the zeal of both Jews and Muslims. But, they do not have the answer to our problems. They have much to say about justice, and as a Palestinian I know how important justice is. But only we Christians, so few now here in Jerusalem, have something to say about love. Love is the only way we can solve our problems here."

Samir's insightful words speak volumes about what should be central to Christianity. They also stand in stern judgment on the contradiction to these words that we too easily find in the church. Almost as soon as Samir had spoken, we entered the Church of the Holy Sepulchre, a place that painfully reflects the brokenness of the body of Christ in microcosm. Inside the ancient building competition is frequently fierce between the several Christian groups who have each carved out their niches in the sacred space, some even forced out of the church itself and up onto the roof. If the church has something to say about love to a divided world, it must first listen to its own message.

The overriding message of Ephesians, it seems to me, is that in order for the church to be an effective part of God's great movement toward uniting all things in Christ, the church itself must experience the unifying power of the love of God revealed in Christ. The communal language of Ephesians stresses that Christian faith is lived out in community. The doxological cast to much of this language accentuates the "mysterious" nature of the church "community." God has done what seems unbelievable, bringing together in one new kind of family so many different parts of the human family. Ephesians exudes with wonder at the divine creation of this new social creature, the "one new person" in Christ.

The doxological language is uttered, however, with a cautious voice. What we know to be true about what God has wondrously done through Christ in the church is not always true to our experience of the church. The mystery of God's new creation includes the puzzle of life together. Living out the vision is not easy.

Ephesians aids our vision of the vision because it is bifocal. With one lens we see clearly the heavenly (divine) side. The church is united to Christ, who has been exalted, and thus is exalted, too. The church has God's own Spirit living inside it. The church is the place where we witness the fullness of God who fills all in all. The church, through Christ, is mystically one with God.

Yet, with the other lens we see also the earthly (human) side. The church we see with our near lens is not yet the church we see with our distance lens. Thus, Ephesians gushes with the language of instruction about how to bridge the chasm. Our status carries responsibility. Who we are as the church obligates us to strive toward the elusive inner unity. Each part of the body is called to contribute its distinctive gift toward achieving the cohesiveness that is vital to the church's functioning as a catalyst toward unity in the larger creation. It is a tall order, and we struggle against the odds, against the powers of this age (you can name them).

The church wages its struggle with bifocal vision. Conscious of the strength of the foe and the frailty of its members, it nonetheless knows its head, its Lord, and is subject to the one who both sits far above all powers and is alive in the weakest of its members. The church knows that it is loved, intimately, by one who considers it as his own body. However fractured it appears or feels, in its depths (though it does not always dwell there) the church knows that it is not alone, isolated, or abandoned. It is one with its Christ, one with its God. One day, it will transcend all divisions and separations when God embraces all in all. But today, it is enough sometimes for its members to hold hands.

COMMISSION ON BAPTIST WORSHIP AND SPIRITUALITY

Worship is the holy experience of encountering God. The BWA celebrates the various biblical forms of worship as a privilege, opportunity, and responsibility for each Christian and every church. Worship shapes our spirituality and our spirituality influences our worship styles and substance.

For five years we worked to understand the 21st century global dynamics of worship and spirituality, and then to offer suggestions for how we can faithfully encourage harmonious growth for seekers and believers from around the world. We were guided by our Baptist heritage, including Trinitarian belief, biblical authority, congregational polity, and a humility to learn from each other. During our Annual Gatherings we heard voices of Baptists from our six global regions. Our sessions were also enriched by each of the settings in which we met, from Kuala Lumpur, to Santiago, to Ocho Rios, to Izmir. In the rich diversity of our world community we sought spiritual discernment for God's guidance.

The term "worship wars," first used in the 1980s, describes what happens when the tensions of a church's diversity become destructive. These tensions are felt globally. We believe there is a better way. The history, cultural contexts, and personalities of church members influence the style/s of worship that congregations use. But when the overarching desire is to honor God and express love through praise, confession, commitment, and thanksgiving, the dimensions of diversity can find center through a spirituality of worship.

We affirmed that worship has many dynamics, including preaching, music, prayer, Scripture reading, healing, communion, baptism, testimony, response invitations, offerings, and community building. Presentations and responses were given by people from each region.

We highlighted that worship and spirituality are interrelated to the whole work of the BWA, even as worship and spirituality are interrelated to the whole life of the local church. Therefore, two sessions were held jointly with other commissions and another session focused on the *Intra-Baptist Relations Report* from the 2013 Ocho Rios gathering.

During the 2012 gathering in Santiago, we met with the Commission on Doctrine and Christian Unity, chaired by Timothy George. We reviewed and celebrated the preaching heritage of Gardner Taylor. Dr. Taylor's preaching significantly impacted the second half of our 20th century world and the ripple effects of this influence continue. During the 2014 gathering in Izmir, our work was enriched by meeting jointly with the Commission on Baptist Heritage and Identity, chaired by Craig Sherouse. We focused on ways that worship in general and preaching in particular reveal our Baptist identity and how our identity shapes our Christian witness.

The *Intra-Baptist Relations Report* focused on how we are to relate with each other. As a commission we connected that document to the important work of spiritually forming mature Christians. With this in mind we offered "Ten Implications" as a summary by which the BWA can enact *The Intra-Baptist Report*. Following is an abbreviated version:

1. The spiritual formation of a unified fellowship, that we may be "an expression of the essential oneness of Baptist people in the Lord Jesus Christ." This "common confession" can shape the fulfillment of our common purpose "before a lost and hurting world."

2. The spiritual formation of a worldwide organization of Baptists, by necessity, includes a working awareness of cultural differences.

3. The spiritual formation of worship that will enable us to obey "God's presence and leadership" in the context for each of our gatherings.

4. The spiritual formation of humility to "guide us in our speaking to others and our listening to others."

5. The spiritual formation of a disciplined passion that enables us to "never degenerate into attacks on the personhood, humanity, or the authenticity of one's Christian faith and commitment."

6. The spiritual formation "to avoid practices or conversations that perpetuate the dominance of one cultural perspective as providing the normative experience or theological perspectives for all members of the BWA."

7. The spiritual formation to develop "lasting and meaningful relationships through thoughtful and prayerful conversations both within and outside of formal meetings."

8. The spiritual formation that in our pursuit of truth "the perceived correction of errors must be done in love."

9. The spiritual formation of Christian decorum that enables conversations to focus on "the intended meaning of statements rather than inaccurate presumptions about what was said."

COMMISSION ON BAPTIST WORSHIP AND SPIRITUALITY

10. The spiritual formation to respect the leadership of conveners and "to respect the diversity and live into the unity that is the gift of the Holy Spirit to the BWA family."

The commission's quinquennium work is exemplified by Joel C. Gregory's ground breaking book, *Baptist Preaching: A Global Anthology*. As a member of our commission, Dr. Gregory selected representative sermons and preaching styles by Baptist preachers from Africa, Asia Pacific, Caribbean, Europe, Latin America, and North America. The four-year project culminated in the study being published by Baylor Press and presented during the BWA's 2014 gathering in Izmir, Turkey. This work is the first of its kind in Baptist life and maybe among all denominations.

Joel Sierra, vice chair, and I are grateful for the contributions of Fausto Vasconcelos and the commission members. They are:

Alan Soden	Gregory Jackson	Monica B. Wango
Barry Morrison	Hilary George	Nathan Nettleton
Bathsheba Stewart	James Heflin	Oliver Pilnei
Carlos E. Cerna	Jennifer Davidson	Randall L. McKinney
Chris Ellis	Joel Gregory	Samson O. Ayokunle
Christopher Z. Dikana	Johnathan O. Hemmings	Samuel Reeves
Deborah Cochran	Johnny B. Hill	Shannon Cowett
Dina Carro	K. Randel Everett	Steve Vernon
Donald Ndichafah	Karin Wiborn	V. Anthony Cadette
Doug Dortch	Karl E. Henlin	Westh N. Rodrigues
Gary Fenton	Lina Andronoviene	Yoo J. Yoon
George Bullard	Michael Catlett	

We hope that our efforts honor God by strengthening the work of worship and spirituality by global Baptists. With awe and wonder, thanks be to God.

D. Leslie Hollon joined the BWA family when he became a member of the Academic and Theological Education Workgroup in 1995, serving until 1999 and again from 2005 to 2010. He served on the METR Commission on Baptist Worship and Spirituality from 2005 until 2015, serving as chair of the commission from 2010 through 2015, during which time he was also a member of the METR Advisory Committee.

CHAPTER 16
EVANGELICAL HYMNODY IN LATIN AMERICA

Joel Sierra Cavazos

Introduction: The triple task

The renewal of the church for mission requires the renewal of worship as a three-fold experience: cultural, counter-cultural and trans-cultural. American Lutheran liturgical theologian Anita Stauffer has defined these three categories to explain the relationship between worship and the world.[1] From her categories it can be inferred that there must be a triple task performed in worship (for which hymns are our main focus).

The cultural task: Contextualization is the task of making Christian worship relevant to the people. It derives its theological foundation from the incarnation of God in Jesus Christ. The Lord Jesus had to learn a human language and be aware of the cultural nuances of a particular social reality. God made the inscrutable universe-founding words understandable to us by the coming of Jesus Christ. Likewise, the Christian church in every culture must accomplish the task of contextualizing the Good News into the cultural languages and means of expression. In addition, the prayers and songs offered in Christian worship must make manifest the incarnation of the Jesus story in such culture. This entails an undertaking of affirming the culture. Lyrical and musical language of each particular culture must be used in expressing the mystery of divine-human relations.

Counter-cultural: The second task performed in worship is a counter-cultural confrontation against the context. Worship is not only an affirmation of the context, but also a prophetic criticism of those elements in the context that must be transformed by the Gospel. Proclaiming the kingdom of God – the Lordship of Jesus Christ – in every Christian worship service, means standing in opposition to all idols.

It is clear that in order to be effective in the counter-cultural task of critically calling the context to repentance, the first task must be performed well. That is,

Christian songs and hymns must be written using the cultural elements of the context in order to be able to unmask false hopes and idolatries in the context.

Trans-cultural: The third task performed in worship in its relation to the world is the affirmation of the trans-cultural nature of worship. God is present and alive in all corners of the world. There are no cultural boundaries to the One True and Holy God. Therefore the exercise of worship unites the local few to the global millions. It is the true globalization of humanity. As opposed to the false one, offered by the market values and the Babel-like human projects of cultural uniformity under the hollow ethics of consumerism.

The human family in all its grand diversity becomes united again as a result of the reconciliation performed by Jesus the Christ on the cross of Calvary. This is what constitutes Christian worship, the proclamation of the kingdom of God in the life, ministry, death and resurrection of the Lord Jesus Christ.

When Christians gather to sing to Jesus in worship there is a series of theological events taking place, as Christopher Ellis has explained it.[2] Christians unite "sacramentally" in one voice, as they share in one proclamation and one spirituality, and "eschatologically" enter the Kingdom of God. Something powerful takes place through the use of hymns and songs in worship.

In addition to the elements described by Ellis, singing together is a means by which God strengthens the church to perform its transforming mission in the world under the leading of the Holy Spirit. Hymns ought to point us to the world. Therefore there is an urgent need to approach this topic with the theological soundness that warrants fruitfulness in the renewal of the church for mission.

I call the contextual dimension of worship "priestly." We sing priestly when our song affirms our culture and our context. The counter-cultural dimension of worship I give the name "prophetic." We sing prophetically when our song criticizes our cultural context. Prophetic hymns are expressions of a Christian stance in prophetic resistance against the currents of our context. I identify the trans-cultural dimension of worship as "kata-holic."[3] We sing kata-holically when our song connects us with the broad people of God of all cultures and of all times. Kata-holic hymns include confessions of faith that belong to the global church.

A Diagnostic View

In general, polarized worship experiences can be found across the Latin American region and across denominational lines. There are at least three poles or extremes: Formality-informality; spiritual-political; individual-social. The first set refers to the atmosphere of the service. Most churches are either too formal and ritualistic or too casual and familiar. The second set refers to whether the service addresses the social realities in time and space or if it is merely a way to escape from such realities. The third set refers to whether the worship experience fosters community or individualism.

In truth, only the first set of extremes is significant enough to be noticed. In the case of the other two sets, only exceptions can be found outside the norm, as most of the churches are on one pole. Most churches develop a worship service that fosters individualism and escapism from the social realities. This has been the effect of the "praise and worship" movement in Latin America.

The impact of the "praise and worship" style has been tremendous in Latin American Evangelical churches. It has shifted the focus of discussion from its more pressing issues (those of the relevance of worship for the renewal of the mission of the church) and into whether or not churches should adopt this or that form of singing and dancing or whether this or that instrumental ensemble is more suited for worship. Many churches have substituted the pulpit for a drum set in the center of the front stage, thus signifying that centrality of the worship gathering has moved from the Word of God proclaimed and celebrated to the instrumental accompaniment of attractive songs during the service.

We are far from the vision of a worshipping people that is affected by worship. There is an indisputable relationship between worship and ethics, and between worship and mission. American ethicist William May argues that people who have been formed by the worship life of the church should think and act distinctively.[4] The truth is that among Evangelicals in Latin America, people have rarely been formed by the worship life of the church. Furthermore, as time passes by, it can be observed that the new generations of Evangelicals do not seem to be ethically different to the rest of the population, nominal Roman Catholics in the majority.

Latin American missiologist Samuel Escobar has pointed out the relationship between worship and mission. A rediscovery of the power and holiness of God, moral transformation in the life of Christians and a potent missionary impulse are the substantial elements of spiritual renewal, whereas emotional outbursts and changes in musical genres or styles of communication are only secondary in comparison.[5] Escobar holds that authentic mission springs out of worship. Everything begins with God.

> [Adoración] es la respuesta reverente y gozosa a la verdad de la Palabra que Dios le envía.[6]

The worship service is an encounter with God. God´s word has been present in the service in the form of hymns, prayers, silences, enthusiasm, preaching and testimonies. It is only natural, then, that Christians would want to run every road to announce God's word to other human beings.[7]

In view of the relationship between worship and ethics and between worship and missionary thrust, it becomes an urgent matter to pay attention to the renewal of worship life, which at this present moment is not in good shape among Evangelicals in Latin America.

Singing in the Spanish-Speaking Worship

In Latin American churches, singing takes place at particular times during the service. Most of the songs are used in praise and during altar calls. However, a distinctive feature of the way songs are used is for greeting people as a welcome gesture and for celebrating birthdays. There is wide opportunity for a more varied use of congregational singing and it is possible to implement more singing during the service that is not only praise or altar calls.

Throughout the history of the Evangelical movement in Latin America there have been at least four stages in the development of congregational singing. These stages slightly correspond to the development of the Evangelical movement in the Latin American region and to the varying theological winds in each era. They do not have inflexible boundaries but they overlap with the preceding and succeeding ones. This is so because the publication of a hymnbook takes several years in the formation as well as in the further distribution among the churches. Because of this, some of the authors that live and work in one stage are known only afterwards.

The first one is **the translation stage** (1880-1930).[8] The main purpose in this stage was to provide the newly formed churches with resources for worship that spoke of God in Evangelical ways. The missionary impulse that carried the Evangelical movement south of the Rio Grande was an extension of the Evangelical mission to the Frontier. Therefore, the theology reflected in these collections of hymns is basically Revivalist. Two strong emphases are placed on the need to battle spiritually against the forces of evil in the world – as a Militant Church – and on the hope of meeting again in the beyond where the Lord awaits us after all this tribulation is over as a Glorious Church. This is interesting because these two emphases are marks of a persecuted church. Persecution (many times violent) on the part of the Roman Catholic population and their leaders was not uncommon in this first stage.

Thomas Westrup and Ernesto Barocio, Baptist leaders in the north of Mexico at that time, as well as Juan Bautista Cabrera from Spain, were the main contributors to this stage. The representative hymnbooks of that era are

CHAPTER 16

the *Himnario Popular* (a Baptist publication under the auspices of the First Baptist Church of Monterrey), and the *Nuevo Himnario Evangélico*, published in 1914 by the American Tract Society under the name of Editorial Caribe, a publishing house based in Costa Rica at that time. This hymnal was a renewal of a previous one published in 1893, the *Himnario Evangélico*. The committee was formed by a combination of American White missionaries and Mexican leaders, and it worked in the midst of turbulence and the social turmoil of the Mexican Revolution. It was a collaborative effort of representatives of several denominations: Baptist, Congregational, Methodist and Presbyterian.

The second stage is one of **pioneering original compositions**. (1930-1970). It was a time when different denominations published their own hymnals. These are basically affirmations of their denominational identities. The *Nuevo Himnario Poular*, of the Baptist Spanish Publishing House (1955), the *Himnario Metodista* (1956), the *Himnario Evangélico Presbiteriano* (1961), the *Himnos de la Vida Cristiana*, of the Christian and Missionary Alliance (1967).

The *Nuevo Himnario Popular* maintains a strong funerary message, though the general theological emphasis of this stage is mainly the counter-cultural separation from cultural influences of the rest of society. The foreword of the *Himnario Evangélico Presbiteriano* explains two criteria for the collection of their hymns: Presbyterian Theology and Exclusión de toda melodía con ritmo mundano a fin de conservar el espíritu de genuina reverencia en el canto sagrado.[9]

This is the ruling criterion in this stage. It is the stage of the first original composition of hymns in Spanish. However, under such theological criterion, the pioneering original compositions of this stage follow the model and influence of North America and Europe. Important names in this stage are Vicente Mendoza and Epigmenio Velasco, Mexican Methodist pastors who wrote original hymns in Spanish.

The third stage is the **theological diversification** (1970-2000). The hymnbooks in this stage have a more diverse span of theological interests, with more attention to life in this world and the churches' responsibility in ministry to the world. There was more involvement of professional theologians in the formation and edition of hymnbooks.

The *Himnario Metodista* (1973) was edited by personnel of the Perkins School of Theology in Dallas, Texas, in the United States. In Buenos Aires, Argentina, an important editorial effort of collaboration among four denominations brought to life the **Cántico Nuevo** (1962), which is notoriously deep in theological implications; however, the main source of hymns is still outside of Latin America. This one is the Latin American hymnbook with more European input in it.

Important names in this stage are Pablo Sosa, Federico Pagura and Alfredo Colom. Sosa and Pagura, both Argentineans, provided excellent translations of hymns as well as original lyrics for the *Cántico Nuevo*. Their contribution is a real milestone in the development of original Latin American hymnody. They also wrote hymns that did not resemble the North American or European models but were original in the musical, lyrical, and theological language. However, most of their hymns were not included in the *Cántico Nuevo* hymnal, but published in smaller collections.[10] Guatemalan Alfredo Colom is one of the most prolific hymn writers of Latin America. His compositions used musical languages of Latin America. He represents an effort to popularize Evangelical worship through the use of native cadences and styles.

The *Himnario Bautista*,[11] published in 1978, is the most recent (or least old) Spanish language hymnbook published by Baptists. It contains 530 hymns and includes an index of guitar chords. This is notable in view of the tension in many churches throughout the Latin American region in relation to the use of guitars in worship.

One important feature of this hymnbook is that it was sponsored by the Home Mission Board of the Southern Baptist Convention and the Baptist General Convention of Texas. This fact is revealing of the missionary attitude of the SBC as well as the general self-perception of Latin American Baptists during the second half of the 20th century. Latin America was seen in 1978 as "home." Local conventions and other Baptist bodies were influenced by this perspective and so the work of cultural contextualization among Latin American Baptists has been a difficult enterprise, which has required much time and effort.

We are now in the fourth stage, **farewell to hymnbooks**. An ever-increasing tendency in most churches is to leave the use of hymnbooks altogether and substitute them with memorized texts or song sheets. In more affluent churches, projectors and screens are used for the lyrics.

Excellent hymnbooks have been published in this stage. *Celebremos su Gloria* (1992) collects most of Alfredo Colom's hymns; it has a creative outlook and a variety of resources for congregational singing. *Mil Voces para Celebrar* (1996), a Methodist hymnal, collects many of the new Latin American hymns that do not follow a North American or European model, as well as many songs from around the world. It is an indispensable resource for any Spanish-speaking church today.

Even though this is a time of abundant production of new songs and hymns, there is a widespread practice of disregarding the hymnbooks altogether and substitute them with recordings from the latest "Christian artist." This represents the risk of losing the liturgical wealth of hundreds of years of hymns and of the hymns of the global church.

A congregation will lose the historical connection by leaving hymnbooks behind. Christians will be in danger of falling into the trap of believing that there is no history behind them. Spiritual pride and historical myopia can result from such an attitude.

Another danger in abandoning hymnbooks is the lack of intercultural liturgical breeding in the local congregation. Hymnbooks make available to local congregations those songs and hymns from the global church. When a local church neglects hymnbooks it is in danger of falling into what Methodist theologian Justo González has dubbed "heretical" in the sense of looking at Jesus only from their own exclusive perspective.[12]

Thus it is necessary to discern how to use the various hymnbooks available in order to enrich the worship service. New songs must be present as well as old ones, national and international, in order to more faithfully perform the triple task of worship: cultural, counter-cultural and trans-cultural.

The Need for the Production of New Hymns

In order to capture the feeling of both leaders and people regarding the topic of renewal of hymns, a survey was prepared and sent to a network of Baptist Latin American theologians and applied to members of a local church in Monterrey.[13] Interestingly, a unanimous affirmative answer was given to the question of whether there is a need for new original hymns among Latin American Evangelical churches.

If more than 80 percent of the hymns you know have been translated into your language, there is a pressing need for more expressions of faith in your native language. Those translations may be beautiful, but they are still translations. There must be a place for international songs in Christian worship, in order to support the kata-holic dimension of worship, but the core of our singing (be it priestly, prophetic or kata-holic) should be produced originally in our language.

Furthermore, the current production of "Praise and Worship" songs is generally too weak in theological foundations.[14] This is another reason why more original hymns – the product of theological reflection and experience – must be written and spread throughout the Latin American region. Most of the songs used today are focused on the individual and not the community. Most do not address the communal nature of the Christian faith. Most lack any reference to the social dimensions and implications of the Gospel.

Some other questions in the survey dealt with the role of the local congregation in the task of renewing worship. Most of the answers in this regard agree that it is a matter which pertains to the local congregation. The experience of worship must be given back to a community of people who know each other and who have gone through phases in life as a family of faith. Huge convocations of masses for "Congresses of worship" among thousands of strangers do not bring any sort of authentic renewal to the devotional life of the Christian.

The production of new hymns may be both a cause and a result of church renewal. It is a cause when the people of God are sensitive enough to listen to the word of God prophesied through the hymns and respond in faith and transformation. It is also a result when as a consequence of God's transforming power, the hearts and minds of Christians are inspired to proclaim God's wonders and messages in new ways with new tunes and new poetic images.

According to Peruvian theologian Juan José Barreda Toscano, if we worship the Lord of Life, we are then compelled to live in community.[15] In general, Evangelicals in Latin America have experienced an intense degree of non-monastic community life through the years, and though a multitude in praise may be quite inspiring and unforgettable, it is in the local congregation that the deeper theological meanings of singing together are experienced.

Those who follow the Lamb are described in the book of Revelation chapter 14 as a singing people. They sing a new song that is their identity mark. They respond to the horrendous forces of the monster in the preceding chapter with a New Song. The New Song is the evidence of their strength to stand in opposition to the monster and to announce a New Reality with great certainty. Jesus Christ is the Lord of the entire Universe; therefore there is hope for life and justice and this hope should be put to music and sung with all the fibers of our being.

CHAPTER 17
LEADERSHIP SAFARI:
THE 21ST CENTURY PASTOR AS LEADER IN WORSHIP AND SPIRITUALITY

D. Leslie Hollon

Preface to the Safari

My new comfort zone is not having a comfort zone. The information, ideas, or circumstances that can coax me into comfort today may be cast into a contrasting context tomorrow. Yet as a Christian and as a pastor, I want to be and need to be a person of consistent character so people know they have a trustworthy shepherd to assist them through life's journey. The same expectation is placed on the church in general and each local congregation in particular.

God and culture are now shaping the 101st generation of Christians as we pursue the 21st century and Christianity's third millennium. In an era variously called post-modern, global-village, post-enlightenment, the information age, every human being is living in a world of fast-paced and constant change. The future shock prophesied in the 1960's by Alvin Toffler arrived with ferocity. Toffler, a futurist, predicted that the pace of change would increase so fast that the human capacity to shape the change – morally, emotionally, and relationally – would be severely tested.

Through this shock, however, faith can steady us and pump adrenaline into our soul. The soul God makes resilient has the inherent capacity to recover from the post-traumatic syndrome that comes to each of us as we venture forth in a world characterized by change. Bumps and bruises come with this territory of turbulent change as we walk through each day's demands and possibilities.

Pulsating through each person is a yearning to know: our purpose, our place, our people, our passion and our plan. These five yearnings serve as an internal compass that are placed by God in our soul as a prevenient grace to keep us tracking toward the Promised Land of spiritual fulfillment. The pastor is called by God to guide people toward the land of promise by showing them that true success is being all God creates us to be and doing all God calls us to do. All other pursuits for fulfillment cause us to miss the mark, which is known in Scripture as sin.

Safari is a Swahili word meaning to travel the adventure. The risk-filled terrains of a safari are jungle, desert, mountains, valleys, plains, rivers and oceans. The terrain of being pastor in the 21st century is also risk filled. The safari image conveys the sensations of certainties and uncertainties that come with our global age. The size of the challenge fits God.

The Holy Spirit is known as the Comforter and Counselor. Spirit is the constant of eternity who can comfort and counsel us with the needed spiritual resources to live effectively in our present world. This Holy Spirit inspired and inspires the Scriptures that reveal God's unchanging message for our ever-changing world. Christ became "the author and finisher of our faith," and offers the salvation by which we can be graced from our sins and transformed into disciples of eternity. These essentials help us as we seek to be Christ's body in Christianity's third millennium.

My presentation particularly aims to assist the spiritual guides of local congregations. Though, the terrain I cover may be interesting to any leader who is committed to helping a community grow in understanding of how to meet the challenges of change through faith dynamics.

To be effective, a pastor must be a person (meaning that one's individuality does not get lost amidst the responsibilities of being pastor) and the person must be a pastor (meaning that he or she is comfortable with the distinctive identity of being pastor). A thorough awareness of this integrated identity helps keep us on track with our private and public safari. This identity aids us in knowing our own promise for purpose, place, people, passion, and plan.

When the pastoral work day is done and I lay in bed, I remember Wayne Oates' dictum, "The promises we keep let us sleep. The promises we break keep us awake." When sleep comes quickly I am grateful for faithfulness. When sleep comes slowly, I close my eyes into God's grace.

A Changing Force, a Timeless Message

The ever-flowing river of life has lessons to teach, observed the Psalmist (Psalms 1, 23, 78 and 137), and all these lessons flow from the glad river of God (Psalm 46:4). In the same era, but standing by a river countries away, a Greek philosopher named Heraclitus said of the river's message, "Everything flows and

CHAPTER 17

nothing stays. . .You cannot step twice into the same river." These currents of change produce within us a love-hate relationship with time. Love, when the change benefits are quick and plenty and costs are minimal. Hate, when the benefits of change are slow and costly. This has always been true. So, Heraclitus also observed that when a stick is held down into the stream, it looks bent when actually it is straight. Our perception of reality may not accurately represent the actual reality.

An example is seen from the Baptist beginnings of the 1600s. The style of worship and music was hotly debated (sound familiar?). England's sterling Baptist pastor, Benjamin Keach, was also a hymnist. Resistance to congregational singing of hymns was the change issue of his day.

Keach cited the precedence of biblical practices for congregational hymn singing but lamented, "Tis no easy thing to break people of a mistaken notion, and an old prejudice taken up against a precious truth of Christ." He and his son subsequently would influence the early story of Baptists in America. His warning to those who opposed change simply because it had never been done that way before was important. People opposed the singing of hymns because they were perceived as carnal and formal. Fortunately, the opposition yielded. As the challenge was for them, so it is for us: how to tailor up-to-date methods for sharing the Gospel without changing the Gospel. This is the call of each Christian generation.

The fast-moving world that God loves in a John 3:16 style, is more diverse and intertwined than ever. As a global community, we have geographically expanded what the Mediterranean world of Jesus' day experienced: a connecting of commerce, communication, language, travel, regionalism, religious pluralism, political statecraft and warfare, ethnic diversity and exported cultures.

Our mosaic world society of 11,000 language groups is wrestling with the blend of globalism, regionalism, nationalism and localism. Massive forces of change are at work. The Gospel march into the next millennium carries awesome challenges if the church is to stay current. By the year 2027 our knowledge base may have expanded 97 percent, meaning that what can now be known is only 3 percent of the knowledge that will be available in sixteen short years. That's why Alvin Toffler and other futurists identify the present as the Third Wave of Civilization, the Information Age. The first wave was the Agricultural Age and the second, the Industrial Age.

Worship, the holy experience of encountering God, collects people from the multiethnic schoolroom, the hard drive office cubicle, the high-tech factory line, the farm, the marketplace, the blended family, the boardroom of corporate mergers, and the interfaith encounter. The worship experience must show worshipers how to live in this kind of world.

What is one to do? Can churches develop opportunities for such a world? Of course! Because the Lord our God, "maker of heaven and earth," long ago sent Christians into the future by way of the Great Commission. When the disciples saw him (Jesus) they worshiped him but some doubted. This was the response of the first-generation Christians to the changing pattern of how things would be. Their doubt was not whether they were looking at the resurrected Christ. The disciples knew this person before them was Jesus Christ. Their question was whether or not they were up to the task He had commissioned them to pursue, "Go therefore and make disciples of all nations ..." (Matthew 28:16-20). This commission is now being handed to the 101st generation of disciples. We too wonder if we are up to the task.

In these uncertain days of change, the best of our heritage reassures us that what brought us to where we are can guide us into tomorrow. Our heritage is values and principles, not methods, and these qualities give us the necessary spiritual insight to see God's leadership in choosing the right ministry designs for the age in which we live. We are guided by principles like biblical authority, self expression of the local church, Christian experiences of conversion and discipleship, mission and evangelism, reconciliation, spiritual gifts and religious liberty. These guiding forces are tailor-made for the age in which we live.

To understand effectively how to pattern these principles for shaping 21st century ministry, we must learn from the spiritual patterns of pioneers who trusted in God's dynamic power. Shapers of the early Protestant era – Martin Luther, John Calvin, Ulrich Zwingli – stressed that churches needed to distinguish between patterns of essential principles and methods (adiaphora). Confusing one for the other petrifies spirit into out dated structure.

As churches that have been entrusted to share the world's most precious message, we must expand our capacities for identifying, understanding and shaping a 21st century style of introducing people to Christian experience.

The following six insights, adapted from futurist Thomas Kuhn and the author of Hebrews, provide guidelines for how to see the changing patterns of history:

- Patterns are common, coming from the past into the present.
- Patterns are useful, providing boundaries and guidelines.
- A successful pattern tends to cause a paralyzing conclusion that this pattern is the only pattern, and other successful patterns aren't possible.

CHAPTER 17

- New patterns usually are formed by people on the fringes, positioned for cutting-edge perspectives.
- Pattern pioneers possess tremendous courage and faith.
- People choose their patterns and live with the consequences.

As Christians and churches grasp the past and present patterns within their communities, their ministry understandings can best be updated. The meaningful old and the exciting new can support each other as parallel models. Then seekers shaped by 21st century patterns won't feel like they are entering a 1950s time warp when they gather as church.

The Call to Purpose by Principled Priorities Through Vision

The renewal of God's vision is underway in the global church by being underway in local churches. We are not waiting to begin church renewal, we have already begun. A Ministry Agenda helps to guide one's progress in shaping the church's structure to facilitate the church's spirit. Renewal stops dead in its tracks when structures control spirit.

Priorities must be established if meaningful, long-range goals are to be accomplished. Priorities emerge from a great many possibilities. The tough decisions are not easy to make but need to be made if the church is to fulfill her ministry potential. We proceed under the premise that effective long range planning for a three to five year period builds upon a congregation's strengths. A church's weaknesses can only be transformed as they are connected to her strengths. Each church has strengths on which to build.

The church's best resource is a talented membership that possesses a fervent faith in God. The young members give the sign of the future, and the senior members give the sign of a vibrant heritage. God has called all of us to make a Gospel difference by building hope and healing hurts.

The church's mission is best clarified by forming a Long Range Planning Team that works as collaborators with the pastor/staff in particular and the congregation in general. Their efforts are divided into four major steps: 1) clarifying and stating the church's vision; 2) analyzing the church and community; 3) developing goals and strategies, based on the gathered information, by which their purpose and objectives can be realized; 4) presenting the work to the congregation for review. After making appropriate revisions through their collaborative process, the congregation can then passionately commit to the vision. Hundreds of hours are invested in the project, and the result is a God inspired direction for the future. Then comes the exciting time to fulfill the vision. Strategic development can focus on the six areas of: Growing, Worshiping, Sharing, Participating, Inviting and Giving. By design, some of the strategies and goals are to be quite specific, and others offer a general direction for action. This tandem approach encourages the entrepreneurial use of spiritual gifts guided by a common vision.

The report should be consistently used as a guide by all working groups within the church. A great tragedy occurs when the ministry agenda simply becomes a collection of promising but unused directions. The entire church is commissioned to the task of being a vibrant source of New Testament ministry. The pastor, church staff, committees, councils and ministry teams are to ensure that they accomplish the agenda that is set before them. Semi-annually, progress reports are to be given by various ministry groups within the congregation. The congregation is to encourage and constructively hold each other accountable.

The Vision Team considers its report to be the first of several phases. The plan is flexible and alterations can be made in light of unforeseen developments and changing conditions. Specific proposals requiring policy change and/or money expenditures are not finally accepted by the adoption of the initial report, but are to be separately considered and approved by the church before proceeding.

By pursuing the vision, the church ensures that her rich heritage of Gospel work continues. The Ministry Agenda serves as the central guide for the fulfilling message of God's reconciling love to the community and world. Success is directly proportional to the faithfulness by which established priorities are pursued.

The Ministry Agenda centers on the organizational basics of: a bias for action, focusing on people, encouraging individual and group creativity, working together, commitment to Gospel values and excellence, mastering the basics, perfecting a simple structure, and releasing the membership to minister from basic biblical beliefs. Through this plan, believers can invest their faith, spiritual gifts, time, money, and facilities into the areas of greatest importance in the church's mission.

Churches are in a great position to face the future, when their plans have truly been a spiritual process that will produce lasting growth in the church, community and the world. The vision, talent, work and prayers of the entire membership are required for the continued success of being faith partners in God's world.

CHAPTER 17

Guiding Principles for the Church's Safari

> We extend the love of Christ by:
> Growing in love for God with all our mind, heart, spirit and body; to love others and ourselves.
> Worshiping with our church family so God's presence may mutually shape us.
> Sharing our spiritual gifts for world shaping ministry.
> Participating in community for the benefit of friendship and spiritual growth.
> Inviting friends to experience God's gift of salvation.
> Giving of time and finances so God's plans will be achieved.

The church's guiding principles provide the basis by which a congregation partners with God to grow the church spiritually, numerically and missionally. The principles are then crafted to strategies and action plans, which themselves must be: 1.) biblical; 2.) sensitive to the Holy Spirit during the stage of research and development when church and society are analyzed; 3.) connected to releasing the empowered faith and spiritual gifts of the congregation.

Spiritual Fulfillment

What does the Promised Land of spiritual fulfillment look like? Where does the safari take us? What exactly are we pursuing? Jesus put it this way to his first followers, "Come and follow me, and I will make you ..." The Latin term for this is *sanctus ficare*, to be made holy. Thus, a church's worship space is called a sanctuary, meaning that a place exists through worship where we can expect the Holy to shape our lives; a place within God's presence where our purpose, people, place, passion and plans are intentionally reshaped by the Holy.

Reflecting upon this, I wrote a blessing which is frequently offered at the close of our worship services:

> As we go: Trust in the Father's love. Live in the ways of Christ. Feel the Spirit's comfort and counsel. Be the people of God who do the work of God. And know the Lord is with you always, even to the end of the age. Amen. Rejoice.

The blessing sends us out with the commission to go and do what we have experienced of God in worship.

Spiritually integrating the worship experience into daily life strengthens our love of God through our mind, heart, body, soul, and loving our neighbor even as we love ourselves. The quest will also show there are other sanctuaries where we can be shaped by the Holy, e.g., a walk in the woods, a get-away place at work/school/home; a special location beyond our normal route where we occasionally travel; a spiritually focused website; and of course, within the sacredness of our own conscience. The duration, intensity, and frequency of spiritual exercise determine the pace of our growth; just as when those characteristics are applied to determine the pace of our physical strength.

The essential role of the pastor is to lead. Lead where? In following Christ. Lead who? The members of a faith community in fulfilling their particular purpose. Lead how? By listening to the Holy Spirit, knowing the Scriptures, studying society, releasing the spiritual gifts of believers, and engaging people's soulful stories. To lead, the pastor must be trustworthy, and trust is built by loving God and the people, an effective work ethic and being a model for growth.

Extraordinary people are actually ordinary people who put forth extraordinary efforts to not only grow personally but to help others with their growth. People of faith in general and Christians in particular are to utilize more potential from our God-given capacity to grow holistically. The pace of change in the 21st century world is too fast for a static mind, body and spirit. The size of the challenge can be met if we will trust God and ourselves to release the latent potential inside of us. This is similar to what Soren Kierkegaard (1813-1855) described as Christ stirring the potential as an anxiety inside of us so we would take a leap of faith. Justin Martyr, the paradigm pioneer in the second century explained this as, "He became what we are in order that we might become what He is." As we remember his life, death, and resurrection, we renew our commitment to let him become within us. William Carey (1761-1834) challenged his pre-global missionary society in England with, "Expect great things from God. Attempt great things for God." The nineteenth century evangelist D. L. Moody commissioned, "The world has yet to see what God can do with one life totally yielded to him." Those last words caught my attention as I read them during my boyhood days along the Texas banks of the Cibolo Creek.

Jesus said in the Sermon on the Mount, "Be ye therefore perfect, even as your heavenly father is perfect (that is grow into complete godliness of your mind and character, having reached the proper height of virtue and integrity)" (Matthews 5:48, Amplified Version). Karl Barth, being encountered by this Christ, and

CHAPTER 17

needing to confront Hitler, wrote, "The seriousness of the Gospel is that it demands a decision." To confront the pressing circumstances of his day, Barth knew that bold decisions could only be made by people of courage and faith.

Arnold J. Toynbee, the 20th century historian, stated that the outcome during paradigm shifts is determined by the response given to the challenge. Pastoral leadership must help Christians mine the potential within them so the right responses are given to the challenge of future shock. Once activated, the new growth enables one to meet the challenges of a post-modern technological world. If we travel back to the future through biblical stories, we see how past paradigm pioneers can show us how to become present paradigm pioneers. Through them God reveals our way forward on the safari.

Noah, for instance, was disrespected by his home country. His greatness was revealed during a moral issue of global proportions. When God showed him what needed to be done, he did it. How? Though courageous faith. So it was when Joshua stepped out from the shadow of Moses and led a bunch of former slaves into freedom. Rahab stepped out from cheapening herself as a prostitute and helped the Israelites enter the Promised Land. David stepped out from being the youngest of eight sons and became Israel's greatest king. Amos stepped out from being a shepherd and became a prophet of godly justice. Matthew stepped out from the tax collectors' table and wrote a Gospel. Peter stepped out from his hatred for non-Jews and boldly led the church to accept Gentile Christians. Mary Magdelene stepped out from her lost place in society and followed Jesus to the cross. Timothy stepped out from his youth and aided the Apostle Paul in establishing churches throughout the Roman Empire. Aquilla and Priscilla stepped out from cultural norms and showed how husband and wife could be equal partners in life.

These and thousands of other stories, illustrate what God can do with followers whose hearts, heads, and hands are empowered by courageous faith. And this kind of faith is a non-negotiable requirement for the 101st generation of Christians. We must not be so foolish to think that because our technological cultures have changed so dramatically from theirs, that the essential character of faith has also changed. No, what must change is our capability to utilize this faith in the 21st century of outer space, cyberspace, virtual reality, bionic body parts, and a worldwide web.

For such a challenge we were born. During the safari we can discover more of what God has waiting in God's creation. If we now use email, fax machines, cellular phones, and digital productions as naturally as we use the radio, television, wired telephones, and compact discs, what awaits us in the future? In an era where we are thinking in terms of multi-universes instead of a single universe, what awaits us? In an era when satellites circling the earth control things on earth, what awaits us? Do we have within us the capacity to expand morally as well as intellectually, to be as wise as well as smart, to be as ecologically minded as we are consumer oriented?

We will benefit by remembering that we are the stewards of God's creation, not owners. Adam and Eve robbed from the Tree of Knowledge because they deceived themselves into thinking that they owned the Garden of Eden. Instead of living as stewards, they became usurpers. The resource of faith, however, keeps us in harmony with creation by aligning us in a right relationship with the Creator.

As God sends us into the future, I am struck by the trust God has in us to co-create with him. It reminds me of a simple phrase I have used through the years to commission our children. "Have fun and use good judgment," is what I have said to Rachel, Ryan and Steven since they were old enough to go outside by themselves. Whether to play next door at a friend's house or to send them around the world, these words have been my reminder: I trust you. Enjoy. Be responsible.

As winter morphs into spring, thanks be to God for our opportunity to green up and grow life. For the privileges and challenges of living responsibly in the era of exponential technological development, we turn afresh to Christ as the timeless one; we turn afresh to Christ as the: the Alpha and the Omega; the One who always was, is, and will be; the author and finisher of our faith. We find our way forward by following the Way, the Truth, and the Life. Our needed moral and spiritual development can then grow exponentially.

We can know the heightened consciousness that comes by what the Apostle Paul shared at the Parthenon in Athens, "In him we live and move and have our being" (Acts 17:28). Traveling into eternity with this basic faith awareness, means we can be trustworthy by daily renewing ourselves to make a Gospel difference. This Gospel difference happens as our personal faith becomes public and as our individuality becomes interdependent with the many people groups who inhabit this earth.   "The great task of magnanimous men and women is to establish with truth, justice, charity and liberty, new methods of relationships in human society – the task of bringing about their peace in the order established by God. We publicly praise such persons and earnestly invite them to persevere in their work with ever greater zeal. It is an imperative of duty; it is a requirement of love." These words were penned by Pope John XXIII in what has become a 20th century classic, Peace on Earth (*Pacem in Terris*).

CHAPTER 17

The requirement of new methods of relationships in human society for the ever changing world in which we live is a challenge bigger than any one of us. The size of the challenge fits the new commandment given by Jesus to his disciples, "Love one another as I have loved you and by this shall all people know that you are my disciples." This is the order established by God. These commissioning words from Jesus form the basis for how we enter eternity one day at a time.

Spiritual Formation

The pastor's essential task in the leadership safari is to guide people in their spiritual formation. Consequently, the pastor is helped from Scripture and Christian history by the following practical outcome questions. They are adapted from the pivotal work of Richard Foster and the marvelous movement called RENOVARÉ.

1. Are people loving God with their entire being and loving others as they love themselves? A church member should know how to love people by how they love God.

2. Are people experiencing a prayer-filled life (intimacy with God, centering one's life, depth of spirituality)? A church member should know how to pray and meditate.

3. Are people leading a virtuous life (personal moral transformation with the power to develop holy habits)? A church member should know how to live virtuously.

4. Are people developing a Spirit-empowered life (finding and nurturing one's spiritual gifts and yearning for the immediacy of God's presence)? A church member should know how to use his/her spiritual gifts and how daily to experience God's presence.

5. Are people pursuing a compassionate life (justice and shalom in human relationships and social structures)? A church member should know how to apply the Gospel in society.

6. Are people encountering a scripturally centered life (focusing on Bible study and faith sharing)? A church member should know how to study and apply the Scriptures, and how to share one's faith.

7. Are people in a *koinonia* life (a community of spiritual friendships)? A church member should know how to relate in spiritual community.

8. Are people living incarnationally in society? A church member should know how to use his or her faith skills (#1-7) in the workplace, school, entertainment areas . The Christian life is 24/7, 365 days a year.

People suffer little danger of being so heavenly minded they are of no earthly good. The reverse is true. We are tempted to be so earthly minded that we are of no heavenly good. By pursuing holistic spiritual formation, represented by these eight areas, we can best know how to translate the ways of heaven into earthly application.

Four Areas of Pastoral Ministry

As a pastor committed to helping people form faith for a 21st century world, I pledge to my congregation the following four commitments:

First, I promise to minister from a life of love. Second, I promise daily to trust God be trustworthy. Third, I promise to work diligently and effectively. Fourth, I promise to grow in my spiritual life and in my abilities as a pastor.

My promises are invested by organizing them through preaching and worship, pastoral care, administration, and mission/evangelism. Though a pastor must be a theoretician and a practitioner, a master generalist, and a selective specialist, he or she must seek to give balanced leadership for children, youth and adults. To do less is to crack the church's foundation by an imbalance of ministry priorities. The stressors bearing on today's church quickly expose any weakness in the church's life. Unnecessary grief can be minimized by a balanced approach. Though no one achieves a perfect balance, the energy saved by the pursuit for balance will be the very energy required to deal with the unavoidable grief of church life. Consequently, these days, eight is my favorite number as it represents the balance of two intersecting circles, symbols of infinity.

The turbulence that accompanies fast paced change can easily throw any of us off balance. But planning our work around these four ministry areas gives us a chance to realign ourselves after one ministry area requires an inordinate amount of time and effort.

Peter Drucker, a futurist and leadership guru, said that data becomes information when it is timely and relevant. Suffocating from piles of data, people are crying for real information. An American today can be exposed in one day to the amount of data an American a century ago would receive in a lifetime. Information provides the necessary knowledge of who, where and when. Instruction explains the how. Interpretation reveals the why. Inspiration breathes in the courage to do it.

For instance, the sermon is to God's divine story line (*imago dei*) within the worshiper. Then personal questions come into focus by the listener seeing more clearly the answers to such questions as, What is God saying to me? – Purpose. Who is involved with me in this story? – People. Where will my decision lead me? – Place. How can I invest myself in this mission? – Passion. How do I do what I now know I am supposed to do? – Plan.

Questions from the First Generation

"How do you like all the people? How did you know God wanted you to be a pastor? How do you help someone believe in God? How old is old enough to be baptized?" These and other "we want to know" questions were asked of me by a first grade Sunday School class.

The questions we ask reveal the desires of our soul and set the context for our experiencing God. Kenneth Scott Latourette, the Baptist church historian who taught at Yale and pioneered studies in global church growth principles, uncovered six essential questions asked by the fifty to sixty million people who lived in the Mediterranean world during Christianity's first three hundred years. Some of the questions are: Who can heal my pain? Who can guide me in this world? Who can grant me eternal life? Who can forgive my mistakes and failures? Who can help my family? Who can guide our society?

By successfully answering these questions, Christianity became the prevailing faith of the Roman Empire. Interestingly, these also are the essential questions of our present age. For the Christian movement to continue growing, churches must effectively answer these six questions because people are experimenting with any possible source to find their answers. We join the world's other seven plus billion people in wanting to know the answers.

God doesn't leave us alone to muddle in uncertainty. Clear directions are given to us so we can know the salvation which heals our aching souls. This clarity happens as we praise God's trinitarian splendor, confess our human frailty, sing our gratitude, search the Scripture for guidance, and live the answers we know so we may find the answers to what we don't yet know.

The Impossible Becoming Possible

The Casa Grande Ruins stand in the sunbaked Sonoran Desert of Arizona (U.S.A.) as testimony that the Hohokam Indians thrived during the 1200s. What enabled them to achieve when survival was challenge enough? As I walked among the ruins three answers emerged: adaptability, hard work and ingenuity. They did what they needed to do with what they had in order to accomplish what they could.

"I can do all thing through Christ who strengthens me," was the promise the Apostle Paul lived. And through his living and those of one hundred succeeding generations of Christians, testimony of Christ's strength stand not as ruins but as the living Church. The Church assembled reveals the nature of God's ability to make our abilities more than what they would be minus the strengthening presence of Christ.

Living in an age called by some as post-enlightenment, we should be reminded of the insight that Roland Bainton, the famed church historian of Yale, wrote for his grandchildren in a book, *Church of Our Fathers*. When describing the Enlightenment era, he warned: "Man is like a clumsy juggler. . .who first drops first one ball and then another. And so the church in trying to decide whether the Christian religion was true forgot what the Christian religion can do." Now is the time to coordinate our faith so the truth and power won't clumsily fall into the abyss of lost opportunity.

Traveling along the precipice of the 21st century and Christianity's third millennium is a safari for all of us. Pastoral leadership seeks to chart the pathways that lead to the promised destination of spiritual fulfillment.

CHAPTER 18
THE LITURGICAL PARTICIPATION OF CHILDREN IN SMALL CHURCHES:
THE THEOLOGY BEHIND IT, AND HOW IT CAN BE DONE

Alison Sampson and Nathan Nettleton

Abstract

The concept of the priesthood of all believers underpins the participation of children in worship. Children who are part of the life of the church are regarded as members of the priesthood; as such, they have pastoral and ministerial gifts to share. Like adults, they need to worship God; and as catechumens, they need to learn about faith.

By being enabled to participate fully in the worship service, children have an opportunity to share some of their gifts; they are encouraged to engage in worship; and they learn the patterns of the faithful.

This paper explores these convictions, partly in theory but primarily in the practice of one small congregation, the South Yarra Community Baptist Church. This small church, with a richly liturgical and sacramental approach to worship has, over the last few years, developed ways of more fully involving the children in the liturgy without dumbing it down. Rather than add children's segments, we have looked for ways that the liturgical experience could be enhanced for everyone by adding additional symbolic actions to the existing components of the liturgy, and then inviting the children, who are much less inhibited about movement, to lead us in these actions. Most of our small group of children is now regularly present and participating for most or all of the service.

Background

Facilitating the involvement of children in the life and liturgy of the church has proved challenging for churches across the board, but in small and under-resourced churches, the challenge can be even greater and much harder to hide. In many larger churches, the approach has been to pay to make the problem go away: we invest in well resourced Sunday School or Kids' Church programs and send the children out to be entertained and educated while we get down to the adult business of worshipping God. A dozen or so years later, they grow out of Sunday School and a large percentage of them disappear, and we are left wondering why children who we thought of as having grown up in the church can't seem to feel at home in it. But, of course, they didn't grow up in the church. We sent them to grow up out there while we were doing our adult things.

Yet alternative approaches are not easy to find, and so those churches that can afford to resource big programs mostly continue to do so. But what of the small and under-resourced churches? Most small churches are simply trying to replicate the patterns of the big churches, perhaps in the hope that if they get the structures right, they'll become a big church too. But in many areas, this doesn't actually work very well, and this is certainly evident when it comes to the involvement of children. It's a bit hard to run a program with different approaches and activities for each age group when you've only got one or two children in each group. And who is going to run it? If your congregation consists of only twenty or thirty adults, it is quite possible that you will not have anyone with the gifts or desire to miss worship regularly and run the children's program. Even if you do, when your congregation is that small it is quite a wrench to remove anybody from the worshipping group, however good the reason. So, even if we believed that sending children out of the liturgy was the best and most desirable thing to do, small and under-resourced churches trying to do so is likely to create more problems than it solves.

Nathan Nettleton is the pastor of the South Yarra Community Baptist Church, a church with what some have called a high-church Bapto-Catholic liturgical style. In the sixteen years he has been there, the average Sunday attendance has fluctuated between about twenty and forty-five people. At the moment, if all the regulars turned up at once, which of course never happens, there are thirty-four of us. Of those thirty-four, seven are children who ages range from seventeen months to years years. One of them is Nathan's daughter, and three of them are the daughters of this paper's co-author, Alison Sampson. Although we have tried approaches such as hiring baby-sitters to look after the children in another room while the liturgy was underway, it has never felt right or worked well for us.

CHAPTER 18

Alison has pushed us to look for better ways. Having grown up as a pastor's kid herself, and now as a mother, writer and theologian, Alison has had the gifts to think through the issues and the personal interest to keep pushing us to face the challenges and find creative solutions. And we and our children are very grateful that she did. Most of our children now stay and participate in the liturgy most of the time, and most of the time most of us are glad they do.

What follows is the theological underpinning of the integration of our children into the service, and a description of how we have put it into practice.

Why Include Children?

Fundamental to the way our church practices worship is the notion of the priesthood of all believers. That is, we take seriously the idea that every participant in the life of the church has pastoral and ministerial gifts to offer the congregation. We take this concept further than most by claiming that, whether or not they are baptized (and in most Baptist churches they are not), children, too, are members of the body of Christ and as such they have gifts to share. As such, too, they have a need to worship God, a need that isn't met by taking them out of the service to engage in Sunday school activities (however excellent the activities).

We believe too that faith is not something we get when we have learned enough doctrine, but is a gift from God, encouraged and nurtured by exposure to the patterns of the faithful. Children and other catechumens obtain this exposure primarily by standing alongside the faithful as they engage in worship; the relationships they build there will carry into all other aspects of church life.

Putting it into Practice

For their sake and ours, children are full participants in our worship service. To enable this, we have had to interrogate our worship practice and find ways to enable their participation, and we have had to be honest about the parts of the service that don't work for them. Overall, we have added more music, movement and activity to our service to encourage their participation; we have provided activities for them to do during the service; and we have changed some of our views on what constitutes a worshipful stance. Our liturgy style is very formal, which many of us once thought of as "adult." However, our children have surprised us with what they are capable of doing. For example, we have a ten minute period of silence, followed by the sermon, every week. We were not sure the kids could manage this, but as we talked about expectations and provided quiet activities for them to do, the kids have shown us they can keep silence, too. We adults have also learned that sitting in silence means learning to embrace small noises in the background as signs of creativity and life.

As we worked to integrate our children without turning our service into one of those "family friendly" affairs, we found that a good service can be accessed on many levels – and that a formal liturgy is, in fact, particularly suited to children. There are several reasons for this. For one, we use the same liturgy for a church season: Advent, Lent, Pentecost, or common time. The only things that change within a season are the readings, a few prayers, the sermon and the hymns. Many of our prayers are sung, whether they are short repeated refrains or the more complex creeds and Lord's Prayer; this makes them simple to memorize. The use of repetition – spoken, sung, structural and visual – makes the service easy to memorize over time, whether or not people can read. Alison's three children have all known and bellowed out parts of the liturgy from the age of two or so.

(The repetition of the formal liturgy also opened up possibilities for the inclusion of languages other than English. We now regularly have some prayers spoken aloud in Mandarin Chinese. It is seamless because everyone else has the English translation in front of them if they can't remember what is being said. Although our Chinese members speak good English, the inclusion of their mother tongue communicates our valuing of their heritage, and is a Pentecost gift to us all.)

During the service, we encourage participation rather than performance. As part of this, every regular attendee has several parts during the service; the effect is that the service is spoken by many voices, with no voice dominating.

Of course, some of our older children already participated in this by taking parts in prayers or readings, and most children joined in the spoken and sung responses. But that's all very verbal and doesn't keep the attention of the younger ones. The little ones needed to be able to do things, and those things needed to be relevant, important, and valued.

Nathan sat down with the service booklet, which includes the texts of our liturgy; went through it page by page; and tried to imagine what could be happening in movement and action while those texts were being spoken or sung. He sought actions that would add rather than detract from what was going on.

He came up with a series of actions for young children that enhance the service. For example, early in our liturgy we have a prayer invoking the presence of the Spirit that is spoken with a sung refrain. As that prayer is spoken and sung, there is a dancing procession around our central altar. We have a processional cross, a processional kookaburra (the kookaburra being Australia's avian symbol of the Holy Spirit), and dancers waving symbolic flames made of sparkly fabric. Our youngest girl recently started enthusiastically joining in the dance, often going around in the opposite direction to the rest and at twice the speed, but that's all good. The Spirit blows where it will and you cannot know where it is going. The flame dancers appear twice more, as the Bible is processed for the readings, and during the eucharistic epiclesis.

When the Gospel is read from the center of the room, it is now surrounded by children reverently holding icons of the four evangelists. When it comes time to set the table, the children line up at the side table, bow before the elements, and then carry them to the central table and set it all out.

We completely changed the way we do the prayers of the faithful. We have instituted a stational approach to the intercessions. After an introductory exhortation to pray, there is about five minutes for people to move around between various stations to offer prayers for different kinds of needs. These stations invite both a prayerful symbolic action and some words. For example, there is a symbolic brick wall, and people are invited to indicate their prayer by pulling a brick from the "wall of oppression" and writing a note or drawing a picture-prayer in the blue sky of freedom about the situation of conflict, injustice or oppression they are praying for. The words or pictures can then prompt other people's prayers; it is not all private devotion.

Although we have five minutes during which we all intercede at these stations, it is not at all uncommon to see a child, or occasionally an adult, go over to one of them and offer a prayer at some other point during the liturgy. The station of a garden and small animals, where we pray for the earth, is especially popular.

So the children have roles in which they can move about – they process with icons; dance as we sing; hold the Bible during the readings; and set the communion table. We celebrate the Lord's Table every week.

Like the adults, our children take pride in and ownership of their roles, and tend to see themselves as participants in the service, rather than as people being entertained. If, at times, they are bored, we are comfortable with that: boredom is something all of us have to work with, and the sooner we learn to deal with it, the better.

As well as giving the children specific roles, we aim to make the service accessible on many levels. For example, we try to engage the different senses, thus broadening the modes of communication. Each week we smell incense, see candles being lit, hear the melodies of deeply familiar songs, and taste freshly baked communion bread. Small changes, such as a more acrid incense and bread baked with bitter herbs during Lent, or a fruity incense and a loaf made with milk and honey for the Easter service, communicate to even very little children that something has changed. If they pay attention, they may work out why.

Our worship space is decorated with religious imagery and icons, giving children (and adults) lots to look at and stimulate their imagination when their attention wanders. They are also free to move about quietly at any time during the service and light candles, hang up prayer flags, play in a sand tray or sit under the communion table. Although we discourage our children from thundering around, and occasionally need to remind them that they are not the center of attention at this time, we don't require them to sit still or maintain absolute silence.

Finally, during the long silence and the sermon, we provide an activity sheet that presents a simple paraphrase of one the lectionary readings, and some suggested responses. They can choose to do one of the suggestions, or they can develop an activity of their own devising. We explicitly name the open option to allow for an authentic response to the story. This openness has been an interesting process, as the kids often say they don't know what to do; but as the silence grows they tend to become absorbed in an idea and create something surprising and beautiful in response.

For these activities, they draw from a set of shoe boxes that contain art and other materials. For example:

- felt tip pens and blank paper
- plasticine to make figurines and models
- correspondence materials (such as paper, envelopes, the church directory, and stamps)
- tangrams, with tangram puzzles related to the week's story
- tiny blank books to rewrite and illustrate the story
- figurines with scraps of cloth to make figures from the story
- beads and beading string to make necklaces, etc., especially for stories to do with treasure, pearls, and other valuables
- a basket of knitting needles and thread, to make knitted squares for AIDS orphans in Africa, or to make God's eyes, or to do a spot of finger-knitting
- and there are many other boxes.

CHAPTER 18

Each week, the boxes are placed in the worship space for the children to work with. We are also building collections of jigsaw puzzles, art books (bookmarked at particular images), and picture story books. These resources are brought in from time to time to match lectionary themes; the children can flick through the books or work on a jigsaw alone or together.

We have certainly found that the activity sheets have helped children tune in to the preaching because on several occasions the preacher has been corrected by a child, mid flight, especially when he has messed up a quote from Harry Potter!

In summary, in our search to find ways to integrate children into the worship service without losing the formal style, we added additional symbolic movements to the liturgy; we provided quiet activities for children to do during the time of silence; and we gradually changed some of our views on what constitutes a worshipful stance.

Final Observations

Including children in the worship service has not all been plain sailing. As much as our children have surprised us with their ability to respect the event, these things cannot be done without some increase in background noise and sudden unpredictable movement, and that has been the cause of some angst for some people.

As the pastor, Nathan is the one they complain to! Most of the answers to these concerns have already been mentioned above, but it should also be noted that it is an important part of our spiritual formation to listen to these concerns and listen for God's wisdom and insight. In addition, Nathan has used the complaints (which have been utterly outweighed by the positive feedback) as an opportunity for pastoral instruction in the purposes of public liturgy and how to engage more fully in it.

Over and over, the concerns are driven by a misunderstanding of the nature of public liturgy. Most of us have grown up with an unacknowledged paradigm which assumes the liturgy should be conducted as perfectly as possible so that nothing will distract people from God; and that it is purely an aid to private devotion. Although there is some overlap between public liturgy and private devotion, they are two different activities that should occupy two different time-slots.

The public liturgy is about offering the communal gift of the entire congregation to God. Everyone has to add his or her contribution to the communal offering or it will not truly be the offering of us all. If we pursue excellence by excluding the contributions of those whose contributions are messy or chaotic or only semi-articulate, then we are offering to God something that to our eyes is more beautiful, but is a lesser offering because its beauty was achieved at the expense of God's little ones. In our church, at least, that is a sacrifice we are no longer willing to make.

We have largely experienced the participation of children in the worship service as a great gift. We included them primarily for their sake, but the rewards have been abundant. In their freedom of movement, children have given us permission to move around the service more freely ourselves. In their avid curiosity and absorption, we have been challenged out of our distraction and encouraged to pay attention. In their hugs and in the way they welcome others in each week, they have modelled loving pastoral care. In their absolute trust, they demonstrate very real faith.

At times, the actions of one child or another has shocked and challenged us, even brought us to tears. One memorable Easter, Nathan's daughter, then about four years old, sobbed inconsolably at the foot of the cross, a poignant reminder of the women who stood watch while Jesus died. We name these actions as gifts, even when they feel like interruptions and challenge our adult preference for quiet participation.

Their presence has reminded us that Jesus came to us as a real little baby, who cried and wore nappies and kept his parents up nights; and that, as a grown man, he welcomed little children, encouraged them to draw near, and instructed his disciples to become more like them, with all their irruptions into the silence, difficult questions, vulnerability, wonder, trust, unquestioning love, and ecstatic expressions of joy.

Our children have been a tangible reminder of what it is to be childlike, and, no matter our age, have challenged each of us to investigate our role as a child of God.

Further, by investigating the accessibility of our service to children, and by broadening our modes of prayer and response, we have learned that worshipping with all our senses offers a fuller experience than that of worshipping with words alone. All of us, not just children, respond to a variety of forms of communication, whether in worship or other aspects of life.

Not every adult functions well in the cognitive realm; not every adult is literate, fluent, or capable of abstract reasoning. By welcoming our children into the worship service and meeting their needs, we have made ourselves more open to adults who operate in more visual or sensory modes, and to adults with disabilities. We have discovered that the marginalization of children from worship can obscure others who are being excluded; bringing children in brings others in, too.

And we are all children in God's eyes. For us as church leaders, the challenge is to take seriously the needs and gifts of all of the children of God – young and old, able and physically challenged, quick witted and slow, tongue-tied and fluent, cerebral and artistic, English speaking and not, and everyone in between – and to find ways for every one of us to be not audience members, but full participants in the life and the worship of the church.

If we are up to the challenge, and challenge it is, the good news is that we might find ourselves becoming the glorious, messy, joyful, chaotic, rowdy, unpredictable, uncontrollable body of Christ, radically inclusive and kaleidoscopic in its gifts – which is exactly we are called to be.

Select Bibliography

- Jensen, David Hadley Graced Vulnerability. A Theology of Childhood. Cleveland: Pilgrim, 2005.
- Mercer, Joyce Ann Welcoming Children. St Louis, MO: Chalice, 2005.
- Miller-McLemore, Bonnie J Let the Children Come. San Francisco: Jossey Bass, 2003.
- Ng, David and Virginia Thomas Children in the Worshiping Community. Atlanta: John Knox, 1981.
- Sampson, Alison The Priesthood of All Believers: An exploration of the ministry of children to the church and its implications for congregations. Melbourne: Zadok Papers no. S186, 2011.
- Westerhoff III, John H Will Our Children Have Faith? New York: Seabury, 1976.
- Yust, Karen-Marie 'More than a Glimpse of Worship' in Liturgy 19 no. 1 2004, pp 21-26.
- Yust, Karen-Marie Real Kids, Real Faith. San Francisco: John Wiley, 2004.

Some Excellent Picture Story Books

- Tomie dePaola Now One Foot, Now the Other (child as agent of care, healing)
- Mem Fox and Julie Vivas Wilfrid Gordon McDonald Partridge (love thy neighbour, child as agent of care)
- Bob Graham Rose meets Mr Wintergarten (love thy neighbour, love thy enemy, child as agent of care)
- Margaret Wild and Peter Shaw Hop, Little Hare! (child as agent of care)
- Liliana Stafford and Stephen Michael King Amelia Ellicott's Garden (love thy neighbour)
- Antonia Barber and Nicola Bayley The Mousehole Cat (self-sacrifice, stilling the storm, love thy neighbour)
- Kim Michelle Toft The World that We Want (creation, stewardship)
- Jeannie Baker Where the Forest Meets the Sea (creation, stewardship)
- Eric Maddern and Paul Hess Nail Soup (hospitality, abundance)
- Reeve Lindburgh and Holly Meade On Morning Wings (a retelling of Psalm 139)
- Julie Vivas The Nativity (Advent, Christmas)
- You can find a longer list of Advent stories (often hard to get, sadly) here: http://lostinastory.blogspot.com/2009/11/advent-list.html.
- You can also visit http://storypath.wordpress.com/about-2/. Click on a theme for a list of books related to the theme. Many of the books are American and not readily available, and some of the links feel tenuous – however, a good resource to flick through of an evening.

Our church website is www.laughingbird.net, and it contains many liturgical resources.

COMMISSION ON EVANGELISM

Led in a very positive way by Fausto A. Vasconcelos, director of the Division on Mission, Evangelism and Theological Reflection (METR), the Commission on Evangelism began its specific walk during the quinquennium of 2010-2015, establishing its goals and desires for the commission as well as presenting many informative papers and provoking subjects in sharing the Gospel of the Lord Jesus Christ with the world. The victories and challenges in different parts of the world were discussed and the commission trusts and hopes that many people will come to Christ as a result of implementation of the commission's desire that all persons come to Jesus Christ as Savior and Lord.

There were numerous events in the past quinquennium in which the BWA evangelism theme of Bread of Life (BOL) was the primary emphasis. The pillars and purpose of the commission for 2010-2015 were:

- The Empowerment of the Holy Spirit (in line with the BWA theme for this quinquennium ("In Step with the Spirit")
- The awareness of the Mandate for Evangelism
- The Holistic Mission of the Church

The Bread of Life Program's purpose was to mobilize Baptists at the local level to:

- Participate in a process to renew their understanding of the mission God in Christ has committed to the church
- Stimulate the desire to bear witness to the multiple dimensions of the church's missional calling in the churches' particular context
- Facilitate the sharing of stories on effective evangelistic engagement in the local area

Some of the Bread of Life events were:

North Haiti Christian University, *Haut Limbé, January 31-February 1, 2013*

The result was a Declaration drafted, presented and receiving enthusiastic reception, proposing the formation of an Alliance of Baptists in Haiti for the purpose of uniting all Haiti Baptists in their common efforts to witness and be a prophetic voice in the country.

First Gathering of Baptist Denominations, *Rio de Janeiro, Brazil, July 22, 2012*

This was the first ever initiative to bring together Baptists of different traditions in Rio. It proved to be a very encouraging initiative. Represented were the Brazilian Baptist Convention, the National Baptist Convention and the Convention of Independent Baptist Churches. Two other groups, the Bible Baptist Fellowship and the Convention of Regular Baptist Churches, were not able to attend, but are open to the initiative. All Baptist groups in Rio together have a total of about 800 local churches/missions. About 150 leaders and church members were in attendance. They were challenged to plan a "Jesus Christ, Bread of Life" outreach action in 2013/2014 involving all local Baptist churches in Rio as a pilot plan for the entire country.

UBLA Congress and Assembly, *Asunción, Paraguay, April 18-21, 2012*

Nine hundred and ninety two registered Latin American Baptist delegates in addition to other worshippers gathered at the Latin American Baptist Congress and Assembly. The presentation of a *"Jesus Christ, Bread of Life"* PowerPoint by the METR director generated enthusiasm and support. Marlene Baltazar da Nóbrega Gomes, president of UFBAL (Latin American Baptist Women's Union) requested a copy of the BOL PowerPoint to post it on the UFBAL website to encourage Latin American Baptist women to Evangelism.

Le Pain de Vie, *Lagos, Nigeria, November 15-16, 2011*

Le Pain de vie, a "Jesus Christ, Bread of Life" training conference on mission and evangelism, was designed specifically for BWA Francophone member bodies in Africa. It reflected, among other truths, on the mandate for evangelism and the holistic mission of the church through the leadership of General Secretary Neville Callam, Youth Director Emmett Dunn and Associate Director for Communications Eron Henry.

Cambodia, *July 11-14, 2011*

This all-day *"Jesus Christ, Bread of Life"* training seminar for sixty-three pastors/leaders of the Cambodia Baptist Union from seventeen provinces around the country were introduced to the BWA vision and mission for evangelism.

APBF Baptist Mission Consultation at Kohima Ao Baptist Church Conference Center, *Nagaland, India, August 24-27, 2011*

There were 135 mission leaders representing 1.3 million members of the thirteen Baptist conventions and associations in Northeast India. This was a follow-up to the Living Water Conference in Singapore in October 2009, now under the *Jesus Christ, Bread of Life* theme, to strategize for evangelism and mission for the region.

In these last five years we have heard wonderful presenters dealing with this vital subject of our lives. In Kuala Lumpur, for example, we heard about church planting, and the case of the Ghana Baptist Convention Home Mission Field by Steve Asante and Emmanuel Mustapha. We discussed the topic, "Missionary Ministry in Asia: Jesus for Eurasia," by Pavlo Unguryan. That year we also heard, "Evangelism & Missions: A Practical Approach," by Daniel Trusiewicz and Timothy H. Lee, professor of missions, Korean Baptist Theological Seminary.

In Ocho Rios, July 2013, the commission dealt with the theme and sub-theme, "In Step with the Spirit: Liberation." Many Jamaicans were present, which made the presentations exciting and wonderful discussions followed each presenter.

Many more keen and interesting subjects on evangelism were presented and discussed over the last five years in other countries like Chile, and Turkey. They were helpful to members of the commission and to the visitors who always make our meetings more vibrant and insightful.

The members of the Commission on Evangelism have much to do. Discovering how to inspire and motivate our Baptist brethren and sisters around the globe to share how persons may come into relationship with God through Jesus Christ and live the life for which they were created is the challenge before us. We can move in that direction, led by the Spirit. May God, through God's Spirit, lead each of us to help bring many to God through the victory of Jesus Christ, the resurrected Son.

Eddy Hallock, commission vice chair, has served as minister of Missions/Evangelism, Tallowood Baptist Church, Houston, Texas, for the last ten years. He pastored for nineteen years in the USA and then served as a missionary in Rio de Janeiro, Brazil, for fifteen years. He served as vice chair of the BWA Commission on Evangelism from 2010-2015.

CHAPTER 19
CHURCH PLANTING AND LEADERSHIP IN EASTERN EUROPE

Daniel Trusiewicz

The European Baptist Federation with the help of its Mission Partners has developed a mission partnership (MP) to facilitate evangelism and the planting of new Baptist churches in Europe, the Middle East and Central Asia. The MP provides funding for suitably gifted people to work as evangelists and church planters in their own countries.

The MP was launched in April 2002 as the response of the EBF to the needs of nations that are open to the Gospel. The number of MP projects has grown steadily throughout the years and the EBF Mission Partnerships has helped start about two hundred new congregations by 2014 and at least ten thousand people have become members of these churches. The MP church planters work in countries of post-communist Eastern Europe, the Baltic nations, the Caucasus and Central Asia, amongst Arabic-speaking peoples of the Middle East and Iraq as well as in Central Europe – particularly among the Roma people.

An important principle is that indigenous church planters are selected and supervised by national Baptist unions. The goal is to start new congregations and thus encourage indigenous leaders for a long run activity. The MP ministry has seen significant fruit in changed lives and transformed communities, which means that virtually thousands have been influenced by the Gospel.

Global statistics show that the number of Christians decreased by almost 1.5 percent while the Muslims increased by nearly 8 percent during the 20th century. This statistic is rather alarming and an appreciation of indigenous mission is the inevitable conclusion from the past as well as a recommended model for successful evangelistic work in 21st century.

In the last decade of the 20th century interesting dynamics of spiritual movement was registered in Eastern Europe that had earlier been suppressed by the atheistic ideology. As new countries declared independence after the collapse of the Soviet Union in 1990 and the introduction of freedom, many new churches were being planted by nationals. For example, in Ukraine, there were about ninety-six thousand members in Baptist churches in 1990 and this number grew to one hundred and fifty thousand in 2004. In the much smaller country of Moldova the number of Baptists doubled during the same period, from eleven thousand to twenty-one thousand. In Armenia, the growth has been even more spectacular as from the handful of 400 Baptists in 1991 they have grown to about five thousand in 2004. The role of MP is to facilitate these efforts of indigenous church planters.

Baptists are significant people movements in the societies of Eastern Europe and indigenous church planters are well mobilized in doing their work. They are most effective because they know the local languages and cultures as well as have natural contacts. It has been a tremendous privilege to witness this and here follow some examples from the mission fields.

Armenia – Unprecedented Growth

This small Baptist union experienced a phenomenal growth since independence in 1991, a sky rocketing development from less than 400 members in 1991 to about five thousand in 2004. More than 100 new congregations have been started there since 1991 and the church planting department has been established in the Baptist Seminary of Yerevan.

The Baptist Union of Armenia owes a lot to the competent leadership of Asatur Nahapetyan, its general secretary, who is very mission minded, relational and a well-organized person. New churches are planted by young and spiritually pioneering Armenian leaders who have been called by God, properly trained and enlisted in this ministry by the union. The need is great indeed as Evangelicals are scarce in Armenia and local people are quite open to the Gospel.

Moldova – Economically Deprived and Spiritually Wealthy

Moldova is regarded to be the poorest nation in Europe; 60 percent of its population live below the poverty level established by the European Union. This totally rural nation has, at the same time, demonstrated a lot of missionary potential. The people are diligent and the land has been farmed very well. The problem is that the country can't sell its produce for a good price and there are no state subsidies for farmers (in case of a drought or similar natural disasters).

The Baptist Union of Moldova was formed when the country gained its independence in 1991 after the breakup of the Soviet Union and numerous new churches have been planted there since. It is also reported that Moldova was

CHAPTER 19

the strongest center of evangelical Christianity in the former Soviet Union with the highest percentage of evangelicals per capita. The best result in Europe is rated when the number of Baptists compared with the density of population! In Moldova, it is more than 1 percent.

Moldova is particularly open for the Gospel despite its material deprivation. Church planting has remained more successful than other countries of Eastern Europe. The indigenous church planters are able to start new congregations during the first two years, however the test usually comes after five years. Fortunately, most church plants do continue after five initial years.

Igor Seremet has successfully planted a new congregation in Anneni Noi and began a school for church planters. Thanks to such leaders the Baptist Union of Moldova membership has doubled during the last 20 years. The union has sent many missionaries to other Russian speaking countries, including the Central Asia.

Ukraine - Second Largest Baptist Union in Europe

Ukraine is numerically the second largest Baptist union in Europe – one hundred and twenty five thousand members who worship in more than two thousand congregations (2014). Those recently planted usually meet in rented halls. The Baptists of Ukraine have started hundreds of new congregations all over the country because the indigenous evangelists demonstrated a mission minded vision as their goal was to double the number of churches and believers.

The first evangelical revival in Ukraine started in the 1830s with the conversion of Onischenko who was a farmer near Odessa. In 1868 Yefim Tsymbal was baptized by Abraham Unger, considered the first Ukrainian baptism. The new movement grew rapidly. In 1926 there were more than one thousand churches. Since 1927 Baptists suffered harsh persecution from the Soviet regime. New opportunities came again with the Perestroyka in 1985, which has resulted in excellent growth. In 1990 there were ninety-six thousand members in more than one thousand churches; by 1995 the number of members grew to one hundred and ten thousand who worshiped in fourteen hundred congregations; and in 2004 the Baptists of Ukraine reported one hundred and fifty-six thousand members in two thousand seven hundred local churches. However by 2014 the number dropped to one hundred and twenty-five thousand members and two thousand four hundred congregations.

Pastor Volodia Omelchuk of Kiev, the capital city of Ukraine, may be regarded as a typical leader and a particularly successful one. He began the church planting work in May 2003. In the beginning there were just a handful of persons on the church planting team who had the goal to start a new congregation, which they called the "Grace." The work was based on home groups and targeted at the youth and young couples. As time passed they developed numerous and effective programs, ranging from contemporary church services to social projects influencing local society, such as the excellent work with young drug addicts and lectures of drug prevention in schools. In 2014 this congregation drew more than three hundred regular attendees. Grace also started two daughter congregations in Kiev, Resurrection the Spirit of Life.

Romania – Numerous and Influential Baptists

Total population is 22.3 million; major religion: Eastern Orthodox, 87 percent; Protestant, 7 percent, Roman Catholic, 5 percent; other and unspecified, 1 percent (2002 census).

The first Baptists in Romania were of German extraction. Karl Scharschmidt, a carpenter by trade, was baptized by Johann Gerhard Oncken in Hamburg in 1845. Later he came to Romania and settled in Bucharest. The Baptist Union of Romania is currently the third largest Baptist body in Europe. Baptists are a mass movement with about one hundred and ten thousand members.

Indigenous church planter George in a town called Pantelimon near Bucharest planted a new congregation from teaching music in a garage. Gradually, the number of people grew and the group developed new ways of ministry, including help to the homeless and the Roma people (Gypsies). Now the church is well established and has its own building. George started another congregation in another town in Romania. He believes that evangelism and church planting is his primary task.

Russia – Huge Distances are Natural Hindrance

Baptists in Russia trace their history to 1867. In 1914 (50 years after the first baptism), they numbered well over one hundred thousand Baptists in spite of the czarist oppression. The Communist revolution gave good grounds for growth and the Baptists counted about two million then. The Soviet government introduced heavy restrictions in the 1960s, including a ban on children attending adult worship. Baptisms were allowed after the age of 18 as well as the required government approval for church leaders.

Indigenous church planter Boris came to Novy Urengoy (Yamal peninsula in Siberia, above the Polar Circle) where oil and gas had been earlier discovered and realized that the indigenous Nyentse people were pushed away from their territories. Fishing and hunting as well as reindeer breeding used to be their traditional way of living. Boris started helping them and found out that they became open to the Gospel. Indigenous missionaries are sharing the Gospel with locals and helping them to find their place in the new situation. Church planting in Siberia may be very fruitful as soon as a missionary gets there across pathless areas.

Belarus- Most Rrestrictive Religious Laws in Europe

The last dictatorship in Europe has the most suppressive religious law. The religious law, which was introduced in 2002, is very restrictive, especially concerning newly planted churches without a permanent building. According to this law a Christian meeting for worship at home is illegal. However within eight years prior to this, 158 new churches were opened. But the new law restricted Baptists from meetings in homes for worship or teaching groups of children who are below 18 years old. Despite these restrictions, the vision of the Baptist union is to plant a Baptist congregation in every town.

Baptist leaders pay a very high price for their faithful witness in Belarus. Obstacles don't stop the spreading of the Gospel. However, the number of young people and children has dropped in Baptist churches of Belarus by about 30 percent since the new law was introduced. Indigenous church planter Pavel paid a sacrificial price so that a new congregation in Senno could have a house of prayer. He took a private loan and invested money in the church building. Often those who organize Christian services in Belarus have to pay fines or they get arrested. However, the example of Belarus shows that churches in Eastern Europe can grow in spite of numerous obstacles.

Azerbaijan – Regular Violations of Religious Freedom

A predominantly Muslim population, Azerbaijan regularly violates freedom of religion. Religious freedom exists only in theory but in practice it is often not respected.

The Baptist movement started in Azerbaijan in 1870. The first Baptist church in the capital city of Baku was planted in 1890 but was only officially registered 1905. The Azeri speaking Baptist churches are not officially recognized currently.

Several pastors who fearlessly preached the Gospel got imprisoned and their families faced many threats. Pastor Zaur spent eight months in detention and was released after thousands of letters from Baptists around the world arrived to the president of the country and a group of Baptist envoys visited to advocate for Zaur.

Lebanon – Help to Rivals

The "pearl of the Middle East" is populated by nearly four million people. About 15 percent are nominal Christians. There are thirty-two Baptist churches in Lebanon with a total of around sixteen hundred baptized Baptist members. Because of the relative freedom of worship in Lebanon, the country is leading Baptist ministry in the Middle East. In the early 1990s the Lebanese Society for Educational and Social Development (LSESD), known as the Lebanese Baptist Society, was established.

The Arab Baptist Theological Seminary (ABTS) is the sole Baptist seminary for the region. The school trains Christian leaders for Arab speaking nations: Lebanon, Egypt, Jordan, Iraq, Morocco, Syria, Sudan, etc. ABTS vision is to see highly committed and well trained Arab leaders, mobilized to serve God, and to positively impact the Middle East and North Africa.

The Gospel is often presented to religious and political rivals. During the war in 2008 Baptists helped even to the followers of Hesbollah and accepted their displaced persons in the Baptist School and the seminary facilities, which was excellent witness. A new well has been built with support from the Baptists in Lebanon after the war. Some evangelists work among the Bedouins who comprise up to 20 percent of Lebanese society. Bedouins are normally the poorest, are often homeless and are usually illiterate who do not have permanent work.

Iraq – Spiritual Opportunities in Spite of Ongoing War

Distribution of Bible is possible and new groups are formed. Affiliated to the EBF, the Baptist Church of Baghdad under the leadership of pastor Ara Badalyan, is growing and planting new congregations in Iraq, both in Baghdad and in the north of the country. There are about three thousand evangelical believers in twelve churches in Baghdad. Several new church plants are in Kurdystan, the mountainous north. The newest initiative is a Christian kindergarten in Baghdad with some plans for an outreach.

People in Baghdad live in constant fear of terrorist attacks that also affect churches. The building of Baptist Church of Baghdad was attacked in 2011. Fortunately no one was killed or injured but the explosion caused serious damage to the facility. Terrorism causes a lot of Iraqi people to leave Baghdad and move to the north of the country or migrate abroad.

CHAPTER 19

Turkey – Pastor with a Body Guard

Christians are a tiny minority in Tureky, with a population of sixty eight million. Ethnicity: 76 percent are Turks; 16 percent are Kurds; 8 percent others. Religion: Islam 84 percent; Non-believers 15 percent; Christians 0.6 percent.

Pastor Orhan Picaclar from Samsun has to face danger every day because he preaches the Gospel in the Muslim dominated nation, in the city of Samsun on the shore of the Black Sea. Several years ago he was kidnapped by Muslim radicals. Since then he also had many death threats pronounced against him. Now he has a police protection and continues the work of sharing the Good News and church planting. The vision is to plant other congregations in Amasya and Ordu. Orhan is married and has an adult son. The Protestant Baptist Church "Agape" from Samsun belongs to the Baptist Association of Turkey, which comprises four local congregations.

Tajikistan – Evangelism Among Muslims

More than 90 percent of Tajik lands are mountains and about 90 percent of the people are Muslims. The population of Tajikistan is about seven million, including a sizable Uzbek minority. The country declared political independence after the collapse of Soviet Union in 1991. Appalling poverty rules, caused by high unemployment. The majority of Tajik men work abroad, mainly in Russia or other countries to provide for their families.

The Baptist Brotherhood of Tajikistan comprises seven local churches and about twenty groups scattered all over the country. The total membership is about five hundred. The largest Baptist church in the country is located in Dushanbe, its capital city. This church has about three hundred members now but used to be about three times bigger, shrinking when the German speaking people moved to Germany.

The whole Bible was translated into the Tajik language only at the end of the 20th century, for the first time in history. Now the Word of God is available in Tajik and many more congregations may be planted as people read the Holy Scripture in their own language. It is a serious challenge to plant a Tajik speaking church mainly because of Muslim apprehension against Christians, so evangelism requires unconventional methods.

Indigenous church planter Mirshakar has found a way of successful evangelistic work among the predominantly Muslim people. He has a good deal of authority and thus has influence on several hundred people. Mirshakar has been successful because he decided to share the Gospel message basically with his extended family who meet regularly for different family occasions.

The primary mission of the Christian church is to go into all the world, preach the Gospel and make disciples (Matthew 28:19-20). Church planting is a natural way to enable this to happen. Even with a handful of resources it is possible to impact thousands and also witness the transformation of societies.

EBF builds bridges of partnerships between churches, conventions, unions, mission agencies and individuals in order to enhance the mission work in the region.

More info from the EBF web site – www.ebf.org

CHAPTER 20
OBSERVATIONS OF A CHURCH PLANTING MOVEMENT IN NORTHEASTERN GHANA

John Drummond

Introduction

Over the past ten years, I have had the honor and the privilege of either leading or serving on more than thirty short term volunteer mission trips on five different continents. On several of those trips I have served alongside missionary and church planter, Emmanuel Mustapha, in the area surrounding Yendi, Ghana. Mustapha, better known as "Muss" to his North American friends, serves as missionary of the Ghana Baptist Convention to the northeastern Ghana mission field and has dedicated his life as a missionary to the indigenous people of that area. Through his ministry, hundreds of evangelical churches have been planted among a diversity of indigenous people groups, and literally thousands have been reached with the gospel of Jesus Christ. The purpose of this paper is to provide an overview of the ministry of Emmanuel Mustapha and the church planting movement that is ongoing in northeastern Ghana so that others may learn from the work that God is doing through his ministry. The information is based on extensive one on one personal interviews conducted with Muss at his home in Yendi, Ghana, during the week of May 13-20, 2011, as well as personal observations and experiences through first hand interaction with Muss' ministry.

A Passion and a Vision

The church planting movement that is currently ongoing in northeastern Ghana did not begin in the minds of men, but through a God-given passion for the people and a vision of how to accomplish the work. From 1999 to early 2005, Muss served near the city of Wa in northwestern Ghana where God began to solidify his calling to the people in the remote regions of northeastern Ghana.

During this time he planted more than forty churches and trained more than twenty-five church leaders, and he learned valuable lessons regarding church planting techniques and the necessity of leadership development. He also directed an extensive social ministry and established an orphanage during his time in Wa. In the midst of this ministry, God began to foster in Muss' heart a passion for the people of northeastern Ghana. This passion prompted a period of intentional, dedicated prayer for northeastern Ghana in Muss' life, and initiated a process of research in that area that began about two years before his eventual relocation to Yendi. Over this two year period, Muss began to gather information about the region, and he made four visits to the region – the first lasting approximately one month, and the remaining visits lasting two to three days. Muss used these visits to the northeastern region to learn about the various indigenous people groups, their cultures, and their religious beliefs. During one visit, Muss intentionally visited on a Sunday so that he could observe the presence and worship of other evangelical denominations in the area. Two of the four visits also involved Muss' entire family so that they too could pray about the potential ministry and have ownership in it. In March, 2005, Muss and his family felt God's peace in their hearts, and they made the move from their home in Wa to the city of Yendi. Yendi continues to serve as the launching point to all of northeastern Ghana for Muss, his wife Felicia, and their four daughters, Olive Jane, Walden, Cindy, and Nellie.

Progression of a Church Planting Movement

Soon after moving his family to Yendi, a house that would serve as Muss' home and ministry base was purchased from the International Mission Board of the Southern Baptist Convention of North America. The house was originally built by the IMB, but was abandoned in the 1960's when the Southern Baptist missionary who used the home relocated away from Yendi. Over the years, the house had been rented and used for many different purposes, but Muss saw it as the perfect location to establish a ministry. Muss' priority was to plant a Baptist church in Yendi, as there were no other Baptist churches in the area. Muss planted this first church, Ditney Baptist, in April 2005, and they began to meet in a church building that was initially constructed by the Nigerian Baptist Association in the 1950s. It was Muss' desire that Ditney Baptist serve as a "mother church" to all of the future church plants, and it continues in that role to the present day.

Aside from his immediate family, Muss had no other Christian leaders or believers to help him in his work. God raised up a local believer, Manasseh

Wumbei, to assist Muss in his ministry to the people of northeastern Ghana. Manesseh has served alongside Muss since 2005, providing critical assistance and leadership to the task of planting churches.

Muss, along with help from his new ministry companion, Manasseh, successfully established the first village church plant, Victory Baptist Church, in the community of Ngondo in May 2005. Soon after this initial village church plant, twelve other villages were identified and targeted, and churches were successfully planted in these communities as well. These thirteen churches began to reach out to neighboring villages, and by November 2005, a total of nineteen churches had been planted. As the churches began to replicate themselves and with continued efforts by Muss and Manasseh to plant new churches, the number of new churches swelled to more than four hundred churches by 2010. Following this same methodology of reproduction, the present goal is to plant an additional one thousand churches by 2015.

Church Planting Dynamics

Most of the churches planted by Muss and his leadership team have occurred among six indigenous people groups—the Konkomba, the Dagomba, the Anufo, the Basare, the Nanumba, and the Gonja. These people live in small communities of approximately two hundred people per village, and individual villages are typically separated by one to three kilometers. Family units live in round earthen structures with thatch roofs, and each village is typically under the leadership of a village chief and his advising elders. The primary occupation is subsistence farming, and except for the occasional trip to the market for necessary supplies, most individuals live out their entire lives within their community.

Because of the social structure within the communities, permission must be granted by the village chief before church planting activities can proceed in an individual village. This permission is typically sought directly by whoever is leading the effort to plant a church in the new community, either by Muss and his leadership team or by church leaders in a neighboring village. A second way that village chiefs are contacted is through Muss' radio ministry, which is based in Yendi. During his broadcasts, Muss offers to plant a new church in any village that desires to have a Baptist church in that community. As a result of these ministry broadcasts, village chiefs will often extend permission and an invitation to come to their village to plant a church. This has proven to be an effective way to reach out to the most remote areas of northeastern Ghana, and has provided a way to communicate with individual villages much quicker than through individual visits.

Once permission to plant a church is granted, a time is set for the people of the village to gather and for the gospel to be shared. Individuals from Muss' leadership team or from a neighboring Baptist church will meet with those who are gathered, often times under a large tree, and share the gospel along with an invitation. From those who choose to receive Christ as their personal Savior, an invitation is given to actually proceed with the planting of a new Baptist church if there is a desire to do so. The new church is given a name, and the new church members choose from among themselves at least one and sometimes two leaders who will be responsible for leading the congregation and for receiving theological and leadership training that is offered through Muss' ministry. Leaders must be born again, respected among their peers, and monogamous, and they typically do their ministry work as they continue to labor to support their families. A meeting place and time of worship is established, and typically one member of the church planting team will return the following Sunday to assist with their first worship service as an individual church. Within a few weeks, a baptism service is established and those who are born again are given the opportunity to be baptized.

From the very beginning, churches are taught the meaning of the "Great Commission," and they are encouraged to share the Good News with surrounding villages. Establishing a mindset of replication early in the church planting process has proven vital to the continued evangelization of neighboring communities.

Initially, church members typically gather underneath a large tree or available structure for worship and Bible instruction. Eventually, most churches desire to establish their own dedicated place of worship, and they will construct a structure at their own expense. Oftentimes, Muss' ministry will assist in providing a roof for the building if the church will provide the land and the actual building structure. This system of cost sharing helps the new church in their desire for a dedicated place of worship without creating an unwanted dependency upon Muss' ministry.

Ministry Organization and Leadership Development

Muss' ministry strategy is divided into four primary components, and is arranged geographically into twelve units, with each unit having an area leader who is responsible for the church planting and ministry activities that are ongoing in the respective area. Both Manessah and another mature believer, Mark, serve as area leaders in addition to their role within Muss' core leadership team. The fundamental component of the ministry strategy is the actual church planting activities, and area leaders are challenged to set goals for church planting in their geographical region and to work through any obstacles that they may encounter along the way. It was the area leaders, not Muss, who set the vision and goal of establishing one thousand new church plants by 2015.

A second component of the ministry strategy is the infrastructure development of the new church plants. This includes church buildings and roofs; Bibles, hymnals, and drum sets for worship; and bicycles and motor bikes for church and area leaders. These items are often in short supply, but are provided in whole or in part whenever funding is available.

A third component of the ministry strategy is social ministry activities. Muss' ministry is not only committed to the Great Commission, but also to the Great Commandment, to "'Love the Lord your God with all your heart and with all your soul and with all your mind.' This is the first and greatest commandment. And the second is like it: 'Love your neighbor as yourself'" (Matthew 22:37-40). Social ministry involves medical missions, the establishment of schools, agricultural and environmental programs, and clean water initiatives. These activities meet very pressing needs in the communities and provide a foundation of goodwill upon which the gospel can be built.

The fourth and final component is also one of the most important, discipleship training and leadership development. From the very beginning, Muss incorporated leadership and theological training into the church planting strategy. Initially, church leaders assembled in Yendi each Friday for theological, pastoral, and doctrinal training. Once the ministry grew too large to accommodate everyone in Yendi, the work was decentralized into the twelve geographical regions, and leader training began to take place monthly within each region under the guidance of the area leaders. In addition to the area training opportunities, Muss also maintains the Ghana Baptist School for Ministry for those local pastors who qualify and desire to be trained and discipled on a deeper level. This program of study takes three years to complete, and students meet in Yendi for ten days every three months where they study through a curriculum that contains twenty-eight different courses covering a wide range of subjects from servant leadership to pastoral instruction to expositional study on individual books of the Bible. Soon, the Ghana Baptist School for Ministry will be expanded to a second location near Salaga through a joint project with the Virginia Baptist Convention of the United States. Currently, there are forty students enrolled in the Ghana Baptist School for Ministry, and more than six hundred who attend the various area training opportunities each month.

A Model of Partnership

Muss' ministry and the church planting movement in northeastern Ghana are *not* dependent upon the resources of North American churches; nonetheless, important partnerships do exist that have contributed to the success of the ministry. Occasionally, short term volunteer mission teams from the United States and other countries will work alongside Muss and his leadership team in planting new churches. The volunteer teams assist in evangelism as well as children's ministry, women's ministry, and leadership training. The mission teams do make important contributions to the church planting process. The indigenous leadership team is encouraged and motivated by the volunteer team's presence, and those receiving the gospel are often humbled at the reality that a mission team from another country would care about them enough to visit their community. Likewise, new church members and leaders are encouraged when they see the volunteer mission team and the indigenous church planting team, two very different groups of people from different walks of life, working together for the purpose of spreading the gospel. This cooperative effort presents a valid, persuasive demonstration of the life changing power of the gospel in the spirit of John 13:35, which says, "By this everyone will know that you are my disciples, if you love one another." Furthermore, through this partnership between Muss and his leadership team and the volunteer mission team, continuity in discipleship among the new church plants is insured, as the indigenous church planting team is committed to follow up ministry, long after the volunteer team returns to their homes. This model stands in stark contrast to well-meaning but misled volunteer teams that work independently without local assistance, leaving a dark vacuum in their wake as new indigenous believers have no hope of discipleship opportunities once the volunteer team is gone.

Partnership opportunities are not limited, however, to U.S. volunteer mission teams. On the contrary, Muss and his leadership team also have a vision of fulfilling the "Great Commission" within their own lives by reaching beyond northeastern Ghana and developing partnerships with local believers in other nations where the gospel needs to be shared. Already, Muss and some of his leaders have partnered with believers in the country of Niger and have traveled to that country to assist with church planting there. Recently, a volunteer mission team from the U.S. working with Muss in Yendi traveled to the country of Togo with several of Muss' area leaders on a joint mission effort to plant seven churches in that country. These ministry partnerships present some exciting opportunities and have already proven effective in reaching even more remote regions with the gospel message.

CHAPTER 20

Challenges

Although God has worked in miraculous ways through the ongoing church planting movement in northeastern Ghana, the work has not been without its challenges. Some of these obstacles can be overcome, while others must be carefully worked through or tolerated.

One of the greatest challenges is the task of discipleship training among the new believers. While the area training opportunities assist in this effort by providing instruction to church pastors and leaders, illiteracy prevents many in the communities from studying the Bible on an individual basis. Communication with the church leaders is often difficult as well, as many have not been educated and are sometimes illiterate themselves. Oral communication and storytelling techniques help with this problem, but do not overcome it.

Before becoming born again believers, most in the community practice African Traditional Religion (ATL). Often marked by divinations and idol worship, these non-Christian practices present challenges both inside and outside the church. Those who declare allegiance to Jesus Christ and who cease their involvement in idol worship and other ATL practices often find themselves alienated and sometimes attacked by non-believing family members and others within the community.

Another traditional practice, polygamy, also presents challenges to the church. New believers who discover that their polygamous relationships do not align with Scripture are often faced with challenging decisions. In addition, those who are in polygamous relationships are not allowed to serve in a leadership position within the church. Such issues must be handled carefully and through much prayer.

Islam presents a significant challenge to evangelical Christianity throughout Ghana, and especially in the northeastern region of the country. Even though an entirely different methodology is utilized, Islam is also rapidly expanding among the individual villages. Although there are exceptions, most villages will not have both an evangelical church and an Islamic mosque in the same village. Once the village chief decides on a direction for the community, other religious efforts within the same community are often shunned. If a community is reached first for Christ, however, this practice becomes a benefit as future attempts to establish Islam in that community are often rejected.

The remoteness of the region and the lack of mobility of those in the community often hinder individuals, especially local church leaders, from traveling to and from training opportunities. While it is desired to equip every church and area leader with a bicycle or a motorcycle, such forms of transportation are often in short supply. Likewise, church planting efforts of churches to surrounding villages are often limited to the geographical area that can be reached either on foot or by bicycle, restricting the effective evangelistic footprint of each church.

Ghana's climatology also presents unique seasonal challenges to church planting activities. Northeastern Ghana experiences two seasons, the dry season and the rainy season. Because their very survival depends on their own ability to cultivate crops during the rainy season, church members and leaders are often occupied with farming activities during the months of June to October. During the peak of the rainy season, torrential rains cause insurmountable destruction to the primitive road system, and villages become completely inaccessible.

Conclusion

Despite the challenges, there is no question that God has initiated and sustained a significant church planting movement among the people of northeastern Ghana, and thousands of indigenous people are now Christ-followers as a result. Through the prayers and passion of Emmanuel Mustapha and his fellow laborers in the work, God has rewarded their faithfulness with a tremendous ministry that continues to bear fruit. Only God knows what the future will bring, but there is little doubt that He will continue to draw the peoples of northeastern Ghana to Himself, and He will continue to use Mustapha and the other leaders as His vessels for the work.

CHAPTER 21
TRANSFORMATION AND GOSPEL IN THE NEW TESTAMENT:
CONTEXTUALIZING THE GOSPEL AND TRANSFORMING THE WORLD

Timothy Hyunmo Lee

Today, "globalization" is a notable feature of the world. Globalization is both a blessing and a problem for Christian mission. Unexpected global immigration and development of traffic and communication provide unprecedented opportunities, which had never been dreamed in the days of the apostles. At the same time, globalization spreads idea of equalitarianism to all nations, ethnic groups and cultures and, as a result, nationalistic attitudes have been fortified.

As a direct result, Christian missionaries are seriously restricted in their access to some nations and to engage in ministry. Hermeneutics, theology and communication formulated by a Western worldview, which were once taken for granted, are gravely questioned. Since the era of Christendom, colonial rule, and imperialism, Western Christianity assumed a triumphalist attitude, consciously and unconsciously.[1] The problem of triumphalism in Christian mission is that the values triumphalists attempt to preserve are not the Word of God, but are theological and cultural understandings that emerged from Western perspectives.

As we move into the new era of globalization, non-Western people are challenging Western Christianity to reconsider two things. The first is to make Christianity their own by taking off the shell of Western culture and putting on their own culture. It is to demand new issues and different understandings from those of Western theologies. Evangelicals have failed to meet both of these two requests. Some evangelicals have been so concerned to preserve the purity of the Gospel and its doctrinal formulations that they have been insensitive to the cultural thought patterns and behavior of those to whom they are proclaiming the Gospel.[2] The point at issue was that they had not recognized that their understanding of the purity of the Gospel and doctrines were partially products of triumphalism. In addition, they failed to pay attention to cultural factors disturbing evangelism and church growth in the field, as Donald McGavran had mentioned. The Willowbank Report mentions, "some people reject the Gospel not because they perceive it to be false, but because they perceive it to be alien."[3]

The second challenge that demands new issues and different understandings requires more serious consideration. First, an illustration. Millard Erickson's textbook on systematic theology, one of the popular books for evangelical students, gives twenty-two full pages to explain the concept of trinity.[4] However, in my estimation, in Asia where the idea of mystery is appreciated, we need only one sentence. One sentence of propositional explanation: "Trinity God exists as three Persons, but one God," would be more than enough. It requires long explanation and polemics to satisfy Western idealists perhaps, but Asians do not need such complicated polemics. Non-Westerners rather, expect to know the different practical issues of the Bible, such as biblical teachings on poverty and injustice. Erickson's thick textbook, with more than thirteen hundred pages, never mentions such issues. The absence is not because the Bible doesn't mention these issues, but because those are not matters of interest for Western evangelicals. Often missionaries scratch where one doesn't itch and wonder why they are not gratified.

Today there is a widespread recognition even among evangelical Christians around the globe that in order for the Christian message to be meaningful to people it must come to them in language and categories that make sense within their particular culture and life situation.[5] It refers to contextualization. Contextualization has to do with how the Gospel revealed in Scripture authentically comes to life in each new cultural, social, religious, and historical setting. In reality, many evangelicals are still suspicious that attempts at contextualization will lead to the compromising of biblical truth, because the term contextualization was coined by ecumenical groups, and their theologies were generally liberal from the evangelical perspective.

However, contextualization is not optional. Although the term contextualization was quite recently coined, the activity of expressing and embodying the Gospel in context-sensitive ways has characterized the Christian mission from the very beginning. This presentation is an attempt to look at the issue of authentic contextualization through the lens of the New Testament.

The missionary model of Jesus Christ shows the best example of contextualization of the Gospel message in the New Testament. John Stott mentions it well in his article, "The Bible in World Evangelization." This shows a standard or example for something, even if not a specific method. The model of Jesus signifies something we should follow without fail. God chose to disclose of himself and his salvation through human language and human culture. Our evangelical doctrine of the inspiration of Scripture emphasizes its double authorship.[6] Men spoke and God spoke. If Jesus used celestial language, supernal rhetoric, and heavenly parable, we cannot understand what the Gospel is all about. Because Jesus spoke in Aramaic, adopted the Jewish rhetoric and utilized Hebrew parables, people can understand the Gospel and be saved. Accordingly, the task of the missionary is to communicate the eternal truth to the target people using language, rhetoric, and parables of their own, in order that they can grasp it. Incarnation is the supreme example of contextualization made by Jesus. God became a human being like us, came into us, and dwelt among us. He became humble, weak, poor and vulnerable. It is the supreme model of evangelization. So should missionaries. Missionaries must become like nationals whom they serve as much as possible, go into them, and dwell among them in order to witness the truth of God. Jesus identified with us, without surrendering his own identity. It shows the model of "identification without loss of identity."[7] Incarnation, inspiration of the Word, and identification of Jesus represents the supreme model of contextualization in modern terms.

However, some of us stay aloof from the contextual model of Jesus, holding on desperately to our own cultural inheritance in the mistaken notion that it is an indispensable part of our identity.[8] Many evangelicals have responded negatively to contextualization due to fear of syncretism. At the same time, we have to note the other side of the coin. Some people excessively respect national culture and diminish the importance of the Gospel or surrender Christian standards and values. This is not Christ's way. Contextualization must fulfill a prophetic role, challenging cultural norms and values. Such confrontation cannot be avoided. There are two perennial fears in the task of contextualization; the fear of irrelevance if contextualization is not emphasized enough and the fear of syncretism if it is taken too far. Contextualization needs the skill of a tightrope walker to maintain balance. Jesus was fully human as well as fully divine.

The contextual model of the early Jesus Christ is repeated in evangelism and missionary work of the apostles and church. The Book of Acts shows the richest illustrations of cultural and theological contextualization. Acts tells the story of a church whose very identity involved expressing the Gospel about Jesus in multiple settings and among different groups of people. Acts shows us a crucial paradigm for the process of contextualization in the early church. The focus in Acts is on witnessing to God's salvation in Jesus Christ among Aramaic and Greek-speaking Jews, Samaritans, God-fearing Gentiles and finally, pagans. The result is that fresh "translations" of the Gospel occur under the guidance of the Spirit as the word of God spans cultural, linguistic and religious boundaries.[9]

Dean Flemming shows well the process of the contextualization in the Acts. I quote some of his points in the following:

Chapters 1-5: to the Jews. In this part, the Christian movement operates within the orbit of Jewish thought to be interpreted in Judaism's own terms. The core of the good news is that Jesus is the Jewish Messiah who will restore the kingdom to Israel (Acts 1:6).

Chapters 6-7: Stephen, the Hellenist. The Gospel began to escape from Judaism and move from Jewish regionalism to universalism.[10] Hellenists took leadership of the Jerusalem church gradually. It seems certain from their Greek names that the seven chosen were Hellenists. A theological movement to Hellenism was accomplished in chapter 15. However, Stephen's sermon in chapter 7 is a convincing example of doing contextual theology for a new situation. He changed the core of Jewish belief. Stephen put forward the offensive claim that the significance of Jesus as the Messiah of Israel essentially superseded that of Moses in the history of salvation: the Gospel of Jesus took the place of the Jewish Gospel of exodus and Sinai as God's concluding, incomparable eschatological revelation.[11]

Chapter 8: Samaritans, a different view on Messiah. Here we can find another example of doing contextualization. The Samaritans had a different messianic expectation from the Jews. Philip, who was one of the "seven" (6:5), linked the Jewish hope for a Messiah and that of the Samaritans by reframing in terms of Jesus as Messiah. He proclaimed "the good news of the kingdom of God and the name of Jesus Christ" (Acts 8:12). He presented the new concept of the Kingdom of God and Christ, the Messiah, which were not the same to that of the Jews, nor that of the Samaritan's.

Chapter 15: Jerusalem Council, from a Jewish to a universal context. The Jerusalem church felt a serious crisis when they heard what Paul and the Antioch church had done in Asia. Paul removed circumcision and keeping laws as requirements for the gentiles. The Antioch church threatened the status quo at Jerusalem. The early church encountered problems between faith in Christ and culture. We can see a pattern of God's people articulating their faith within an intercultural context in chapter 15, which carries implications for the church in any generation. Flemming suggests seven elements from the story of the Jerusalem Council, which influence contextual theologizing.

1. The work of the Spirit in the community as the context for creative theologizing

2. The appeal to the church's experience of God's activity

3. The role of Scripture in guiding the community
4. Contending for the truth of the Gospel
5. Compromise on nonessential issues for the sake of unity and fellowship
6. The role of the community and its leadership
7. The church's contextualizing of the Gospel is missional, ecclesial and transformational[12]

These elements should function as the guiding principles in our contextualization.

Chapters 13, 14, 17: Three sermons of Paul, contextualization in Asia Minor. The central focus of the second half of the Book of Acts is Paul's preaching in the Roman colony and administrative center of Pisidian Antioch. We can find three sermons of Paul in this part: the synagogue preaching at Pisidian Antioch (Acts 13; 13-52); preaching to pagans at Lystra (Acts 14:8-20); and preaching at Athens (Acts 17:16-34). As we carefully compare these three sermons of Paul, the excellent examples of contextualization in both form and meaning can be uncovered.[13] The first sermon speaks to Jews and the second sermon to pagan gentiles who are indigenous Lycaonians, and the last sermon to pagan Greek gentiles heavily influenced by Stoic and Epicurean philosophy. Paul uses different descriptions of God, different core concepts of salvation, different rhetorical styles, different cultural resources, and tailored themes. Although it is not easy to elaborate all the details of the sermons due to time limitations, I want to show you, as an example, Paul's different descriptions of God depending on the audience. To the diaspora Jews in Pisidian Antioch, he talked about "the God of this people of Israel chose our fathers" (13:17) who was active in Israel's history and who had fulfilled the promise to their fathers (13:32-33). To the pagan gentiles in Lystra, "the living God, Creator of all things," (14:15) who was a gracious provider and sustainer of human life, was presented. To the Greek gentiles in Athens, Paul insisted the God who was ruler of nature and history, the universal judge, was not confined to human temples or made by human hand.

I want to move to talk about the second issue: The need for contextualization in culturally sensitive ways is well recognized among evangelicals today, although it is yet to be fully developed.

Perhaps the serious problem is a lack of theological contextualization rather than a cultural one. Recent interpreters of Paul have viewed him as a pastoral theologian, a task theologian, a missionary theologian, a hermeneutical theologian. In other words, Paul was a contextual theologian.[14] The work of Paul is a masterful case of contextualization in ways that communicate central truths of the Gospel in a variety of ways, depending on the particular situation. Most church members in the early days were Jews. For them, Jesus was the Messiah, the promised deliverer of Israel. Their faith was to restore themselves as a people of God through the forgiveness of their sins. However, as the Gospel crossed over the boundary of the Jews, the understanding of Jesus as the deliverer of Israel could be a puzzle for gentiles. Moreover, Jewish belief was based on national identity and lineage. Circumcision and keeping laws symbolized this tradition. But gentiles no longer accepted Jesus only as a deliverer of Israel. The new faith demanded transformation. It had nothing to do with Jewish lineage and tradition. In other words, the Gospel of death and resurrection demanded new theologizing in a Hellenistic world. It was Paul who had done the contextualization of the Gospel in the new culture. Jesus is the Lord of all. "Was a man already circumcised when he was called? He should not become uncircumcised. Was a man uncircumcised when he was called? He should not be circumcised. Circumcision is nothing and uncircumcision is nothing. Keeping God's commands is what counts" (1 Cor. 7:18-19). First Corinthians features a series of what may be called "case studies" in doing contextual theology in which we find the Gospel speaking to the whole range of concrete issues.

Today, theological contextualization is still a hot potato for evangelicals. In the 1980s, theological contextualization was a matter of concern for evangelical groups in the face of theological attacks from ecumenical theologies. Since the 1990s, when the thrust of liberation theology had weakened, evangelical concern for theological contextualization has faded, even though it has not completely vanished away. However, we still have an urgent need to develop refreshed and healthy evangelical contextual theologies.

Although the need to contextualize the Gospel is obvious, in actual practice it is difficult, as I have already mentioned. Blinded by our own ethnocentrism and ecclesiastical hegemony, it is very difficult to cultivate the art of listening and learning from those different from ourselves. But the spirit of humility is a fundamental requirement for contextualization. Contextualization brings to us a challenge: How do we carry out the great commission and live out the great commandment in the world of cultural diversity, with the Gospel that is both truly Christian in content and culturally significant in form? Darrel Whiteman suggests that contextualization leaves us with three challenges: (1) contextualization should change and transform the context – this is the prophetic challenge; (2) contextualization should expand our understanding of the Gospel because we now see the Gospel through a different cultural lens – this is the hermeneutic challenge; (3) contextualization should change cross-cultural witness because people will not be the same once they become part of the body of Christ in a context different from their own – this is the personal challenge.[15]

In the same way that Jesus emptied himself and lived among us, we must be willing to do likewise as we enter another culture with the Gospel and discover what the Holy Spirit has been doing before we arrived. Our common goal is to contextualize the Gospel and transform the world in Christ Jesus.

CHAPTER 22
TRANSFORMATIONS IN THE WEST:
SOME REFLECTIONS FROM 'DOWN UNDER' WEST

John Beasy

The Motto of the Australian Baptist "Global Interaction" Mission Agency, as Westerners ministering in Asia and Africa, is axiomatic to how people must also be introduced to the transformative Gospel in the West, and then engaged in ongoing discipleship: "Empowering Communities to discover their own distinctive ways of following Jesus."

Context: What is the West?

This term has been understood in the past largely as the culture of any country that is part of "the Western world"; the core understanding being that such a country has had a European heritage/history with the original core influence being the Roman and Greek empires. However, a major feature of modern Western culture is the diversity of races found within it. The USA, the UK, France, Canada and Australia are prime examples of Western countries.

Consumerism, materialism and hyper-individuality are strong Western values. The West has seen an erosion from valuing community and thriftiness, to hyper individualism, mobility, excessive spending and digital connection. As Sine well notes in *The New Conspirators* "hyper-individualism is one of the cardinal virtues of the global economy and has been a major force in undermining our values of neighborliness, community and mutual care." (Sine, 2008, pp141)

With the rise of Social Networking sites like MySpace, Facebook, Twitter, and Instagram, the Western world has never been as well connected as today. The USA, UK and Australia are the highest percent users of social media. Yet paradoxically, the West has connection without community.

Australia is a prime example of the West and represents hard soil for sowing the Gospel. The God of the Aussie West is Consumerism, Accumulation and Individualism, i.e. "Meism."

CHAPTER 22

This does not suggest that opportunities for sharing the Gospel toward transformed lives are redundant. In fact, the Christian church may be better positioned than imagined to respond biblically, and with impact, within the dominant consumer-driven, individualistic values of the secularized Western front. Christian research in Australia shows that people are not closed toward spirituality. In fact Jesus remains the most palatable commodity of Christianity among those who are skeptical of the Christian faith. However, despite a level of spiritual openness, there are some major roadblocks to people travelling to Jesus through the pathway of the church.

- Institution and structure are viewed with cynicism.
- Sexual abuse has done untold damage to the church's brand.

Further at a time when the Western heart is crying out for more meaning and relational connection, many churches continue to feed the prevailing God of individualism, and fail to speak with a prophetic counterculture voice. MY salvation, MY favor, MY extraction. What God has for ME dominates over a genuine sense of yielded followship of Jesus as LORD of all.

Unfortunately a concern toward whole life transformation and authentic discipleship gets limited space.

A further challenge in the West is that even when churches have sought to relate more outwardly to the community, they have become more proficient in demonstrating the Gospel, yet less so at declaring the good news. Action without announcement has become more prevalent.

Into all this, theologians such as Michael Frost, Dallas Willard and NT Wright have spoken solidly, challenging the Western church to rediscover its mission, and once again become communities of transformation where Jesus is embraced as Lord over all life. There is a growing call for a more biblical approach, which repositions the rightful reign of the Kingdom of God and Jesus' saving presence in everyday life as our primary concern to advance.

A growing awareness of *Missio Dei* and the place of the church as the prime agent within God's mission, has heightened a growing awareness that true mission is necessarily integral, requiring both the declarative and demonstrative elements of the Gospel. As in the life of Jesus, being, doing and saying remain integral to our task.

Key Consideration: What Unique Mission Space Emerges from the Western context?

Mission Space 1: - Community Connection

Meaning and relationships must drive missional engagement. Western culture presents a platform upon which authentic followers of Jesus can promote a contra culture that has a primary concern toward genuine relationships and authentic community. The creation of opportunities to connect with people and build a sense of neighborliness, community, and mutual care becomes a key missional space.

Mission Space 2: - Prophetic Voice

Marketers everywhere are convincing young adults to embrace a life of high status, high fashion and high luxurious living, which is to their economic, social and spiritual peril. In pursuing counter cultural models of meaning, the church has the opportunity to regain a prophetic voice and challenge the cultural trends of individualism and injustice that damage and dislocate.

The church has an opportunity to lead the charge in allowing better images of biblical faith to define the notions of the good life. This is above all a prophetic call. As the biblical narrative shapes our view of what it means to live life well, it also becomes the lens through which the inherent errors of a culture that values consumption and accumulation may be seen.

Key Consideration: What Models of Missional Engagement may be most Effective?

Models of mission must be those that enable connections to be deeper, meaningful and relevant.

Essentially people in the West are seeking genuine relationships, meaningful causes, healthy choices and spiritual meaning. Mission in the West must become far more intentional and innovative in helping people discover Jesus within pursuit of these life aspirations.

In this regard many perceived Community Service needs and aspirations about meaning, well-ness and healthy relationships, align well with Christian values and practice. An innovative church with relevant community programs becomes well placed to be an effective connector to local communities.

Jesus' self-proclaimed mandate in Luke 4:16-21 reflects the focus needed on the whole person. He speaks directly into the hunger seen in the West for holistic care. Namely a focus on spiritual aspects – the personal redemption of our spirits; physical aspects – the redemption of our bodies and all creation; social aspects – the healing of our relationships and societal ills; emotional aspects – our feelings and self-beliefs.

As disciples in the West, we should dare to believe and follow the mandate that Jesus actually intends to make "All things new" (Col 1:19-20, Eph 1:10; 2:22; Heb 2:8). Local innovative models will arise naturally where followers of Jesus view themselves as community connectors, powerfully demonstrating the reality of the Gospel by placing emphasis on meaning; exploring creative solutions in the context of local community; forging effective community partnerships and connecting to the deepest cry of the human heart for intimacy and purpose.

Real Transformation?

A Key question remains, Will all this focus on innovation, alerting, creating curiosity and integral mission actually lead to true transformation? The sad reality is that the Western posture is very weak in what it may take for true transformation to be realized. In our preoccupation with "results," pace and solutions, we do not have long attention spans. Nor are we generally reflective, contemplative or disciplined enough to allow the time and space for maturation. Spiritual practices are rarely fostered. In the want for fast fixes and demonstrated spiritual "victory," a lifelong process of apprenticeship with Jesus is rarely affirmed or rigorously pursued. There has been a tendency to celebrate being safe in God through conversion, yet to baulk at what it will take to become sound in the life of Christ at all levels of our being.

Such a process of transformation, or as Dallas Willard terms it, "A Renovation of the Heart' while a Western longing, seems yet a long away off, unless the presenting mission spaces of community connection and prophetic voice are embraced more widely and rigorously by the church.

COMMISSION ON BAPTIST HERITAGE AND IDENTITY

The Commission on Baptist Heritage and Identity (HIC), which deals with the history of the international Baptist movement and our current Baptist identity, had a full quinquennium. In addition to papers and presentations at our four Annual Gatherings, we also worked on two major projects: writing and posting online short histories of our BWA member bodies, and a 21st Century Baptist identity statement. HIC also helped to plan and lead historical tours of Melaka, Malaysia, Baptist sites of Jamaica, and ancient Christian sites of Turkey and Greece.

The HIC website, www.bwa-baptist-heritage.org, now has numerous short cameos about the origins and development of Baptist work in various countries. Our webmaster, David Parker of Australia, works diligently to keep our site updated and useful. Our 21st Identity Project intended to utilize hard data, which was to be gathered through another commission survey of representatives of our BWA member bodies. When that survey did not work out, our Identity Project came to a halt. Excellent identity materials have been gathered and discussed as part of our papers in our Annual Gatherings. It remains for the new HIC to determine whether this 21st Century Identity Project will continue.

HIC has a tradition of focusing on the Baptist history of our host country in the opening commission session at Annual Gatherings. This has proven to be a very popular session. It helps orient Baptists of the world to our host country, and is also well attended by local Baptists. The new Commission on Religious Freedom also started the practice of focusing on the religious liberty stories of the host country. Several sessions in the quinquennium were held jointly with the Commission on Religious Freedom, as we shared the stories of local Baptist history, identity and religious freedom. There was strong synergy from these joint sessions.

In Kuala Lumpur, Malaysia, in 2011, we had a joint session with the Commission on Religious Freedom on the history of the Malaysian Baptists. Brian Talbot of Scotland presented a paper entitled, "Baptists and the King James Version of the Bible: 400 Years of Shared History." A response by Stephen Jennings of Jamaica included another extensive paper on the Bible and slavery. David Parker of Australia presented a paper, "Mapping a 21st Century Global

Identity," the first of three papers of the 2010-2015 quinquennium on this project topic.

In Santiago, Chile, in 2012, Victor Aguilar of Chile presented a paper, "The History of Baptists in Chile." Parrish Jacome of Ecuador presented a paper, "A Latin American Baptist Identity." Both of these papers are available on our HIC website in both English and Spanish. David Parker presented, "Mapping a 21st Century Global Identity, Part II." And Daniel Carro from Argentina and the USA presented a review of Justice Anderson's new book, *An Evangelical Saga: Baptists and Their Precursors in Latin America*. We also had a Skype interview with Justice Anderson.

In Ocho Rios, Jamaica, in 2013, Doreen Morrison of the United Kingdom and Glenroy Lalor of Jamaica made a presentation on the "History of Jamaican Baptists." This was particularly significant for Baptist history and missiology. They made the strong case that the freedman, George Liele, who came from the USA as a missionary to Jamaica in 1783, was the first Baptist missionary, preceding William Carey's mission to India by a decade.

All of the METR commissions participated in a roundtable of presentations and discussions on trends in missiology and theology. Ken Edmonds of Australia presented a paper and PowerPoint presentation on "The First Baptist Place of Worship: The Great Bake House in Amsterdam, circa 1598." Delroy Reid-Salmon of the USA presented a paper, "The Caribbean Baptist Diaspora." Fred Anderson of the USA presented a paper, "free indeed: Virginia Baptists and Slavery." And David Parker presented via Skype another paper that related to our HIC project, "Mapping a 21st Century Global Identity, Part III."

In Izmir, Turkey, in 2014, no formal papers were presented at any of our three sessions. We held a joint session with the Commission on Religious Liberty, led by Turkish pastor, Ertan Cevik, with two other Turkish pastors participating, on the topic, "Baptist Life in Turkey and the State of Religious Freedom." Our second session was a joint session with the Commission on Baptist Worship and Spirituality. Joel Gregory of that commission led a presentation on his recent book, entitled, *Global Baptist Preaching and its Implications for Baptist Identity*. Our third session was a panel discussion by Middle Eastern leaders on the topic, "The History and Identity of Middle Eastern Baptists Since 1990."

The commission has enjoyed particularly strong relationships among its members. We are grateful to the METR leadership that has helped us toward our joint goal of being "In Step With the Spirit" during the quinquennium. The papers from the Annual Gathering sessions, 2011-13, are available on our website. We hope the Spirit will use the papers, discussions and relationships to further the cause of God's in-breaking Kingdom, and to strengthen the work of Baptist churches.

Craig A. Sherouse, commission chair, is senior pastor, Second Baptist Church, Richmond, Virginia, USA.

CHAPTER 23
THE KING JAMES BIBLE AND BAPTISTS OVER 400 YEARS[1]

Brian R. Talbot

The King James Version was commissioned in 1604 at the Hampton Court Conference, a gathering called by the new monarch of the United Kingdom with a view to easing tensions that had existed in the Elizabethan Church of England. The new King, James I (of England & VI of Scotland), accepted a proposal for the commissioning of a new Bible translation put to him by the leading Puritan scholar at the conference, John Reynolds (1549-1607), president of Corpus Christi College, Oxford.[2] Why did Reynolds call for a new Bible translation when the Geneva Bible was so popular amongst devout Protestant Christians? It is likely that he wished to see a replacement for the version that was most common in parish churches in England, the Bishops' Bible. Archbishop Matthew Parker (1504-75) had asked the previous monarch, Elizabeth I, to authorize this Bible alone for reading in church since "in certain places be publicaly used some translations which have not been labored in your Realm, having inspersed divers prejudicial notes." He wanted "to draw to one uniformity." This version was not a work of particularly high merit, though this was unlikely to have been the reason why the Queen declined his request, but its significance in this context is that James required it to serve as the basis of the 1611 revision of the English Bible.[3] Parker, together with Edmund Grindal (1519-83), Bishop of London, made a concerted effort to restrict the supply of Geneva Bibles in order to encourage usage of the Bishops' Bible. However, "his [Parker's] lack of confidence [in it] sealed the fate of the Bishops' Bible."[4] It is probable therefore, that Reynolds wanted a version of the Bible that would gain general acceptance throughout the land, something that did not happen with the previous Bishops' Bible. It would have greatly surprised him how long it would take before the King James Version became accepted as the "Authorised Version" in the United Kingdom.

The Geneva Bible was the most popular English language version in the years leading up to 1611. Between 1560 and 1611 there were sixty-four separate editions of the Geneva Bible or New Testament produced.[5] By way of contrast with the Bishops' Bible, between 1583 and 1603 only seven editions of the Bishops' Bible were produced compared to fifty-one of the Geneva edition.[6] The fundamental motivation for the production of the Geneva Bible was to make the Bible accessible and intelligible to a lay readership. In addition, it contained marginal notes that proved both immensely popular and helpful to its Protestant readership during the great religious controversies of Elizabethan and Jacobean England. It is generally agreed that this Bible version was the best in the English language at that time.[7] As a result, when the King James Bible appeared in print sometime between March 1611 and February 1612 very few British Christians would have been aware of its arrival. The launch of the new Bible version took place without any fanfare. In fact even the Stationer's Company that printed it did not record the actual date of first publication. For them it was simply a revision of the Bishops' Bible, the Anglican Church's official Bible.[8] The earliest description of this version was given in February 1612 where it was described as: "a great Bible of the new translation."[9] The origins of this translation (KJV) of the Scriptures was, therefore, much more humble than would have been expected by its later devotees.

In the light of its low-key launch it is no surprise that this Bible version struggled to claim support from the vast majority of Protestant churchgoers in the United Kingdom. In fact the very first time it was included in a formal list of English-language Bible versions was as late as 1645, where it was referred to as "the last translation procured by King James" or "the new translation," and uniquely, "the reformed and revised edition of the Bible."[10] Throughout the first half of the seventeenth century the Geneva Bible was the version of choice not only of the Puritans in England, but also their counterparts in America and on the European mainland. The spiritual ancestors of those Christians, who in a later era would refer to themselves as Evangelicals, would almost unanimously have chosen the Geneva Bible as their preferred English-language translation. A good illustration of the esteem in which the Geneva Bible was held by Protestant Dissenters was related in a satirical pamphlet published in 1642. The story concerned Thomas Williams who ran a haberdashers shop in Oxford. In December 1641 a fire broke out in his shop. Smelling smoke, Mr. and Mrs. Williams went downstairs to investigate the problem. They saw their goods on fire, including their highly valued Geneva Bible. The booklet reported that this couple could more easily have accepted their losses had the burned Bible "been a copy of the KJV with the Apocrypha and [if it had been] bound with a copy of *The Book of Common Prayer*."[11] Here is an excerpt from Thomas Weaver's satire on the plight of this Dissenting couple.

CHAPTER 23

5. He heard some cry, Fire, fire, amaine,
   and said that were he slack,
   Great John of All trades would againe
   be brought to his first pack:
   Then hasting downe to see what burn'd,
   the smoke did almost stop
   His breath: the new Exchange was turn'd
   to a Tobacco shop.

6. His wife came downe at that report,
   her cloaths hung in such pickle,
   As she were new come from the sport
   after a Conventicle:
   And first in these flames she espide
   a pure Geneva Bible,
   With gilded leaves, and strings beside,
   that were not contemptible.

7. But with lesse griefe he could have seen't,
   as he then said to some one,
   Had but the Apocrypha beene in't
   and Prayers that we call Common:
   The Practice there of Pietie,
   and good St Katherine Stubs
   Were martyr'd, which oft quoted hee
   had heard in severall Tubs.[12]

The Geneva Bible became enormously popular with more than seventy editions published between 1560 and 1640. In England alone more than half a million copies were sold of the Geneva Bible. It was crucial for its availability that it was printed in the country between 1576 and 1640. The Geneva Bible was also the first English-language Bible published in Scotland, in 1579. However, although the Bible was in English, the dedication of the General Assembly of the Church of Scotland was in the Scots language.[13] This was the Bible of choice of most evangelical Protestants. No wonder the KJV struggled to make an impact in such an unsympathetic spiritual environment.

There were, though, additional reasons for the unattractiveness of this new Bible, in comparison with the much loved Geneva version. William Laud,

Archbishop of Canterbury from 1633-1645, was a militant Arminian who loathed the Calvinistic theology of the study notes of the Geneva Bible. Laud drew attention to the primary reasons, he believed, were behind the popularity of this version that was imported from the printing presses of Amsterdam. He wrote: "For the books which came thence were better print, better bound, better paper, and for all the charges of bringing, sold better cheap. And would any man buy a worse Bible dearer, that might have a better more cheap?"[14] Laud, for these reasons, banned the printing of the Geneva Bible in England by the King's Printer, Robert Barker, who had a monopoly at that time on Bible production and who had invested substantially in the KJV and needed it to become a commercial success. Without the legal restrictions imposed on the printing and importation of the Geneva Bible, it is likely that the KJV would have had very little commercial success.

There were two other reasons for the promotion of the KJV at the expense of this more popular version. The first of these related to the proclamation of 1541 specifying a need for Bibles "of the largest and greatest volume" for use in parish churches.[15] There were only three Bibles printed successively with the required specifications, the Great Bible, the Bishop's Bible and the KJV. Between 1612 and 1641 only the KJV was available to meet this requirement. It was referred to as "a Bible of the latest edition." "The last translation," or "a Bible of the largest volume." It is interesting that in the first half of the seventeenth century the people of that era were having some difficulty distinguishing between the KJV and the Geneva Bible in terms of the translation of the text, but by contrast found it relatively easy to distinguish the KJV as an artefact.[16] The second of these was the continuing objection by the Royalists to the study notes and theological comments on the text of the Geneva Bible. William Laud, after making reference to James I's criticism of the notes, stated that this issue was just as pressing in the 1640s. He observed "that now of late these notes were more commonly used to ill purposes than formerly and that that was the cause why the High Commission was more careful and strict against them than before."[17] In the light of the execution of Charles I a few years later in 1649, the political concerns of Laud and his colleagues appeared to be well grounded. However, William Prynne, a Puritan with more evangelical and Low Church sympathies, while accepting that the annotations were a cause of conflict, suggested that the real issue was a fear on the part of Laud and his supporters that these comments on the biblical text "should over-much instruct the people in the knowledge of the Scriptures."[18] By the mid-seventeenth century there had been no significant debate over the alleged superiority or inferiority of the KJV as a Bible translation. Differences of opinion concerned the study notes accompanying the biblical text of the Geneva Bible. The more fervent and Bible-centered Protestant Christians retained their affection for the older version at home, but it was the KJV that regular worshippers heard read, Sunday by Sunday, in the local parish church. This version was now accepted and respected, and crucially after three decades of usage was one with which British Christians were increasingly familiar.

Baptists and the Early Years of the King James Version

Is there any evidence of Baptist connections with or usage of the KJV in the first half of the seventeenth century? It is clear that this is a field in which very little research has been done on this particular subject, but it is likely over time that a proportion of Baptists would have had access to this new Bible version, although it is most likely that it would not have displaced the Geneva Bible in their affections. At the present time, the earliest known reference to the KJV in the work of a Baptist at that time came in *An Appendix to a Confession of Faith 1646* produced by Benjamin Cox and appended to the 1646 edition of the *First London Confession*.[19] Cox (1595-c.1664) had been an ordained Anglican clergyman, and appointed a lecturer (on the Bible) at Barnstaple in Devon between 1620 and 1627. While serving as a curate at Sampford Peverill, Devon, during the 1630s it is likely he became acquainted with a group of Baptists in the nearby community of Tiverton. However, by the 1640s he had joined first the General Baptists, having been convinced at that stage of a general redemption of humankind, before identifying with the Particular Baptists from December 1645.[20] In 1646, Cox wrote an appendix to accompany the second printing of the First London Confession of Faith, first issued by a group of seven London Particular Baptist congregations two years earlier in 1644. This document was written by this elderly minister "for the further clearing of truth and discovery of their mistake who have imagined a dissent in fundamentals where there is none" amongst English Particular Baptists.[21] In a paragraph addressing some individuals who had claimed that God was the author of evil, Cox expressed his clear disagreement with this position. "It is a great sin to say that God is the author of sin." After citing a number of Bible verses to support his argument, Cox turned to the text alleged to support this claim. "As touching that place which is here objected against us, viz. Amos 3:6, 'Shall there be evil in a city and the Lord hath not done it?'" He turned to the alternative reading in the KJV as the preferred option. "We conceive that it is either to be rendered according to the last translation in the margin, 'Shall there be evil in a city, and shall not the Lord do somewhat?' or else that it is to be understood only of the evil of punishment, and not of the evil of sin."[22] Cox, as a Dissenter, together with his congregation, would normally have preferred the Geneva Bible for public worship; however, he both owned and used a KJV in his studies. It is likely that Cox was representative of educated Baptist leaders by the 1640s in consulting the newer version, but preferring the long-established one. Further studies, though, are required before this hypothesis can be confirmed.

A second Baptist with a connection to the KJV in the 1640s was the little-known printer, Henry Hills (c1625-1690).[23] Hills was a controversial figure whose religious allegiance appeared to change over the years when it became advantageous to him for professional reasons. Christopher Anderson, noting his engagement as a Bible printer by Charles II, stated that: "his moral character seems to have been far from correct...[he] had actually been employed in printing the Scriptures, and according to report, shamefully incorrect."[24] Anderson drew attention to Hills' Anglican connections and especially his later shameful Roman Catholic ties. "The displeasure of the God of Truth he had brought upon himself," but this careful Baptist scholar omitted any reference to Hills' earlier Baptist connections![25] Hills was associated with leading London Baptist William Kiffen as early as July 1642 and was a member of Kiffen's congregation for most of the Commonwealth era. He was first employed by Sir Thomas Fairfax in Oxford in 1647, then by the Army and the Council of State in 1653. In later years he was employed by Oliver and then Richard Cromwell. However, after the restoration of the monarchy in 1660, Hills discovered strong Anglican convictions that ensured that he served in the same capacity as an official printer of Charles II. Remarkably this leading printer retained his post under James II after declaring his acceptance of Roman Catholic beliefs! When James II fled to France in 1688 his official printer also went into exile in the same country. Hills died in France in November 1689. Beginning in 1647 and continuing up to 1689, more than 900 titles, including various editions of the King James Bible, bear the name of Henry Hills on their imprint. A number of Baptist titles, together with other radical works were produced between 1648 and 1673, including *A Confession of Faith of Several Churches of Christ in the County of Somerset* (August 10, 1656), under the guidance of Particular Baptist minister Thomas Collier. It is probable that his most important Baptist publication was *The Humble Apology of Some Commonly Called Anabaptists* (January 28, 1661). This document was issued by seven London Baptist causes in the immediate aftermath of the revolt of the Fifth Monarchists led by Thomas Venner, who had tried to overthrow the restored monarchy in January 1661. The inevitable defeat of the plotters resulted in more than forty deaths caused by this conflict and the subsequent execution of all those implicated in this uprising. It is important to note that Hills was one of five signatories from William Kiffen's congregation within this pamphlet who stressed their loyalty to the King.[26] Hills' interest in the KJV was professional as a printer. It is ironic that a Dissenter who most probably preferred the Geneva Bible spent a large proportion of his professional life promoting the sale and usage of the KJV.

Baptists in the Era of the Consolidation of the King James Version

The KJV consolidated its position as the predominant Bible version both in the home as well as the church in the second half of the seventeenth century. This process took place as a result of two events. The first was the lack of availability of Geneva Bibles. After 1644 this version was neither printed in the United Kingdom nor officially imported from the Netherlands.[27] The second and equally important fact was the absence of requests for its recall, even after the departure of Laud and the execution of Charles I in 1649, together with the establishment of the Commonwealth in the early 1650s. It is significant that the eight editions of the Bible with the Geneva notes, printed between 1642 and 1715, all contained the KJV text.[28] In this era, more than half a century after the KJV had first appeared, the public perception of its main rival had changed in England. No longer was the Geneva Bible automatically the people's version, it was now seen more as one associated with the Puritans and with an anti-Royalist agenda.[29] In the seventeenth century although they were very familiar with the Geneva Bible and used it extensively, even radicals associated with the Dissenting tradition and Oliver Cromwell's regime had adopted the KJV as their primary Bible version. Two examples will illustrate this point. John Milton (1608-1674), the great scholar and writer of such well-known works as *Paradise Lost* and *Paradise Regained*, vehemently opposed the established church and supported the execution of Charles I, yet his personal Bible was a 1612 edition of the KJV printed by Robert Barker. It is this version of the Bible that predominates in biblical citations in his literary endeavors.[30] John Bunyan (1628-1688) was brought up in very humble circumstances, yet this Baptist preacher became the author of numerous works, including the best-selling religious book (apart from the Bible) in the English-speaking world, *Pilgrim's Progress*. His biblical citations are almost certainly either from the Geneva or KJV Bibles. Yet it is clear that the Bible he used most was the KJV. In his 1665 work *The Holy City Or The New Jerusalem*, for example, Bunyan included a lengthy quotation of the biblical text from Revelation 21:10-22:4 to aid his readers in studying this topic. It would be natural for him to choose his preferred Bible version for this purpose.[31] The vast majority of biblical quotations in *Pilgrim's Progress* or in his spiritual autobiography, *Grace Abounding to the Chief of Sinners*, come either from the KJV or from language shared by these two versions. It is probable that Milton and Bunyan were the first two major English Dissenting writers who were predominantly influenced by the KJV.[32] However, Bunyan continued to use the Geneva Bible alongside the KJV with regular citations of the older version in his works.[33] For example, II Peter 1:17-19 (Geneva Bible) is probably cited from memory in his early work, *A Few Sighs from Hell*.[34] There are even occasions when he is quoting the Bible from memory and his quotation of a text is a combination of the Geneva and KJV renderings. This is seen in his expository comments on the story of the Rich Man and Lazarus (Luke 16:19-31).[35] In line with other Puritan and Dissenting ministers Bunyan had a high view of Scriptural authority,[36] but he was very open about accepting marginal readings of both the Geneva Bible[37] and the KJV,[38] if he felt they were justified. He also made a couple of references to William Tyndale's translation of the Bible.[39] The Bible version so closely associated with the monarchy and the established church had become the favored version of radicals and dissenters like Bunyan and Milton.

In the eighteenth century, as in the previous one, variant texts of the KJV had circulated with unacceptable levels of printers' errors. Nonconformists, in particular, had drawn attention to them. William Kilburne had assembled a formidable list of typographical errors in his *Dangerous Errors in Several Late printed Bibles*, as early as 1660.[40] He was, though, only one of many writers to draw attention to this problem. Baptist minister Henry Jessey (1601-63), who was known as a "living concordance" of the original languages of the Bible, spoke for many Protestant Churchmen of his day when he stated that it is "our duty to endeavour to have the whole Bible rendered as exactly agreeing with the original as we can attain."[41] Yet there was a lack of political will to embrace the necessary wholesale revision of the KJV text in circulation at that time. John Wesley (1703-91), the leading Methodist minister, revised the New Testament text of the KJV in 1755 and made as many as twelve thousand modifications of it.[42] Philip Doddridge (1702-1751), the well known biblical expositor and Congregational minister, also drew attention to the need for the revision of the KJV text in the preface to volume one of his popular work, *The Family Expositor* (1739). In its six substantial volumes, published over a period of seventeen years, the Northampton minister proposed a significant number of revisions to the KJV text.[43] Progress on this subject was most closely associated with the work of two scholars F.S. Parris, Fellow of Sidney College, Cambridge, and Benjamin Blayney, Fellow of Hertford College, Oxford, who produced revised texts for their respective university presses, two of the three permitted Bible publishers, in 1743 and 1769. Blayney's edition, that incorporated Parris's modifications, soon became the universally accepted text of the KJV that has hardly altered since that time. "This has been referred to often since as the standard edition."[44] This version differed from the 1611 text in no fewer than 24,000 places. However, many of the changes were simply the correction of accumulated printers' errors, though others were more substantial changes. What is remarkable is that these alterations were accepted by the Christian public without significant criticism. This signalled that the KJV had not yet become a sacrosanct cultural icon, a status that would be bestowed by some Christians at a later date.[45]

Baptists and the Era of Adulation of the King James Version

Its Wonderful Language

The publication of Blayney's modified text in 1769 was the event that stilled the many critical voices raised against the language and accuracy of the KJV.[46] In addition, a number of other factors began to emerge that enhanced the status of this biblical text. First of all, beginning around 1780, the classical taste that had dismissed the writings of the seventeenth century as unsophisticated began to take a delight in past works for their own sake. An unknown writer to *The Critical Review*, in January 1787, while still suggesting that the KJV did not achieve the highest literary standards, nevertheless, argued that:

> The defect in idiom we cannot allow to be a fault; it raised the language above common use and has almost sanctified it; nor would we lose the noble simplicity, the energetic bravery, for all the idiomatic elegance which a polished age can bestow…Our attachment to this venerable relic has involuntarily made our language warm.[47]

Critical accuracy in the text now combined with changing cultural tastes that placed greater value on the "relics" of the past, led to the KJV being viewed with greater favor in the wider social context of that day. It was not only secular and literary figures that were placing greater value on the KJV. Vicesimus Knox, the Anglican headmaster of Tonbridge School in Kent, argued with respect to the KJV, that "its antiquity is a greater source of strength than any correction of its inaccuracies would be" and that "the present translation ought to be retained in our churches for its intrinsic beauty and excellence."[48] This new mode of thinking and use of early seventeenth-century language was adopted by some Evangelical Christian ministers, for example, Edward Irving, the most popular London clergyman in the 1820s. He deliberately adopted the linguistic forms found in the KJV.[49] Baptist scholar, Christopher Anderson, declared; "As far as the English language and the art of printing were concerned, everything else in the form of human composition, or in the shape of a book, was reduced to a thing of comparative insignificance."[50] Across the Atlantic prominent Southern Baptist minister, William T. Brantley (1787-1845), offered similar paeans of praise. "It is our heart's desire and prayer to God, that this venerable monument of learning, of truth, of piety and of unequalled purity of style and diction, may be perpetuated to the end of time, just as we have it now."[51] In such a social context as this, modernization of the language of the KJV was out of the question.

The KJV and British Identity

A second reason for the enhanced respect for the KJV was its growing association with national pride and identity. The French Revolution of 1789 had shaken the confidence of the British establishment with very real fears that the upheaval across the English Channel might erupt "in England's green and pleasant land." Some of the more radical Evangelicals such as Scottish landowner and Baptist layman Robert Haldane welcomed these changes, in the hope that the toppling of Roman Catholic governments in Europe might lead to greater freedom to preach the Gospel in those lands, though he needed to assure anxious colleagues that he was not wishing to promote a revolution at home.[52] Political concerns had escalated further with the rising threat from Napoleon Bonaparte in still Catholic France. Militant Protestantism was the natural way to assert a distinctive religious and political identity.[53] France through ignorance of the Scriptures, it was assumed, had not adopted the Protestant faith. By contrast, the King James Bible came to be viewed as a symbol of national identity. It was distinctly Protestant. Roman Catholics would not accept it and preferred their own Douai-Rheims editions. When Bible verses were reproduced in educational literature in Catholic Ireland, they gave passages in both the Douai-Rheims and the KJV.[54] However, more enlightened Evangelical Protestants, such as Scottish Baptist Christopher Anderson, recognized that the Catholic Irish primarily had legitimately objected to the use of Protestant catechisms in their schools and when a further step was taken, the production of the Bible in their native Irish language, there was a much greater degree of openness to work with the Protestant teachers and preachers. Anderson saw it as a scandal that the Bible had not been provided for the Irish in their own language.[55] However, he also lauded the success of the Bible of every "British Christian."

His Bible, at this moment, is the only version on which the sun never sets... on the banks of the Ottawa and St Lawrence, as well as Sydney, Port Philip and Hobart Town; before his evening rays have left the spires of Quebec and Montreal, his morning beams have already shone for hours upon the shores of

CHAPTER 23

Australia and New Zealand ... while the sun is sinking on Lake Ontario; in the eastern world, where he has risen in his glory on the banks of the Ganges, to the self-same Sacred Volume, many who are no less our countrymen have already turned ... Here unquestionably, is the most elevated point of view in which Britain can be viewed- the only true summit of her greatness.[56]

The KJV's identification with a sense of British identity had hindered its acceptance amongst the Irish Catholics. By contrast, it had the opposite effect on the majority of Protestant Christians in mainland Britain.

The KJV and Mission

A third reason was the formation of the British and Foreign Bible Society (BFBS) in 1804. Christians of the full range of Evangelical Protestant traditions supported this venture. However, one of the principal people with the vision for this work was Joseph Hughes (1769-1833), minister of a village congregation, Battersea Baptist Church, near London, from 1797 until his death. Hughes supported a range of evangelical and ecumenical ventures to promote the Christian faith. For example, he was one of the pioneers of Sunday Schools in Scotland, setting one up while studying at King's College, Aberdeen, in 1789, based on new initiatives in children's work he had seen in England, and was the founder of the Surrey Mission Society in England in 1798.[57] In May 1799 this Baptist minister was in attendance at a missionary meeting held in the Independent Surrey Chapel, London, and heard the preacher, Independent minister George Burder, lament the lack of a society that could promote and produce religious tracts. The following day a meeting was held to form such a mission agency, at which Hughes was a prominent participant. He was appointed secretary of the newly formed Religious Tract Society (RTS) for thirty-four years until his death. In its first full year of operations the RTS printed and distributed two hundred thousand tracts in the English language and took in subscriptions the substantial sum of four hundred and sixty-seven pounds. The growth of this mission agency under Hughes' leadership can be illustrated by the fact that in 1832 in excess of fourteen million tracts were distributed in nearly eighty world languages. In total, in his lifetime, one hundred and ninety seven million pieces of Christian literature were written using the KJV as its biblical text. This work was an outstanding success.[58] It was at a meeting of the RTS in 1802 that the shortage of Bibles for ordinary people in the churches was raised that led to the formation of the BFBS two years later. Hughes, himself, was the principal mover of this initiative, writing a pamphlet "The Excellency of the Holy Scriptures," in support of this cause. Hughes advocated the formation of a society composed of

Christians of all denominations "with the sole object of giving the Word of Life to the nations." His tract was widely circulated and received a strong favorable response, leading to the launch of the BFBS.[59] He was appointed one of its secretaries.

The growth of Evangelicalism in the early nineteenth century led to a large increase in the production of Bibles for personal use, at a price ordinary people could increasingly afford. English Congregationalist John Campbell, in 1844-45, recorded a list of some of the necessities of life required in the 1840s: "light postage, quick transit, cheap Bibles, and cheap Periodicals, for the millions of England."[60] Numerous societies were established to promote particular Christian causes. The BFBS believed that no barrier of language, cost or supply should hinder access to the means of salvation to potential readers. Over a period of around sixty years it transformed the contemporary printing and binding trades, becoming a Victorian institution in its own right. The initial motivation for the formation of the society was to overcome the scarcity of Welsh-language Bibles in Wales.[61] However, this challenge soon pointed to the even greater need for Bibles in other parts of the world.[62] The Bible Society histories reveal the extraordinary creative efforts to take Bibles not only to the English-speaking world, most notably in the British Empire countries, but also to other parts of the world.[63] This vision for exporting copies of the Scriptures led to a renewed enthusiasm amongst middle-class Christians for distributing KJV Bibles and New Testaments at home amongst the largely unreached poorer neighborhoods of various towns and cities. Members of BFBS auxiliaries were entitled to obtain a number of copies of Bibles at the cost price, greatly increasing access amongst the population to the Bible.[64] The BFBS was by far the largest pan-evangelical organization in the UK at that time. As early as 1824 there were no less than 859 BFBS auxiliaries, together with 500 Ladies' organizations promoting its work; in 1832 it had more than 100,000 subscribers.[65] In the present context it is important to note that the one English-language version it published and promoted was the KJV. In addition to this significant step, was the decision to publish the Bible without note or comment, although allowing for cross-references and alternative textual readings in the margins, as had been the practice since Benjamin Blayney's revision in 1769.[66] After various editions prior to Blayney's work, this revision of the KJV text became the agreed text accepted and increasingly valued by all English-speaking Protestant Christians. The advent of the BFBS, in the first few decades of the nineteenth century, had in large measure ensured that a high proportion of the population of the United Kingdom who wished to own a Bible could have access to a copy of the KJV. It was not the only Bible version in print, but for the vast majority of Evangelical Christians in Britain, for all practical purposes, it was viewed as the Bible.

Baptists in America were equally enthusiastic about the formation of a Bible Society in their country. Baptists and paedo-baptists joined forces to form the American Bible Society (ABS) in 1816, at a meeting in New York. In line with the policy of the BFBS, their Bibles were published without notes or comments and the only English language copies published would be of the version now in common use, that is, the KJV.[67] The quality of the editions of the Bible produced by the ABS, together with the quantity of its output was acknowledged as the industry standard by the late 1820s.[68] The missionary vision of the ABS was clear in 1829 – to provide a Bible for every household in the land. Its *Fourteenth Annual Report* declared: "A Bible to every household must be the motto of each [auxiliary] Society, and must be sounded through all our borders, until every soul in the whole land has access to this fountain of life."[69] By 1830 the ABS was printing as many as 300,000 KJV Bibles a year at a time when the population was thirteen million.[70] Baptists were active in the work of the ABS. Spencer Cone, a Baptist minister from New York, for example, was one of the society's corresponding secretaries between 1834 and 1836. Baptists were also generous in their donations for this cause. It has stated that more than $170,000 was donated by American Baptists to the work of the American Bible Society between 1816 and 1836.[71]

The Bible version long established in the USA, as in the United Kingdom, was of course the KJV. As early as the 1640s New England Puritans had adopted the KJV instead of the Geneva Bible. For the next two centuries the KJV would reign supreme in the affections of American Protestants.[72] It was spoken of with a reverence unique to this English-language version. "Divine Providence [was] marking out to this country the true and only path to universal usage of the Sacred Volume, whether in this or in any other land. It was the Bible, but it must be without note and comment."[73] The mass production of Bibles by the ABS in the early nineteenth century confirmed the KJV as the standard of American Baptists.[74] They were as supportive of its promotion and use in mission as any other Protestant denomination in that country. An additional agency, the Baptist General Tract Society, was formed on February 25, 1824, "to disseminate evangelical truth and to inculcate sound morals by the distribution of tracts."[75] It complemented the work of the Bible Societies assisting Baptists in evangelistic endeavors not only in America, but also in Canada and Mexico, and further afield in Europe, Africa and South America.[76] American Baptists, whether with whole Bibles or smaller pieces of Gospel literature in the KJV, communicated their faith with clarity and enthusiasm in the first half of the nineteenth century.

Baptists and Controversies and the King James Version

The promising launch of the Bible Societies did not continue as harmoniously as might have been expected and Baptists were at the center of the controversies that arose. In America difficulties emerged when American Baptists presented an application for funds to the ABS, in August 1835, to assist the printing of a Bengali language Bible, prepared by William Yates, a Baptist missionary in Calcutta, in line with the Burmese version of the Scriptures, in which the Greek word βαπτιζω and its cognates were translated "immerse" and "immersion." After months of discussion, the board of the ABS voted on March 17, 1836, to award the sum of $5,000 for this purpose, with a clear restriction. They would only support translations that conform to the "common English version… and that all the religious denominations represented in this Society can consistently use and circulate said versions in their several schools and communities."[77] Although other Christian bodies were happy with this decision, it was inevitable that American Baptists would reject this restriction. Three hundred and ninety delegates from Baptist Churches met in Philadelphia in April 1837, to organize their own agency for printing and distributing the Scriptures. It was called the American and Foreign Bible Society (AFBS). Spencer H. Cone, pastor of Olivet Street Baptist Church, New York, 1823-1841, was elected its president and Charles G. Sommers, New York, its first corresponding secretary. William Colgate, a prominent manufacturer, was the first treasurer.[78] However, although this Baptist agency was happy to support overseas Bible translations that rendered βαπτιζω in a manner deemed satisfactory to Baptists, a majority of its members had no desire to produce a revised version in English. A vote taken in May 1850 confirmed this policy. A minority of its members withdrew and formed yet another agency, the American Bible Union (ABU), with the object to "procure and circulate the most faithful versions of the Scriptures in all languages throughout the world."[79] Both agencies struggled to find adequate financial support from Baptist churches. Battles over Bible translation policy in American Baptist ranks raised serious questions about the propriety of possessing denominational Bibles. The ABU did produce a translation of the New Testament in 1862-1863 that translated βαπτιζω as "immerse,"[80] but there was no chance of this translation replacing the KJV in American Baptist churches. This unfortunate controversy was resolved at a Bible Convention in Saratoga, New York, in May 1883, when it was decided that the American Baptist Publication Society would handle Bible work at home and foreign distribution would take place under the auspices of the American Baptist Missionary Union.[81]

British Baptists also participated in painful controversies over the Bible and translation policies at that time. The Apocrypha Controversy which unfolded between 1821 and 1825 concerned whether it had been the intention of the BFBS to circulate Bibles exclusively containing the sixty-six agreed books of the Old and New Testaments or whether additional non-canonical books could be bound with them, under certain circumstances, for distribution in parts of Continental Europe. The strongest pressure to exclude the Apocrypha came from the Edinburgh and Glasgow auxiliaries of the BFBS, led by Baptist layman Robert Haldane. Already chafing at the control of the English parent body and its unwillingness to devolve some measure of control of their work to its constituent auxiliaries, this issue was seen as a matter of principle on which a stand needed to be taken. These men and their colleagues were convinced that a breach of promise had occurred by the addition of the Apocrypha, in particular with respect to various editions of a French Bible in which Haldane had taken a particular interest. Unfortunately the parent body declined to revert to its original position of excluding the Apocrypha and instead chose to maintain ties with Continental Bible Societies who took a different viewpoint in this controversy. As a result the Scottish auxiliaries withdrew from the parent body, eventually uniting as the National Bible Society of Scotland in May 1861. The rules for membership in Scottish ranks were tightened in 1831 to ensure that all officeholders were both Protestants and held orthodox views concerning the Trinity.[82] A further secession from the ranks of the BFBS in England had occurred in 1831 when the parent body declined to break ties with Continental Bible Societies that had a significant number of Unitarians in their auxiliaries. Around that time a number of British mission agencies tightened their rules for membership concerning the Trinitarian issue and over the propriety of offering public prayers in committee meetings to God in the name of Christ.[83] The core issue was the authority of Scriptures and Baptists on both sides of the Atlantic felt strongly about these topics. However, the more fundamental question of whether the KJV itself ought to be revised was now increasingly being heard. Could Baptists and other Christians come to a common mind on that topic or would further fragmentation of Christian ranks occur?

Baptists and the Calls for Revision of the King James Version

As the nineteenth century progressed there were an increasing number of voices calling not for a new translation to replace the KJV, but rather for a revision and the correction of at least some of the more obvious errors in the text. Here many individuals could be cited, but a few examples will be given. The sentiments expressed at a meeting of the Virginia and Foreign Baptist Bible Society in June 1850 was representative. "Whilst the feeling appeared to be in favor of the present version – several brethren admitted that it had serious defects and that an improved version prepared in a way that would secure public confidence and approbation was a most desirable object."[84] However, this was a change in opinion as a majority of American Baptists, as late as 1838, were opposed to such a step. In response to the concerns of a Massachusetts Baptist congregation, in March 1838, the AFBS board instructed corresponding secretary Charles Sommers to write a letter to the church indicating that they had no intention "to prepare at some future day a new or amended version of the English Scriptures."[85] However, just over a decade later there had been a decisive shift of opinion on this topic. A report in the *New York Recorder*, in June 1850, produced a similar favorable response to a revised Bible version from Baptists in that city. The Baptist editor of that periodical claimed that a majority of Baptists in both the AFBS and the ABU would also support work on a revision. He added that he "will receive such a translation with thankfulness and willingly aid in its circulation in any feasible way."[86]

The impression must not be given that all Baptists were in favor of the revision. Some were fearful that a revision could only make matters worse, possibly destroying the good relations between Evangelical Protestants,[87] or that the KJV would be withdrawn from print if a new version was produced. William Colgate at an ABU gathering in 1857 admitted concerning the minority party opposed to revision: "I thought it would meet with great opposition at first. But I did not think it would be so fierce. People have made more noise and said more against it than I expected."[88] These negative fears were unfounded, according to Edward Underhill, secretary of the British Baptist Missionary Society, in a letter to Cone in New York. Underhill declared: "I rejoice much in the prospect of an English version."[89]

Most Baptists observed the movement toward the production of a revised Bible text, but a few were active participants in this process. One good example of the latter was Thomas Curtis, an English Baptist schoolmaster and publisher, who wrote to Cambridge University Press in 1832 because he claimed they were "circulating grossly inaccurate copies, if copies they may be called, of the Authorized Version." He claimed to have identified thousands of errors, not counting mere typographical ones.[90] Some critics could be easily ignored but not Curtis. He organized a committee of Dissenting clergymen to assist him in pressing for reform. They produced a pamphlet in 1833, addressed to the Bishop of London, entitled *The Existing Monopoly*. They wished to break the monopoly of the three printing agencies that controlled the production of the Bible. By 1855 two-thirds of American Baptist periodicals advocated reform, a movement that was especially strong amongst Southern as opposed to Northern Baptists.[91] Silas Mead and H.J. Lambert, Australian Baptists in Adelaide, both criticised the

AV and called for a new translation in 1868.[92] However, Dissenters alone were not powerful enough to produce a change on this subject, but by the 1850s the momentum had shifted in the direction of a revised version. By the time Anglican scholar J.B. Lightfoot, Hulsean Professor of Divinity at Cambridge, advocated reform, charging the translators of the KJV with "an imperfect knowledge of Greek grammar" in 1871[93], it was inevitable that the reformers would win the day. Charles Spurgeon, the most prominent Baptist preacher of his generation strongly supported a revised text. He declared:

> If God's Word is worthy of all reverence it is a crime of the highest magnitude to dilute it with error; and the sin is grievously increased, when the error is so apparent that the wayfaring man is aware of it. The cant and fudge which cries out against the least alteration of the old version of our forefathers, as if it were positive profanity, are nothing to me. I love God's Word better than I love King James' pedantic wisdom."[94]

The vast majority of Baptists, together with a similar proportion of Christians of other traditions favored this revision. As a result a first official Bible translation in English since 1611 would be produced. A new era in Bible production and revision was about to commence.

Baptist Responses to the Publication of the Revised Version

When in the 1880s the Revised Version (RV) was completed, sales figures for the Revised Version (RV) were astonishingly high. In London, two million copies, half of them orders from America, were sold in the first four days alone. In the USA, New York City had the highest sales, but other northeastern cities also saw brisk trading. Boston booksellers sold twenty thousand copies on the first day and Philadelphia's early sales exceeded one hundred thousand copies. In the Southern States, despite a severe economic depression, sales were still encouraging. Yet denominational assemblies were reluctant to pronounce on the RV. American Baptists were the only denomination that formally endorsed the Revised New Testament. It was, though, in church magazines and denominational newspapers that the endorsements for the revision were found in America.[95] Charles Spurgeon's review of the new version was mixed. He judged the RV as "strong in Greek, but weak in English."[96] Sales in New Zealand were also strong. C. Dallaston, pastor of Oxford Terrace Baptist Church, Christ Church, gave a lecture on the new version to his congregation. In his conclusions he said:

> The authorised version, notwithstanding all its imperfections, is truly loved, and to many it will be a sacrifice, indeed, when another is allowed to take its place. This revised version will have to win its way; its worth

will have to be recognised by the members of our churches before it receives its due appreciation.⁹⁷

An article on the Revised New Testament, in the February 1882 issue of the *New Zealand Baptist,* noted: "Notwithstanding all that may be said against the new translation, it must be admitted that in a multitude of passages, the meaning of the writers is much more apparent; what might have been obscure has been cleared away, the truth shining forth with greater brightness."⁹⁸ On the completion of the Old Testament, the same periodical heartily endorsed it and after offering examples of textual improvement concluded that it: "should prove sufficient to induce all who [love the Bible] that they HABITUALLY USE the Revised Old Testament [sic]."⁹⁹ A reviewer in the English *Baptist Magazine,* described the RV as "a decided literary success."¹⁰⁰ Contemporary review articles of the New and Old Testaments of the Revised Version were also praised in the pages of *The Queensland Baptist,* Australia, with no apparent negative criticisms printed in its pages.¹⁰¹ Henry Fox, at a meeting of the Devon Association of Baptist Churches in Totnes, England, delivered a paper praising the new version in June 1881. The assembled gathering of Baptists, at the end of his paper, passed a resolution offering "thanks to Almighty God for His great goodness in permitting the labours of the New Testament Revision Committee to be successfully completed…"¹⁰² John Clifford, the prominent English General Baptist minister, while acknowledging the number of people using the RV in personal devotions, enthusiastically wished "a speedy introduction of the Revised Version into family worship, Sunday Schools and our public services."¹⁰³ It was inevitable that the growth in usage of the new Bible version would be gradual. Henry Fox predicted that it would be "many years before the New Version has been generally adopted for use in public worship as well as private reading."¹⁰⁴ It was noticeable after its publication that the RV was the version chosen as a gift to present to church members being honored in some way, for example, for years of service as an organist or choir-master.¹⁰⁵ New Zealand Baptist congregations were encouraged to persist with using the RV for public Scripture readings, despite the fact that it has "marred the music of the Authorised Version."¹⁰⁶ Some ministers made a point of illustrating how the RV has improved the text of Scripture, for example, American Baptist minister, Dr A.J. Gordon, of Boston, in a sermon on "The Ministry of Women."¹⁰⁷ Yet, despite the warm welcome given to this new translation, it did not displace the KJV in the affections of the vast majority of churchgoers, nor did it replace it on the majority of church lecterns or in the typical church pew. The KJV was still predominant amongst Baptist Christians at the end of the nineteenth century.

CHAPTER 23

Baptists and the KJV in the Twentieth Century

In the twentieth century an increasing number of Bible translations took a share of the market for Bibles. The American Standard Version (1901) was commended, but despite its many endorsements the uptake of this version was modest.[108] A minority of more progressive British Christians were attracted, for example, to the translations of individual scholars such as R.F. Weymouth (1903) or James Moffat (1913), or after the Second World War to the version produced by J.B. Philips and most recently Eugene Peterson's *The Message* (2002). However, these versions were never seriously considered for use in churches. The most significant of the numerous new translations included the Revised Standard Version, first published in the USA in 1952. It was widely accepted in the UK, as well as in the USA, because its language echoed the KJV and was also suitable for public reading,[109] though it received strong criticism from many Conservative Evangelicals.[110] By 1990 more than fifty-five million copies of this version had been sold.[111] The Good News Bible (GNB, 1976), written in more contemporary English and a simplified vocabulary has proved particularly popular in the wider Christian community and in schools in the United Kingdom, but the New International Version (NIV, 1978) is the one that has attracted the greatest support from Baptists and other Evangelicals,[112] and now tops the best seller list of English-language Bibles. This is true not just in Western Europe, but also in other parts of the world. Amongst Malaysian Baptists, for example, usage of the KJV began to decline significantly in the 1980s, with the NIV predominant by the early 1990s in the English-language congregations.[113] However, especially in the USA, there has been some scholarly Evangelical support, together with strong popular sales figures for a revised KJV, *The New King James Version* (1982),[114] although some scholars have questioned whether it is accurate to call it a further revision of the KJV, rather than a new translation.[115] The NKJV has also been popular with a more conservative strand of Australian Evangelicals.[116] In the last quarter of the twentieth century a survey was conducted amongst Scottish Churches, in 1984, to ascertain which Bible versions were most commonly used. The KJV at 40 percent came top, followed by the New English Bible at 23 percent (popular with Episcopalians); and the Good News Bible at 20 percent, largely due to a significant take up amongst Church of Scotland congregations. Three versions were prominent amongst Scottish Baptists. The NIV unsurprisingly came top with 53 percent, yet overall as a new version had only been taken up by 6 percent of Scottish Churches; the RSV second for Baptists with 33 percent and the KJV third with 27 percent.[117] A follow-up survey in 1994 about Bible version usage revealed that the percentage of congregations using the KJV had declined to 17 percent from 40 percent in a decade, though it was still the third most popular version in the pews. In second place overall was the GNB with 24 percent. Topping this poll was the NIV with 35 percent. Amongst Scottish Baptists the RSV had almost disappeared at 3 percent, almost certainly losing ground to the NIV which came first with a 76 percent uptake. The KJV was the only other Bible version with a significant uptake in Baptist Churches at 12 percent, but still it was rapidly loosing its market share.[118] It is unlikely that Scottish Baptists are unrepresentative of the majority of their Baptist colleagues in other English-speaking countries.[119] Assuming the accuracy of this claim, it is clear that by the end of the twentieth century the KJV is rapidly disappearing from our pulpits and pews.

Where does this leave the KJV in the twenty-first century? There will be clear memories of significant Baptist leaders like Martin Luther King whose famous speeches drew on the KJV in particular. Utterances like: "We cannot be satisfied as long as a Negro in Mississippi cannot vote and a Negro in New York believes he has nothing for which to vote. No, no we are not satisfied, and we will not be satisfied until justice rolls down like waters and righteousness like a mighty stream." This is a quotation from Amos 5:24 in the KJV. Another example comes from King's "I have a Dream" speech that reached its crescendo with the quotation of Isaiah 40:4-5, again from the KJV.[120] It is probable that support for the 1611 version will only decline gradually for the foreseeable future as there are still a significant number of older churchgoers in particular who are fiercely loyal to the version with which they grew up, but younger people will prefer newer translations. How will the KJV be viewed in the wider culture of the English-speaking world? It is most probable that it will be lauded most for its literary excellence. A representative commendatory article appeared in the British tabloid newspaper *Metro,* in the approach to the 400th anniversary of the publication of the KJV, by journalist Graeme Green, in which he from a secular perspective viewed the significance of the KJV. He wrote:

> The tome, which first went on sale on 2 May, 1611, took previous English language versions and created a definitive Bible that became the most influential book ever written, a cornerstone of British society, permeating everything from art and literature to politics and morality, here and around the world."[121]

Of this we can be certain, the KJV has a secure place both in British history and in the culture and religious heritage of the English-speaking world.

Brian Talbot, "The King James Bible and the Baptists Over 400 Years," *American Baptist Quarterly,* vol 30 no 1 - 2 (Spring - Summer 2011): 108-133.

CHAPTER 24
"FREE INDEED!"
VIRGINIA BAPTISTS AND SLAVERY:
HOW A STATE BAPTIST HISTORICAL ORGANIZATION COMMEMORATED THE 150TH ANNIVERSARY OF EMANCIPATION

Fred Anderson

Emancipation of the slaves in the United States became a signal event in history – first, for the enslaved who were then free; for the Republic which finally was living up to the ideals for which it stood; and even for the Baptists in a slave-owning state such as Virginia. Emancipation was a signal event in the history of Virginia Baptists for several reasons, including the fact that in the immediate months following the end of slavery, 57 percent of the membership of the churches left the rolls. Over the next five years some 250 new churches were planted by the newly-freed people among Baptists in Virginia alone. These new churches were constituted by a people who largely were penniless and illiterate. It is a remarkable story of massive church planting that is reminiscent of the early Christian church.

Despite the signal event, emancipation and the rise of the black church has been a largely overlooked story by the very keepers of Virginia Baptist history. With the 150th anniversary of the Civil War and emancipation upon us, the two organizations that I lead devoted time, energy, creativity and resources to commemorate the anniversary and to examine these overlooked topics.

Let me share that the two organizations are the Virginia Baptist Historical Society (the oldest and largest of the various state Baptist historical organizations in the United States. Across the years it has amassed a large collection of materials including black Baptist association records) and the Center for Baptist Heritage & Studies (founded at the beginning of 21st century to be focused upon education through programming, exhibits, conferencing and the creation of resources and publications). The two organizations work hand-in-glove and the two joined for this special project. The two also are agencies or "ministry partners" of the Baptist General Association of Virginia which also is the parent body of the University of Richmond where both organizations are housed in a building provided by Woman's Missionary Union of Virginia expressly to house the Virginia Baptist Historical Society, and to serve as a living memorial to the Virginia Baptist ministers who were imprisoned for their faith in the 1700s.

We called the project "free indeed!" from the snippet of Scripture – "if the Son therefore shall make you free, ye shall be free indeed!" John 8:36 – and it was to commemorate the anniversary in three ways:

Name Registry

For many years I have wanted to have an index of the names found in the old church records in the Society's collection. We have about 4,000 original church record books, the minutes and rolls kept by the clerks of the churches, and about 250 of these were from the antebellum period. I wanted to have a list of the names found within those manuscript books and so I assigned one of my colleagues, Michael Whitt, special projects assistant, the task of pulling out the names and placing them into a user-friendly database. It required about three years of work but today we have a registry of more than 51,000 names – blacks, slave and free; white surnames – arranged by county and then by church. It is in hardcopy and in a digital format. It is valuable for social historians, local church historians and family researchers. Recently the Richmond Area African American Genealogical Society came calling and one researcher shouted when he found his great-great grandmother. Another recent visitor discovered her ancestors but she learned that they were not slaves, they were free people of color but the descendant had never known this fact. And so we have the name registry.

Book

As my colleague, Michael Whitt, was gathering the names, he would interrupt my work to tell me about some interesting story hidden in the old church records until finally I told him to write them down and maybe we would publish a book. Indeed we did! Michael wrote the bulk of the text and together we edited and proofed and published "free indeed!" – the book – which gives a lengthy account of the relationships between whites and blacks within the Baptist churches of Virginia prior to emancipation.

Our Society has been publishing an annual journal for 50 years but this edition, the 50th, was the first to give serious attention to the story of the enslaved and how slavery was regarded and treated by white Baptists in Virginia. We

CHAPTER 24

also included several previously unpublished manuscripts within an appendix including two eye-witness accounts to slavery and the churches as written by two white ministers in the 1870s, placed in our collection and largely forgotten. They tell about preaching on the plantations, about black preachers and about relationships between the races. Other items in the appendices include John Leland's account of slavery in Virginia; the testimony of a black preacher from the 1850s on why he became a Baptist; the remembrances of a noted white pastor, Robert Ryland, who led a black congregation; and a history of black Baptists in Virginia written in the 1920s and buried in the state Baptist paper. The book totals 229 pages and includes illustrations. And so now we have the registry and the book.

Exhibit

Along the way, we began to identify unique and interesting items within the Historical Society's vast collection that would be effective in a public exhibit. We selected about 50 such items – artifacts, manuscripts, church records, photographs, and other illustrative material – which would capture the interests of visitors. We commissioned a young Baptist artist to create original art work for the exhibit. We opened the exhibit in January 2012 and plan to continue the exhibition through this calendar year (2013).

We have had hundreds of visitors including numerous church and civic groups. The groups have included those who otherwise may never have visited our Historical Society, several African-American churches have brought groups for personalized tours of the exhibit, school groups have come, some directors of missions in various district associations deliberately have invited black and white pastors to come together, African-American historical and genealogical groups have toured the exhibit, and on and on. One WMU group from a Richmond area church came; and when the leader arrived she said she wished she had invited the women's organization from the black church which had come out of her church. I told her it was too late for that day but it was not too late to plan another visit and she did; a group of the black women came with her.

While on a day trip to Washington, D.C. with my wife, there was a group of about 20 high school age kids, predominately black and a few whites, along with some adult chaperones. We were on the same train together, by happenstance were at the same restaurant together, seated across from one another, and then on the same train coming home at the end of the day. I made their acquaintance and discovered that they were part of a program trying to get school dropouts to work on their GED and to have a part-time job. I invited the group to come see "free indeed!" and they did, one young man pronounced it "awesome" and put a dollar in the donation box. We talked about slave days but we also talked about the world of work today. It was a tour which was serendipitous. There were many experiences in year one of "free indeed!"

A retired high school history teacher, a Baptist herself, spent hours reading every line of every label in the exhibit. The African-American history consultant for the Virginia Historical Society came at 10 o'clock and left at 3 o'clock, reading every label and commenting upon the unique items in the exhibit. From that visit, a friendship was forged and the history consultant became a featured speaker in a conference we sponsored in May; without the exhibit and the name project, I doubt our paths would have crossed. We placed a signboard at the front door, a board shaped in the likeness of an African-American woman of yesteryear and she carries a chalkboard with lively notes about the exhibit. The signboard has brought in a multitude of casual visitors, university students and professors and campus visitors, who otherwise would have never darkened the doors of the Virginia Baptist Historical Society.

When international visitors come to the Virginia Baptist Mission Board, which is located about two miles from our building, they frequently are brought by a Mission Board staff member to visit the Historical Society; and of course, over the last year and half, they have seen the story of blacks and whites worshipping together in antebellum times. One dark-skinned Panamanian Baptist toured the exhibit and left, remarking that it made him sad to learn about slavery. I replied that he should feel glad that these people triumphed over terrible trials.

And so our "free indeed!" project includes a name registry, a book and an exhibit. The book and the exhibit look at the trials and triumphs of Virginia's enslaved and freedmen and they also offer an examination of the relationships between white and black Baptists in Virginia. There are heart-rending stories. There are good stories and bad stories. There are beautiful accounts and ugly accounts. Together they are form a shared history between whites and blacks.

Let me give you a visual representation of "free indeed!" Instead of creating a PowerPoint illustration and bringing a laptop and projector, I have decided to rely upon something I first saw as a child in the primary department of the Sunday school in my home church – indeed, all I really ever needed to know I gained from the primary department – that God is love and that Jesus loves me. I remember sitting in those little chairs in a semi-circle while a tall, stately woman named Mrs. Callaway turned the pages of beautiful color illustrations of whatever Bible story was the lesson of that Sunday. And so I will use her method.

CHAPTER 24

Early History of Black Baptists in Virginia

Remember that there were Africans in Virginia before there were Baptists! Every school child in Virginia has learned that the first slaves arrived in 1619. It was not until 1699 that there was documented evidence of Baptist preaching in the colony although there may have been Baptists in Virginia as early as the 1680s. It was in 1714 that the first church was constituted so Africans were in Virginia at least 60 to 100 years before the Baptists.

In the exhibit we go back to the first documented evidence of black members of Baptist churches in Virginia. "Negro Adam," property of Thomas Dodson, was the first black who can be documented in one of the church records at the Virginia Baptist Historical Society. He was dismissed from Broad Run Baptist Church near Warrenton, Virginia, in the central part of the state, in May 1764 because he had gone to another community. The following month two more came into the fellowship, "Negro Dick" and "Negro Sarah," both of whom belonged to the Dodsons. Likely there were earlier black Baptists in Virginia but these are the first whose names survive in the Baptist archives.

Why were the enslaved and free blacks, people like Adam, Dick and Sarah, drawn to Baptist churches? They found a degree of freedom. It was not perfect freedom but it was more than they would have found in other churches and certainly in the larger culture. Just like the whites, they were considered sinners saved by grace and were accepted into the fold. They could express their religious convictions, offer professions of faith, seek baptism and join the church – and their names could be recorded in "the book" – they may have thought it was the Lamb's Book of Life but it really was the church clerk's record book. Just the recording of names within the book accorded the enslaved a degree of human dignity, of recognition and acknowledgment, which they did not find in the larger world. In the Baptist churches they found that even in chains they were "free indeed" in Christ. They were members of the earthly church and bound for the heavenly land. They had come into the Kingdom of God! They received from the church a spiritual education that provided sustenance in their state and elevated them, if only within their psychic, to a greater sense of worth.

In the 18th century in Colonial Virginia there was only one church permitted by law, the Anglican Church, the Church of England, which was the Established Church of Virginia. Baptists were tolerated at times and in certain places and they openly were persecuted, beaten, whipped, imprisoned, at other times and in other places. Most of those persecutions were aimed at white Baptists and especially to the preachers. Some 40 Baptists, again primarily ministers, were imprisoned or otherwise severely persecuted. But we also have found an account of African slaves stripped and whipped for having dared to hear a Baptist minister preaching from his jail window. And so, blacks also paid a price for religious liberty.

The people of the Established Church considered Baptists to be the lowest of the low, the meanest of the mean. Some reckoned that if you would leave these dissenters alone they would fall out among themselves and surely their religious society would come to nothing in the end. In the mid to late-1700s, Baptists in Virginia tended to be anti-slavery either for economic or moral reasons. Although Anglicans despised the Baptists, they seemed content to send their slaves to the Baptists for spiritual education. And the Africans found a welcoming attitude among the Baptists. I believe the Africans felt at home within the Baptist churches of Virginia because they and the white Baptists shared the same social strata of those who were despised by the ruling class. Surely blacks recognized that white Baptists were held in contempt and they must have felt some affinity.

They also found an appealing worship style that was lively and spirited as compared to Anglican services. The white Baptists of the 1700s were given to whoops and hollers and heart-warming hymns and the black Baptists used to being demonstrative in their own African religions must have felt at home. White Baptists were welcoming to blacks as if they had illuminated the front porch of the meetinghouse. In some churches blacks were appointed deacons, albeit over their own people. In many of the churches there was separate seating, which accounts for the addition of galleries to many a country meeting house. The churches without balconies often put up a partition to separate the races although we have found accounts of blacks and whites sitting on the same pews and thinking nothing of it. We found one interesting account of a church that had separate seating in the usual pattern with the whites on the first floor and the blacks in the balcony but which decided on at least one given Sunday to switch. Maybe the whites just wanted to experience the worship service from a different vantage point.

After studying the period, we also have concluded that the vast majority of blacks participated in worship services held outdoors in arbors. We have read reminiscences of white Baptist preachers who made regular appointments to preach on scattered farms. It makes sense. After all, most of the country churches had more black members on the roll than they had seating; and it would have been challenging at best to transport and accommodate huge numbers of slave worshippers. We are told that most slaves on the farms and plantations were given one outfit of clothing for a year and, therefore, they probably would not have had clean clothing to make them presentable in church. We believe that

CHAPTER 24

the slaves who attended church services were the trusted house servants and carriage drivers.

In 1890, the founder of the Virginia Baptist Historical Society, Charles Hill Ryland, requested white ministers who had preached to blacks in slave days to write their remembrances. These were placed in the files of the Historical Society and until our "free indeed!" project, they were not used. They provide a first-person, eye-witness account, albeit paternalistic and from the white perspective, of a relationship between the races within the Baptist community.

William Cauthorn Hall was one of those ministers who recorded his memories. Let me share just a few of his remembrances from the entire document which we have included in the "free indeed!" book. These are William Hall's words:

> I have never seen the day when the worship of God was not as free for the black people as for the whites. A great deal of preaching in those early days for whites as well as blacks was done under arbors with rough seats both in summer and winter. The negroes attended as freely as the white people and generally in larger numbers. There were no restraints imposed upon them, so far as I know, but the negroes kept together in the congregation and if they were sometimes crowded into the white part of the congregation there was no complaint made about it. I have seen the master and servant occupying the same seat and worshipping together. The negroes did not seek those places and push themselves into them, but where room was wanting it was accorded to them, and no one thought of objecting to the partial mingling together. They were worshipping God, and social distinctions were ignored.

> Sometimes masters and servants would be converted at the same meeting and in the joy of their first love all distinctions were lost sight of, and they rejoiced together in the love of a common Saviour. This religious familiarity did not appear to have the least tendency to interfere with the relations existing between master and servant, but only made them feel more interested in each other. The master felt for his servant the kindness of a Christian brother, and the feeling was reciprocated by the servant. There relations were made more desirable and their interests mutually advanced by the grace of God in their hearts.

> It was always the custom of the negroes to treat everything about religion with the greatest reverence. I never heard one make a joke of anything that was sacred, and the songs of those who professed religion were piously religious. They sung wildly sometimes but the songs were religious.

The white minister's recollections were lengthy and he laboriously had written it in long hand. When transcribed and then set into a smaller font, it still took up 25 pages of our "free indeed!" book. Allow me to read one passage that gives a word-picture of the times. It took place at a country church about 50 miles or so from the state capitol and I have spoken at that church and can picture the scene from 163 years ago. The pastor of the church, William H. Taylor, is buried just in front of the stately brick church and his grave is surrounded by an iron fence and maintained as a shrine. Here is how William Hall described the scene:

> I was assisting Rev. Wm. H. Taylor in a protracted meeting held [in 1850] at Mount Zion church, in Buckingham county, of which he was pastor. On that morning a large crowd had gathered and as the church would not hold all the whites, provision had been made for the negroes in the grove. There were four preachers present beside the pastor, and he requested that one of them should go to the grove and preach. I told him that I would go if it was his wish.
>
> He replied, 'No, my brother, I want you to preach in the house this morning, and besides that, you are not a good negro preacher, I know that, if you don't.' After further consultation, seeing that the other brothers were unwilling to go, I told him that he had better send me, and that I would do the best I could for them.
>
> When we went forward the negroes were singing the hymn commencing 'Jesus I love thy charming name,' which always had an inspiring effect upon me. I took my position by the side of a log on the lowest extreme of the congregation. I was accustomed to preaching under similar circumstances and tried to shake off the wet blanket that Bro. Taylor had unintentionally thrown over me, which was forgotten as soon as the services commenced.
>
> We had several hymns sung and prayers offered before the sermon. One of the hymns, 'Am I a soldier of the cross,' was sung so heartily and followed by an earnest soul stirring prayer, that I felt really anxious to begin the part assigned to me in the service. Here I will make an extract from my journal of that date, 'Preached in the morning to the colored people ... from Acts 4:12. 'Prepare to meet thy God.' Had much liberty in speaking to them and hope that much good was done. While I was preaching to them I could see the tears running down their cheeks.
>
> When I commenced my sermon, I felt in my heart that the Lord was with me. He gave me unusual liberty in saying before the minds of the listening crowd a plain presentation of gospel truth. It was my aim to

CHAPTER 24

impact sufficient light for salvation to every one present if they should never hear another sermon. There was no excitement on the part of any. I talked to the people as the Lord enabled me, and I have never seen more earnest attention in any congregation before or since. I had reason to believe that the truth spoken was according to the mind of the Spirit, and that the people's hearts were opened to receive it. The Lord was manifestly with us. I enjoyed it then and it does my heart good now to remember the happy occasion.

At the close of my sermon I requested that one of the colored brethren should lead in prayer. Such a prayer I have seldom ever heard. As we walked back to the church [one of the ministers] said to me, 'If that man's prayer is answered, neither you or any of your descendants will ever lack any good thing in this world or in the world to come.' [Another man said] 'Yes and if they will do as you have told them not one of them will be lost.' I preached in the church that afternoon with encouraging success, but I did not enjoy the presence of the Lord as I did in the morning. I thank the Lord for the many similar sermons in my ministry.

In a search of the hundreds of old records, we have found that very rarely was the word "slave" used. The churches referred to them as "servants." It was a euphemism in a society that did not want to acknowledge the very practice upon which it was established. In other words, they would deny slavery by calling slaves "servants." In early church records the black members often were listed along with the whites; but in time, most clerks made separate listings of white and "colored" males and females. In most cases, the clerks recorded the names of the slave owners beside the name of the slave member, and in most of those early records, the slave owners were not Baptists and, therefore, not members of that Baptist church. Slaves had to produce a permission slip from their master in order to be baptized, which seems contrary to Baptist principles and doctrine; however, it was another acknowledgement that in view of society and the law, slaves were considered property. No one would want to put another person's property at risk by placing it under water! We also have read letters from slave owners to the Baptist pastor offering an assessment of the slave's genuine or seemingly lack of sincerity in their professed conversion. One such letter praised one servant for his profession of faith and cautioned that another's was mere superstition and suggested that the latter slave needed pastoral counseling.

Let it be forever said that blacks found the releasing presence of Jesus Christ within the Baptist experience and it was a spiritual release that enabled them to survive in the world beyond church walls. Yes, they were "free indeed" in Christ, a freedom that transcended everything and lasted forever. It was the ultimate expression of freedom.

The earthly reality was quite different from the inward spiritual freedom. But actual physical freedom could have come much earlier. If the country had followed the lead of Virginia Baptists, slavery might have been abolished much sooner and a war averted. Indeed if the membership of the Virginia Baptist churches had followed their own leadership, the course of history may have been different.

In 1785 the General Committee, which was an early Virginia Baptist attempt at organization, passed a resolution declaring "hereditary slavery to be contrary to the word of God." Five years later, in 1790, the General Committee endorsed a resolution authored by John Leland, the great Baptist statesman, which condemned slavery and urged that "the horrid evil" be removed. Leland believed so strongly in his own resolution that he owned no slaves and instead worked his children on his farm. There were others who opposed slavery in the late 18th century; but in the early 19th century attitudes and politics hardened in defense of the peculiar institution. Also, we have concluded that it was not so much that the Baptists became pro-slavery as it was that more slave owners became Baptists so their view in time predominated.

In the 18th-century Virginia Baptists actually were, in a word, abolitionists. In the exhibit is the resolution authored by John Leland and adopted by Virginia Baptists that condemned slavery as an evil and sought for its abolishment. The document was written 75 years before emancipation. These are the words John Leland wrote and which Virginia Baptists adopted:

> Resolved, that slavery is a violent deprivation of the rights of Nature, and inconsistent with a republican government; and therefore recommend it to our brethren to make use of every legal measure, to extripate the horrid evil from the land, and pray Almighty God, that our Honourable Legislature may have it in their power, to proclaim the general jubilee, consistent with the principles of good policy.

Another anti-slavery Virginia Baptist minister of the period was David Barrow, one of the persecuted ministers. He wrote and published a pamphlet in 1808 in which he condemned the practice of slavery. He also authored his own political creed in which he stated: "holding, tyrannizing and driving slaves I view as contrary to the laws of God and nature." In his creed, he wrote; "I believe the natural equality of man, except in some monstrous cases." He envisioned

CHAPTER 24

"that desirable time when [slaves] will be delivered from the iron talons of their task-masters and joyfully put off the galling yoke of slavery." Eventually he left Virginia for the frontier of Kentucky where he could work his own children on the farm and not endure ridicule of his neighbors for not owning slaves.

Another evidence of the anti-slavery attitude of 18th century Virginia Baptists is found in the minutes of 1797 of the Dover Baptist Association, once the largest district association of Baptists in the world, in which churches were encouraged "to unite with the Abolition Society in proposing gradual emancipation."

With Leland's resolution on everyone's mind, Baptists of the Roanoke Association met in June 1790 and adopted the following resolution:

> Respecting the strong remonstrances Against slavery, and the manner in which they have taken it up unanimously agreed to remonstrate, as Christians, against oppression as we discover the same, and that we are heartily disposed to be under the influence of the spirit of humanity, yet nevertheless, we believe it would be a very gross violation thereof ... to emancipate our slaves promiscuously without means or visible prospects of their support. That tho' we are not unanimously clear in our minds whether the God of nature ever intended, that one Part of the human species should be held in an abject state of slavery to another part of the same species: yet the subject to us is so very abstruse and such a set of complex circumstances attending the same, that we suppose [neither] the general committee nor any other Religious Society whatever has the least right to concern therein as a society, but leave every individual to act at discression. In order to keep a good conscience before God, as far as the Laws of our [land] will admit; and that it is the indispensable duty of masters to forbear and suppress cruelty, and do that which is just and equal to their servants.

Some Baptist associations shied from the topic. Some shunted it off to the state, declaring it was a matter for the legislature and not for a religious society. Some were more discerning and forthcoming. The Portsmouth Association in 1796 declared that man's greatest problem was "covetousness" and proceeded to explain:

> Covetousness leads Christians, with the people of this country in general, to hold and retain, in abject slavery, a set of our poor fellow creatures, contrary to the laws of God and nature.

The next year, in the summer of 1797, the Baptists in Northern Virginia's Ketocton Association had laid their crops by and were ready to consider the fate of those folks who labored on the crops. They answered a query from a church about Divine Law:

> Is Hereditary Slavery a transgression of the Divine Law? Answered in the affirmative. Is not the Bondage of the Africans amongst us, a species of Hereditary Slavery? And consequently, the continuation of the practice a transgression of the Divine Law? Answered also in the affirmative.

The Ketocton appointed a committee consisting of six of their most prominent members and asked for a plan of gradual emancipation. The committee drafted such a plan which included the following provisions:

1. All slaves 14 years and under to be free at 22 years of age.
2. All above 14, and under 20, to be free at 25.
3. All above 20, and under 25, to be free at 28.
4. All above 25, to serve 5 years.
5. All born after this date shall be entitled to the same rights and privileges as children born of Negroes before heretofore emancipated.
6. All who have been purchased with money, shall serve ten years from the time of such purchase.

By the next year, the association had succumbed to the idea that such a plan among church members was not practical and the whole concept of emancipation should be left to the legislature.

The generation that was so adamant in pushing for an end to slavery was passing off the scene. It had been the same generation that had provided the foot soldiers for the Revolution against England. It was a generation of enlightened ideas. It was led among Baptists by courageous pastors who practiced what they preached and abhorred the ownership of a human being by another human being. But the leaders of that generation were leaving Virginia, Leland for his native state of Massachusetts and Barrow for Kentucky.

In the 1700s, there were numerous African preachers including "Negro Lewis" of the Northern Neck of Virginia, and in the Historical Society's collection there is an account of his preaching to about 300 people and displaying his preaching gifts which "exceeded many white preachers." The account comes from one of the most valuable items in our collection, an 18th century manuscript book called *Dozier's Textbook*. Richard Dozier was the overseer for the wealthiest man in

CHAPTER 24

Colonial Virginia, Robert Carter; and Dozier had a hobby. He enjoyed going to hear Baptist preachers and recording their sermon texts and noting the results of the sermons. In *Dozier's Textbook* there is an entry for May 26, 1782, in which he wrote:

> I went in the evening to hear a negro (called Lewis) speak. He spake by the way of [exhorting] to abt. 400. I think with the greatest sensibility I ever expected to hear from an Ethiopian he pointed out the state man was in by nature and laid before us the Evidence of a sinful nature … and entreated them to rest not in a unconverted state but come & accept X [Christ] by faith that they might be reconciled of God.

Another remarkable black preacher of the times was Jacob Bishop who served for awhile as a minister of a mixed congregation in Portsmouth, Virginia. He attended the meetings of the Portsmouth Baptist Association in the 1790s. From the history of the Kehukee Baptist Association there is this description:

> In 1795, there came a black preacher from Northampton county, in Virginia, whose name was Jacob Bishop. The brethren and friends in that county gave him money to buy his freedom, which he did; and soon after bought his wife's. And when he came to Norfolk he bought his eldest son's freedom. His preaching was much admired both by saints and sinners, for some time wherever he went.

In 1792 the Roanoke Baptist Association actually purchased a man named Simon in order to set him free to preach. The Association explained: "We think him ordained of God to preach the Gospel." The original manuscript book is in our exhibit and thus far it is the only reference we can discover to this black preacher named Simon.

Indeed for most of the blacks mentioned in our name registry the notation from the old church records remains the only evidence that they ever existed. Their names cry out to us to let us know that they once walked the same ground and declared the same faith.

All of the advancements for black preachers and black congregations were challenged after the Nat Turner insurrection of 1831 in Southampton County in Virginia. The state passed harsh laws requiring the presence of white males if blacks gathered for worship and for white pastors to preside over black congregations. In that period, Robert Ryland, a white minister and president of the Baptist school, Richmond College, became the pastor of the First African Baptist Church of Richmond which was a large congregation of upwards of 2,700 members.

Ryland wrote his own catechism for blacks and a copy is in the exhibit. Published in 1848, it is titled *The Scripture Catechism for Coloured People.* It covers questions on the Bible and Christian doctrine which can be answered by a simple yes or no; but Ryland also expected his congregants to give the Scripture text to back up their answer so in an age when to teach reading and writing to slaves was illegal, they must have memorized the answers. It has been interesting to watch people as they tried to answer the questions in the catechism. Many 21st century Christians would not be able to know all the answers.

Here is a sample of some of the questions and answers:

> Question: Is the belief of a God the first step necessary for us to be religious? YES He that cometh to God must believe that he is, and the he is a rewarder of them that diligently seek him. Heb. 11. 6.

> Has God revealed himself to mankind? YES That which may be known of God is manifest unto them; for God showed it unto them. Rom 1.19.

> Was this revelation through his works sufficient to teach man the saving knowledge of God? YES The heavens declare the glory of God ... There is no speech nor language where their voice is not heard ... Their line has gone out through all the earth. Psalm 19.2-4.

Maybe we need a negative answer. Here is another question: "Did this revelation come from human wisdom? NO The prophecy came not in old time by the will of men; but holy men of God spake as they were moved by the Holy Ghost." 2 Pet. 1.21.

There were numerous stories of one-on-one relationships between blacks and whites. One of the interesting stories comes from a church named Nomini in Westmoreland County, Virginia. An itinerant preacher named Henry Toler came into the area while a Samuel Templeman was away on business. Toler converted Templeman's mother and wife or as he later recalled the situation: "On my return it appeared to me that the world was turned upside down. I found the whole family alarmed and earnestly inquiring what they should do to be saved." Among those who had been converted was his "favorite servant-man" named Cupid. The servant got religion in a powerful way and began exhorting himself to the other slaves.

> I could hear him at all hours of night singing, and it tormented me. On a Sunday night I heard a loud talking in the kitchen, and went round back of the house to listen, and lo! He was lamenting his poor master's situation, that if he died unconverted, he would be eternally miserable; it raised my anger to such a pitch, I cam to the resolution that I would,

in the morning, chastise him for his insolence. Thus, I returned, and to bed. I have often wondered at the goodness and forbearance of God. In the morning, by light, I took my whip, and went to the stable, determined to execute my threat. The moment I set foot on the sill of the door, I caught his eye fixed on me; he was a very humble man. 'Master,' says he, 'I hope you won't be angry; I want to talk with you.' I was disarmed in a moment, and told him he might say what he pleased; I dropped my whip, and have never seen it since. He commenced with his experience, (the first I have ever heard); I found something working in my heart that I had never felt before, assenting to the truth of what he said. I was thoroughly convinced that if I died without such religion as Cupid had experienced, I should be miserable forever; he broke out in a warm exhortation, and I was obliged to turn away, lest Cupid should see my tears. I returned to the house, and told my wife that if she would get the Bible and call the family together, I would try to worship God. This was joyful news to her.

Samuel Templeman, converted through the testimony of his slave, became a Christian and, in short order, a Baptist minister. He preached and ministered throughout a large territory encompassing some four counties and had a lasting influence upon the region.

There were about 20 independent black Baptist churches in Virginia prior to emancipation but most of blacks were in mixed congregations. One of the independent churches was Second African Baptist Church of Richmond which came from Second Baptist Church, a church constituted in 1820. Twenty-six years after its founding, the black members, some 57, formed a separate church. This was five years after the First Church had helped create First African for its black members, a move that nearly cost the white pastor, Jeremiah Bell Jeter, his position and his reputation among the other clergy of the city.

The Second African Church had a chapel which the white members of Second had their slaves build for the new church. Like the First African, the Second African was served by a white pastor until after the Civil War. Among the treasures found within the minutes of the mother church, Second Baptist Church, is the original constitution of the new black Second church. It is the only written constitution that we have discovered of one of Virginia's antebellum black Baptist churches. Among the articles in the constitution is the following:

> The Second Baptist Church shall annually appoint a committee of twenty-four male members to aid in the religious instruction & discipline of the Second Coloured Baptist Church. The Pastor of this

Church shall be a white Baptist minister of good standing … selected by a majority of the members of the Coloured Church, and approved by the committee of the Second (White) church. Meetings for public worship must be held in the day time.

The new church was received into the local district association.

In an age when church discipline was the order of the day, the old church records contain examples of blacks being disciplined, just as whites were disciplined, for a variety of infractions. Some were excommunicated and just like the whites, blacks often expressed repentance and were readmitted into the fellowship. There were even cases of blacks bringing their masters before the church for offenses against them. In 1772 the Meherrin Baptist Church in Lunenburg County heard a case of inappropriate behavior. A married slave couple accused their white mistress of "the sin of anger & unchristian language" as well as parting a black man and his wife. The mistress expressed her regret and the church and the black couple accepted it.

In 1780 at a church business meeting at South Quay Baptist Church in Southampton County, a slave owner named John brought charges against his slave Nero for disobedience and harsh language. Nero also brought charges against the master for misconduct. Both were censored by the church.

In 1842-43, the long winter was made livelier at Sperryville Baptist Church in the mountains of Rappahannock County. A female servant confided to someone that her master had made "corrupt propositions." When brought before the church, the master insisted that he was merely testing the servant's virtue and "did not intend to carry out his proposition to the woman if she had assented."

The very fact that blacks could dare to bring charges against their masters within a Baptist church indicated the heightened freedom they experienced within the membership.

In his *Virginia Chronicle* of 1790, John Leland indicted the attitude regarding slave marriages. He wrote:

> The marriage of slaves is a subject not known in our code of laws. What promises so ever they make, their masters may and do part them at pleasure. If their marriages are as sacred as the marriages of freemen, the slaves are guilty of adultery when they part voluntarily, and the masters are guilty of a sin as great when they part them involuntary, and yet while they are property, it is not in the power of the masters to prevent their being forced apart.

CHAPTER 24

The Baptist General Committee considered the matter of slave marriages in a statement of 1788. Before the Committee was the question: "Is it allowable for a member possessing slaves who are about to remove to a distant part of the world, and for such member to part man and wife?" The answer: "It is not allowable and when a member is about to remove he shall use his utmost endeavors to keep man and wife together, and if such a member fails therein, he shall be dealt with as an offender and excluded from society." Coan Baptist Church in Westmoreland County altered the wedding vows of slaves to read: "until death or removal."

Another related issue to marriages was the selling of slaves and the destruction of family structure. State laws did not recognize slave marriages but the churches did or otherwise they would have been condoning adultery. In 1817 one of the country churches, Lyle's Baptist Church in Fluvanna County, described a situation in which a white member had sold "his negro man Phil" and it resulted in "a burden on the church." In the selling of a slave, a church member was torn away from the fellowship. Once slaves were relocated they could produce their "church letter" in seeking membership in another Baptist church.

David Roper, the founding pastor of Second Baptist Church of Richmond, "disposed" of a slave in 1821 and the church considered the question of "whether the Church conceives any circumstances that will justify a member of this Church in purchasing or selling a Slave?" The church concluded: "Resolved that we do not regard the late disposal of a slave by Bro. D. Roper to be either reprehensible or contrary to any regulation of the Church."

In 1837 Antioch, a church in the plantation country of Charlotte County, decided "that we view the practice of trading in slaves for the sole purpose of gain as contrary to the spirit of the Gospel & to its interest, therefore we will not hereafter connive at it in our Members."

What was the status of the blacks, slave or free, within the churches? They were members but the churches were governed by white males. It would be decades after the War before white females participated in business sessions. They largely were penniless yet in some cases masters allowed their slaves to work extra time and earn small amounts of money. There was more opportunity for this among town and city slaves who labored in industries. With a few cents in their pockets, black members were expected to contribute to the church and its causes. In the journal of the missionary Luther Rice in 1819-20 there is a notation that he received a small amount of money for mission from "a free woman of color." At Emmaus Baptist Church in New Kent County, "the colored members" presented a request "that they might be allowed to contribute towards defraying the expense of the church, and that the church should say how much and when it should be paid." The church decided that fifty cents per quarter for a free person and 12 ½ cents per quarter for a slave was a worthy offering unto the Lord.

In many churches blacks were appointed as deacons, albeit having oversight of their own race. In the early 1800s, Williamsburg African Church and Gillfield, a large and important independent black church in the city of Petersburg, both inquired of their district associations whether slaves could serve as deacons. It was determined that they could have the same service in a church as a free person.

One of the epoch stories out of Virginia during slavery is the colonization movement. For some it appealed as a great humanitarian project. For others it was a convenient way to rid the state of the slave problem and the blacks themselves who by that time were not native Africans but persons born in what had become the United States of America. They were Americans and Virginians even if they did not have the status of citizenship.

One such native Virginian was Lott Cary who was born in 1780 a slave in Charles City County, an area of vast plantations between Williamsburg and Richmond. At his grandmother's knee he had learned about the One in whom all men and women are "free indeed." He came to Richmond to work in the tobacco warehouses and joined the First Baptist Church of the city. He soon began preaching "at candlelight" at First Church. The famous missionary Luther Rice even encouraged him and loaned him money, which the black minister repaid. His master allowed him to earn money and in time he accumulated enough to purchase his own freedom and that of his wife and son.

Lott Cary and his friend, Collin Teague, and others were taught in an evening school conducted by William Crane, a white Baptist who was a member of the Second church of Richmond. Crane encouraged Cary and Teague to consider going to Liberia. The little group met in Crane's house and constituted the first Baptist church for Monrovia, Liberia, calling it Providence. The new church was transplanted from Richmond to Africa. Lott Cary's story in Liberia assured him a place in history.

Another fascinating story out of the colonization movement is the freeing of the slaves of a Baptist minister by the name of Thaddeus Herndon of Northern Virginia. He and his wife, Mary Fannie, freed slaves worth, in crass material terms, some $30,000, which was a fortune. But the rest of the story reflects a humanitarian spirit. The Herndons bought their freed slaves the good they would need – clothing, bedding, tools, equipment and books including a family Bible for each family. Thaddeus reckoned that there was a bond between him and his slaves: "We have lived together," he declared. "We have grown up together." The Herndons transported their slaves to the ship, held a prayer meeting on the ship, and Mary Fannie gave each family a journal book in which she had recorded that slave family's history, noting the dates when their children were born. To one of the slaves, a man named Washington, the former master pleaded: "Write to me, Washington, you can write. I have furnished you with paper. Keep a journal."

The Liberia movement was fraught with controversy, crises and disasters. It also had its brighter side in the planting of a Baptist witness in the country. By 1857 the Liberia Baptist Association listed 17 member churches with nearly 1,000 members. Many of the prominent Liberian Baptists were from Virginia and indeed one section of the country was named Virginia.

In our exhibit we placed a copy of the constitution of the Republic of Liberia printed in Philadelphia in 1848. It contained some revolutionary ideas that had not found full expression in the land they had left. Section 1 read: "All men are born equally free and independent and have certain natural, inherent and unalienable rights among which are the rights of enjoying and defending life and liberty, of acquiring, possessing and protecting property and of pursuing and obtaining safety and happiness." Section 3: "All men have a natural and inalienable right to worship God according to the dictates of their own consciences, without obstruction or molestation from others…" Section 4: "There shall be no slavery within this Republic. Nor shall any citizen of this Republic, or any person resident therein, deal in slaves…" It all sounded Jeffersonian but without deception.

The four years of war by whatever name Southerners and Northerners chose to call it created destruction in Virginia where much of the battles were fought and affected the Baptist churches. Congregations were depleted; white males went off to fight; meeting houses were destroyed; records were lost; and several ministers were imprisoned. As Union forces swept through some areas, blacks ran away or as the records of Walnut Grove Baptist Church near Richmond state: "Gone with the enemy."

By war's end, the course of rebuilding began. In our exhibit we placed the eye-witness account of Julia Wilber, a member of the Rochester [New York] Ladies' Anti-Slavery Society who visited the former Confederate capital a month after it fell. She brought boxes of clothing to place upon the walking skeletons of the emancipated folk. She wrote: "As soon as the slaves were made free by the advance of the Union army, the masters refused to keep the old and disabled who had been worn out in their service, and sent them to this place to die. They also turned off the sick and the young children. Some of the old people looked more like moving bundles of rags than like human beings." She gave away 600 new garments to the people.

Blacks were now free indeed, even free to form their own churches and, in time, associations and state conventions. There were some whites who wanted to perpetuate the old order and were reluctant for blacks to leave the churches. The Rappahannock Association in an area of large farms and plantations met in the summer of 1865 and accepted the following report: "The issue of the war has not changed, or even in the least modified, our views with reference to the scriptural Lawfulness of slavery. Southern Christians have always drawn their defense of the institution from the word of God ... The time may have, and probably has, arrived, when God sees fit in His excellent wisdom, to abolish slavery in this country." When one of the member churches advanced the inquiry as to whether or not its black members should be required or encouraged to withdraw membership, the Rappahannock decided "that separate organizations of the colored members of our churches, should, at present, neither be required nor encouraged."

On the other hand, in the Appomattox Association, another area with a large black population, Daniel Witt, one of the fathers of the Baptist General Association of Virginia, recommended that "the churches, quietly and promptly, organize their colored membership into separate and independent churches, and endeavor to exert such a supervision over them as is consistent with their separate and independent organization."

The Middle District Association just below Richmond tried its best to retain the Midlothian African Church and prevent its withdrawing. "We believe that such a course will be injurious alike to the church and the religious interests of the colored people within the circle of its influence. Convicted of this fact, we feel that an earnest effort should be put forth to dissuade them from their present intention."

But the blacks were gone. At first, there was a mass exodus from the mixed churches and out of the existing associations. Some few blacks remained in some of the churches until as late as the 1880s.

Immediately after the war, two district associations were formed by the free people: the Shiloh around Richmond and the Norfolk Union for the Tidewater region. They were mirror images of the earlier associations that now would be composed of white churches. In its first report, the Shiloh in August 1865 listed the number of church members within its ranks as 9,674 and the number in Sunday schools was about 2,500. In three years, the Shiloh listed a total membership of 25,122 within 75 churches. In 1868 the Norfolk Union Association listed 11,767 members.

Within the first five years after emancipation, there were about 250 new churches planted by blacks, a tremendous undertaking by a people who had been considered as inferior.

In addition, blacks were adamant that their ministers receive theological education and a seminary was started in what had been the infamous slave jail in Richmond. A black Baptist newspaper was published, calling itself the *Shiloh Herald*, in contrast to the existing *Religious Herald* with its white editors and white subscribers. In our exhibit we placed the first issue of the newspaper. The *Shiloh Herald* declared that it entered "the arena of journalism with malice to none and charity to all, not as a rival but as an aider." The black Baptist denomination in Virginia had been birthed.

The founder, publisher and editor of the *Shiloh Herald* was a fascinating man named Henry Williams. He was born a child of free parents in Spotsylvania County, Virginia, on October 13, 1831. Just two months earlier Nat Turner, a slave preacher, led an insurrection in Southampton County, Virginia, in which about 60 whites were killed. The short-lived rebellion created widespread fear among white Virginians. Severe laws were passed that restricted activities of blacks. No longer could they gather for worship unless there where white men present. No longer could they be taught to read and write. Henry Williams' parents decided to flee to Ohio and there Henry spent his youth.

The story was handed down that as a youth he ran away from home to visit Africa. He soon became homesick and boarded the first ship back to America. He pictured the scene for his hearers: "On reaching the ship, my manner of getting aboard was to be by climbing a rope. There I was, dangling between the sky and the sea with hungry sharks awaiting my fall. I finally succeeded in getting aboard." It was after reaching home that he became converted to Christianity and soon began preparation to enter the ministry.

Without benefit of formal education, he was self-taught and self-made. He became an itinerant missionary and traveled on foot including a missionary journey of 40 miles. He joined the secretive Underground Railroad and "personally led and transported on his back and shoulders many of his race from one station to another on the way to Canada, traveling day and night, through rain and snow."

In 1865, with the Civil War over, he made a missionary journey as far as Petersburg. He happened to meet someone from Gilfield Baptist Church, an independent black Baptist church which dates to perhaps 1797, who invited him to preach. It seems that the church was "waiting for a pastor to whom a call had been extended and whose arrival was long overdue." The expected new pastor never arrived and Henry Williams suddenly found himself called as the pastor. It was November 1865. His wife, Madeline Carter Williams, joined him and a new era began in the life of Gilfield and for black Baptists in Virginia.

Annie Williams, a contemporary of the pastor and a teacher in the Sunday school, once recalled that upon his arrival in Petersburg, "in a speech on the Poplar Lawn, now Central Park, he advised us as a people just liberated, to devote ourselves, our time, our all, to material progress, the acquisition of prosperity, trades and education, and above all to make friends of our neighbors among whom we live, rather than seek political advancement." She continued: "In fact [pastor urged us] to leave politics alone. From this he made enemies. But did he not see the end from the beginning?"

"His strong points were a wealth of common sense, an incompatible honesty, steadfast in honorable purpose, an untiring industry, all supplemented by the highest order of physical, moral and Christian courage. He was of the stuff martyrs are made."

A newspaper in his time also admitted that the Baptist pastor had his enemies but added: "They were enemies because he told them the truth."

In 1870 he was elected to the Petersburg City Council. And in the same year he launched *The Shiloh Herald*, which declared on its masthead that it was "devoted to vital godliness and sound morality."

Gilfield members revered him. Through personal appeals and hard work, he led the church which had about 1,200 when he arrived to receive 5,781 new members with 4,455 by baptism at his hands. He not only was the pastor but also the superintendent of the church's large and vital Sunday school which enrolled about 700. At one point the church members took up a special collection to furnish the pastor with a horse and buggy to be used in visiting the flock.

Henry Williams was a recognizable figure on the streets of Petersburg. He was a physically big man, slightly stooped, and possessed a commanding voice. In his long pastorate he kept the church and school "free from broils, factions and dismemberment and free from debt." In the 1870s he led the church to build a large new building which was debt-free within a year. He even suggested that the church make its own bricks to save costs. During his pastorate, the church established four branches in the countryside beyond Petersburg. He was considered the father of the Virginia Baptist State Convention and the organizer of two district associations of black churches.

CHAPTER 24

Within his community, he led a movement to hire black teachers for black schools. He took a particular interest in the poor of Petersburg and found ways to help them.

He served Gilfield Baptist Church for 34 years until his death in February 1900 at age 68. He witnessed tremendous changes within his own lifetime as slavery vanished and freedom offered new challenges.

In the minutes of the Norfolk Union for 1868 there was a greeting from Williams of Shiloh. He summarized the spirit of the black Baptists of Virginia: "Pray for us, dear brethren, that peace may dwell within our walls and prosperity within our palaces, and that we may all stand fast in the liberties wherein we have been made free, and that we may not again be entangled in the yoke of bondage." Henry Williams might as well have said: We are free indeed!

Acknowledgement is made to my colleague, R. Michael Whitt, special projects assistant at the Virginia Baptist Historical Society, who followed through with his assignment to compile the name registry and who wrote the narrative which the Society published under the title "free indeed!"

Relishing their new full freedom, the blacks constituted new churches, associations, a newspaper, a seminary and eventually a college.

It has taken 150 years for black and white Baptists to begin to form a new humanity. More and more traditionally black churches are joining the Baptist General Association of Virginia or, at least, becoming dually aligned with it and the historically black state associations, the State Convention and the General Convention. It is almost as if the porch light has been turned on and the welcoming mat swept.

CHAPTER 25
HISTORIA DE LOS BAUTISTAS EN CHILE

Victor Aguilar Reyes

Introducción

Al tratar de escribir algunas líneas sobre el origen y desarrollo de la obra Bautista en Chile, presentando una panorámica breve de los hechos más relevantes, quisiera hacerlo con tal acierto que el recuerdo de su vivencia resulte un homenaje para esa historia y también para cada uno de aquellos visionarios, pioneros, aguerridos y sacrificados hermanos que, con su modo de ser, forjaron esa historia bautista que deseo compartir brevemente con ustedes. Fue difícil al comienzo emprender una inesperada gran obra, en especial porque los apreciados pioneros debieron enfrentar grandes impedimentos. Eran pocos, no contaban con los medios económicos, el pueblo donde surgió la primera obra bautista en el sur de nuestro país era de reducida población y, lo que era peor que todo, los trabajos de los hermanos participantes no estaban en la misma localidad. La mayoría de los pioneros trabajaba en el campo, desde donde concurrían a los cultos que se realizaban en aquel pueblo y en otras ciudades del sur de Chile. Con gran entusiasmo y duro trabajo evangelizador lograron finalmente levantar una numerosa obra bautista que se extendió por todo Chile. A partir de sus inicios esta obra comenzó a tomar contactos con otras iglesias bautistas independientes, estrechando y fortaleciendo aún más el carácter nacional de las iglesias bautistas en nuestro país, sin olvidar el valioso y gran apoyo misionero que brindó la Convención Bautista del Sur de los Estados Unidos. La presencia poderosa de Dios en la vida de nuestros recordados hermanos y líderes bautistas chilenos, sumada al valioso apoyo misionero desde Estados Unidos, lograron establecer el inicio, el desarrollo y la final consolidación de una gran presencia bautista en nuestro país.

Tres grandes organizaciones bautistas independientes se cuentan en la actualidad en Chile: la Unión de Iglesias Evangélicas Bautistas de Chile, la

CHAPTER 25

Corporación de Iglesias Evangélicas Bautistas Misión Chilena y las Iglesias Bíblicas Bautistas.

Diego Thomson

La historia y herencia bautistas en Chile comenzaron con la llegada del gran educador Diego Thomson en 1821, considerado el primer bautista en llegar a nuestro país. En esta breve presentación sólo consideramos los hechos más sobresalientes e importantes que permitieron el comienzo, el desarrollo y la consolidación de esta gran presencia bautista en nuestro país con que contamos actualmente.

Diego Thomson llegó a Buenos Aires, Argentina, en 1818. Su deseo era servir a Jesucristo mediante la promoción de las Sagradas Escrituras y la implantación de un sistema de educación popular. Para él un sistema de educación centrado en la Biblia era la pieza clave para el avance cultural de cualquier pueblo. Instalado ya en Argentina, desde Buenos Aires Thomson envió a Chile en 1820 los primeros 240 Nuevos Testamentos en español que se recibieron en nuestro país.

El éxito que Thomson logró en Buenos Aires al desplegar con entusiasmo 100 escuelas para cinco mil niños de ambos sexos, llamó la atención del Gobierno Chileno de aquel entonces. Así fue que el libertador Don Bernardo O'Higgins le invitó en 1821 a visitar Chile, convirtiéndose así en el primer bautista que se tiene registro en llegar a nuestro país. La invitación de O'Higgins fue con el propósito que Diego Thomson empezara también en Chile una serie de escuelas populares con el sistema Lancasteriano que había realizado con tanto éxito en Argentina. El sistema hacía honor al maestro cuáquero Lancaster, de nacionalidad inglesa. Su método de enseñanza consistía en que el maestro instruía a los alumnos más aptos, los que a su vez daban lecciones a los menos adelantados. Todo ello se hacía usando como libro de texto la Biblia. El recordado y extrañado misionero Don Roberto Cecil Moore recuerda en sus memorias que "la primera Biblia que entró legalmente a Chile fue traída por Diego Thomson con la expresa autorización del Presidente O´Higgins, en 1821".[1]

A pesar de la exigente oposición de la Iglesia Católica Apostólica Romana, Thomson permaneció en Chile por casi un año. Desde aquí se preocupó también por la importación y distribución de la Palabra de Dios. Sin lugar a dudas, Thomson fue el precursor de la obra educacional evangélica en Chile. Cuidadosa y sabiamente se dedicó a expandir las enseñanzas del Nuevo Testamento bajo el sistema Lancasteriano, ya que el fuerte control y oposición de la Iglesia Católica no permitía que se dieran las condiciones para llevar adelante un trabajo evangélico abierta y tranquilamente.

Más allá de toda oposición, gracias a este método de enseñanza y al apoyo de Don Bernardo O´Higgins, Thomson logró dar comienzo a la primera escuela con este nuevo sistema, la que se inició el 18 de septiembre de 1821, con un número de 200 alumnos. Se llamaba "Escuela Normal Lancasteriana" y se reunía en la capilla de la Universidad de San Felipe, hoy en día el edificio del Teatro Municipal de Santiago.

A fines de 1821 Thomson fue reemplazado por Don Antonio Eston, que también llegó a Chile contratado por el Gobierno para seguir trabajando en el área educativa, lo cual realizó por varios meses más. La segunda escuela lancasteriana en Chile se fundó en las casas que habían pertenecido a la Compañía de Jesús, donde hoy se levanta el ex – Congreso Nacional. La escuela de Valparaíso se abrió en junio de 1822 y llegó a contar con 130 alumnos.

Por su favorable trabajo educativo en Chile, Thomson se ganó la ciudadanía chilena, la cual le fue otorgada por el propio Don Bernardo O´Higgins, el 31 de mayo de 1822. El 18 de junio del mismo año Thomson partió desde Valparaíso con dirección al Perú. Desgraciadamente, producto de la fuerte y titánica influencia y autoridad de la Iglesia Católica en nuestro país, el sistema Lancasteriano no logró aquí el mismo éxito que había logrado en Argentina.

Colonización Alemana

Durante la presidencia del General Manuel Bulnes, que abarcó dos períodos consecutivos: el primero, de 1841 a 1846; y el segundo, de 1846 a 1851; se produjeron las primeras inmigraciones de alemanes hacia el sur de Chile. La inmigración de los alemanes a Chile se inició principalmente gracias a la llamada "Ley de Inmigración Selectiva" que fue dictada en 1845 durante el gobierno de Bulnes. Su propósito era traer a personas con un nivel sociocultural medio y alto para colonizar los territorios del sur de nuestro país. Los colonos que llegaron eran personas muy trabajadoras, esforzadas, y emprendedoras. Muchos trajeron sus capitales para ser invertidos principalmente en el desarrollo de la agricultura y la industria. Si bien las inmigraciones de colonos alemanes en un principio fueron esporádicas y escasas, con la intervención del Gobierno dichas inmigraciones tomaron fuerza y continuidad, logrando con el tiempo una gran comunidad de colonos alemanes esparcidos en diferentes lugares del sur de nuestro país, manteniendo y cuidando su cultura y también sus creencias religiosas.

Según el historiador Isaías Valdivia, "En el año 1884 llegaron al Sur de Chile algunos colonos alemanes, que emigraron del Continente Viejo, para establecerse en los lugares denominados El Salto, Contulmo y Quillén Viejo. Varias familias de estos colonos eran bautistas y las más distinguidas eran: las familias Reinicke,

Roloff, Berg, Meier y Lichtenberg".[2] Una vez asentadas en nuestro territorio estas familias comenzaron a desarrollar y desplegar sus conocimientos y habilidades para emprender negocios, lo cual les permitió una estabilidad económica y una vida familiar tranquila y normal en el nuevo país que los acogía. Dicha tranquilidad y normalidad se vería en un par de años más tarde impresionada por un avivamiento evangelizador iniciado por algunos de los colonos.

Avivamiento Bautista Alemán

Según Roberto Moore, "Un laico de gran espiritualidad, Felipe Meier, levantó un avivamiento entre los colonos y ellos organizaron a lo menos tres iglesias bautistas en ésta década, una de éstas en Quillen, otras en Contulmo y Victoria".[3] Así también lo expresa Isaías Valdivia al señalar que: "De ésta modo y después de algunos años de labor incansable se organiza la primera Iglesia Bautista Alemana, en la colonia de Contulmo, en el año 1892. A medida que seguían trabajando entre sus conciudadanos, el Señor les bendijo con nuevos convertidos. En la colonia de "El Salto" se fundó la segunda iglesia, el 20 de Julio de 1894".[4]

La organización de estas iglesias, cuyos cultos en un principio se realizaban en idioma alemán, no fue el único resultado de dicho avivamiento. Algunos colonos alemanes comenzaron a gestar la idea de realizar sus cultos en lengua castellana con el propósito de evangelizar y educar también a los chilenos en el menaje evangélico de Jesucristo. Fue así que Wenceslao Valdivia abrazó las doctrinas y principios bautistas, siendo bautizado en 1896 por inmersión en la iglesia bautista de Quillén, gracias a la labor que realizara el colono alemán bautista Don Enrique Reinike. Valdivia es considerado el primer bautista chileno.

En éste mismo sentir, escribe Humberto Muñoz, "Los hermanos José y Germán Lichtenberg llevaron su celo hasta el grado de organizar algunos cultos sencillos en castellano, los domingos en la tarde, para los chilenos".[5] Roberto Moore agrega que "Hasta donde se sabe, esta fue la primera predicación bautista en castellano llevada a efecto en Chile. De los esfuerzos de estos jóvenes salieron varios de los primeros predicadores bautistas chilenos, entre otros, Abraham Chavez y Juan Antonio Gatica".[6] Isaías Valdivia también destaca a los siguientes hermanos: Gualberto Mella, Nieves Zapata, José Sáez, Pedro Barra, Erasmo Rodríguez, doña Rosa de Lagos, Manríquez y otros".[7]

Bautistas y Aliancistas

Roberto Moore recuerda, además, la llegada del primer misionero Aliancista: "Un menonita, Henry L. Weiss, que hablaba alemán, por iniciativa personal llegó con su esposa, vía Panamá, a Concepción, en abril de 1897. Un misionero presbiteriano le había sugerido comenzar obra en el sur de Chile".[8] Weiss fue el primer misionero de la recién formada Alianza Cristiana y Misionera en llegar a nuestro país. "Una comisión de colonos del avivamiento (alemán) lo conquistó como su líder espiritual, instalándose...en Victoria. Comenzó su trabajo que pronto se tornó ministerio de predicación a los chilenos".[9]

Sin muchos conocimientos del idioma y sin ningún apoyo económico desde Estados Unidos, H. Weiss inicia igualmente la obra evangelizadora contando con la gran colaboración de los bautistas alemanes ya instalados en Chile. Este proyecto evangelizador se fundó sobre éste núcleo alemán predominantemente bautista, permitiendo la extensión de las creencias bautistas hacia los chilenos que se encontraban principalmente en Contulmo, Quillen, el Salto y Victoria. Roberto Cecil Moore lo recuerda así: "Recién había llegado la Alianza Cristiana y Misionera que incorporó a sus filas a unas pocas iglesias bautistas de habla alemana y otras de habla castellana que los inmigrantes alemanes habían fundado en el distrito alrededor de Victoria-Temuco y Osorno-Puerto Varas".[10] Así comenzaron a propagarse las doctrinas y principios bautistas al sur de nuestro país, considerando y reconociendo a nuestros hermanos bautistas alemanes como los iniciadores del movimiento bautista en Chile.

Guillermo MacDonald

En 1888 llegó a Chile el hermano bautista escocés Guillermo MacDonald. Su propósito inicial fue servir como profesor contratado por el gobierno en la colonia inglesa de Púa. Roberto Moore recuerda que "ya la obra de la Alianza Cristiana y Misionera había crecido con la llegada de otros misioneros y la expansión hacia el sur hasta Osorno. MacDonald entró a la misión en 1899. Aunque la Alianza no era bautista, se había basado sobre el núcleo alemán que lo era. Además, gran parte de sus misioneros pertenecía a la denominación bautista. MacDonald trabajó eficazmente con ellos por siete años. Según parece, MacDonald, de todos los misioneros, era el favorito entre los pastores chilenos y trabajó especialmente en el distrito más cercano de su residencia, en la zona al norte y sur de Temuco".[11]

Aunque MacDonald comenzó su obra evangelizadora en Chile al interior de la Alianza Cristiana y Misionera, no dejó de sentir su incomodidad por sus diferencias en aspectos relacionados con el trabajo administrativo, eclesiástico y doctrinal que los Aliancistas estaban llevando en aquel entonces. La historiadora Elisabeth Pacheco escribe: "Desde hacía algún tiempo, MacDonald venía sosteniendo controversias doctrinales y dificultades concernientes al régimen de administración de las iglesias con algunos de sus colegas. Estas desavenencias culminaron en una conferencia que tuvo lugar a principios del año 1908 en la ciudad de Valdivia. Algunos de los misioneros desaprobaban la actitud de MacDonald de pedir ayuda para la obra a una iglesia bautista del extranjero. MacDonald, en cambio, se apoyaba en que cada sector era autónomo, según el régimen administrativo de la misión, por lo tanto, le asistía el derecho de pedir sostén a cualquiera fuente evangélica, puesto que la misión de la Alianza no era otra que una agrupación de iglesias evangélicas, sostenidas por entidades de diversa índole evangélica".[12]

También R. Cecil Moore se refiriere a la situación de Guillermo MacDonald con otras palabras: Pero él no estaba conforme. Sus colegas le acusaban de deslealtad al saber que él esta escribiendo a diversas partes del mundo, a Inglaterra, a Canadá y a Estados Unidos, tratando de hallar respaldo para una obra netamente bautista. MacDonald les respondía que él no era culpable de deslealtad siendo que la constitución misma de la Alianza dejaba libre a cada misionero para buscar ayuda entre los de su secta.

Fundación de la UBACH

Pronto hizo crisis el problema. MacDonald presenció, o supo de primera mano, que otro misionero de la Alianza había bautizado a un niño de pecho. Por ambos lados vino la ruptura. En sesión anual, a principios de 1908, la Alianza tomó una acción decisiva en contra de MacDonald. Pero parece que él a su vez ya había enviado su renuncia como misionero de ellos. Cecil Moore recuerda que "había tenido acaloradas discusiones en varias ocasiones en las reuniones generales de pastores y misioneros; gran parte de los pastores chilenos estaban convencidos de la validez de los argumentos de MacDonald y se unieron con él en el rompimiento con la Alianza en enero de 1908".[13] Esto trajo como resultado la salida o retiro formal de Guillermo MacDonald de la Alianza, pero él no saldría sólo, unos 300 hermanos y líderes bautistas también se retiraron.

Los que se habían retirado de la Alianza comenzaron a reunirse y organizarse en un pequeño terreno que pertenecía a la propiedad de MacDonald en la localidad de Freire. Entre estos 300 hermanos bautistas se destacaron por su importante labor: Wenceslao Valdivia, Abraham Chávez, Juan Antonio Gatica, José Tenorio Espinosa, David Mancilla, Juan Domingo Alvarez, Joaquín Mora, José Ramírez, y el industrial Enrique Reinicke.

MacDonald rápidamente visitó varias de las iglesias, y el 26 de abril de 1908 se organizó una Convención en Cajón, en donde se fundó la Unión Evangélica Bautista de Chile. Fueron representadas en aquella ocasión las iglesias de: Lastarrias, Gorbea, Molco, Mune, Cajón y un grupo de hermanos de Huilio. En aquella importante convención fundacional se encontraba el misionero bautista

W. G. Bagby, miembro de la Convención Bautista del Sur (USA), que estaba trabajando en Brasil. Bagby viajó a Chile en esa ocasión para participar como Asesor Fraternal en dicha importante convención.

MacDonald, considerado como el principal fundador de la obra bautista en nuestro país, junto a sus hermanos y líderes que lo acompañaron, comenzaron rápidamente a trabajar por la expansión del evangelio en Chile, de acuerdo a las doctrinas y principios bautistas. Poco tiempo después los bautistas de Chile liderados por MacDonald se pusieron en contacto con los bautistas de Argentina y de Brasil. Estos últimos ya estaban relacionados con la Convención Bautista del Sur (USA). Firmaron un convenio con la Foreign Mission Board de los Bautistas del Sur, que se materializó con la llegada de los primeros misioneros norteamericanos a Chile en 1917. Cabe recordar que en un principio la obra bautista en nuestro país también contó con la cooperación de los bautistas de México y Cuba.

Crecimiento Cronológico de la UBACH

1914 - El 7 de Junio de éste año se organizó la Primera Iglesia Bautista de Temuco. En esa reunión presidió el pastor Juan Domingo Alvarez, fue nombrado secretario Manuel Valderrama, y tesorero José Mercedes Ulloa.

1917 - La Junta de Misiones Foráneas de la Convención Bautista del Sur de los Estados Unidos envió a los primeros misioneros: Los esposos Guillermo y María de Davidson, quienes iniciaron la obra bautista misionera en la ciudad de Santiago siguiendo la visión y orientación de Guillermo MacDonald.

1917 – Abril. Fue incorporada como miembro de la Unión Bautista de Chile la Iglesia de Valdivia, en la cual el pastor Juan Domingo Alvarez prestó colaboración como misionero.

1919 - W. E. Davidson y esposa; el misionero Frank Marrs y esposa; y el pastor Polidoro Aguilera y esposa, organizaron en el mes de enero la Primera Iglesia Bautista de Santiago de Chile. Cecil Moore, sin embargo, recuerda que esta iglesia, según Acta, "registra su organización bajo el pastorado de Abadón Pacheco el 20 de Abril de 1920, y la iglesia observa esta fecha como su aniversario. Probablemente se trate de una reorganización".[14]

1919 - En agosto de ese año la Primera Iglesia Bautista de Concepción se unió a la Convención Bautista de Chile.

1919 - En octubre llega junto a su esposa el destacado misionero Roberto Cecil Moore a Valparaíso, quien se traslada a la capital, para apoyar en un principio en la educación bíblica a los hermanos de la Primera Iglesia Bautista de Santiago.

1920 – En enero el misionero R. Cecil Moore, se traslada a Concepción para

CHAPTER 25

apoyar las obras en aquel sector.

1920 – A finales de éste año llegó a Chile la misionera Agnes Graham. Don Guillermo MacDonald vio la necesidad de crear una escuela para educar especialmente a los hijos de los hermanos y líderes bautistas. Para lograrlo estableció contactos con la Convención Bautista del Sur de los Estados Unidos y logró recibir recursos para comprar un terreno y construir el primer edificio de lo que sería más tarde el Colegio Bautista de Temuco. Además logró la designación de una maestra misionera, Miss Agnes Graham, como su primera directora. Ella organizó la administración y docencia de dicho Colegio. Cecil Moore recuerda que "en 1920 el analfabetismo en Chile era casi el 50%. Durante los años del servicio de Agnes Graham y el Colegio Bautista este porcentaje fue reducido a la mitad; ciertamente esto se debió a muchos factores, pero también es cierto que Agnes Graham y sus colegas tuvieron una apreciable parte en este logro tan deseable".[15]

1921 - El misionero José Lancaster Hart y esposa inician el Instituto Bíblico en su propio hogar de residencia en la ciudad de Temuco. Dicho instituto preparó bíblica y teológicamente a los pastores y líderes de la obra bautista. Moore escribe que "la señora Hart prestó eficaz cooperación en este esfuerzo, como también en el Colegio Bautista y a muchas otras fases de la obra. En 1934 se cambió a Concepción por un tiempo, pero año y medio más tarde se trasladó a Antofagasta para abrir un nuevo campo en el Norte Grande".[16]

1921 – El 11 de octubre se creó la Sociedad Evangélica Bautista (SEB) compuesta por los misioneros extranjeros provenientes de la Foreign Mission Board, Richmond (USA).

1921- El 26 de octubre de éste mismo año fue organizada la Segunda Iglesia Bautista de Santiago. Los miembros fundadores fueron: Salomón Mussiett Musalem, Berta Canales de Mussiett, Guillermo Davidson y María de Davidson, Claudina de Villanueva, Manuel Morales, Felicita Valdés, Luis Carrasco, Juana Ulloa, Manuel González, Irene Flores, Carmen Bruna y Luisa Medina de Rubio.

1923 – Para éste año ya existían 29 iglesias con 1.154 miembros; 12 sociedades de señoras y 10 uniones de jóvenes.

1923 – Nace la Unión Femenil Bautista Misionera en Concepción y en 1924 se aprueban sus Estatutos en Temuco, siendo su primera Presidenta la hermana Ceferina de Fernández y como Secretaria General la misionera Maria Moore.

1925 – Se inicia formalmente la Junta de Publicaciones "El Lucero", en Concepción.

1926 – El 8 de mayo se organiza la Primera Iglesia Bautista de Talca con seis miembros, liderados por el misionero Santiago McGavock y Juan Vallette. Ese mismo día fue elegido pastor el joven hermano J. Vallette, quien estaba casado con la hermana del pastor Abdón Pacheco, la señorita Milagro Pacheco. Al día siguiente se agregarían 13 nuevos miembros más, bautizados por el pastor y misionero S. MacGavock.

1929 - Bajo la dirección del misionero W. Q. Maer se organiza la Primera Convención de Jóvenes en la Ciudad de Temuco.

1931 - Nace la Revista "La Ventana" siendo María de Moore, la Directora de ésta publicación.

1933 – Se inicia la Junta de Préstamos y Edificación para las iglesias bautistas de Chile.

1934 – Se inician los Institutos Femeniles.

1936 - El 15 de marzo de éste año fue organizada la Primera Iglesia Bautista de Valparaíso contando con la presencia de los pastores Guillermo MacDonald, Santiago McGavock, Salomón Mussiett, y delegaciones de la Primera y Segunda iglesia de Santiago. Los miembros fundadores fueron: Pastor Isaías Valdivia, Carlos Espinoza y señora, Francisco Cárdenas y señora, Julia Cárdenas E., Edelmira Sánchez, Catalina Cuadra, Guillermina de Figueroa, Elisa Gutiérrez, Adela Sánchez, Ernesto Labrín y Eduvina Albornoz.

1937 – Se inicia la Primera Iglesia Bautista de Antofagasta bajo la dirección del misionero José Lancaster Hart con la ayuda de Tennese de Hart, Maximino Fernández y Ceferina de Fernández. En Antofagasta existía un grupo de 16 hermanos protestantes que estaban a cargo del Pastor metodista-presbiteriano Emeterio Báez. "Emeterio Báez decidió irse al sur y pidió a Hart se hiciera cargo de este grupo".[17] La mayoría de estos hermanos fueron ganados para la causa bautista y en 1938 dicha iglesia lograría un pequeño local como templo.

1938 – Lamentablemente por causa de un accidente mecánico se produjo el fallecimiento del destacado pastor Maximino Fernández el 5 de febrero del mismo año. "El pastor Fernández fue reemplazado por su más logrado discípulo: el joven misionero pastor, predicador y colportor sureño: Manuel Gaete Muñoz".[18] El pastor Manuel Gaete Muñoz llegó a Antofagasta en septiembre de este mismo año, e inició la obra misionera en casi todo el norte de Chile, incluyendo Iquique y Tocopilla. Apoya la pequeña obra bautista de Chuquicamata e inicia la futura iglesia en Pedro de Valdivia, ente otras.

1938 – W. Q. Maer inicia el Primer Campamento de Verano en el pueblito de Labranza.

CHAPTER 25

1938 – Empezó la enseñanza teológica en el Seminario, siendo su primer Rector el misionero Sr. MacGavock. En este mismo año se colocó la primera piedra del edificio del Seminario en calle Argomedo 312 en la ciudad de Santiago.

1939 – Se inician las Escuelas Bíblicas de Vacaciones, siendo su primera directora María de McConnell. En 1941 asumió la Rectoría del Seminario y Docencia el destacado Hermano Honorio Espinoza, para darle un nuevo y renovador impulso a la educación teológica al pueblo bautista en Chile.

1944 - En julio de éste año llegó el pastor misionero Manuel Gaete a Copiapó, dedicándose a predicar el evangelio de Jesucristo y concretar una pequeña obra en ésta ciudad. Además, extendió las doctrinas y principios bautistas en las regiones de Atacama y Coquimbo.

1945 – Se edificó el Hogar permanente del Centro Bienhechor de Antofagasta, donde empezó a funcionar la "Escuela Básica N° 8, Peggy Hart", siendo la Directora de éste Centro la Srta. Lois Hart.

1955 - Se Inaugura el Hogar Bautista en Chillán, siendo su primera Directora la hermana Carolina Arancibia.

1956 - El Pastor Alizandro Vega con su familia inician una obra el 6 de mayo del mismo año, inaugurándose la actividad bautista en Puerto Montt con la asistencia de varios hermanos, entre los que se cuentan Pablo Navarrete, Eusebio Castillo, Lastenia de Castillo, Estelita Díaz de Vega, Sara y Ester Castillo.

1956 - Se constituye la Primera Iglesia Bautista de Ñuñoa con 29 miembros registrados, después de haber comenzado como Misión en 1950, siendo cabeza la Misionera María Pimm de Moore.

1965 – Se Inaugura el Consultorio de Salud Infantil en Antofagasta, siendo su primera Directora la señorita Lois Hart.

1970 – Nace la Junta de Evangelización, destacándose el misionero Evans Holmes y el hermano Lamar Tribble para el desarrollo de su misión. Sus comienzos se iniciaron en 1964 en el Tabo y en la convención de 1965 se nombró un comité de evangelización. En 1966 se nombró la Comisión Coordinadora Nacional de Evangelismo.

1974 – Apoyo a la Junta Militar. El pastor Luis Mussiett Canales, Presidente de la Convención Bautista de Chile, junto a otros altos líderes de organizaciones evangélicas, firman la Declaración de Apoyo al legítimo Gobierno de las Fuerzas Armadas. Esta Declaración de la Iglesia Evangélica Chilena es entregada al General Augusto Pinochet, el 13 de diciembre de 1974. En dicha declaración se destaca lo siguiente:

"El pueblo evangélico no puede guardar silencio ante la orquestada acción del marxismo... al calumniar vilmente a nuestro Gobierno, como carente de los más mínimos principios de derechos humanos...arma que el marxismo ateo está utilizando para desconocer la legitimidad de nuestro Gobierno...

1. Chile cayó en forma audaz en las garras del marxismo...
2. El pronunciamiento de las Fuerza Armadas...fue la respuesta de Dios a la oración de todos los creyentes que ven en el marxismo la fuerza satánica...en su máxima expresión.
3. Los Derechos Humanos están garantizados en Chile por la "Declaración de Principios de la Junta de Gobierno" y ha quedado demostrado a través de más de un año...
4. ...reconocemos entonces como autoridad máxima en este país al Gobierno de la Junta Militar, el cual, al liberarnos del marxismo, vino a dar respuesta a nuestras oraciones.

Elevamos nuestras oraciones al Altísimo para que El guíe a nuestros gobernantes...

1978 - Nace el comité COMPLA, encargado de planificar y coordinar las actividades de la obra, reuniéndose 2 veces al año. Lo conforman 41 personas y lo preside el Presidente de la Convención (UBACH). Este comité estudia, corrige, aconseja y recomiendan las acciones y políticas a seguir antes que un asunto llegue a la Asamblea Convencional.

1995 - La Convención Bautista del Sur de los Estados Unidos deja completamente su apoyo y colaboración formal con la UBACH. La Sociedad Evangélica Bautista entrega en donación todos los bienes materiales o propiedades (El Tabo, Lincarray, etc.) a la UBACH, encontrándose en estos momentos en una etapa ya final. Una de las características más sobresalientes de la Sociedad Evangélica Bautista fue el gran apoyo bíblico y teológico que proveyeron a las iglesias bautistas de Chile. Toda la literatura, en especial la de la Escuela Dominical y el Expositor Bíblico.

La hermana Raquel Contreras, esposa del ex-Rector Guillermo Catalán, durante su presidencia tuvo como lema: "Unidad en la Diversidad", si bien era el énfasis pero no la visión de la UBACH. Durante su presidencia se produjo el perdón y la reconciliación entre las dos convenciones bautistas de Chile, la UBACH y las Iglesias Bautistas Nacionales.

2010 - (Julio) La UNAPAB (Unión de Pastores Bautistas de Chile) aprobaron el Ministerio Pastoral de la mujer bajo las mismas normas y condiciones que los hombres.

2011 - La UBACH retoma las relaciones con la Convención Bautista del Sur, bajo nuevas condiciones de trabajo en lo que respecta a misiones y educación.

Contribuciones de la UBACH

La Unión de Iglesias Bautistas de Chile en la actualidad continúa con su crecimiento, educación, fraternidad y administración de manera estable y consolidada. Es sin duda alguna la entidad religiosa evangélica bautista de mayor representación en nuestro país. Cuenta con una sólida Unión Nacional de Jóvenes Bautistas, una gran Unión Femenil Bautista Misionera, y un sólido Seminario Teológico donde se preparan los actuales y futuros líderes de la obra bautista en Chile. Esta prestigiosa Unión Bautista de Chile cuenta además con una Junta Nacional de Publicaciones y una Junta de Educación Cristiana nacida y organizada en la Convención de 1954, reemplazando a la Junta de Escuelas Dominicales. Cuenta también con una Junta de Préstamos y Edificación, una Junta de Evangelización, un prestigioso Colegio Bautista en Temuco, y un Consultorio en Antofagasta.

Convención de Iglesias Bautistas Nacional de Chile

(Ex Misión Chilena)

En el relato de todo hecho histórico existen variadas versiones de los hechos. Así también existen diversas versiones sobre cómo se inició la Convención de Iglesias Bautistas Nacional de Chile, también conocida como la Convención de Iglesias Bautistas de la Misión Chilena.

Una de las versiones narra la historia de que tres hermanos problemáticos fueron expulsados de la UBACH en 1927 y de esta forma nació la Convención Nacional. De acuerdo con esta versión uno de los tres problemáticos era el pastor Ismael Neveu. De acuerdo con mis investigaciones, sin embargo, él no era uno de ellos.

Otra versión cuenta de las diferencias que el pastor Ismael Neveu tenía con los misioneros en relación con la administración de recursos, lo cual hizo que se fuera en 1940.[19] La versión de la historia que prefiero contar es la que tiene inicios en 1937.

Crecimiento Cronológico de la Convención Nacional

1937 – Ismael Neveu Z., junto a su familia y los hermanos: Pablo Guajardo y su esposa Dina Cereceda, Pablo Parada y su esposa Margarita, Segundo Parada y Eusebio Isla, inician una obra bautista independiente en el pueblo de Cherquenco.

1939 – La naciente Iglesia Bautista Nacional de Cherquenco liderada por el pastor Ismael Neveu, junto con el importante y activo apoyo del hermano Eusebio Isla B., logran a fines de éste año un poco más de 100 miembros.

El pastor Neveu contacta 4 iglesias bautistas independientes para iniciar relaciones fraternales con éstas. Estas iglesias fueron:

Iglesia	Encargado
Tomé	Francisco Parra
Concepción	José Martín Sepúlveda
San Bernardo	Clemente Navarrete
Chillán	Justo Valdebenito

Estas cinco iglesias bautistas decidieron finalmente unirse (Cherquenco, Tomé, Concepción, Chillán y San Bernardo) para trabajar juntas principalmente en pro de la fraternidad, evangelización y apoyo mutuo. De ésta manera comienza el Movimiento Bautista Nacional que, a través de los años contactarían otros grupos bautistas independientes e iniciarían obras misioneras en otros sectores del país.

1942 – Nace la revista "Luz Apostólica", iniciativa que impulsó el pastor y misionero Ismael Neveu Z., con el propósito de mantener el contacto y unidad entre las iglesias.

1947 – En Cherquenco, los líderes de las iglesias del Movimiento Bautista Nacional impusieron las manos sobre el pastor Ismael Neveu, y lo ordenaron Misionero Nacional.

1948 – El hermano Germán Durán V. fue designado Presidente de la Juventud de las Iglesias Bautistas Nacionales, cargo que ocupó hasta el mes de enero de 1960.

1949 – (Abril) El hermano Ricardo Escobar es aceptado por la asamblea de las iglesias bautistas nacionales, junto con su iglesia que contaba en ese entonces con 21 miembros, que se reunían en la ciudad de San Bernardo.

1949 – Las iglesias del Movimiento Bautista Nacional, se reúnen en la ciudad de Temuco el 18 de septiembre de ése mismo año, para dar comienzo

CHAPTER 25

formalmente a éste Movimiento a una Corporación que se denominará: "Misión Bautista Chilena". Para ésta fecha ya contaban también con las iglesias de: Curacautín, Lanco, Panguipulli, Collipulli, Perquenco y Temuco.

1951 – En la concentración de las Iglesias Bautistas Nacionales realizada en Lanco, se ordenó Pastor Misionero al hermano Eusebio Isla Burgos para el trabajo evangelístico.

1952 – En una reunión extraordinaria se llevó a cabo la "Primera Asamblea Anual de la Convención de Iglesias Bautistas de la Misión Chilena", aprobándose sus Estatutos en la ciudad de San Bernardo. También, es nombrado como primer Presidente de la reciente Convención de Iglesias Bautistas de la Misión Chilena el pastor Gerardo Calderón Hernández.

1954 – El 14 de mayo de ese año la Convención de iglesias Bautistas de la Misión Chilena lograrían la Personalidad Jurídica, ajustándose a los Estatutos aprobados por el Ministerio de Justicia.

1960 – Para éste año ya habían nacido y añadido las siguientes iglesias: Talca (Pastor Marcial Miranda), Reumén, Púa, Traiguén y Segunda de San Bernardo (Pastor Juan Bustamante Galleguillos)

1960 – De la Primera Iglesia Bautista Misión Chilena de San Bernardo, nació la iglesia de Lo Espejo y de ésta iglesia nació la iglesia de Lo Valledor. Así, también nació de la Primera Iglesia Bautista M. Ch. de San Bernardo la iglesia de Los Cóndores de Chile y de ésta última nació la iglesia El Sembrador.

1965 – En la 14ª Asamblea Anual de la Convención de Iglesias Bautistas de la M. Ch. en la ciudad de Talca, el hermano Germán Durán Valdebenito es elegido Presidente de dicha Convención, cargo que ocupa hasta 1990, dando cumplimiento a 25 años como presidente. Durante su presidencia se destacó por representar a la Convención Bautista Misión Chilena, en Brasil, Argentina, Uruguay, Puerto Rico y Estados Unidos. Apoyó la educación teológica y pastoral entre los líderes y pastores de la Misión Chilena, así como también la cordialidad, fraternidad y trabajo conjunto en pro del fortalecimiento entre las iglesias bautista nacional.

1966 – Se nombró Pastor Evangelista de la Convención Bautista Misión Chilena al hermano Norindo Avila M., de la iglesia de Lanco.

1974 - El Vicepresidente de la Convención Bautista Misión Chilena, Pastor Ricardo Escobar junto a otros altos líderes de organizaciones evangélicas, firman la Declaración de Apoyo al legítimo Gobierno de las Fuerza Armadas. Esta Declaración de la Iglesia Evangélica Chilena es entregada al General Augusto Pinochet, el 13 de diciembre de 1974.

1981 – Es fundado el Instituto Teológico Bautista por el pastor Job Isla Sandoval, comenzando con 12 alumnos en la casa del hermano Germán Silva Pávez. Al año siguiente la Convención apoya dicho proyecto educativo financieramente, arrendando establecimientos para el desarrollo de la educación Bíblico-Teológica.

1985 – Para éste año la Convención Bautista Misión Chilena ya contaba con nuevas iglesias tales como:

Región Metropolitana:

La Roca, Esmirna, El Redentor, El Cortijo,

Sur de Chile:

Laja, Los Angeles, Yumbel, Monte Aguila,

Curihue, Pilinhue, y Rucamilla.

1994 – Acuden a la Asamblea Anual de la Convención de Iglesias Bautistas de la Misión Chilena, el Presidente de las Iglesias Bautistas Americanas (ABC) Don Héctor González en compañía del Director del Área Latinoamericana el pastor José Norat de Puerto Rico, quienes firmaron el Convenio entre ABC y la Misión Chilena, para trabajar principalmente en la Educación Teológica.

1995 – Llegan los primeros Misioneros: El Pastor Esteban y Sheila de Heneisse, para hacerse cargo del Instituto Teológico Bautista Misión Chilena. Con su llegada logran darle un nuevo y renovado impulso en cuanto al contenido teológico, y gracias a su gestión dicho instituto logra su incorporación como miembro a la Asociación de Seminarios e Institutos Teológicos del cono Sur de Latinoamérica.

1999 - Llegan los misioneros Juan y Kristina de Gutiérrez en reemplazo de los pastores Heneisse, para continuar la educación teológica.

2000 - Llegan los misioneros Carlos y Mayra de Bonilla para dedicarse a la docencia del Instituto principalmente en reemplazo de los misioneros Gutiérrez.

2000 - Los misioneros Dwight y Bárbara de Bolick, ha centrado su trabajo en el mejoramiento de las condiciones de vida de las iglesias del Distrito de Los Lagos, especialmente utilizando las destrezas adquiridas en sus estudios de negocios para concentrarse en el desarrollo económico sustentable especialmente entre los mapuches.

2003 - Una de las características de la Misión Chilena, es su estilo conservador en el aspecto litúrgico. De las 50 iglesias de la Convención Bautista Nacional (Misión Chilena) casi la mayoría de las iglesias se identifica con esta tendencia, y solo unas pocas iglesias, ubicadas en la Región Metropolitana mayormente, se inclinan por un estilo de liturgia carismática. Estos mismos hechos han producido ciertas tensiones entre los líderes y pastores, pero superadas finalmente. El conflicto más grave aconteció, a partir de éste año, cuando algunos pastores de la ciudad de Santiago, adoptaron de manera radical el modelo Visión Celular G-12 de César Castellanos, acabando con el gobierno congregacional y marginándose de los trabajos y objetivos de la convención. Esto derivó de manera lamentable la salida o retiro finalmente de por lo menos 5 iglesias.

2004 - Este año el trabajo de los misioneros entrega sus primeros frutos ya que asumen el liderazgo del Instituto Teológico y sus profesores solo chilenos entre los cuales se nombra a Susan Calliñir, Lucila Alvarez, Patricia Cofre y Víctor Aguilar.

2006 – Este año se realizó una reconciliación con la UBACH durante la Asamblea Anual de Panguipulli. Durante este tiempo también la Convención Nacional trabajó con el programa de evangelización Hay Vida en Jesús a nivel latinoamericano.

2008 – La primera mujer pastora fue ordenada el 8 de marzo de este año. La pastora Margarita Campos convirtiéndose en la primera mujer bautista ordenada por la Junta de Pastores de la Convención Nacional, actualmente existen 5 mujeres ordenadas y otras en el proceso de ordenación.

2010 – El Terremoto de febrero impacto severamente nuestro país y nuestras iglesias, pero por este medio se logró descubrir un nuevo tipo de ministerio, el de servicio de reconstrucción y ayuda a la comunidad a través de equipos voluntarios.

Contribuciones de la Convención Nacional Bautista

Actualmente la Convención Nacional Bautista continúa su crecimiento, educación, fraternidad y administración de manera estable y consolidada. Aunque es una convención pequeña, está realizando un trabajo importante. Cuenta con una sólida Unión Nacional de Jóvenes, una gran Unión Femenil Bautista que trabaja en diversas áreas como evangelismo y trabajo con adolescentes, un sólido Instituto Teológico que trabaja muy cercano a las Iglesias locales, un grupo consolidado de voluntarios que trabajaron en reconstrucción luego del terremoto, una Junta de Evangelización, varios colegios bautistas y jardines infantiles, un ministerio reconocido socialmente con los indígenas del Pueblo Mapuche, y ha sido la primera convención en reconocer el ministerio pastoral de la mujer por medio de la ordenación pastoral de mujeres. Cuenta con pastores, líderes y gente dispuesta a la fundación y fortalecimiento de la Iglesia y el Reino de Dios en la tierra.

Conclusión

Como se ha podido apreciar, el trabajo de poner en escrito más de doscientos años de historia es complejo.

La historia de los Bautistas se matiza de muchas historias de hombres y mujeres valientes y esforzados quienes hicieron crecer el evangelio entre sus más cercanos, comenzando en pueblos pequeños y extendiéndose a lo que encontramos ahora, una gran cantidad de iglesia en diversas ciudades del país.

Se observa un crecimiento sólido, marcado por la estructura Bautista de educación, libertad, autonomía y firmeza en la propagación de los principios bautistas.

La historia nos insta a continuar con la obra de engrandecimiento del Reino, siguiendo los principios bíblicos que tiñen nuestra identidad Bautista.

Bibliografía

Anderson, Justo. Historia de los bautistas, Tomo III. El Paso Texas: CBP, 1990.

Condell de Pacheco, Elizabeth. Guillermo MacDonald, el apóstol de la frontera. Segunda edición del Comité de Publicaciones de las Organizaciones Femeninas Bautistas de los Países Hispanoamericanos, 1956.

Encina, Francisco A. Resumen de la Historia de Chile, ediciones Zig-Zag, 10ª edición, Tomo II, redacción, iconografía y apéndices de Leopoldo Castedo, Santiago-Chile, 1974.

Moore, Roberto C. Recuerdos, vivencias de un misionero bautista, Santiago, Chile, 1978.

Moore, Roberto C. Vida de Agnes Graham, Santiago, Chile, 1954.

Moore, Roberto C. Hombres y Hechos Bautistas de Chile. Editoriales Evangélicas Bautistas, Santiago: Imprenta siglo XX, sin fecha.

Principios Bautistas: Herencia y Desafío para la iglesia de hoy, Tiempo Nuevo, cuaderno de estudios bíblicos N°1. Instituto Teológico Bautista, Departamento de Publicaciones, Santiago, Chile, enero, 1997.

Varios Autores, Diamantes Bautistas, un libro para los 75 años de la Convención Evangélica Bautista de Chile, 1908 - 1983, Convención Evangélica Bautista de Chile, Editorial Universitaria, Santiago, 1983.

CHAPTER 26
IDENTIDAD BAUTISTA LATINOAMERICANA, APROXIMACIONES Y DESAFÍOS

Jose Parrish Jacome Hernandez

> El momento ha llegado cuando se debe dejar el narcisismo histórico, o sea, la introspección denominacional, para vernos en el marco del cristianismo moderno. Por demasiado tiempo, ha prevalecido un complejo de inferioridad histórico, que a veces, ha resultado en un complejo de superioridad denominacional.
>
> *Justo C. Anderson*

Las últimas décadas han sido espacios de constantes diálogos entre varias denominaciones históricas inquietas por lo que consideran la necesaria reflexión de su identidad, una preocupación que ha sido considerada innecesaria en ciertos círculos por ser contraria al espíritu de globalización reinante en el mundo.

Esta tensión busca lidiar entre la necesidad de seguir reafirmando en las nuevas generaciones aquellos pilares que sustentan ese sentido de pertenencia tan válido, con el idealismo que llamando a la unidad cristiana, pretende desconocer toda pertenencia y relevancia de una búsqueda de sus raíces.

América Latina vive esta dinámica fruto de un crecimiento numérico significativo de creyentes identificados con la iglesia evangélica, donde la diferenciación cada vez ha sido más compleja de precisar, en especial cuando la medida se establece en función de las prácticas litúrgicas que en un momento se levantaron como indicadores útiles para la distinción, pero que en la actualidad ya no cumplen esa función.

Allí radica la necesaria búsqueda de los pilares que siempre serán los distintivos de una iglesia que respondiendo a su ADN mantiene esa impronta que la caracteriza y orienta en su diario transitar. Esta exploración no deja de ser desafiante cuando se requiere mover lo que en la superficie puede confundir o desconocer el verdadero fundamento.

Esta relevación también requiere la objetividad de quienes realizando esta tarea levantan auténticos principios que superando todo valor que responde a un momento histórico o cultural en particular, sea capaz de encontrar los elementos que independiente del marco visible, conserve un fondo sólido coherente con su identidad.

Considerar el marco histórico es pertinente para un acercamiento que anhele descubrir lo que hace de una congregación local, una iglesia bautista, asumiendo el desafío siempre vigente del tiempo, contexto, cultura, enriquecidos con una interacción bíblica y teológica capaz de responder a estas y otras demandas que no pueden ser desconocidas.

Una Visión Retrospective

La tarea de precisar la identidad de un grupo, etnia, conglomerado social, puede ser un trabajo complejo o no tan laborioso en la medida en que se cuente con estudios serios que permitan una aproximación al tema con basamentos comprobados y no simplemente con especulaciones arbitrarias.

En este sentido la riqueza de nuestra denominación está avalada por historiadores formados académicamente y respetables por su credibilidad, que lograron reconstruir aquellos elementos vitales para la conformación de una identidad que establezca parámetros claros de distinción.

Justo C. Anderson, en su obra Historia de los Bautistas, sistematiza lo que distingue como los siete principios fundamentales que sustentan nuestra comprensión de ser creyentes y ser miembros de su iglesia. Estos principios dejan una marca imborrable para que todo acercamiento en búsqueda de una identidad los considere.

El principio Cristológico, Bíblico, Eclesiológico, Sociológico, Espiritual, Político, Evangelístico, constituyen esa huella que en el ejercicio reflexivo de una fe viva, los creyentes que conformaron las primeras congregaciones bautistas cimentaron como los pilares sobre el cual se levantaría toda su interacción como iglesias.

> La lealtad del evangelio histórico y la libertad en su expresión – firmeza y flexibilidad – son las características sobresalientes del testimonio bautista. Se adaptan perfectamente bien a la época espacial, que desea estar segura y, al mismo tiempo, libre. Es una época que necesita fundamentarse en la revelación de Dios, pero, asimismo, acostumbrarse a las nuevas formas de una era cibernética.[1]

Esta mirada no puede quedarse en el pasado de forma estática, tiene que tener la capacidad de generar diálogos y respuestas a una sociedad que sigue presentando sus agonías y cuestionamientos a la fe cristiana que recurre al marco histórico para anclarse y no desafiarse a recuperar ese sentido de urgencia que caracterizó a sus antecesores.

En ese sentido la necesidad de un liderazgo capaz de sintonizar con los requerimientos que se presenten será siempre determinante para que el proceso histórico continúe manteniendo esa riqueza que se nutre de una presencia donde la palabra y la acción sean el principal eje sobre el cual se siga construyendo una clara identidad.

Un Tutelaje Necesario

La presencia de los bautistas en esta parte del continente se registra desde el siglo XIX, donde las diversas sociedades misioneras de los Estados Unidos de América, Inglaterra, y Canadá, principalmente, comienzan a enviar parejas con la finalidad de iniciar su trabajo de plantación de iglesias, en lo que se consideraba un campo blanco.

Rápidamente esta presencia fue ganando auge, en medio de necesidades muy sentidas, donde la educación, salud, economía familiar, y emprendimientos micro empresariales, fueron la tónica de vinculación a una denominación que procuraba instaurarse en esta parte del mundo, con un mensaje de esperanza que requería expresiones concretas y no solamente palabras.

Esta realidad local fue entendida mejor por aquellas organizaciones misioneras bautistas que por su trasfondo histórico y teológico, establecieron vínculos de apoyo en los campos donde la urgencia era inminente, dejando un legado que las generaciones posteriores pudieron disfrutar como un recurso propio.

Una gran parte de países se beneficiaron del talento humano que llegó en la figura de los misioneros bautistas, educadores, médicos, enfermeras, teólogos, y pastores, a quienes era posible identificar una vocación tan marcada que contagiaba a los pocos nacionales que en ese primer momento formaban parte de un movimiento que luchaba por levantar raíces autóctonas.

La figura del misionero fue determinante en la construcción de una identidad bautista en la región, convirtiéndose en el prototipo a seguir. Más tarde se van mostrando ciertas diferencias ancladas al ámbito cultural y fundamentación teológica, aspectos vitales que con el pasar de los años se profundizarán entre unos y otros bautistas en el continente.

La hegemonía fue posible en la medida que los misioneros respondieran a un patrón común. Cuando las sociedades misioneras o juntas de las convenciones bautistas con trabajo foráneo eran diversas en un mismo país, sin embargo, se comenzaron a notar diferenciaciones entre los ejes que los misioneros manejaban.

Esta realidad, lejos de afectar una expansión, pudo mostrar la riqueza invaluable de los bautistas, aquella diversidad que fundamentada en su ejercicio de fe que reconociéndose como sacerdote delante de Dios, realiza responsablemente y con libertad de conciencia su elección dentro de su marco interpretativo de las Escrituras.

Un Crecimiento Desafiante

La hegemonía casi absoluta de la iglesia Católica Romana a principios del siglo XX sufrirá su mayor golpe en nuestro continente fruto de los movimientos políticos que en muchos de los países se fueron gestando, donde la consecución de un estado laico establecía un nuevo marco para las expresiones de fe diversas.

Es en este periodo donde muchos historiadores manifiestan que la identidad de los grupos evangélicos y de forma particular los bautistas se establecen, debido a una mayor participación del componente nacional capaz de seguir replicando con la facilidad de su propio lenguaje el mensaje de transformación del evangelio.

Este crecimiento no fue de orden similar en todos los países, destacándose el fenómeno de Brasil, donde todos los parámetros antes establecidos fueron rotos, al llegar a un desarrollo numérico que bordeó el 600% entre los años 1911 al 1938, motivado por una serie de factores muy particulares donde la incidencia del evangelio respondió a una demanda espiritual y social de sus habitantes.

Este aspecto en menor escala fue dándose en otros países, donde la necesidad de comenzar a capacitar a este contingente local se tornó en el desafío más notorio para un conglomerado de misioneros que habiendo crecido asumían otro rol dentro la conformación de las primeras organizaciones que comienzan a tener forma.

La formación del liderazgo va a convertirse en el eje a considerar para preservar un crecimiento que en muchos casos superó las expectativas o en otras circunstancias fue mostrando la poca asimilación que se había realizado con la realidad, quedándose como un movimiento religioso transcultural, sin sabor propio alguno.

En mi lectura allí radica uno de los aspectos que afectó a un desarrollo armónico de unos países y otros, evidenciándose esa capacidad intuitiva que algunos misioneros tuvieran a diferencia de otros para ir generando un proceso donde la formación y el acompañamiento al nacional vaya formando un mecanismo sólido para evitar una malsana dependencia que no permita la madurez requerida.

Es allí donde la identidad incorpora elementos que no siendo gravitantes en este ámbito fueron dando forma al pensamiento, acción y reflexión de quienes buscaban preservar un modelo no en los principios bíblicos – teológicos que si bien eran compartidos, no influían tanto como la figura de su depositario, fiel, inequívoco, sabio, justo, cualidades que en la mente de muchos bautistas latinoamericanos terminó por idealizar la figura de los misioneros americanos, en su gran parte.

Un periodo donde el crecimiento numérico no significó avance organizacional necesariamente, mostrando que la dependencia financiera, organizacional, teológica, impedía que la identidad fuera enriqueciéndose con los elementos muy propios de la cultura y realidad latinoamericana.

Una Realidad que no Puede Ignorarse

La realidad de nuestro continente ha cambiado sustancialmente provocando un sentido de pertenencia que por mucho tiempo fue muy débil, este espíritu de reencontrarse con sus raíces, no es ajeno a la realidad de la fe, donde esta dimensión está dispuesta a validar las vivencias más allá de un entendimiento que fue heredado, reconociéndose la necesidad de cuestionarse lo que en su momento era inamovible.

Hablar de una única identidad bautista en el continente latinoamericano es complejo, es posible que por varias décadas el liderazgo de los misioneros foráneos matizara una comprensión de lo que significa ser bautista, enfocando elementos tan visibles que los trascendentales, incidentales, estando allí no tenían el mismo impacto.

Esta identidad en algunos casos creo cultura, una que por mucho tiempo oscureció o despreció la propia al considerarla atentatoria contra la fe que se profesaba. Esto generó un anacronismo tan severo que unido a ese pietismo muy propio de la mayoría de las organizaciones misioneras que llegaron a nuestro continente, fueron formando una separación abrupta del contexto y realidad que se quería influenciar, teniendo el contacto mínimo que permita evangelizar y nada más.

El protestantismo latinoamericano, está marcado por ese carácter puritano – pietista – evangélico del cristianismo evangélico mundial cuyas raíces históricas se encuentran en el movimiento pietista de los siglos XVI y XVII en Inglaterra y el gran avivamiento del siglo XVIII en los Estados Unidos. El pietismo mismo representaba un intento muy importante por reformar la herencia protestante, y su influencia ha dejado una impresión distintiva en el cristianismo de América Latina.[2]

El giro desarrollado por la Junta Misionera Foránea de los Bautistas del Sur a finales de la década de los 80 y principios de los 90 redundó en una crisis, que al pasar de los años, me atrevo a señalar es reconocida como positiva para la mayoría de los países, porque empujó a una construcción propia de su entendimiento y quehacer ministerial, donde partiendo de un modelo innegable, se fue contrastando cuanto era evangelio y cuanto cultura.

Este proceso se unió a un movimiento que en todo el continente se gestaba en medio de las otras denominaciones e iglesias libres o de corte independiente, en donde la denominada latinoamericanización del protestantismo se fue gestando a partir de la década del 70, ganando fuerza y relevancia en las dos décadas posteriores.

Desde el liderazgo hasta las estructuras organizativas, pasando por los temas de culto y los métodos de difusión, el protestantismo evangélico del continente ha asumido un sabor propio cada vez más ajustado a los patrones culturales locales de cada región o país de América Latina.[3]

La añoranza atrapa a quienes recuerdan con nostalgia los años cuando los misioneros guiaban, cantaban, tocaban el piano, resolvían los problemas, compraban las terrenos, un tiempo donde ser bautista eran prácticas litúrgicas que muchos vieron amenazadas cuando la llamada pentescotalización o carismatización de las iglesias históricas penetró con fuerza, afectando lo que para muchos es la auténtica identidad bautista.

Un rostro en constante construcción

El pasado tiene su riqueza, indiscutible, incuestionable, presta a iluminar los grandes dilemas y controversias que todo tiempo tendrá, incorporando al dialogo aquellos elementos que nunca dejarán de ser gravitantes para mostrar los postulados que frente a un mundo en constante cambio se requieren presentar.

Acepto como innegable la herencia bautista que por medios de los principios bíblicos que sustentamos en la denominación, históricamente han servido para sustentar rasgos de una identidad común, presta a ser manifiesta cuando la centralidad de cada uno de estos pilares de nuestra fe se vean amenazados o requieran ser proclamados como palabra profética una vez más.

Lo desafiante se provoca cuando esa identidad común pretende desconocer los rasgos particulares, propios, necesarios, para que ese evangelio sea pertinente a un tiempo y momento donde el mensaje liberador de Jesús y su reino, incorporen los elementos que desde el principio fueron integrados a una vivencia que no se desentiende de sus raíces étnicas, ni culturales.

Desde esa óptica existen aspectos que están y seguirán en construcción en cuanto a esa identidad, donde el sabor latinoamericano no se pierde al tener que enfrentar con esperanza a son de salsa, merengue, tango, cueca o zamba, las grandes desigualdades de un continente rico en recursos naturales, reconocido como el reservorio natural del mundo por sus grandes extensiones de tierras cultivables, pero al mismo tiempo desangrado por la corrupción, violencia, injusticia, donde sobrevivir es el único desafío que muchos tienen en las grandes ciudades.

Es posible que muchos se sigan preguntando si es válido responder a una inquietud que busca respuesta de lo que implica ser bautista en nuestro continente, polarizado por dos posiciones o más en las cuales la descalificación, desconfianza, constante sospecha, impide el disfrutar de la bendición de ser miembros del pueblo de Dios. Dios quiera que investidos de su gracia, estemos dispuestos a proclamar y demostrar el evangelio del reino, sin limitación, ni temor alguno.

> Ser bautista hoy, es ser bautista como fueron los que nos antecedieron, gente libre de ataduras denominacionales, gente que se dio la libertad de pensar y buscar respuestas concretas a los problemas de la sociedad a la luz de la Biblia. Ser bautista es pensar únicamente bajo la dirección de la lectura bíblica que se abre en diálogo con la vida misma, vivir y enseñar la centralidad de Jesucristo, vivir y enseñar el sacerdocio del creyente. En resumidas cuentas ser bautista es luchar porque El evangelio una vez dado a los santos se encarne en cada persona y así ser instrumentos de Dios para un pueblo que está perdiendo la esperanza.[4]

La identidad bautista latinoamericana lejos de perderse, se ha ido dinamizando incorporando un ejercicio de reflexión – acción, donde la dinámica de ser iglesia sigue animando a muchas congregaciones a replantearse su compromiso con la comunidad, uno que implique escuchar, observar, acompañar, donde la postura de autosuficiencia o superioridad se deja de lado, reconociendo que nuestra interacción con los que están en las calles debe ser de igual a igual.

Un rostro bíblico, donde las Escrituras no se pierden, en una centralidad que reconoce a Jesús como Señor y modelo innegable de ministerio, incidiendo sobre el pobre, la viuda, el huérfano, el menesteroso, donde los despreciados son acogidos e integrados, los niños reconocidos como signo y señal del Reino, las mujeres creación de Dios con iguales derechos y responsabilidades.

Un rostro humano, multiforme, heredero de una herencia bautista donde la diversidad nunca ha sido un inconveniente, más bien siempre fue asumido como algo que fortalece, enriquece y aporta al crecimiento, asumiendo la realidad de ser un continente diverso donde indios, mestizos, inmigrantes, blancos o negros, aceptan su responsabilidad de responder a la fe que nos ha sido dada con la certeza que nuestro campo de misión son las calles, los barrios, las ciudades, los campos, donde la injusticia y la desigualdad nos invitan a no ser neutrales, sino tomar una posición radical como Jesús lo hizo a favor de los más necesitados.

Un rostro moderno, que en algunos casos no quiere un membrete, rótulo, distintivo denominacional, no por vergüenza, ni por desestimar su herencia, aunque su teología y práctica es innegablemente bautista, apelando a una realidad cierta del tiempo en que vivimos, donde el denominado posmodernismo ha permeado fuertemente lo que en su momento caracterizó a las grandes iglesias y movimientos históricos, entre ellos los bautistas.

> Percibimos que el cristianismo protestante, en su versión actual, tiene una constitución atípica en lo que respecta a la continuidad histórica de la tradición protestante. Es un cristianismo que, al parecer, nos ha llegado – y continúa llegando – por carriles distintos de los que usó el protestantismo hasta bien entrado el siglo XX. Se puede pensar incluso que este cristianismo está conectado con la generación de los últimos treinta años y desligado del protestantismo de la sola gracia, la sola Escritura y la justificación de la fe Por eso la preservación de la fe en ese estilo no significa mantener la fe en la pureza doctrinal como se ha entendido tradicionalmente.[5]

Un rostro sensible, capaz de involucrarse con pasión en todo aquello que implique la lucha por diversas causas, en donde la vida en todas sus expresiones esté inmersa, mostrando un compromiso que no se desentiende de lo que mantiene vivo el corazón del creador, el hombre, la naturaleza, la creación en pleno.

Un rostro interconfesional, presto a hacer presencia en todo esfuerzo que tiene como finalidad visibilizar el reino de Dios y su justicia, alejado de toda postura sectaria que elude su responsabilidad en el aquí y ahora que no puede esperar. En ese sentido somos llamados a participar de todo diálogo y esfuerzo que tenga esa finalidad, sin el temor a ser juzgado por quienes no admiten ningún contacto con otras expresiones de fe.

CHAPTER 26

Esta construcción evidencia lo que somos como pueblo bautista latinoamericano, donde los paradigmas del pasado deben reconocer un tiempo innegable, dispuesto a reconocer el aporte de quienes cruzando fronteras estuvieron dispuestos a reconocerse como protagonistas y no meros espectadores.

Un bautista innegable, pastor, maestro y teólogo, el doctor J. L. Garrett comentó proféticamente en la década del 70, lo que en nuestro continente no podemos soslayar: El gran ejército de jóvenes que entrará a nuestras iglesias después de 1970 cree que la unidad cristiana es más importante que las diferencias denominacionales. No podemos asumir que nuestra mentalidad del pasado será la del futuro.[6]

Estos atrevidos pincelazos no pretenden agotar la riqueza de una identidad que sigue en mi lectura en una construcción dinámica y constante, producto de un continente joven, presto a seguir buscando respuestas a necesidades que lejos de satisfacerse, continúan demandado atención, entre quienes con una riqueza innegable como los bautistas se atreven a caminar con el pueblo, sintiéndose y mirándose como uno de ellos.

NOTES
CHAPTER 1

[1] *The Nature and Mission of the Church: A Stage on the Way to a Common Statement*, Faith and Order Paper No. 198 (Geneva: World Council of Churches, 2005). This study document supersedes a previous document, *The Nature and Purpose of the Church: A Stage on the Way to a Common Statement*, Faith and Order Paper No. 181 (Geneva: World Council of Churches, 1998). Hereafter cited as NMC. All references to NMC will be noted in the text by reference to the section (§) rather than the page. An online version is available at http://www.oikoumene.org/en/resources/documents/wcc-commissions/faith-and-order-commission/i-unity-the-church-and-its-mission/the-nature-and-mission-of-the-church-a-stage-on-the-way-to-a-common-statement.html.

[2] *Baptism, Eucharist and Ministry*, Faith and Order Paper No. 111 (Geneva: World Council of Churches, 1982). Hereafter cited as BEM.

[3] D. M. Baillie, *God Was In Christ* (New York: Charles Scribner's Sons, 1948) 133-40; and Bruce D. Marshall "Trinity," chapter in *The Blackwell Companion to Modern Theology*, ed. Gareth Jones (Oxford: Blackwell Publishing, 2004), 186.

[4] Fiddes, "Church and Trinity: A Baptist Ecclesiology of Participation," chapter in *Tracks and Traces: Baptist Identity in Church and Theology* (Carlisle: Paternoster, 2003), 65-82, and Fiddes, "A Personal God and the Making of Community," chapter in *Participating in God: A Pastoral Doctrine of the Trinity* (Louisville: Westminster John Knox Press, 2000), 11-61; Stanley Grenz, *The Named God and the Question of Being; A Trinitarian Theo-Ontology* (Louisville, KY: Westminster John Knox Press, 2005), and Grenz, *The Social God and the Relational Self: A Trinitarian Theology of the Imago Dei* (Louisville: Westminster John Knox Press, 2001), 334-335; Frank Rees, "Trinity and Church: Contributions from the Free Church Tradition," *Pacifica* 17 (October 2004): 251-67; and Nigel G. Wright, *Free Church, Free State: A Positive Baptist Vision* (Milton Keynes: Paternoster, 2005), 4-6. Although not a Baptist, Miroslav Volf has offered a constructive baptistic-free church communion ecclesiology, which as the subtitle of his book suggests, displays the church as the image of the Trinity, in Volf, *After Our Likeness: The Church as the Image of the Trinity* (Grand Rapids: Eerdmans, 1998), especially chapter 5, "Trinity and Church," 191-220.

⁵ David J. Bosch, *Transforming Mission: Paradigm Shifts in Theology of Mission* (Maryknoll: Orbis Books, 1991), especially 390; Graham Hill, *Salt, Light, and a City: Introducing Missional Ecclesiology* (Wipf & Stock, 2012); Gary V. Nelson, *Borderland Churches: A Congregation's Introduction to Missional Living* (Danvers, MA: Chalice Press, 2008); Ed Stetzer, *Planting Missional Churches* (Nashville: B&H Publishing, 2006); Daniel Vestal, *It's Time: An Urgent Call to Christian Mission* (Atlanta: Cooperative Baptist Fellowship, 2006). With the exception of Bosch, who was a pioneer in missional thinking, the Baptist conversations about missional ecclesiology has followed the lead of Lesslie Newbigin, *The Open Secret: An Introduction to the Theology of Mission*, revised ed. (Grand Rapids: William B. Eerdmans, 1995), and the Gospel and our Culture Network, viz., George R. Hunsberger and Craig Van Gelder, eds., *The Church Between Gospel and Culture* (Grand Rapids: Eerdmans, 1996); and Darrell L. Guder, ed. *Missional Church: A Vision for the Sending of the Church in North America* (Grand Rapids: Eerdmans, 1998).

⁶ G. Ernest Wright attributed the phrase "Unitarianism of the Second Person" to Elton Trueblood, who applied it to the Christology invoked at the First Assembly of the World Council of Churches which met in 1948 at Amsterdam, in *The Old Testament and Theology* (New York: Harper and Row, 1969), 24. However, two years earlier H. Richard Niebuhr delineated three Unitarianisms in Christianity (i.e., of the Father, the Son, and the Spirit) in "The Doctrine of the Trinity and the Unity of the Church," *Theology Today* 3 (October 1946): 371-84.

⁷ See my essays, "God in Three Persons: Baptist Unitarianism and the Trinity" *Perspectives in Religious Studies* 33 (Fall 2007): 323-44; and "Back to the Future of Trinitarianism?" in *Theology in the Service of the Church: Essays Presented to Fisher H. Humphreys*, ed. Timothy George and Eric F. Mason. Macon: Mercer University Press, 2008, 36-61.

⁸ Karl Barth, *Church Dogmatics*, I/1, trans. G. W. Bromiley (Edinburgh: T. & T. Clark, 1975), 346.

⁹ Geoffrey Wainwright has argued that a return to trinitarian doctrine is essential for the church to be the church, in "The Doctrine of the Trinity: Where the Church Stands or Falls," *Interpretation*, 45.2 (April 1991): 117-132.

¹⁰ For an excellent summary of various ecclesiological visions and versions see Dennis M. Doyle, *Communion Ecclesiology* (Maryknoll: Orbis Books, 2000).

¹¹ Volf, *After Our Likeness*, 2-3.

¹² Friedrich Schleiermacher, The Christian Faith, 2nd ed., trans. and ed. H. R. Macintosh and J. S. Stewart (Philadelphia: Fortress Press, 1976), § 24, cited by Volf in *After Our Likeness*, 159.

NOTES

[13] Thomas Helwys, *Synopsis fidei, verae Christianae Ecclesiae Anglicane, Amsterdamiae*, 9, in Burrage, *The Early English Dissenters*, 2:183. Subsequent Baptist confessions emphasize the church as gathered community, see e.g., First London Confession (1644), XXXIII, in William L. Lumpkin, *Baptist Confessions of Faith*, revised ed. (Valley Forge: Judson Press, 1969), 165.

[14] W.T. Whitley, *A History of the British Baptists*, (London: C. Griffin and Company, 1923), 4.

[15] *The Orthodox Creed* (1678), XXX, in Lumpkin, *Baptist Confessions of Faith*, 318-19.

[16] Walter Shurden, *Proclaiming the Baptist Vision: The Church*, ed. Walter Shurden (Macon: Smyth and Helwys, 1996), 143.

[17] "The Baptist Doctrine of the Church," 2, A Statement approved by the Council of the Baptist Union of Great Britain and Ireland, March 1948, in Roger Hayden ed. *Baptist Union Documents 1948-1977* (London: Baptist Historical Society, 1980), 5-6.

[18] E. Roberts-Thomson, *With Hands Outstretched: Baptists and the Ecumenical Movement* (London: Marshall, Morgan & Scott, 1962), 35-36. The work of Ernest Payne and Robert Walton might in part be described as a retrieval of the catholic spirit of the early Baptists in Payne, *The Fellowship of Believers: Baptist Thought and Practice Yesterday and Today*, enlarged ed. (London: Carey Kingsgate Press, 1952), and Walton, *The Gathered Community* (London: Carey Press, 1946). Philip E. Thompson has similarly made an effort to reclaim the catholicity of the early Baptists in "A New Question in Baptist History: Seeking a Catholic Spirit Among Early Baptists," *Pro Ecclesia* 8/1 (1999): 51-72.

[19] Ernest A. Payne, *The Baptist Union: A Short History* (London: The Carey Kingsgate Press, 1959), 223.

[20] "Toward a Common Expression of Faith: A Black North American Perspective," *American Baptist Quarterly* 4 (December 1985): 389-96.

[21] Volf, *After Our Likeness*, 154-58.

[22] Wright, *Free Church, Free State*, 233.

[23] Payne, *The Fellowship of Believers*, 37.

[24] Baptist confessions, catechisms, and sermons have tended to use the language of "ordinances," although early Baptists used a variety of almost interchangeable terms to describe baptism and the Lord's Supper, frequently invoking the language of sacrament, see e.g., *The Orthodox Creed*, XIX, XXVII, XXXIII, in William L. Lumpkin, *Baptist Confessions of Faith*, revised ed. (Valley Forge: Judson Press, 1969), 311-13, 317, 321. One of the most striking references states

that as Israel "had the manna to nourish them in the wilderness to Canaan; so have we the sacraments, to nourish us in the church, and in our wilderness-condition," *The Orthodox Creed*, Article 19, in Lumpkin, *Baptist Confessions of Faith*, 311-12. For an example of recent explorations in sacramental theology, see the essays in Anthony R. Cross and Philip E. Thompson, eds. *Baptist Sacramentalism* (Carlisle: Paternoster Press, 2003).

[25] "The Baptist Doctrine of the Church," 5.

[26] John E. Colwell, *Promise and Presence: An Exploration of Sacramental Theology* (Milton Keynes: Paternoster, 2005); and Wright, Free Church, Free State, 94-101.

[27] Robert Hall, Terms of Communion, I.III, in *The Works of Robert Hall* (London: Henry G. Bohn, 1851), III:45. As Peter Morden has recently shown, the theology and practice of evangelical Baptist leader, Charles Haddon Spurgeon, on the Lord's Supper was sacramental, in "The Spirituality of C. H. Spurgeon: II Maintaining Communion: The Lord's Supper," *Baptistic Theologies* 4/1 (Spring 2012): 27-50, especially 41-45.

[28] Orthodox and Catholic theology maintains that the episcopal office is necessary for the ecclesiality of the church, following Ignatius, that the church is gathered around the bishop, *To the Symrneans*, 8, in *The Apostolic Fathers, Ante-Nicene Fathers*, (Grand Rapids: Wm. B. Eerdmans, 1979), 1:90. Volf contends that from the standpoint of a free church ecclesiology, ordained ministry "does not belong to the esse of the church," *After Our Likeness*, 248. Nigel Wright echoes Volf, but continues that for Baptists, "ministers belong most certainly to the bene esse of the church, to that which promotes its well-being, upbuilding and growth," *Free Church, Free State*, 172.

[29] For example, Arthur Dakin argued for a functional view of ministry in *The Baptist View of the Church and Ministry* (London: Baptist Union, 1944), 10, 15-24. Ernest Payne contended for the necessity of ordination for right order, in *The Fellowship of Believers*, 55. John Colwell has offered a thoroughly sacramental account of ordination, in "The Sacramental nature of Ordination," in *Baptist Sacramentalism*, Cross and Thompson eds., 232-38.

[30] Daniel Turner, *A Compendium of Social Religion of the Nature and Constitution of Christian Churches*, 2nd ed. (Bristol: W. Pine, 1778), 49-50.

[31] Irenaeus, *Against Heresies*, III.3.1; The Ante-Nicene Fathers (Grand Rapids: Wm. B. Eerdmans, 1979), 1:415. Irenaeus does not limit the succession of ministry to the bishops, but includes presbyters as a communal sign of continuity with apostolic faith and practice, *Against Heresies*, III.2.1, IV.26.2; ANF, 1:415, 497.

NOTES

[32] *BEM*, IV.B.38.

[33] William Bradford, *History of Plymouth Plantation, 1620-1647*, 2 vols, ed. William Chauncey Ford (Boston: Houghton Mifflin Company, 1912), 1:20-22. Following Bradford's account, Champlain Burrage showed the covenanting at Gainsborough occurred in the beginning of the year 1606/1607, in *The Early English Dissenters*, 1:231-32.

[34] Smyth, *The Character of the Beast*, in *The Works of John Smyth*, 2:645.

[35] Thomas Helwys, *A Short Declaration of the Mystery of Iniquity* (1611/1612), ed. Richard Groves (Macon: Mercer University Press, 132.

[36] Paul Fiddes provides a clear and concise account of the covenant origins of Baptist ecclesiology, in *Tracks and Traces*, 21-47.

[37] Martin Luther, in *Luther's Works*, 36:113 Various early Christian baptismal liturgies contain ritual anointing of the baptized, sometimes accompanied with the reading from 1 Peter 2:9-10 that proclaims that the baptized are a royal priesthood, in Edward Charles Whitaker, *Documents of the Baptismal Liturgy*, (London: SPCK, 1997), 2-7, 30-35, 110-123, 194-196.

[38] Augustine, On the Epistle of John 1.2; in The Nicene and Post-Nicene Fathers (Grand Rapids: Eerdmans, 1978), VII: 461.

[39] E. Y. Mullins, *The Axioms of Religion* (Philadelphia: Judson Press, 1908), 53.

[40] Winthrop S. Hudson, "Shifting Patterns of Church Order in the Twentieth Century," in *Baptist Concepts of the Church*, ed. Winthrop Still Hudson (Philadelphia: The Judson Press, 1959), 216.

[41] Hudson, *Baptists in Transition: Individualism and Christian Responsibility* (Valley Forge: Judson Press, 1979), 20.

[42] The old suspicion of Pentecostalism has dissipated though it has not altogether disappeared. In 2006 the International Mission Board of the Southern Baptists approved a policy excluding candidates who speak in tongues or have a private prayer language from appointment as missionaries. In response some Baptists in the United States have formed Pentecostal enclaves within their denomination, like Holy Spirit Renewal Ministries (formerly the American Baptist Charismatic Fellowship) or the Fullness movement among Southern Baptists. Others have founded new denominations like the Full Gospel Baptist Church Fellowship. The Pentecostal waves have also affected the global Baptist family, and with each successive wave comes a new controversy. In some countries like Argentina and Brazil there are two separate Baptist denominations: one charismatic and another non-charismatic. In the post Soviet era, Baptists and Pentecostals, who

were once forced together into a common denominational body, have split again into separate unions, though they continue to live out the struggles and tensions of their history of strained relationships.

[43] Molly T. Marshall, *Joining the Dance: A Theology of the Spirit* (Valley Forge, PA: Judson Press, 2003) 6-7; Clark Pinnock, *Flame of Love: A Theology of the Holy Spirit* (Downers Grove, IL: InterVarsity Press, 1996) 22.

[44] William C. Turner, *Discipleship for African American Christians: A Journey Through the Church Covenant* (Valley Forge, PA: Judson Press, 2002), xv.

[45] James Wm. McClendon, Jr., *Ethics: Systematic Theology*, Volume I, revised ed. (Nashville: Abingdon Press, 2002), 30; McClendon, *Doctrine: Systematic Theology*, Volume II (Nashville: Abingdon Press, 1994), 45-46.

[46] McClendon delineated three senses of catholicity. The first (and earliest) sense of catholic (καθολικos) is a generic usage (usually designated with a lower case "c" = catholicity$_1$) and is roughly equivalent to the term "universal." It denotes the way of life comprised of "belief, worship, and morals" that is well-rounded or typical as opposed to one-sided or partial. The second sense of catholic is an inclusive usage which has come to carry basically the same meaning as "ecumenical" (οἰκουμενε), that is, a way of speaking about all churches summed up as one. This second sense of catholicity initially conveyed a more restricted sense of the inhabited earth, and corresponds to the etymological meaning of catholic as "whole" (Kath hollou = catholicity$_2$). In modernity this sense of catholicity$_2$ designates ecumenism as pursued by interchurch cooperation. The third sense of catholic is as a proper name for the Catholic Church (Roman or otherwise) which usually appears written with an upper case "C" (catholicity$_3$). McClendon (and Yoder) argued for a radical catholicity in which "the believers church or baptist style of life typically displays such wholeness or catholicity1 as to make for catholicity$_2$," in James W. McClendon, Jr. and John Howard Yoder, "Christian Identity in Ecumenical Perspective," *Journal of Ecumenical Studies* 27 no. 3 (Summer 1990): 561-80. See also McClendon, "What is A Southern Baptist Ecumenism?" *Southwestern Journal of Theology* 10 no. 2 (Spring 1968): 73-78.

[47] See Fiddes, *Participating in God*, 262-64.

[48] Fiddes, *Tracks and Traces*, 70.

[49] Doyle, *Communion Ecclesiology*, 13, 11-22.

[50] First London Confession (1644), preface, in Lumpkin, *Baptist Confessions of Faith*, 155.

[51] C. René Padilla, *Mission Between the Times: Essays on the Kingdom* (Grand Rapids: Eerdmans, 1985); Padilla, "A New Ecclesiology in Latin America," *International*

NOTES

Bulletin of Missionary Research, 11 no 4 (October 1987): 156-164; Padilla. *The Local Church, Agent of Transformation : An Ecclesiology for Integral Mission* trans. Brian Cordingly (Buenos Aires: Ediciones Kairós, 2004); Samuel Escobar, *Christian Mission and Social Justice* (Scottdatle: Herald Press, 1978); Escobar, "Evangelical Theology in Latin America: The Development of a Missiological Christology," *Missiology* 19, no. 3 (July 1991): 315-32; Escobar, "Missionary Dynamism in Search of Missiological Discernment," *One in Christ* 35 no. 1 (1999): 69-90; Escobar, *Changing Tides: Latin America and World Mission Today* (Maryknoll: Orbis, 2002); Escobar, *The New Global Mission: The Gospel From Everywhere to Everyone* (Downers Grove: InterVarsity Press, 2003); and Orlando E. Costas, *Liberating News: A Theology of Contextual Evangelization* (Grand Rapids, Mich.: Eerdmans, 1989).

[52] Escobar, *The New Global Mission*, 13.

[53] Escobar, *The New Global Mission*, 126-27.

[54] *The Lausanne Covenant* (1974), 1. http://www.lausanne.org/en/documents/lausanne-covenant.html.

[55] David J. Bosch, *Transforming Mission: Paradigm Shifts in Theology of Mission* (Maryknoll: Orbis Books, 1991), 390.

[56] Craig Van Gelder, ed. *The Missional Church and Denominations* (Grand Rapids: William B. Eerdmans, 2008), 148.

[57] Lesslie Newbigin, *The Open Secret: An Introduction to the Theology of Mission*, revised ed. (Grand Rapids: William B. Eerdmans, 1995), 29. Newbigin's assessment of the West has been followed by observers who are specifically interested in reaching the post-Christendom culture of North America. E.g., George R. Hunsberger and Craig Van Gelder, eds., *The Church Between Gospel and Culture* (Grand Rapids: Eerdmans, 1996); and Darrell L. Guder, ed. *Missional Church: A Vision for the Sending of the Church in North America* (Grand Rapids: Eerdmans, 1998).

[58] Karl Barth, *Church Dogmatics*, IV/3.1, trans. G. W. Bromiley and T. F. Torrance (Edinburgh: T. & T. Clark, 1961). Barth begins his account of "Jesus Christ, The True Witness," §69, with a reference to William Carey as key to understanding of the radically missionary church that proclaims the good news of God's reconciling work in Jesus Christ, *Church Dogmatics*, IV/3.1, p. 25.

[59] Escobar makes this same point in his article on the mission of the church in theological conversations between Catholic and Evangelicals, "Missionary Dynamism in Search of Missiological Discernment," 81.

[60] Karl Rahner, *The Trinity*, trans. Joseph Donceel (New York: Continuum, 1974), 22.

[61] Steven R. Harmon, *Towards Baptist Catholicity: Essays on Tradition and the Baptist Vision* (Milton Keynes: Paternoster, 2006), 89-110.

[62] Augustine, SERMO CCLXXII, in die Pentecostes postremus. Ad Infantes, de Sacramento, in *Patrologia Latina* (Paris: J.P. Migne), 38:1246-48.

[63] BWA press release on Elstal meeting. http://bwanet.org/bwa.php?m=news&p=news_item&id=283.

[64] Neville Callam, "Significance of BWA as an Ecclesial Movement," *BWA News* (15 May 2008), http://www.bwanet.org/bwa.php?m=news&p=news_item&id=383.

CHAPTER 2

[1] All citations from *The Church, Towards a Common Vision* refer to the numbered paragraphs in the document, and will be included in the body of the paper.

[2] Cardinal Charles Journet, Introduction, *The Church of the Word Incarnate* (1955), http://www.ewtn.com/library/THEOLOGY/CHWORDIN.HTM.

[3] Ibid.

[4] Ibid. Journet's full statement reads, "Taken formally and ontologically such expressions as those of Origen and Augustine and Catherine might seem to mean that 'Christ sins and has always sinned in His members'—a proposition condemned by the twenty-second session of the Council of Basle. It can be said that Christ lives, suffers, and sanctifies Himself in His members. It cannot be said that He sins in His members."

[5] Cited in Thomas Buffer, S.T.D., "The Mariology of Cardinal Journet (1891-1975) and Its Influence on Some Marian Magisterial Statements," http://campus.udayton.edu/mary/buffer03.htm. Buffer adds: "[Journet's] entire theological work would serve this initial vision, as he sought to make known precisely and scientifically what St. Catherine knew through intuition."

[6] As stated in the Catholic Catechism, *ex opere operato* ("by the work worked") means that "the sacrament is not wrought by the righteousness of either the celebrant or the recipient, but by the power of God," cited in Susan K. Wood, *One Baptism, Ecumenical Dimensions of the Doctrine of Baptism* (Collegeville, MN: Liturgical Press, 2009), 69. According to Wood, its intent is not to underwrite a "magical" view of the sacraments, but to uphold the conviction that "Christ and the Spirit are the principal actor (principal cause) in the sacrament through the agency of the sacrament (instrumental cause)," 69. Understood in this light, *ex opere operato* does not deny the necessity of faith but indicates that the object of faith

is Christ and the Spirit rather than the purity or perfection of the minister or laity.

[7] Augustine, *Augustine: Later Works*, ed. John Burnaby (Philadelphia: Westminster, 1955), 256.

[8] Cited in *The Catholic Encyclopedia*, Vol. V ed. Charles Herbermann, et. al. (NY: Robert Appleton, 1909), 129. Augustine is favorably describing the position of Tichonius who "assailed on all sides by the voices of the holy pages, awoke and saw the Church of God diffused throughout the world, as had been foreseen and foretold of her so long before by the hearts and mouths of the saints."

[9] Personal correspondence, Dennis Doyle, University of Dayton, June 2013.

[10] According to Elizabeth Groppe, Congar embraces a "people of God ecclesiology" that "contributes to our awareness of the church's sinfulness and failings." Groppe goes on to describe Congar's position, however, as follows: "Insofar as the church is a divinely established institution, it is pure and sinless, but, insofar as the church is composed of people, it is marred by pride, egoism, and human weakness," in Elizabeth Groppe, *Yves Congar's Theology of the Holy Spirit* (Oxford: Oxford University, 2004), 127.

[11] Dennis Doyle, "Journet, Congar and the Roots of Communion Ecclesiology," 58 *Theological Studies* (1997): 473. Doyle notes that both Journet and Congar's influence can be seen in Vatican II's *Lumen Gentium* on this topic, specifically §8: "While Christ, holy, innocent and undefiled knew nothing of sin, but came to expiate only the sins of the people, the Church, embracing in its bosom sinners, at the same time holy and always in need of being purified, always follows the way of penance and renewal," 478.

[12] Rowan Williams, "Insubstantial Evil," Robert Dodero and Robert Lawless, eds. *Augustine and His Critics, Essays in Honour of Gerald Bonner* (New York: Routledge, 2000), 118.

[13] Robert C. Walton, "The Community of the Church," in Curtis W. Freeman, James Wm. McClendon, Jr. and C. Rosalee Velloso da Silva, eds., *Baptist Roots, A Reader in the Theology of a Christian People* (Valley Forge, PA: Judson Press, 1999), 333.

[14] Ibid., 334.

[15] Brian Daley makes a similar point about the oneness of the church. He states that though unity "is hindered or clouded by our sinfulness and 'slowness of heart' (Luke 24:25)," it nonetheless "already exists among us as God's gift." Our calling is to allow this unity "to become more fully evident in the way Christians look

upon each other, articulate their faith, carry out their worship, and act in the world," in Brian Daley, "Rebuilding the Structure of Love: The Quest for Visible Unity among the Churches," in *The Ecumenical Future*, Carl E. Braaten and Robert W. Jenson, eds. (Grand Rapids: Eerdmans, 2004), 74.

[16] See, for example, the Baptist Union of Sweden commentary on *BEM* and the eucharist: "There is, it seems to us, a tendency towards sacramentalism in this document. Eager to clarify the meaning of the eucharist, the document gives to this sacrament such a comprehensive function and such a unique position that other elements of Christian worship and Christian experience are eclipsed, such as prayer, Bible study, praise, service and fellowship," in Max Thurian, ed. *Churches respond to BEM, Volume IV, Official responses to the "Baptism, Eucharist and Ministry' text* (Geneva: World Council of Churches), 206.

[17] This task has been addressed already by Baptist theologians in a variety of ways. See, for example, Stephen Harmon, *Towards Baptist Catholicity, Essays on Tradition and the Baptist Vision* (U.K.: Paternoster, 2006/Eugene, OR: Wipf and Stock, 2006), Anthony Cross and Phillip Thompson, *Baptist Sacramentalism, Studies in Baptist History and Thought* (Eugene, OR: Wipf and Stock, 2007) and Christopher Ellis, *Gathering, A Theology and Spirituality of Worship in Free Church Tradition* (London: SCM Press, 2004).

[18] Henri De Lubac, *Corpus Mysticum: The Eucharist and the Church in the Middle Ages* (IN: University of Notre Dame, 2007). De Lubac links this understanding to an over-emphasis on the eucharist as the "mystical body" to the exclusion of the whole church as also a "mystical body" (where "mystical" is here understood as both real and mysterious), 116.

[19] Ibid., 116.

[20] Catherine Pickstock, *On the Liturgical Consummation of Philosophy* (Oxford: Blackwell, 1998), 166.

[21] Cited by Brandon O'Brien, "From Soul Liberty to Self-reliance: John Leland and the Evangelical Origins of Radical Individualism," in *American Baptist Quarterly* 27, 2 (Sumer 2008): 144.

[22] Pickstock, 162.

[23] Ibid., see 164-166.

[24] Ibid., 165-166.

[25] Alexander Schmemann, *For the Life of the World* (New York: National Student Christian Association, 1973), 18. Schmemann writes, "Man is a hungry being. But he is hungry for God...So the only natural (and not "supernatural") reaction

of man, to whom God gave this blessed and sanctified world, is to bless God in return, to thank Him, to see the world as God see it and—in this act of gratitude and adoration—to know, name and possess the world," 14 and 15.

[26] Irenaeus of Lyons engages an understanding of "recapitulation" in his refutation of the Gnostics. Joel Kurz nicely summarizes recapitulation: "Christ submitted himself to Adam's circumstances and achieved the reversal of the events which led to death and the sullying of creation. Creation and redemption coexist within the divine economy, so Christ's restoration of creation and humanity occurs within the matrix of movement toward the eschatological fulfillment and consummation. By assuming Adam's flesh and successfully retracing his events, Christ was initiating and executing the process of recapitulation," in Kurz, Joel R. "The Gifts of Creation and the Consummation of Humanity: Irenaeus of Lyons' Recapitulatory Theology of the Eucharist." *Worship* 83, no. 2 (March 2009): 122.

[27] This passage is from Rauschenbusch's prayer, "Thanks for Creation," cited in Stanley Hauerwas, *A Better Hope, Resources for a Church Confronting Capitalism, Democracy, and Postmodernity* (Grand Rapids, MI: 2000), 240. For an account of baptism and creation, see especially Paul Fiddes, "Baptism and Creation," in Paul Fiddes, ed. *Reflections on the Water, Understanding God and the World through the Baptism of Believers* (Macon, GA: Smyth & Helwys, 1996), 47-68. Fiddes states, "Both creation and incarnation therefore tell us that the God who relates Himself to human beings also has a kind of relation, and evokes a kind of response, within created reality at every level," 58. For an analysis of how grace fulfills the "deepest longing of our nature"—our hunger—see John Milbank, *The Suspended Middle, Henri de Lubac and the Debate concerning the Supernatural* (Grand Rapids, MI: Wm. B. Eerdmans, 2005), 26.

[28] Ellis, Gathering, 178.

[29] Eleazar Clay, *Hymns and Spiritual Songs, Selected From Several Approved Authors* (Richmond: John Dixon, 1793) cited in Philip Thompson, "Re-envisioning Baptist Identity: Historical, Theological, and Liturgical Analysis," *Perspectives in Religious Studies* 27, no. 3 (Fall 2000): 291-292.

[30] They have been "concerned about what they see as the danger of ritual to claim for human action what should be wholly subject to the sovereignty of God," in Ellis, *Gathering*, 211.

[31] Historically, this view has been taught by Augustine. More recently, however, The International Theological Commission of the Roman Catholic Church states, that "the Catechism [1992] teaches that infants who die without baptism are entrusted by the Church to the mercy of God, as is shown

in the specific funeral rite for such children." This conviction, they state, should not be used to negate the necessity of baptism or to delay it. See "The Hope of Salvation for Infants who Die without Being Baptised," http://www.vatican.va/roman_curia/congregations/cfaith/cti_documents/rc_con_cfaith_doc_20070419_un-baptised-infants_en.html

[32] Anthony Cross, *Baptism and the Baptists, Theology and Practice in Twentieth-Century Britain* (Waynesboro, GA: Paternoster, 2000), 454-455. The full quotation reads: "[Baptists'] theology of baptism is subordinated to their evangelistic enthusiasms, for they emphasize the importance of conversion but not the act of initiation into the church," 455. Cross adds that that "overwhelming majority of Baptists writing on baptism have done so within the ecumenical context," which suggests they hold an "ambivalent attitude toward baptism." They defend believers baptism, on the one hand, but on the other, pay little attention to the rite, 455.

[33] Anthony Cross, *Baptism and the Baptists,* 457. The full context reads: "The emphasis placed on baptism continues to centre on the candidate.... This individualism has meant Baptists have continued to find difficulty in expressing the provenience of God's grace the and corporate dimension of the rite.... The corporate dimension [of baptism] continues to revolve around the congregation as predominantly spectators of that which the candidate is doing."

[34] See, for example, Stanley K. Fowler, *More Than a Symbol: The British Baptist Recovery of Baptismal Sacramentalism* (Eugene, OR: Wipf and Stock, 2007); Christopher Ellis, in *Gathering*, op. cit, as well as "Believer's Baptism and the Sacramental Freedom of God," in Fiddes, ed., *Reflections on the Water*, op. cit.; James W. McClendon, "Baptism as a Performative Sign," *Theology Today*, 23, no. 3 (October 1966): available online at: http://theologytoday.ptsem.edu/oct1966/v23-3-article6.htm. For an excellent description and engagement with some of the debate surrounding baptism as symbol or sacrament, see Anthony Cross, *Baptism and Baptists*.

[35] Christopher Ellis, "Believer's Baptism and the Sacramental Freedom of God," 38.

[36] Cited by Philip Thompson, 291-292. Recorded by Morgan Edwards, *The Customs of Primitive Churches –or- A Set of Propositions Relative to the Name, Material, Constitution, Power, Officers, Ordinances, Rites, Business, Worship, Discipline, Government &c. of a Church; to Which are Added Their Proofs from Scripture, and Historical Narratives of the Manner in Which most of them Have Been Reduced to Practice* (Philadelphia: n.p., 1774) Luther's well-known "Flood Prayer" relates similar themes: "We pray through the same thy groundless mercy that thou wilt graciously behold this N. and bless him with true faith in the spirit so that by

means of this saving flood all that has been born in him from Adam and which he himself has added thereto may be drowned in him and engulfed, and that he may be sundered from the number of the unbelieving, preserved dry and secure in the holy ark. Amen."

[37] Neville Callam, cited in *The Report of the International Conversations between The Anglican Communion and The Baptist World Alliance, Conversations Around the World, 2000 – 2005* (London, UK: The Anglican Communion Office, 2005), 58.

[38] *Baptism, Eucharist and Ministry*, Faith and Order Paper No. 111, World Council of Churches, Geneva, 1982, http://www.oikoumene.org/fileadmin/files/wcc-main/documents/p2/FO1982_111_en.pdf, 3. A similar statement can be found in a recent Catholic Catechism which states, "Though we have taken the example of the baptism of adults, because the meaning is clearest there, infant baptism is far and away the most common," *A New Catechism, Catholic Faith for Adults* (New York: Seabury, 1969), 250.

[39] Susan K. Wood, *One Baptism, Ecumenical Dimensions of the Doctrine of Baptism* (Collegeville, MN: Liturgical Press, 2009), 174.

[40] Ibid.

[41] McClendon, 9.

[42] Geoffrey Wainwright, *Embracing Purpose: Essays on God, the World and the Church* (London: Epworth, 2007)184. Wainwright acknowledges that recognition of the saints would necessarily involve questions about "canonization," and this would become part of the dialogue about "the condition of the faithful departed in general."

[43] John Paul II, *Ut Unum Sint* (1995), §84. 1995. www.vatican.va/holy_father/john_paul_ii/encyclicals/documents/hf_jp-ii_enc_25051995_ut-unum-sint_en.html.

[44] I am grateful to Jenny Howell for her emphasis on this point in her essay, "Reading History with the Saints: An Examination of McClendon's 'Biography as Theology,'" delivered at "Baptists and History," annual meeting of Young Scholars in the Baptist Academy, Prague, July 24, 2011.

[45] James Wm. McClendon, Jr., *Biography as Theology, How Life Stories Can Remake Today's Theology* (Nashville, TN: Abingdon, 1974), 134, my emphasis.

[46] McClendon discusses Jordan's rich and varied understandings of the term "koinonia," which Jordan came to mainly through his study of the Greek New Testament. These include "participation" and "communion," as well as a sharing of a community's goods and life in the Holy Spirit. Another use related to the sacrifice of Christ: "Easters of a sacrifice in Israel were koinonoi (sharers) of that sacrifice...," 129.

[47] See my *Attending the Wounds on Christ's Body, Teresa's Scriptural Vision* (Eugene, OR: 2012).

CHAPTER 3

[1] *The Church: Towards a Common Vision.* Faith & Order Paper 214 (Geneva: WCC publications, 2013). All paragraph numbers refer to this edition.

[2] *The Word of God in the Life of the Church.* A Report of International Conversations between The Catholic Church and the Baptist World Alliance 2006-2010, *American Baptist Quarterly* 31 (2012), §§11-12.

[3] Loreli F. Fuchs, SA, *Koinonia and the Quest for an Ecumenical Ecclesiology* (Grand Rapids: Eerdmans, 2008), 252.

[4] Vatican II, Unitatis redintegratio, 3, in Austin Flannery, O.P., (Ed.), *Vatican Council II: The Conciliar and Post Conciliar Documents* (Dublin: Dominican Publications, 1977), 455-6; *Ut Unum Sint*, 11 (London; Catholic Truth Society, 1995), 16.

[5] *The Nature and Mission of the Church.* Faith and Order Paper 198 (Geneva, WCC, 2005), para. 24, p. 22.

[6] Cf. *The Nature and Mission of the Church*, 17(d).

[7] *Word of God in the Life of the Church*, §16.

[8] E.g. William Bradford, *History of Plymouth Plantation, 1620-1647*, ed. W.C. Ford (2 volumes; Boston: Massachusetts Historical Society, 1912), vol. 1, 20-22; The *Faith and Practise of Thirty Congregations, Gathered According to the Primitive Pattern* (London: Will Larnar, 1651), 52, in W.L. Lumpkin, *Baptist Confessions* (Philadelphia: Judson Press, 1959), 183; *A Confession of the Faith of Several Churches of Christ (The "Somerset Confession")* (London: Henry Hills, 1656), XXIV, in Lumpkin, *Baptist Confessions*, 209. For exposition, see Paul S. Fiddes, 'Walking Together. The Place of Covenant Theology in Baptist Life Yesterday and Today', in *Tracks and Traces. Baptist Identity in Church and Doctrine* (Milton Keynes: Paternoster, 2003), 21-47.

[9] See the *Particular Baptist Confession of Faith* (1644), art. XLVII, in Lumpkin, *Baptist Confessions, 169.*

[10] Paragraphs 10 (local ecumenical covenant), 17-18, 45 (Old and New covenants).

[11] See Thomas Helwys, *A Short Declaration of the mistery of the iniquity* (n.pm.:, n.p., 1612), 46; Robert Hall, *An Apology for the Freedom of the Press and for General Liberty* (1793), repr. in Olinthus Gregory (ed), *The Works of Robert Hall*, Vol. III (London: Holdsworth and Ball, 1832), 121-38.

[12] Balthasar, Hans Urs von, *Theo-Drama. Theological Dramatic Theory*. 5 Volumes (San Francisco: Ignatius Press, 1988-98),Vol. IV, 330.

[13] Ibid., 329.

[14] See *Conversations Around the World. Conversations between the Anglican Communion and the Baptist World Alliance*, 44-51. Similarly, see *Dialogue between the Community of Protestant Churches in Europe (CPCE) and the European Baptist Federation (EBF) on the Doctrine and Practice of Baptism*. Leuenberg Documents 9 (Frankfurt: Verlag Lembeck, 2005), 19-22; *Pushing at the Boundaries of Unity. Anglicans and Baptists in Conversation* (London: Church House Publishing 2005), 31-57; *The Word of God in the Life of the Church*, §§101-4.

[15] Note that the *Catechism of the Catholic Church* states (1229), 'becoming a Christian has been accomplished by a journey and initiation in several stages'.

[16] E.g. Phil. 1:6, Eph. 4:30, Rom. 5:9-10, 8:24, 13:11, 2 Tim. 2:10, 1 Pet. 1:9.

[17] Aquinas, *Summa Theologiae* 1a2ae.57.4-5; cf. 2a2ae.47.1.

[18] Aquinas, *Summa Theologiae* 2a2ae.47.14; 1a2ae.58.1-4.

[19] Aquinas, *Summa Theologiae* 2a2ae.8.1-2; 2a2ae.17.1-3; 2a2ae.18.2; 2a2ae.23.1-2.

[20] Prov. 8:22; Wisd. 6:16; Sir. 24:1-22. See Paul S. Fiddes, *Seeing the World and Knowing God. Hebrew Wisdom and Christian Doctrine in a Late-Modern Context* (Oxford: OUP, 2013), 175-203.

[21] *Joint Declaration on the Doctrine of Justification. Phase III of the International Lutheran-Roman Catholic Commission on Unity (1986-1993)*, 1990: §15.

[22] *Joint Declaration*, §17.

[23] *Joint Declaration*, §16.

[24] Helwys, *Short Declaration of the mistery of iniquity*, 'The principal matters handled in the Booke', recto; and 49.

CHAPTER 4

[1] As in The *Word of God* itself, the "Catholic Church" here is shorthand for the Roman Catholic Church.

[2] See §§3-6.

[3] §§1, 4.

[4] See "The Status of this Report", p. 2.

⁵ See especially fn. 7, p. 8.

⁶ §§72-131; quotation from overall title of section.

⁷ §13.

⁸ §13.

⁹ The report in fact does something like this in §§32-3, relating the different understandings of the sanctity of the church to a shared agreement that "Christ is the source and goal of the holiness of the church and its members."

¹⁰ To add an anecdotal example, I wrote part of this paper whilst a guest at a Baptist training institution; the student who had previously inhabited the room I was given had chosen to nail a very traditional crucifix to the wall above the bed. The staff were a little surprised when I informed them of this, but the fact that a Baptist ministerial student can find, and not be embarrassed to find, meaning and devotional help in a crucifix is a nice illustration of the point I am making here.

¹¹ There is indeed a lengthy quotation from *Dei Verbum* in §62.

¹² The report notes a degree of Baptist unhappiness with the term "sacrament," and so uses "sacrament/ordinance" where specifying points of agreement; this is rather clumsy, but the reason for doing it is sound, and so I have followed it here.

¹³ See Jeff Astley, *Ordinary Theology: Looking, Listening, and Learning in Theology* (London: Ashgate, 2003).

¹⁴ See my Whitley Lecture, *Tradition and Renewal in Baptist Life* (Oxford: Whitley Publications, 2003).

¹⁵ See particularly *Lumen Gentium* §§60-65.

¹⁶ Comité mixte baptiste-catholique en France, *Marie*, Documents Episcopat 10 (Paris: Le Secretariat Général de la Conférence des Évêques de France, 2009), §59.

¹⁷ Jean Calvin, *The Institutes of the Christian Religion*, ed. John T. McNeill and trans. Ford Lewis Battles (Philadelphia: Westminster, 1960), III.20.24; in the surrounding sections Calvin is eloquent about various abuses, and of course insistent on Christ as the only mediator of our intercession to the Father, but, inasmuch as requests for prayer are proper between believers, his only argument against asking the saints in glory to pray for us as we do our sisters and brothers on earth is the lack of access.

¹⁸ This was very evident in the nineteenth century; it has died away to some extent now, but it is not hard to find the sentiment in certain urban areas, in particular, still.

NOTES

CHAPTER 5

[1] Dr. McCall's long-time assistant, Clara McCart, who was known for her sense of propriety said surprisingly of this venture, "Well, we'll have to see if it burps or beeps!"

[2] In approaching the king, McCall had to climb up some steps and reached for a post to steady himself without knowing that touching the post was forbidden to all except royalty. Dr. McCall argued that his name "Duke" made him royalty. Evidently his shrewd legal arguments were convincing enough that he was only required to pay the minimum fine of slightly less than two shillings.

CHAPTER 6

[1] Unless otherwise stated, all scripture quotations are from the New English Translation (NET) version of the Bible.

CHAPTER 8

[1] All Scriptures are taken from the NRSV and in the Old Testament are modified to translate the divine name as Yahweh, rather than as "the LORD".

CHAPTER 9

[1] Tom Nevin, 'Nedbank's chief kicks over a hornet's nest', http://www.exacteditions.com/read/african-banker/issue-21-31755/50/2, accessed 20 June 2014.

[2] http://www.zapiro.com/cartoon/800762-120412mg, accessed 17 June 2014.

[3] http://www.reuelkhoza.co.za/, accessed 16 June 2014). For more on ubuntu, culture and Christian faith see Kretzschmar (2008 & 2010) and Miller (2013).

[4] http://www.reuelkhoza.co.za/attunedleadership.html, accessed 30 June 2014.

[5] Sometimes called NPOs (Non Profit Organisations), CBOs were traditionally called para-church organisations. More recently the term Faith Based Organisations (FBOs) is also used.

[6] Some organisations, such as the International Red Cross, began as Christian organisations. It was founded in 1863 Jean-Henri Dunant, who also involved with the Young Men's Christian Association.

[7] See Meier (2014) for an excellent discussion of the differences between transforming (Burns) and transformative (Bass) leadership.

⁸ For a discussion of pastoral dysfunction see Hall (1997:240-253).

⁹ Unless, of course, one is part of a social system that values and rewards family connections and loyalty to the party or dominant ideology over and above proven competence.

¹⁰ http://www.ketsdevries.com/author/articles/, accessed 17 June 2014.

¹¹ See Ciulla (2000) and Kretzschmar (2012) for a discussion of ethics in the workplace.

¹² For a critique of a narrow understanding of the 'bottom line' as short term economic profit making and the proposal of a 'new' bottom line, see the clip, http://www.youtube.com/watch?v=9Uy9OBVpc6Y, accessed 20 June 2014.

¹³ Rigby, Rhymer, 'Worn-out executives need a place to think', http://www.ft.com/cms/s/0/8b6bed84-d63c-11dc-b9f4-0000779fd2ac.html#axzz36CwtZwv4, accessed 1 July 2014.

¹⁴ http://www.ketsdevries.com/biography/, accessed 16 June 2014.

¹⁵ https://flora.insead.edu/fichiersti_wp/Inseadwp1989/89-37.pdf, accessed 1 July 2014.

¹⁶ See Kaminiów & Haenze (2013:119).

¹⁷ http://www.xpand.eu/xpand-schweiz/angebote/leaders-of-influence/, accessed 16 June 2014.

¹⁸ http://www.xpand.eu/fileadmin/user_upload/xpand_ch/LoI-CH_Broschuere.pdf, accessed 16 June 2014.

CHAPTER 10

¹ Paper presented to the Commission on Theological Education and Leadership Development of the Baptist World Alliance, meeting in Kuala Lumpur on 7 July 2011.

² Jürgen Moltmann, *Theology of Hope: On the Ground and the Implications of a Christian Eschatology*, trans., James W. Leitch (London: SCM, 1967).

³ Rob Bell, *Love Wins: A Book About Heaven, Hell, and the Fate of Every Person Who Ever Lived* (New York: HarperOne, 2011).

⁴ See my article, "Beyond Bebbington" where I argue that contemporary evangelicalism is in danger of being reduced to a movement of passionate piety. Brian Harris, "Beyond Bebbington: The Quest for an Evangelical Identity in a Postmodern Era," *Churchman* 122, no. 3 (2008).

NOTES

[5] Examples of the work of some of the new atheists include Richard Dawkins, *The God Delusion* (Boston: Houghton Mifflin, 2006); Sam Harris, *Letters to a Christian Nation* (New York: Random, 2006); Christopher Hitchens, *God Is Not Great: How Religion Poisons Everything* (New York: Twelve, 2007).

[6] David Kinnaman and Gabe Lyons, *Unchristian: What a New Generation Really Thinks About Christianity... And Why It Matters* (Grand Rapids: Baker, 2007).

[7] For a discussion of and rationale for the conclusion that we live in a 'post-Christendom' era, see Stuart Murray, *Church after Christendom* (Carlisle: Paternoster, 2004); Stuart Murray, *Post-Christendom* (Carlisle: Paternoster, 2004).

[8] For a very different (and far more positive) interpretation of the churches contribution to society, see Alvin J. Schmidt, *Under the Influence: How Christianity Transformed Culture* (Grand Rapids: Zondervan, 2001).

[9] A simple but thought provoking introduction to the topic is found in Dave Andrews, *People of Compassion* (Blackburn, VIC: TEAR Australia, 2008).

[10] So, for example, Jim Wallis, speaking of the mixed legacy of Evangelicalism, laments, "Evangelicals in this century have a history of going along with the culture on the big issues and taking their stand on the smaller issues. That has been one of the serious problems of evangelical religion. Today, many evangelicals no longer just acquiesce to the culture on the larger economic and political issues, but actively promote the culture's worst values on these matters." Jim Wallis, *The Call to Conversion* (Herts: Lion, 1981), 25.

[11] The following three paragraphs are a slightly modified form of part of a brief newspaper article I wrote in 2007. Brian Harris, "When Faith Is the Problem," *The Advocate*, April 2007.

[12] See for example Stanley J. Grenz, *Revisioning Evangelical Theology: A Fresh Agenda for the Twenty First Century* (Downers Grove: Inter Varsity Press, 1993); Stanley J. Grenz and John R. Franke, *Beyond Foundationalism: Shaping Theology in a Postmodern Context* (Louisville: Westminster John Knox Press, 2001).

[13] Clark H. Pinnock, "Biblical Texts - Past and Future Meanings," *Journal of the Evangelical Theological Society* 43, no. 1 (2000).

[14] Stephen L. Carter, *The Culture of Disbelief: How American Law and Politics Trivialize Religious Devotion* (New York: Basic Books, 1993).

[15] Denise Bradley and others, *Review of Australian Higher Education* (Canberra: DEEWR, 2008), 21.

[16] Ibid., 20.

[17] Yao Li and others, "China's Higher Education Transformation and Its Global Implications," *Vox* (2008).

[18] This is why Grenz named his overview of theology *Theology for the Community of God*. Stanley J. Grenz, *Theology for the Community of God* (Nashville: Broadman and Holman, 1994).

[19] George Marsden, *The Outrageous Idea of Christian Scholarship* (New York: Oxford University Press, 1997).

[20] Philip K. Dick, *The Dark Haired Girl* (Shingletown: Mark V. Ziesing, 1988).

CHAPTER 12

[1] Lumpkin, ed., *Baptist Confessions of Faith* (Valley Forge, Pa.: Judson Press), 301.

[2] Petr Chelcicky, "The New of Faith," in Curtis Freeman, James W. McClendon, Jr., and C. Rosalee Velloso Ewell, eds., *Baptist Roots: A Reader in the Theology of a Christian People* (Valley Forge, Pa.: Judson Press, 1999), 23.

[3] *The New Hampshire Confession*, 1833, X, Of Sanctification, in William L. Lumpkin, ed., *Baptist Confessions of Faith* (Valley Forge, Pa.: Judson Press, 1999).

[4] Bill J. Leonard, *Baptist Questions, Baptist Answers: Exploring Christian Faith* (Louisville: Westminster John Knox Press, 2009), 33.

[5] Basil of Caeasarea, *The Book of St. Basil the Great on the Holy Spirit*, ed., C. F. H. Johnston (Oxford: Clarendon Press, 1892), 51-4.

[6] William P. Alston, "The Indwelling of the Holy Spirit," in *Divine Nature and Human Language* (Ithaca, NY: Cornell University Press, 1989), 223.

[7] Significant contributions in this area include Romanus Cessario, *The Moral Virtues and Theological Ethics* (Notre Dame, IN: University of Notre Dame Press, 1991; Jean Porter, *The Recovery of Virtue: The Relevance of Aquinas for Christian Ethics* (Louisville: Westminster /John Knox, 1990); Peter Kreeft, *Back to Virtue* (San Francisco: Ignatius Press, 1992; Josef Pieper, *The Four Cardinal Virtues* (Notre Dame, IN: University of Notre Dame Press, 1954.

[8] See Augustine, *Of the Morals of the Catholic Church*, in Whitney J. Oates, ed., *Basic Writings of Saint Augustine*, vol. 1, (New York: Random House, 1948); see as well Stanley Hauerwas, *Character and the Christian Life: A Study in Theological Ethics* (Notre Dame, IN: University of Notre Dame Press, 1975); Stanley Hauerwas, *A Community of Character: Toward a Constructive Christian Social Ethic* (Notre Dame, IN: University of Notre Dame Press, 1981); Joseph J. Kotva, Jr., *The Christian Case for Virtue Ethics* (Washington, D.C.: Georgetown University Press, 1996); Gilbert C. Meilaender, *The Theory and Practice of Virtue* (Notre

Dame, IN: University of Notre Dame Press, 1984); H. Richard Niebuhr, *The Responsible Self* (New York: Harper & Row, 1963); Samuel K. Roberts, *In the Path of Virtue: The African American Moral Tradition* (Cleveland: The Pilgrim Press, 1999); Michael Slote, *From Morality to Virtue* (New York: Oxford University Press, 1992).

[9] Deontological ethics, or ethics of duty, judges the morality of an action based on the action's adherence to rules; consequentialist or teleological ethics judges the rightness of an act according to its consequences.

[10] Stanley Hauerwas, *A Community of Character* (Notre Dame, IN: University of Notre Dame Press, 1981), 114.

[11] Ibid., 115.

[12] Hauerwas, *Character and the Christian Life*, 11.

[13] Martin Luther King, Jr., "Our God is Able," in *Strength to Love* (New York: Harper & Row, 1963).

[14] Joseph Kotva, Jr., *The Christian Case for Virtue Ethics* (Washington, D.C.: Georgetown University Press, 1996), 21.

[15] John Walvoord's study, *The Doctrine of the Holy Spirit: a study in Pneumatology* (Dallas, TX.: Dallas Theological Seminary, 1943) was one such work. The virtues were understood primarily as "spiritual gifts," with little sensitivity to the formative transformation that the believer had to undergo in order to demonstrate embodiment of these "fruits of the Spirit."

[16] James Wm. McClendon, Jr., *Biography as Theology: How Life Stories Can Remake Today's Theology* (Nashville: Abingdon Press, 1974).

[17] Francis Wayland, *The Elements of Moral Science* (Cambridge, MA.: Belnap Press of Harvard Univ. Press, 1963), 83.

[18] Wayland, *Elements*, 150.

[19] Wayland, *Elements*, 86.

[20] Wayland, *Sermons to the Churches*, 150.

[21] Wayland, *Sermons to the Churches*, 61.

[22] Wayland, *Sermons to the Churches*, 82-83.

[23] Wayland, *Sermons to the Churches*, 154.

[24] Wayland, *Sermons to the Churches*, 252-53.

[25] Billy Graham, *The Holy Spirit: Activating God's Power in Your Life* (Waco, TX: Word Books, 1978).

26 Ibid., 81.

27 Ibid., my italics.

28 Ibid., 99.

29 Ibid., 85.

30 Ibid., 86.

31 Ibid., 88.

32 Ibid., 88.

33 Ibid., 219.

34 Ibid.

35 Ibid., 82.

36 Ibid., 82.

37 Ibid., 220.

38 T. B. Maston, *Why Live the Christian Life?* (New Orleans: Insight Press, 1996, 1974).

39 T. B. Maston, *Right or Wrong?* (Nashville: Broadman Press, 1955), 8.

40 Ibid., 8.

41 Ibid., 8.

42 Ibid., 42.

43 Ibid., 7.

44 Maston, *Right or Wrong?*, 8.

45 Ibid., 41.

46 Ibid., 24.

47 Ibid., 25.

48 Ibid.

49 Ibid.

50 Maston, *Why Live the Christian Life?*, 83.

51 Ibid., 84.

52 Ibid.

53 Ibid.

NOTES

CHAPTER 13

[1] For the basic idea of this paper, I am indebted to Michael Rogness, "Proclaiming the Gospel on Mars Hill" *Word & World* 27 (3, 2007) 274-294. http://ehis.ebscohost.com/eds/delivery?sid=b2c812d6-0d53-4bf0-9326-c1fb9c07888f%40se, accessed 2/6/2012.

[2] Of course, an oral tradition has evolved that the preaching, teaching, and evangelism has to have certain terms and phrases or it's not the real thing. The problem is we have developed a whole glossary of "church speak" which increasingly does not communicate with those "out there" and more and more does not communicate with those "in here" in the church. The phenomenon of insider language and actions moves in the direction of exclusion rather than inclusion. Paul's language and actions always moved in the direction of openness and inclusion.

If one is attempting to bridge the gulf between academia, church-speak, and the culture around us, no better resource for help is Tex Sample, *Ministry in an Oral Culture—Living with Will Rogers, Uncle Remus, and Minnie Pearl* (Louisville, Kentucky: Westminster/John Knox Press, 1994).

Harry L. Lucenay, pastor of Kowloon International Baptist church, Kowloon Tong, Hong Kong, notes " in "Preaching the Truth Across Cultures," *Window*, Spring, 2009, vol. 12, No. 1, 8, an important point for all of us toward what is more and more cross cultural extension of the kerygma, "In the United States I worked with children who were afraid of dying and young adults who were ashamed of what they had done. Both had real desires to get their hearts right with God but their motivations were very different. In Asia, a personal relationship with God may be felt to be more important than salvation from damnation."

[3] Howard Thurman, Jesus and the Disinherited, (Boston, Mass: The Beacon Press, 1976), 29.

[4] See, for example, http://rhetoric.eserver.org/aristotle/. As well, George Hunter, *The Celtic Way of Evangelism: How Christianity Can Reach the West...Again* (Nashville, Abingdon Press, 2000); cf, Thomas Cahill, How the Irish Saved Civilization: *The Untold Story of Ireland's Heroic Role from the Fall of Rome to the Rise of Medieval Europe* (New York, New York: Nan A. Talese, 1995). Especially, Edward Farley, *Deep Symbols: Their Postmodern Effacement and Reclamation* (Valley Forge, Pennsylvania: Trinity Press International, 1996), 70.

[5] Harry Emerson Fosdick, *The Secret of Victorious Living* (New York, New York: Harper ChapelBook, 1966),7.

[6] John Claypool, *The Preaching Event* (Waco, TX: Word Books, 1980), 45.

[7] See Martin E. Marty, "Cultural Dominance," *Sightings*, email newsletter (divsightings@gmail.com), 5/7/2012. As well, review David Kaplan's chapter, "The Law of Cultural Dominance," in *Evolution and Culture*, Marshall G. Sahlins & Elman R. Service, eds., (Ann Arbor, MI: University of Michigan Press, 1960), 69-92. Also helpful is Mark Oppenheimer, "When American Faith transcended Differences: In 'Bad Religion,' Ross Douthat Criticizes U. S. Christianity," *New York Times*, April 18, 2012, http://www.nytimes.com/2012/04/19/books/in-bad-religion-ross-douthat-criticizes-us-christianity.html, accessed 5/7/2012.

[8] Claypool, 28. Elizabeth J. Morgan in "Effective Preaching: An Ethical Obligation," *Christian Ethics Today*, February 2002, 23, drew particular attention to the need to consider emotions: "Ethical treatment of emotion distinguishes between exploitative manipulation and legitimate persuasion. The Apostle Paul warned against the 'meaningless talk' of sophists in 1 Timothy 1:6. Sophistry relies on manipulation through exaggeration and distortion of fact, and it appeals to personal gain through spectacular promises; it encourages imagination over reality; it over-magnifies fear, sentimentality, anger, and false optimism ... an ethical passion energizes words and stimulates images that actualize reality, that make abstract truth concrete and thus motivate healthy moral response. The ethicist does not take advantage of the hearers' senses by distortion and histrionics, but neither are the senses ignored. Making the delicate choice of passionate words is precisely the juncture where the speaker's integrity must prevail."

[9] Garry Wills in his *Head and Heart: American Christianities* (New York, New York: Penguin Press, 2007), 3 outlined the fruition of Western Culture's emphases which eventuated in this dichotomy. At least in American Protestantism, the impact of the Enlightenment provided the basis for those theological perspectives which emphasized the head. More emphases on experiential religion particularly after the American religious awakenings gave impetus to heart language. Wills notes that at different times these head and heart perspectives have been "... identified by different terms—liturgical vs. pietist, ecclesial vs. revivalist, high church vs. low church, elite vs. populist, rational vs. emotional, studied vs. spontaneous, Modernist vs. Fundamentalist, immanent vs. apocalyptical, and so on."

According to Timothy L. Smith's classic treatment *Revivalism and Social Reform: In Mid-Nineteenth-Century America* (Nashville: Abingdon Press, 1957), a shift did occur about the time of the ending of the Civil War. The revivalists' emphases and energies began to denounce not just personal sin but social issues, as well. Though seminaries began developing more studies involving sociology, however, the philosophical divide continued and evolved by the 1920s into the Fundamentalist-Modernist controversy, another either-or dynamic. A most interesting account of one of those who moved from rigid fundamentalist thinking to a quite different expression of Christian faith is in Frank Schaeffer, *Crazy for God: How I Grew Up as One of the Elect, Helped Found the Religious Right, and Lived to Take All (or Almost All) of It Back* (Cambridge, MA: Da Capo Press, 2008).

[10] Preparing for the trip to this meeting gave me opportunity to explore a few of Santiago's contemporary cultural dynamics. One of those was finding the narratives about Camilla Vallejo, the Communist student leading a movement for better access to a quality higher education. I have to identify Vallejo's efforts with a piece of the kerygma, the Gospel, Good News. I recognize, however, that because she is a Communist many Baptists and other Christians will dismiss her efforts. Such an illustration does present the reality for all of us as to how we begin communicating the kerygma in a given culture not our own—that is, finding touch points for conversation, relationship, and kerygma.

[11] David J. Schlafer and Timothy F. Sedgwick, *Preaching What We Practice: Proclamation and Moral Discernment* (Harrisburg, Pennsylvania: Morehouse Publishing, 2007), 155.

[12] See Claypool, pp. 55-81, and his chapter "The Preacher as Gift-Giver" as he delineates the difference between gift-love and need-love—with the strong suggestion not to allow need-love to drive one's preaching.

[13] www.baylor.edu/mediacommunications/news.php?action=story&story=111222, accessed 5/24/2012, demonstrated that "Although high levels of narcissism can impair ethical judgment regardless of one's religious orientation or orthodox beliefs, narcissism is more harmful in those who might be expected to be more ethical." See Majorie J. Cooper and Chris Pullig, "I'm Number One! Does Narcissism Impair Ethical Judgment Even for the Highly Religious?" Journal of Business Ethics, published online February 16, 2012, http://www.springerlink.com/content/u0k76hw8x37h7562/, accessed 5/24/2012.

[14] See David G. Benner, *Spirituality and the Awakening Self: The Sacred Journey of Transformation*, (Grand Rapids, MI: Brazos Press, 2012) for a description of the human's journey toward fulfillment being brought along through a deeper consciousness of God.

[15] Stanley Hauerwas, *A Cross-Shattered Church: Proclaiming the Theological Heart of Preaching* (Grand Rapids, Michigan: Brazos Press, 2009), 12: "I have ... increasingly come to the recognition that one of the most satisfying contexts

for doing the work of theology is in sermons. That should not be surprising because throughout Christian history, at least until recently, the sermon was one of the primary places in which the work of theology was done. For the work of theology is first and foremost to exposit Scripture. That modern theology has become less and less scriptural, that modern theology has often tried to appear as a form of philosophy, is but an indication of its alienation from its proper work. I am, therefore, making these sermons available not only because I think they are my best theological work, but because I hope they exemplify the work of theology."

[16] Schlafer and Sedgwick, 149, maintain that "Preaching toward moral formation requires a community of practices that offers its members clear alternatives to those that are prevailing or taken for granted.""Preaching moral discernment, as evidence by the earliest narratives of communal discernment, is a matter of discovering, embodying, and proclaiming Christian faith as a new way of life, fully lived in relationship with God." Whether one uses the Antiochs or Mars Hill as a starting place, there are basically four major themes emitting from Scripture, and picked up by the historic Baptists, I have to say: Kerygma (the proclamation of the Gospel and I would add as Francis of Assisi said, "Preach the Gospel, even if you have to use words"; Didache (teaching the Gospel); Diakonia (caring for people for the sake of the Gospel); and *Koinonia* (supporting, encouraging, deferring, and submitting to one another for the sake of the Gospel).

[17] Schlafer and Sedgwick, 151-52: "The shift in authority has been ushered in by the enlightenment and other sweeping changes that have brought us to the twenty-first century. Science, education, communications, competing claims and counterclaims—these question traditional authority. Credibility rests upon making sense of things, not on a leader saying something is so. The preacher's authority is not now taken for granted but is granted in response to his or her ability to convey claims about God, to make connections, and to draw out implications. Christian moral discernment is thus effected by a reframing of what is happening and what possibilities for action might deepen life in Christ."

[18] James M. Childs, Jr., *Preaching Justice: The Ethical Vocation of Word and Sacrament Ministry*, Harrisburg, Pennsylvania: Trinity Press International, 2000), xi.

[19] Walter Brueggemann, *The Word Militant: Preaching a Decentering Word* (Minneapolis, MN: Fortress Press, 2007), 34.

[20] Daniel C. Maguire, *The Moral Core of Judaism and Christianity: Reclaiming the Revolution,* (Minneapolis, MN: AugsburgFortress, 1993), 48.

[21] David P. Gushee and Robert H. Long, *A Bolder Pulpit: Reclaiming the Moral*

Dimension of Preaching (Valley Forge, PA: Judson Press, 1998), 4.

[22] John S. McClure, *Other-Wise Preaching: A Postmodern Ethic for Homiletics*, (St. Louis, Missouri: Chalice Press, 2001), 30.

[23] Ronald J. Sider and Michael A. King, *Preaching About Life in a Threatening World*, (Philadelphia, Pennnsylvania: The Westminster Press, 1987), 11.

[24] Paul Heibert, *Transforming Worldviews: An Anthropological Understanding of How People Change* (Grand Rapids, Michigan: Baker Academic, 2008), 11-12. Heibert maintained, that in the nineteenth century, "Many missionaries looked for evidence that people were truly converted, such as putting on clothes,; giving up alcohol, tobacco, and gambling; refusing to bow to ancestors; taking baptism and communion, and attending church regularly. Such changes are important as evidence of conversion, but it became clear that these did not necessarily mean that underlying beliefs had changed."

"... In the twentieth century, Protestant missionaries began to stress the need for transformations in people's beliefs. People had to believe in the deity, virgin birth, and death and resurrection of Christ to be saved. They had to repent inwardly of their sins and seek the salvation Christ was offering to those who believe. Right beliefs were seen as essential to Christian conversion, and missions set up Bible schools and seminaries to teach orthodox doctrine."

CHAPTER 14

[1] David W. Bebbington, *Evangelicalism in Modern Britain: A History from the 1730s to the 1980s* (London: Routledge, 1989), pp. 5-17.

[2] David F. Ford & Rachel Muers (eds), *Modern Theologians: An Introduction to Christian Theology Since 1918* (third edn; Oxford: Blackwell Publishers, 2005), p. 236.

[3] "Editors' introduction," in Lewis Mudge & James Polding (eds), *Formation and Reflection: The Promise of Practical Theology* (Minneapolis: Fortress Press, 1987), p. xvi.

[4] Dan R. Stiver, "Theological method," in Kevin J. Vanhoozer (ed.), *The Cambridge Companion to Postmodernism* (Cambridge: Cambridge University Press, 2003), p. 170.

[5] Ibid., p. 170.

[6] Ibid., p. 171.

[7] Ibid., p. 175.

8 Stephen B. Bevans, *Models of Contextual Theology* (2nd edn; Maryknoll, NY: Orbis Books, 2002), p. 17.

9 Patricia O'Connell Killen & John de Beer, *The Art of Theological Reflection* (New York: Crossroad, 2004), p. 52.

10 Elaine Graham, Heather Walton & Frances Ward, *Theological Reflection: Methods* (London: SCM Press, 2005), p. 10.

11 Ellen T. Charry quoted in ibid., p. 9.

12 Ellen T. Charry, *By the Renewing of Your Minds: The Pastoral Function of Christian Doctrine* (New York: Oxford University Press, 1997), p. 18.

13 Brian D. Robinette, "Discerning the mystery of God," in J.J. Mueller (ed.), *Theological Foundations: Concepts and Methods for Understanding Christian Faith* (2nd edn; Winona, MN: Anselm Academic, 2011), p. 44.

14 For example, see Stanley J. Grenz & John R. Franke, *Beyond Foundationalism: Shaping Theology in a Postmodern Context* (Louisville: Westminster John Knox Press, 2001); David K. Clark, *To Know and Love God: Method for Theology* (Wheaton: Crossway Books, 2003); and Norman R. Gulley, *Systematic Theology: Prolegomena* (Berrien Springs: Andrews University Press, 2003).

15 Brian Harris, "Why method matters: Insights from the theological method of Stanley J. Grenz," *Crucible 2* (1), Nov 2009. Available at http://www.ea.org.au/site/DefaultSite/filesystem/documents/Crucible/Harris%20-%20Why%20Method%20Matters%20-%20Crucible%202-1%20November%202009.pdf.

16 Ibid.

17 Stanley J. Grenz & John R. Franke, *Beyond Foundationalism: Shaping Theology in a Postmodern Context* (Louisville, KY: Westminster John Knox Press, 2001), p. 13.

18 Stanley J. Grenz, *Revisioning Evangelical Theology: A Fresh Agenda for the Twenty First Century* (Downers Grove: IVP, 1993); Stanley J. Grenz, *Theology for the Community of God* (Nashville: Broadman & Holman, 1994); Stanley J. Grenz, *Renewing the Center: Evangelical Theology in a Post-Theological Era* (Grand Rapids: Baker, 2000); and Stanley J. Grenz & John R. Franke, *Beyond Foundationalism: Shaping Theology in a Postmodern Context* (Louisville, KY: Westminster John Knox Press, 2001).

19 Grenz & Franke, *Beyond Foundationalism*, p. 27.

20 Harris, "Why method matters," p. 9.

21 Grenz died suddenly in his sleep on 12 March 2005. See http://en.wikipedia.org/wiki/Stanley_Grenz.

NOTES

22 Grenz & Franke, *Beyond Foundationalism*, pp. 57ff.

23 Grenz, *Revisioning Evangelical Theology*, pp. 87-88.

24 Harris, "Why method matters," p. 5.

25 Ibid.

26 Grenz, *Revisioning Evangelical Theology*, p. 112.

27 Harris, "Why method matters," p. 6.

28 D.A. Carson, *The Gagging of God: Christianity Confronts Pluralism* (Grand Rapids: Zondervan, 1996), p. 481.

29 Harris, "Why method matters," p. 8, summarizing Grenz, *Revisioning Evangelical Theology*, pp. 95-97.

30 Harris, "Why method matters," p. 9.

31 Ibid., p. 9.

32 Thomas C. Oden, *The Word of Life* (San Francisco: Harper & Row, 1992), pp. xv-xx.

33 Harris, "Why method matters," p. 10.

34 Nicholas Wolterstorff, *Reason Within the Bounds of Religion* (Grand Rapids: Eerdmans, 1976).

35 Harris, "Why method matters," p. 12.

36 Stanley J. Grenz, "Participating in what frees: The concept of truth in the postmodern context," *Review & Expositor* 100 (4), Fall 2003, p.

37 Harris, "Why method matters," p. 12.

38 Harris, "Why method matters," p. 13.

39 Harris, "Why method matters," p. 14.

40 James W. McClendon, Jr, *Ethics: Systematic Theology* (vol. 1 of 3; revised edn; Nashville: Abingdon Press, 2002).

41 Source unknown.

42 Mark A. Bowald, "Grace," in Kevin Vanhoozer et al (ed.), *Dictionary for Theological Interpretation of the Bible* (London: SPCK/Grand Rapids: Baker Academic, 2005), p. 269.

43 Richard B. Vinson, Richard F. Wilson & Watson E. Mills, *1 & 2 Peter, Jude* (Macon, GA: Smyth & Helwys Publishing, 2010).

44 J. Daryl Charles, *The Unformed Conscience of Evangelicalism: Recovering the Church's Moral Vision* (Downers Grove: IVP, 2002), pp. 158f.

45 Ibid., p. 170.

46 Robert Harvey & Philip H. Towner, *2 Peter & Jude* (Downers Grove: IVP, 2009), p. 137.

47 Richard J. Bauckham, *Jude, 2 Peter* (Waco, TX: Word Books, 1983), p. 338.

CHAPTER 15

1 Though I do not consider this paper worthy, I dedicate it to the memory of my beloved professor, Frank Stagg.

2 Evelyn and Frank Stagg, *Woman in the World of Jesus* (Philadelphia: The Westminster Press, 1978), 256.

3 *Nichomachean Ethics*, V, 1134b, 9-18; VIII, 1160b, 23-31; VIII, 1160b, 32-1161a, 8.

4 *Politics*, I, 1253b, 1-14; I, 1259a, 40-1260b, 25; I, 1260a, 8-20; III, 1278b, 33-40; III, 1279a, 17-22.

5 David Balch has pointed out the significance of Aristotle's discussion of the household for understanding the philosophical milieu for the domestic codes found in the New Testament. He concludes, essentially, that Aristotle included discussion of the household because it was a standard topos in such works. He failed to note how Aristotle actually used the topos. Aristotle included discussion of the household not simply because it was a standard topic or because he had a primary interest in household management but because it was functional as a proof in his argument about the workings of the state. David L. Balch, *Let Wives Be Submissive: The Domestic Code in 1 Peter*, SBL Monograph Series, vol. 21 (Chico CA: Scholars Press, 1981), pp.34-35.

6 John H. Elliott, *Home for the Homeless: A sociological Exegesis of 1 Peter, It's Situation and Strategy* (Philadelphia: Fortress Press, 1981).

7 I have presented a fuller explanation of my interpretation of the Colossian household code in an earlier publication: "Heuristic Haustafeln: Domestic Codes as Entrance to the Social World of Early Christianity. The Case of Colossians," in *Religious Writings and Religious Systems,* Volume 2, ed. Jacob Neusner et al. Atlanta: Scholars Press, 1989.

8 Some of the interpretation presented here regarding the Ephesian household code appears in an earlier publication: "Introducing the Letter to the Ephesians," in *Interpreting Ephesians for Preaching and Teaching*. Ed. Scott Nash (Macon: Smyth & Helwys, 1996).

9 Wesley Carr, *Angels and Principalities: The Background and Meaning and*

Development of the Pauline Phrase hai archai kai hai exousiai. Society for New Testament Studies Monograph Series 42 (New York: Cambridge University press, 1981), 93-98, discusses the way in which the Christology of Ephesians has determined the cosmology. Christ rules from the heavenlies, yet the sphere of his rule primarily involves the earth, the place where the church lives.

[10] Cf. Walter Wink, *Engaging the Powers: Discernment and Resistance in a World of Domination* (Philadelphia: Fortress Press, 1992).

[11] D. C. Smith, "The Ephesian Heresy and the Origin of the Epistle to the Ephesians," *Ohio Journal of Religious Studies* 5 (1977): 93-94.

[12] This is a point well made by John Paul Sampley, *"And the Two Shall Become One Flesh": A Study of Traditions in Ephesians 5:21-33"* (Cambridge: Cambridge University press, 1971), 154ff.

CHAPTER 16

[1] Anita Stauffer, "Culture and Christian worship in intersection", *International Review of Mission*, Geneva: Jan 1995 Vol.84, Iss. 332-333 page 1.

[2] Christopher Ellis, *Gathering: a theology and spirituality of worship in Free Church tradition* London: SCM Press; 2004 pages 164-169.

[3] This term is used by Justo González in *Desde el Siglo y hasta el Siglo: esbozos teológicos para el siglo XXI [From Age to Age: theological sketches for the 21st century]* 2ª Ed. México: El Faro; 2006.

[4] William May. "Liturgy for life: the political meaning of worship." *Christian Century* August-September, 2001 page 26.

[5] Samuel Escobar. *De la adoración a la misión.* [From worship to mission] Electronic page of Artencel, Música en Selección. Accessed: June 2005, www.artencel.com/+ff-12.htm, page 1.

[6] [Worship is a reverent and joyous response to the truth of the Word that God sends]. Ibid. page 7

[7] Ibid. page 8.

[8] It begins with the birth of native Protestant congregations in Latin America which needed singing material for their worship services.

[9] [Exclusion of all melodies with mundane rhythm in order to preserve a spirit of genuine reverence in holy singing] *Himnario Evangélico Presbiteriano* [Evangelical Presbyterian Hymnbook] México: Casa de Publicaciones "El Faro"; 1961.

[10] *Canciones de Fe y Compromiso*, [Songs of Faith and Commitment] (Three booklets) published by Comunidad Teológica de México; and *Cancionero Abierto*, [Open

Songbook] (Five booklets) published by ISEDET in Buenos Aires.

[11] *Himnario Bautista* [Baptist Hymnal] El Paso, TX: Casa Bautista de Publicaciones; 1978. Also published as *Himnario de Alabanza Evangélica [Hymnal of Evangelical Praise]* for its use outside of Baptist churches.

[12] Justo González. *Desde el Siglo y hasta el Siglo: esbozos teológicos para el siglo XXI [From Age to Age: theological sketches for the 21st century]* 2ª Ed. México: El Faro; 2006 page 127.

[13] The network is called RIBET: (Red de Instituciones Bautistas de Educación Teológica) [Network of Baptist Institutions of Theological Education].

[14] Refer to the work of Marva Dawn, *Reaching out Without Dumbing Down: a theology of worship for this urgent time*. Grand Rapids: Eerdmans; 1995.

[15] Juan José Barreda Toscano, "Hacia una teología bíblica de la celebración litúrgica" [*Towards a biblical theology of the liturgical celebration*] in *Unidos en Adoración: la celebración litúrgica como lugar teológico*, [United in Worship: the liturgical celebration as theological locus] Buenos Aires: Kairós; 2004, page 158.

CHAPTER 21

[1] Triumphalism is the attitude or belief that a particular doctrine, religion, culture, or social system is superior to and should triumph over all others. Triumphalism is not an articulate doctrine but rather a term that is used to characterize certain attitudes or belief systems by parties such as political commentators and historians.

[2] Bruce J. Nicholls, *Contextualization: A Theology of Gospel and Culture* (Vancouver: Regent College Publishing, 2003), 8.

[3] *The Willowbank Report: Lausanne Occasional Papers*, No. 2 (Wheaton: Lausanne Committee for World Evangelization, 1978), 13.

[4] Millard J. Erickson, *Christian Theology* (Grand Rapids: Baker Book House, 1985), 321-42.

[5] Dean Flemming, *Contextualization in the New Testament: Pattern for Theology and Mission* (Downers Grove: InterVasity Press, 2005), 13.

[6] Ralph Winter and Steven C. Hawthorne, eds., *Perspectives on the World Christian Movement,* third edition (Pasadena: William Carey Library, 1999), 23-4.

[7] Ibid., 24.

[8] Ibid.

[9] Dean Flemming, *Contextualization in the New Testament*, 30.

¹⁰ Stephen B. Bevans and Roger P. Schroeder, *Constants in Context: A Theology of Mission for Today* (Maryknoll: Orbis Books, 2004), 18-9.

¹¹ Martin Hengel, *Acts and the History of Earliest Christianity* (Philadelphia: Fortress Press, 1980), 73.

¹² Dean Flemming, *Contextualization in the New Testament*, 48-53.

¹³ Stephen B. Bevans and Roger P. Schroeder, *Constants in Context*, 27-30. Flemming also provides an excellent chart of comparison of Paul's sermons in his book, 86-8.

¹⁴ Dean Flemming, *Contextualization in the New Testament*, 89.

¹⁵ Darrell L. Whiteman, "Editorial: Contextualizing the Gospel," *Missiology: An International Review* vol. XXV no. 1 (January 1997): 4; emphasis added.

CHAPTER 23

¹ Some material used in this paper has also contributed to B.R Talbot, "The King James Bible: A Reflection on 400 Years of its history," *Evangelical Review of Theology*, 35.4 (October 2011).

² William Barlow, The Summe and Substance of the Conference Which It Pleased His Excellent Majestie to have with the Lords, Bishops and Other of His Clergie at Hampton Court, 14 January 1603 [1604]. See also 'To the Reader', the Preface to the first edition of 1611, *The Holy Bible 1611 Edition* (Nashville: Thomas Nelson, 2010), p. vii. Details of the exchange are given in D. Daniell, *The Bible in English* (London: Yale University Press, 2003), 432-436.

³ S.L. Greenslade, ed., *The Cambridge History of the Bible: The West from the Reformation to the Present Day* (Cambridge: Cambridge University Press, 1963), 159-161.

⁴ A.W. Pollard, *Records of the English Bible* (London: Henry Frowde, 1911), 40.

⁵ Daniell, *Bible in English*, 369.

⁶ A. McGrath, *In The Beginning: The Story of the King James Bible* (London: Hodder & Stoughton, 2001), 128-129.

⁷ For example, McGrath, *In The Beginning*, 118-119; Greenslade, *History of the Bible*, 159; D. Wilson, *The People's Bible* (Oxford: Lion Hudson, 2010), 68; F.F. Bruce, *The English Bible* (London: Methuen, 1963), 90-92.

⁸ D. Norton, *The King James Bible: A Short History from Tyndale to Today* (Cambridge: Cambridge University Press, 2011), 133.

[9] Pollard, *Records of the English Bible*, 66.

[10] Preface, possibly by Downame, to *Annotations upon all the Books of the Old and New Testament*, fols. B3ʳ-B4ʳ· cited by Norton, *King James Bible*, 134.

[11] Cited by L. Kreitzer, "William Kiffen and the Prodigal Printer Henry Hills: Publish Abroad: Printing and the King James Bible," chapter twelve in L. Kreitzer, *William Kiffen and his World* (Part.2; Oxford: Centre for Baptist History and Heritage, 2012).

[12] "A Satire of Thomas Williams" in Thomas Weaver's *Songs and Poems of Love and Drollery* (1654), in Kreitzer, "William Kiffen and the Prodigal Printer Henry Hills." I am thankful to Dr Kreitzer for providing a pre-publication copy of this work.

[13] G. Campbell, *Bible: The Story of the King James Version 1611-2011* (Oxford: Oxford University Press, 2010), 26-27.

[14] W. Laud, *Works*, Vol. IV, 263; quoted by Norton, *History of the English Bible*, 91. Puritan and London bookseller, Michael Sparke, who imported Bibles from Continental Europe, in defiance of the Government restrictions on this trade, strongly opposed the practice of printing monopolies and from the opposite theological point of view to Laud mentioned the same reasons as the Archbishop for the popularity of the Geneva Bible (*Scintilla*, 1641; reprinted in A.S. Herbert, *Historical Catalogue of Printed Editions of the English Bible, 1525-1961* (London: The British and Foreign Bible Society, 1968), 183-187.

[15] Pollard, *Records of the English Bible*, 23.

[16] Norton, *History of the English Bible*, 92.

[17] Laud, *Works*, Vol IV, 262; quoted by Norton, *History of the English Bible*, 92.

[18] W. Prynne, *Canterbury's Doom* (London, 1646), 181; quoted by Norton, *History of the English Bible*, 92.

[19] I am grateful to Dr Stephen Holmes, Senior Lecturer in Theology, University of St Andrews, for drawing my attention to Cox's use of the KJV.

[20] S. Wright, *The Early English Baptists, 1603-1649* (Woodbridge, Suffolk: The Boydell Press, 2006),117-119. M. Tolmie, *The Triumph of the Saints: The Separate Churches of London 1616-1649* (Cambridge: Cambridge University Press, 1977), 61. M.K. Bell, *Apocalypse How? Baptist Movements during the English Revolution* (Macon, Georgia: Mercer University Press, 2000), 90.

[21] *The First London Confession of Faith 1646 edition with an Appendix by Benjamin Cox* (Rochester, New York: Backus Books, 1981), 23.

22 *First London Confession of Faith 1646 edition with an Appendix by Benjamin Cox*, 26.

23 Most of the information on Henry Hills was provided by Dr Larry Kreitzer, Regent's Park College, Oxford.

24 *The London Printer's Lamentation or the Press Opprest and Overprest,* 1660; C. Anderson, *The Annals of the English Bible in Two Volumes* (London: William Pickering, 1845), Vol.1, 555.

25 Anderson, *Annals of the English Bible*, Vol.1, 555-557.

26 Kreitzer, 'William Kiffen and the Prodigal Printer Henry Hills', 1-16.

27 Campbell, *Bible: The Story of the King James Version*, 125.

28 H. Hamlin, 'Bunyan's biblical progress', in H. Hamlin & N.W. Jones (eds), *The King James Bible after 400 Years* (Cambridge: Cambridge University Press, 2010), 214.

29 J. N. King & A.T. Pratt, "The materiality of English printed Bibles," in Hamlin & Jones, *King James Bible after 400 Years*, 88. See the discussion of some of the Geneva notes on this topic in McGrath, *In the Beginning*, 141-148.

30 J.P. Rosenblatt, "Milton, Anxiety, and the King James Bible," in Hamlin & Jones, *King James Bible after 400 Years*, 181-201.

31 J. Bunyan, *The Holy City Or The New Jerusalem*, in G. Offor, ed., *The Works of John Bunyan* (Edinburgh: Banner of Truth, 1991 [1854]), Vol.3, 399-400.

32 Hamlin, "Bunyan's biblical progress," 202-218.

33 C. Hill, *A Turbulent, Seditious, and Factious People: John Bunyan and his Church* (Oxford: Oxford University Press, 1988), 169.

34 J. Bunyan, *A Few Sighs from Hell or The Groans of a Damned Soul* (1650), in Offor, ed., *John Bunyan*, Vol.3, 710.

35 Bunyan, *A Few Sighs from Hell*, 677.

36 For example, Hill, *John Bunyan and his Church*, 169.

37 For example, *The Saint's Privilege and Profit* [published posthumously in 1692], in Offor, ed., *John Bunyan*, Vol. 1, 657; *A Discourse of the Building, Nature, Excellency and Government of the House of God* (1688), in Offor, ed., *John Bunyan*, Vol.2, 582.

38 For example, *The Work of Christ As An Advocate* (1688), in Offor, ed., *John Bunyan*, Vol.1, 183; *A Treatise on the Fear of God* (1679), in Offor, ed., *John Bunyan*, Vol.1, 471; *The Desire of the Righteous Granted* , [published posthumously in 1692], in Offor, ed., *John Bunyan*, Vol.1, 759; *A Holy Life The Beauty of Christianity* (1684),

in Offor, ed., *John Bunyan*, Vol.2, 530.

[39] *The Acceptable Sacrifice Or The Excellency of a Broken Heart* (1689), in Offor, ed., *John Bunyan*, Vol. 1, 695; *Differences about Water Baptism No Bar to Communion* (1673), in Offor, ed., *John Bunyan*, Vol.2, 642. This second reference does not mention Tyndale by name, but almost certainly is referring to his translation (and possibly others prior to the publication of the Bishop's Bible), as Offor indicates in his notes.

[40] Campbell, *Bible: The Story of the King James Version*, 127-128.

[41] E. Whiston, *The Life and Death of Mr Henry Jessey* (London, 1671), 45-47; quoted by Norton, *History of the English Bible,* 98-99.

[42] Daniell, *Bible in English,* 536.

[43] I. Rivers, "Philip Doddridge's New Testament," in Hamlin & Jones, *King James Bible after 400 Years,* 124-145.

[44] Anderson, *Annals of the English Bible,* Vol. 2, 560.

[45] Campbell, *Bible: The Story of the King James Version,* 132-142. D.W. Bebbington, "The King James Bible in Britain from the Late Eighteenth Century," 1. I am grateful to Professor Bebbington for allowing me to read a copy of this as yet unpublished paper, prepared for *"The King James Bible and the World It Made, 1611-2011" Conference at Baylor University, Texas, April 7-9, 2011. The next section of the paper was significantly influenced by this study.*

[46] Campbell, *Bible: The Story of the King James Version,* 146.

[47] *The Critical Review,* 63 (1787), 40, quoted by Norton, *History of the English Bible,* 241.

[48] Vicesimus Knox, *Essays, Moral and Literary* (1778), 266-267; quoted by Norton, *History of the English Bible,* 243.

[49] E. Irving, *Babylon and Infidelity Foredoomed of God* (2 vols; Glasgow: for Chalmers and Collins, 1826), 1, 308, quoted by Bebbington, 'King James Bible', 3.

[50] Anderson, *Annals of the English Bible,* Vol.2, 562.

[51] William T. Brantley D.D., *Objections to a Baptist Version of the New Testament* (New York: J.P. Callender, 1837), 6. I am indebted to the American Baptist Historical Society, Mercer University, USA, for access to a number of documents used in this study. See also C.D. Weaver, "Brantley, William T(heophilus)," in D.M. Lewis, ed., *The Blackwell Dictionary of Evangelical Biography 1730-1860* (2 vols; Oxford: B. Blackwell, 1995), Vol. 1, 134.

[52] R. Haldane, *Address to the Public concerning Political Opinions* (Edinburgh, 1800).

NOTES

[53] Bebbington, *King James Bible*, 4.

[54] A.S. Herbert, *Historical Catalogue of Printed Editions of the English Bible, 1525-1961* (London: British and Foreign Bible Society, 1968), 346.

[55] For example, C. Anderson, *The Native Irish and Their Descendants* (London: William Pickering, 3rd ed. 1846), 68.

[56] C. Anderson, *The Annals of the English Bible in Two Volumes* (London: William Pickering, 1845), Vol.1, xi. A similar view of the Bible's significance on an even wider stage, is given in V. Mangalwadi, *The Book That Made Your World* (Nashville: Thomas Nelson, 2011).

[57] "Joseph Hughes, M.A., Originator of Useful Works" in S.A. Swaine, *Faithful Men* (London: Alexander & Shepheard, 1884), 139-141.

[58] John Leifchild, *Memoir of Joseph Hughes, A.M.* (London: Thomas Ward & Co., 1835), 180-183.

[59] Swain, *Faithful Men*, 144-145. See also E.P. Clipsham, "Hughes, Joseph," in D.M. Lewis, ed., *The Blackwell Dictionary of Evangelical Biography 1730-1860* (2 Vols; Oxford: Blackwell, 1995) Vol.1, 580.

[60] A. Peel, *These Hundred Years A History of the Congregational Union of England and Wales 1831-1931* (London: Congregational Union of England and Wales, 1931), 135-139.

[61] D.E. Jenkins, *The Life of the Rev. Thomas Charles of Bala* (3 vols; Denbigh: Llewelyn Jenkins, 1908), Vol. 2, 492-529.

[62] Leifchild, *Joseph Hughes*, 192-195.

[63] There are many works which could be cited here. One example, in typescript manuscript, is G.A. F. Knight, "The History of the National Bible Society of Scotland, Part I: 1809-1900," 1-120.

[64] L. Howsam, *Cheap Bibles: Nineteenth Century Publishing and the British and Foreign Bible Society* (Cambridge: Cambridge University Press, 1991), 35-39.

[65] R.H. Martin, *Evangelicals United: Ecumenical Stirrings in Pre-Victorian Britain 1795-1830* (Metuchen, New Jersey: The Scarecrow Press, 1983), 91-92.

[66] Martin, *Evangelicals United*, 112.

[67] These guidelines were reported in the *Second Annual Report of the American and Foreign Bible Society* (New York: John Gray, 1839), 50.

[68] P.C. Gutjahr, *An American Bible: A History of the Good Book in the United States 1777-1880* (Stanford, California: Stanford University Press, 1999), 90.

69 *Annual Report,* American Bible Society 1830, 530-531, cited by Gutjahr, *American Bible,* 19.

70 M. Bragg, *The Book of Books: The Radical Impact of the King James Bible 1611-2011*(London: Hodder & Stoughton, 2011), 166.

71 T. Armitage, *History of the Baptists* (New York: Bryan Taylor & Co., 1887), 895.

72 H. Stout, "Word and Order in Colonial New England" in N.O. Hatch & M.A Noll, *The Bible in America: Essays in Cultural History* (New York: Oxford University Press, 1982), 19-38; cited by P.J. Thuesen, *In Discordance with the Scriptures: American Protestant Battles over Translating the Bible* (Oxford: Oxford University Press, 1999), 30.

73 Anon, *An Argument sustaining the Common English Version of the Bible* (New York: John A. Gray, 1850), viii.

74 W. Wyckoff, *Revision of the English Scriptures* (New York, n.p., n.d. [1850s?]), 6. See also W. H. Brackney, *Historical Dictionary of the Baptists* (Lanham, Maryland: The Scarecrows Press, 1999) 65.

75 *The Columbian Star,* March 6, 1824; cited by D.G. Stevens, *The First Hundred Years of The American Baptist Publication Society* (Philadelphia: The American Baptist Publication Society, n.d [1924?]), 5.

76 Stevens, *First Hundred Years,* 16.

77 "Resolution of the Board of Messengers of the American Bible Society, 17 February 1837" cited in the *First Annual Report of the American and Foreign Bible Society* (New York: John Gray, 1838), 13. See also R. Torbet, *A History of the Baptists* (London: The Carey Kingsgate Press, 1966), p. 278.

78 *First Annual Report of the American and Foreign Bible Society,* 3.

79 H. Vedder, *A Short History of the Baptists* (Philadelphia: The American Baptist Publication Society, 1907), 338-339.

80 Thuesen, *In Discordance with the Scriptures,* 47.

81 Torbet, *History of the Baptists,* 279.

82 W.C. Somerville, *From Iona to Dunblane: The Story of the National Bible Society of Scotland to 1948* (Edinburgh: National Bible Society of Scotland, 1948), 21-23. F. Macdonald, "Bible Societies," in N.M. de Cameron et a.l eds., *Dictionary of Scottish Church History and Theology* (Edinburgh: T. & T. Clark, 1991), 71-72.A. Haldane, *The Lives of Robert and James Haldane* (Edinburgh: Banner of Truth, 1990 [1852]), 513-545.

83 A.J. Brown, *The Word of God Among All Nations: A Brief History of the Trinitarian*

NOTES

Bible Society 1831-1981 (London: Trinitarian Bible Society, 1981), 7-25.

[84] "Report of Virginia and Foreign Baptist Bible Society,'" June 1850, in the *Religious Herald*, 13 June 1850. This is the Baptist newspaper published in Virginia. I am grateful to Dr Frederick Anderson, Executive Director of the Virginia Baptist Historical Society, for access to articles from this periodical.

[85] Anon, *An Argument sustaining the Common English Version of the Bible*, 16.

[86] *New York Recorder* article, reprinted in the *Religious Herald*, June 20, 1850.

[87] Brantley, *Objections to a Baptist Version of the New Testament*, 64-66.

[88] "[William] Colgate's Reasons for Revision," No. 23 (New York: American Bible Union, 1857), 1.

[89] *Religious Herald*, April 4, 1851.

[90] Thomas Curtis to the Secretaries of the Cambridge University Press, January 27, 1832, quoted by Howsam, *Cheap Bibles*, 111-112.

[91] *Religious Herald*, May 10, 1855.

[92] *Truth and Progress*, July 1868, 144-148; November 1868, 222; cited by Ken Manley, "'Sound the Battle Cry!' –Australian Baptists and the Bible," I am grateful to Dr Manley for allowing me to see a copy of this unpublished paper.

[93] J.B. Lightfoot, *On a Fresh Revision of the English New Testament* (London: Macmillan and Co., 1871),80; cited by Bebbington, "King James Bible," 9.

[94] Charles Haddon Spurgeon, preface, in Hannah C. Conant, *The English Bible: History of the Translations of the Holy Scriptures into the English Tongue with Specimens of the Old English Versions* (London: Arthur Hall, Virtue and Co., 1859), x-xi.

[95] Thuesen, *In Discordance with the Scriptures*, 51-54.

[96] *Evangelical Repository and Bible Teacher*, 58, (October 1881), 153; cited by Thuesen, *In Discordance with the Scriptures*, 55.

[97] C. Dallaston, "The Revised Version of the New Testament," *New Zealand Baptist*, (September 1881), 113-114.

[98] William Morgan, Pukekohe East, Auckland, "Can That Faith Save Him?" *New Zealand Baptist*, (February 1882), 17.

[99] *New Zealand Baptist*, (August 1885), 120-121.

[100] J.S. "The Revised Bible," *Baptist Magazine*, (July 1885), 316-323.

[101] *The Queensland Baptist*, articles between 1881 and 1904. I am grateful to Dr David

Parker for checking the records of this newspaper on this subject for this paper.

[102] H.C. Fox, *The Revised Version of the New Testament* (Plymouth: William Brendon and Son, n.d. [1881]), 2.

[103] J. Clifford, "The Revised Version of the New Testament," *General Baptist Magazine*, (June 1881), 250-253.

[104] Fox, *Revised Version of the New Testament*, 7, 12.

[105] For example, to Miss Firth and Mr Frew in Wellington Baptist Church, *New Zealand Baptist*, (March 1887), 39.

[106] H.H. Driver, "Our Sabbath Worship," a paper read at a Baptist Union of New Zealand conference in Christchurch, on 13 November 1888, and published at the request of the Assembly, *New Zealand Baptist*, (January 1889), 9-12.

[107] A.J. Gordon, "The Ministry of Women (concluding section)," *New Zealand Baptist*, (May 1895), 70-71.

[108] Thuesen, *In Discordance with the Scriptures*, 69-72.

[109] Daniell, *Bible in English*, 738-743.

[110] A good Evangelical scholarly example is American Presbyterian O.T. Allis in his *Revision or New Translation? Revised Version or Revised Bible?* (Philadelphia: Presbyterian and Reformed Publishing Company, 1948).

[111] Thuesen, *In Discordance with the Scriptures*, 152.

[112] D.A. Carson makes this point in his *The King James Version Debate: A Plea for Realism* (Grand Rapids: Baker, 1979), 84. It has also been strongly marketed with books like K. Barker, ed., *The Making of a Contemporary Translation* (London: Hodder & Stoughton, 1987), advocating its cause.

[113] Information provided by Dr John Kok, Kuala Lumpur Baptist Church, July 7, 2011.

[114] A.L. Farstad, *The New King James Version in the Great Tradition* (Nashville: Thomas Nelson, 1989). From the same school of thought came a critical appraisal of the NIV in E. Radmacher & Z. Hodges, *The NIV Reconsidered* (Dallas: Redencion Viva Publishing House, 1990).

[115] J.P. Lewis, *The English Bible From KJV to NIV* (Grand Rapids: Baker, 1982), 329-362.

[116] B. Zwartz, "The Book That Changed The World," *THE AGE*, May 27, 2011, 11. *THE AGE* is an Australian newspaper, based in Melbourne, Victoria. I am grateful to Ken Edmonds for a copy of this publication.

[117] J. Drane, "Bible Use in the Scottish Churches," in P. Brierley & F. Macdonald, *Prospects for Scotland: From a Census of the Churches in 1984* (Bromley, Kent: MARC Europe, 1985), 26-29.

[118] P. Brierley & F. Macdonald, *Prospects for Scotland 2000* (London: Christian Research, 1995),

[119] The King James Version is still the predominant version amongst Baptists in the Bahamas. I am grateful to Clinton Minnis for drawing my attention to this fact, July 8, 2011.

[120] S.S. Montefiore, *Speeches that Changed the World* (London: Quercus, 2005), 151-2.

[121] G. Green, "The King James Bible to celebrate 400th Anniversary," *Metro,* April 26, 2011, accessed on May 4,2011 at http://www.metro.co.uk/lifestyle/861738-the-king-james-bible-to-celebrate-400th-anniversary#ixzz1LQrjRyPO.

CHAPTER 25

[1] Cecil Moore, *Recuerdos, vivencias de un misionero bautista*, Santiago, Chile, 1978, 37.

[2] Isaías Valdivia, *Wenceslao Valdivia: Primer Bautista Chileno*, Valparaíso, Chile, 1947, 19.

[3] Roberto C. Moore, Los Evangélicos en marcha…en América Latina, Editorial *Librería el Lucero*, Santiago-Chile, 1959, 71-72.

[4] Isaías Valdivia, 19

[5] Humberto Muñoz R., *Nuestros Hermanos Evangélicos*, Segunda edición, Editorial Salisina, Santiago-Chile, 1984, 106-107.

[6] Roberto C. Moore, 71-72.

[7] Isaías Valdivia, 18.

[8] Diamantes Bautistas, UBACH, Santiago-Chile, 1983. 21.

[9] Diamantes, 21.

[10] Roberto C. Moore, Recuerdos…, 37-38.

[11] Cecil Moore, *Hombres y Hechos Bautistas de Chile*, Imprenta siglo XX, Santiago-Chile, s/f., 10.

[12] Elizabeth Pacheco, *Guillermo MacDonald; el apóstol de la frontera*, Segunda edición, Comité de Publicaciones de las Organizaciones Femeninas Bautistas de los Países Hispanoamericanos, 1956, 55.

[13] Cecil Moore, *Hombres…*, 10-11.

[14] Cecil Moore, *Hombres…*, 37-38.

[15] Cecil Moore, *Hombres…*, 50.

[16] Cecil Moore, *Hombres…*, p.53.

[17] Diamantes, p.12.

[18] Diamantes, p.13.

[19] Justo Anderson, *Historia de los bautistas*, Tomo III. El Paso Texas: CBP, 1990, p. 157.

CHAPTER 26

[1] Justo C. Anderson, *Historia de los Bautistas.* Tomo I, (El Paso, Texas: Casa Bautista de Publicaciones, 1978) 113.

[2] Pablo A. Deiros. *Historia del cristianismo en América Latina.* Primera Edición, (Buenos Aires, Argentina: Fraternidad Teológica Latinoamericana, 1992), 789.

[3] Deiros, 794.

[4] Juan Carlos Cevallos. *Ponencia Los Bautistas y su Mensaje.* Quito, Ecuador: Convención Bautista Ecuatoriana, 1992).

[5] Arturo Piedra, Sidney Rooy, y H. Fernando Bullón. *Hacia donde va el protestantismo; Herencia y prospectivas en América Latina.*) Buenos Aires, Argentina: Fraternidad Teológica Latinoamericana. 2003), p 51.

[6] Glenn Hinson. "Southern Baptists and Ecumenism", *Review and Expositor* LXVI, 3, Summer 1969, 287.

CONTRIBUTING AUTHORS

Victor Aguilar Reyes is a theologian and psychologist who serves as the General Coordinator of the Community for Ecumenical Spirituality and Reflection in Chile.

Fred Anderson is executive director at the Virginia Baptist Historical Society and the Center for Baptist Heritage and Studies at the University of Richmond in the United States.

John Beasy is Senior Pastor at Enfield Baptist Church, Adelaide, Australia; founder of Life Well Ministries; and National President of Australian Baptist Ministries.

Rod Benson is an ordained Baptist minister, consultant ethicist and social justice advocate based in the Blue Mountains, west of Sydney, Australia.

"DA" is living in a Central Asian country working among Iranian and Azeri peoples.

John Drummond is a member and overseas mission team leader of the St. Andrew Baptist Church in Panama City, Florida, USA, where he is a real estate developer.

Paul S. Fiddes, a former Principal of Regent's Park College, Oxford, 1989-2007, is Professor of Systematic Theology at the University of Oxford, England.

Curtis W. Freeman is Research Professor of Theology and Director of the Baptist House of Studies at Duke University Divinity School, Durham, North Carolina, USA.

Robert I. Garrett holds the Piper Chair of Missions at Dallas Baptist University, Texas, USA, where he directs the M.A. program in Global Leadership.

Brian Harris is Principal and head of Department of Ministry and Practice at Vose Seminary in Perth, Australia.

D. Leslie Hollon is senior pastor of Trinity Baptist Church, San Antonio, Texas, USA.

Stephen R. Holmes, a Baptist minister, is Senior Lecturer in Theology at the University of St. Andrews, Scotland.

Jose Parrish Jacome Hernandez is General Secretary of the Union of Baptists in Latin America and senior pastor of Israel Baptist Church, Guayaquil, Ecuador.

Louise Kretzschmar teaches in the Department of Philosophy, Practical and Systematic Theology at the University of South Africa, Johannesburg, South Africa.

Timothy Hyunmo Lee is Professor of Missions at Korea Baptist Theological Seminary, Daejeon, South Korea, and Mission Committee Chairman of the Asia Pacific Baptist Federation.

Faith Linton, author and educator, is a member of the Board of the Bible Society of the West Indies, in Kingston, Jamaica.

Robert Scott Nash is the Columbus Roberts Professor of New Testament in the Roberts Department of Christianity, College of Liberal Arts, Mercer University, Macon, Georgia, USA.

Nathan Nettleton is pastor of the South Yarra Community Baptist Church in Melbourne, Australia. He teaches liturgical studies at Whitley College in the University of Melbourne.

Elizabeth Newman is Eula Mae and John Baugh Professor of Theology and Ethics and Director of the Master of Theological Studies program at the Baptist Theological Seminary in Richmond, Virginia, USA.

Samuel K. Roberts was the Anne Borden and E. Hervey Evans Professor of Theology and Ethics at Union Presbyterian Seminary in Richmond, Virginia, USA. He died February 24, 2015.

Alison Sampson is Associate Pastor of the South Yarra Community Baptist Church in Melbourne, Australia, and a public health expert.

Joel Sierra Cavazos, Pastor of Comunidad Bautista Jireh in Monterrey, Mexico, is a former vice president of the Baptist World Alliance.

Courtney Stewart, an ordained minister and General Secretary of the Bible Society of the West Indies, lead the Jamaica Bible Translation project.

Brian R. Talbot is Extraordinary Associate Professor, Department of Theology, North West University, South Africa and Minister of Broughty Ferry Baptist Church, Dundee, Scotland.

William M. Tillman, Jr., former T. B. Maston Chair of Ethics at Hardin-Simmons University in Abilene, Texas, is Director of Theological Education for the Baptist General Convention of Texas, USA.

Daniel Trusiewicz, a Baptist minister in Poland, is Coordinator of Mission Partnerships in the European Baptist Federation.

CONTRIBUTING AUTHORS

R. Glenn Wooden is a member of the Third Horton Baptist Church and Associate Professor of Old Testament at Acadia Divinity College, Wolfville, Nova Scotia, Canada.

www.ingramcontent.com/pod-product-compliance
Lightning Source LLC
Chambersburg PA
CBHW071645090426
42738CB00009B/1428